Hitler's
Volkssturm

Hitler's Volkssturm

The Nazi Militia and the Fall of Germany, 1944–1945

David K. Yelton

University Press of Kansas

can

© 2002 by the University Press of Kansas
All rights reserved

Published by the University Press of Kansas (Lawrence, Kansas 66049), which was organized by the Kansas Board of Regents and is operated and funded by Emporia State University, Fort Hays State University, Kansas State University, Pittsburg State University, the University of Kansas, and Wichita State University

Library of Congress Cataloging-in-Publication Data

Yelton, David K., 1960–
    Hitler's Volkssturm : the Nazi Militia and the fall of Germany,
1944–1945 / David K. Yelton.
        p. cm. — (Modern war studies)
    Includes bibliographical references and index.
    ISBN 0-7006-1192-4 (cloth : alk. paper)
        1. Nationalsozialistische Deutsche Arbeiter-Partei. Deutscher Volkssturm—
History. 2. World War, 1939–1945—Germany. 3. Germany—History,
Military. 4. Germany—History—1933–1945.
    I. Title. II. Series.
    DD253.8.V64 Y45 2002
    940.54'1343—dc21   2002006163

British Library Cataloguing in Publication Data is available.

Printed in the United States of America

10 9 8 7 6 5 4 3 2 1

The paper used in this publication meets the minimum requirements of the American National Standard for Permanence of Paper for Printed Library Materials Z39.48-1984.

For Denise, Katie, Allyson, and Emily

Contents

Abbreviations

Abt.	*Abteilung* (branch or detachment)
a.D.	*außer Dienst* (retired)
Adj.	adjutant
Adm.	admiral
AG	*Amtsgruppe* (office group)
AHA	Allgemeines Heeres Amt (General Army Office)
AK	*Armeekorps* (army corps)
Allg.	*Allgemeine* (general)
AOK	*Armee Oberkommando* (army command or headquarters)
Arb.	*Arbeit* (work or labor)
Art.	*Artillerie* (artillery)
Ausb.	*Ausbildung* (training)
AWA	Allgemeine Wehrmachtamt (General Armed Forces Office)
Az.	*Aktenzeichen* (document identification number)
BA	Bundesarchiv
BA-Ko	Bundesarchiv Koblenz (German Federal Archives, Koblenz)
BA-MA	Bundesarchiv-Militärarchiv (German Federal Military Archives, Freiburg im Breisgau)
Bd.	*Band* (volume)
Bde.	brigade
BdE	*Befehlshaber des Ersatzheeres* (Commander of the Replacement Army)
BrB. or Br.B	*Brieftagebuch* (listing of communications)
Btn.	battalion
Btnfü.	*Bataillonführer* (Volkssturm battalion leader)
BzA	*Bezirksamt* (local government district office)
Cav.	cavalry
Ch.	*Chef* (chief)
ChHRü	Chef Heeres Rüstung (Chief of Army Armaments)
CIOS	Combined Intelligence Objective Subcommittee
CO	commanding officer
DAF	*Deutsche Arbeits Front* (German Labor Front)
Dep.	*Deponierung* (records group)
Dir.	*Direktion* (directorate)

Div.	division
DRK	Deutsches Rotes Kreuz (German Red Cross)
DtVs	Deutscher Volkssturm
DVst	Deutscher Volkssturm
Ers.	*Ersatz* (replacement)
Feldbtn.	*Feldbataillon* (field or active duty battalion)
Feldkomp.	*Feldkompanie* (field or active duty company)
FHO	Fremde Heere Ost (Foreign Armies East)
FS	*Fernschreiben* (teletype)
geh.	*geheim* (secret)
Gen.	general
GenKdo.	*Generalkommando* (army corps headquarters)
Genltn.	*Generalleutnant* (major general)
Genmaj.	*Generalmajor* (brigadier general)
GenQM	*Generalquartiermeister* (General Staff Chief Supply and Administrative Office)
GenSt	*Generalstab* (general staff)
GenStdH	Generalstab des Heeres (General Staff of the Army)
GG	General Gouvernement (General Government, i.e., occupied Poland)
gK. Chefsache	*geheime Kommandosache, Chefsache* (extremely highly classified material)
Gkdos.	*Geheime Kommandosache* (top secret command matter)
gKdos.	*geheime Kommandosache* (classification term for top secret command matter)
GLA	Generallandesarchiv (General State Archives)
Gltg.	*Gauleitung* (Nazi regional administrative office)
Gltr.	*Gauleiter* (regional NSDAP leader)
Gren.	*Grenadier*
GRs.	*Geheime Reichssache* (top secret government matter)
gRs.	*Geheime Reichssache* (top secret government matter)
Gstbfü.	*Gaustabsführer* (Gau Volkssturm Chief of Staff)
GStdH	Generalstabs des Heeres (General Staff of the Army)
H.	Heer (army)
Hauptabt.	*Hauptabteilung* (main branch)
HDL	*Hauptdienstleiter* (NSDAP rank equivalent to Gauleiter)
HG or HGr	*Heeresgruppe* (army group)
HJ	*Hitler Jugend* (Hitler Youth)
HMSO	His/Her Majesty's Stationery Office
Höh.	*Höheres* (senior or higher)
HöhArtKdo	Höheres Artillerie Kommando (Senior Artillery Command)
HöhKdo	Höheres Kommando (Senior Command)

HPA	Heerespersonalamt (Army Personnel Office)
HQ	*Hauptquartier* (headquarters)
HSSuPF	Höheres SS und Polizeiführer (Senior SS and Police Commander)
HStA	*Hauptstaatsarchiv* (Main State Archives)
HVA	Heeresverwaltungsamt (OKH's Army Administration Office)
Ia	operations section
Ib	supply and administration section
Ic	intelligence section
IfZG	Institut für Zeitgeschichte
In.	*Inspektion* (inspectorate)
Inf.	infantry
Inl.	*Inland* (domestic)
Insp.	*Inspekteur* (inspector)
IPW	interrogation of prisoner of war
Kdo.	*Kommando* (command)
Kdr.	*Kommandeur* (commander)
Kdt.	*Kommandant* (commander)
KG.	*Kampfgruppe* (battle group)
Kgeh.	NSDAP secret security classification
Kofü.	*Kompanieführer* (Volkssturm company leader)
Komp.	*Kompanie* (company)
Korück	*Kommandeur des rückwartiges Heeresgebietes* (commander of army rear areas)
Kr.	Kreis (NSDAP county administrative area)
Krltg.	Kreisleitung (NSDAP Kreis office)
Krltr.	*Kreisleiter* (NSDAP Kreis leader)
Krstbfü.	*Kreisstabsführer* (Kreis Volkssturm Chief of Staff)
KTB	*Kriegstagebuch* (war diary)
LA	Landesarchiv (State Archives)
Ldsbef.	*Landesbesfestigung* (fortifications)
Lfd.	*Laufend* (continuous)
LHA	*Landeshauptarchiv* (Main State Archives)
LRA	*Landratsamt* (district magistrate's office)
Ltn.	*Leutnant* (lieutenant)
LWA	*Landeswirtschaftsamt* (state economic office)
MIA	missing in action
Mob.	*Mobilisation* (mobilization)
mot.	*Motorisiert* (motorized)
MS	manuscript
NA	National Archives
NCO	noncommissioned officer

Nr.	*Nummer* (number)
NS	National Socialist
NSDAP	Nationalsozialistische Deutsche Arbeiter Partei (National Socialist German Workers Party)
NSFK	Nationalsozialistische Flieger Korps (National Socialist Flyers Corps)
NSFO	Nationalsozialistische Führungsoffizier (National Socialist Leadership Officer)
NSKK	Nationalsozialistische Kraftfahr Korps (National Socialist Motor Corps)
OB	*Oberbefehlshaber* (commander)
OBdM	Oberbefehlshaber der Marine (Supreme Commander of the Navy)
Oberinsp.	*Oberinspekteur* (senior inspector)
Oberltn.	*Oberleutnant* (first lieutenant)
OberQM or ObQM	*Oberquartiermeister* (quartermaster of an army or army group; also Deputy Chief of the General Staff in OKH)
ObKdo or Okdo	*Oberkommando* (high command)
Og.	Ortsgruppe (NSDAP town-level group)
Ogltr.	*Ortsgruppenleiter* (leader of NSDAP ortsgruppe)
OKH	Oberkommando des Heeres (Army High Command)
OKL	Oberkommando der Luftwaffe (Air Force High Command)
OKM	Oberkommando der Marine (Naval High Command)
OKW	Oberkommando der Wehrmacht (Armed Forces High Command)
OLGP	*Oberlandesgerichtspräsident* (head of regional superior court)
Op(s).	operations
OQu	see OberQM
Org.	*Organisation* (organization)
OSS	Office of Strategic Services
Ost Dok	Ost-Kokumentation (collection of reminiscences of Germans in the former eastern territories)
OT	Organisation Todt
Pg.	*Parteigenosse* (Party member)
PK	Partei Kanzlei (Party Chancellery)
POW	prisoner of war
PrBrRep.	Preussische Brandenburgische Repositorium (Prussian-Brandenburg Records Collection)
Pro.	propaganda

Prop.	propaganda
PW	prisoner of war
Pz	*Panzer* (armored)
PzAK	*Panzer Armeekorps* (armored corps)
PzAOK	*Panzer Armeeoberkommando* (armored army command)
PzGren	*Panzergrenadier* (armored infantry)
PzGrenDiv	*Panzergrenadier Division* (armored infantry division)
QM	*Quartiermeister* (quartermaster)
QMzbV	*Quartiermeister zur besondere Verwendung* (quartermaster for special purposes)
Qu.	*Quartiermeister* (quartermaster)
RAD	Reichsarbeitsdienst (Reich Labor Service)
RB	Reichsbahn (German National Railway)
RBDir	Reichsbahndirektion (German National Railway district)
Regt.	regiment
Rept.	report
RFSS	Reichsführer SS
RG	Record Group
Rk.	Reichskanzlei (Reich Chancellery)
RM	*Reichsminister* or *Reichsministerium*
RMfRuK	Reichsministerium für Rüstung und Kreigsproduktion (Reichs Ministry for Armaments and War Production)
RMfVuP	Reichsministerium für Volksaufklärung und Propaganda (Reichs Ministry for Popular Enlightenment and Propaganda)
RPA	Reichspropagandaamt (Reichs Propaganda Office)
RS	*Rundschreiben* (circular)
Rü or Rüst	*Rüstung* (armament)
RüA	Rüstungsamt (Armaments Office)
RüInsp	Rüstungsinspektion (Armaments Inspectorate)
RüKdo	Rüstungskommando (Armaments Command)
RüKomm	Rüstungskommando (Armaments Command)
RüStab	Rüstungsstab (Armaments Staff)
RVK	Reichsverteidigungskommissar (Reich Defense Commissar)
RWK	Reichswirtschaftskammer (Reich Economic Chamber)
RWM	Reichswirtschaftsministerium (Reich Economic Ministry)
SA	Sturmabteilung (Storm Troopers)
SD	Sicherheitsdienst (Security Service)
Sec.	section
SHAEF	Supreme Headquarters Allied Expeditionary Force
Sipo	Sicherheitspolizei (Security Police)
SKL	Seekriegsleitung (Naval War Staff)

SS	Schutzstaffel
StA	Staatsarchiv (State Archives)
Tgb.	*Tagebuch* (diary)
TN	Technische Nothilfe (Technical Emergency Aid)
TO&E	table of organization and equipment
Uffz.	*Unteroffizier* (sergeant)
UK	*Unkriegsverwendungsfähig* (not suited for military service, draft deferred, or exempt)
USSBS	United States Strategic Bombing Survey
Verw.	*Verwaltung* (administration)
VGD or VEDiv	*Volksgrenadier* Division
Vs.	Volkssturm
VsBtn	Volkssturm *bataillon* (battalion)
VsKomp	Volkssturm *kompanie* (company)
WEA	*Wehrersatzamt* (Conscription and Recruiting Office)
WE-Lager	Wehrertüchtigungslager (Premilitary Training Camp)
WFSt	Wehrmacht Führungsstab (Armed Forces Command Staff)
Wi.	*Wirtschaft(s)* (economy or economic)
WK	Wehrkreis (Replacement Army Area)
WvW	Wehrmachtverlustwesens (Armed Forces Casualties Branch)
zbV	*zur besondere Verwendung* (Special Purpose)
Z-Karte	*Zuteilungskarte* (Z-Card, Volkssturm deferral or deferment card)

Preface

This study began in the fall of 1984 as a paper topic for Gerhard L. Weinberg's graduate seminar at the University of North Carolina. It grew into a master's thesis, then a doctoral dissertation, and finally a book manuscript. In the beginning the fact that scholars had written little on the Volkssturm seemed justification enough for the project. My goal then was simply to explain the purpose of the Volkssturm and why it failed. As the work has matured, however, I have come to see the Volkssturm as more than simply a failed militia created by a desperate regime bent on prolonging an irretrievably lost war. It is a window into better understanding Nazi Germany, its leaders, and its people in World War II's turbulent final phase.

While labeling the Volkssturm a failure or desperate is not inaccurate, neither is it a complete explanation. My research has led me to conclude—contrary to much existing scholarship on the period—that Nazi Germany's leadership began to formulate and implement a relatively coherent strategy in the late summer of 1944. This strategy aimed at winning the war, but in a peculiarly National Socialist manner. The plan called for creating a stalemate that would prolong the war, maximize enemy casualties, and ultimately collapse the supposedly inferior Allies' morale. Nazi leaders envisioned the Volkssturm playing a critical, dual role in this strategy. First, they intended it to be a militia, mobilizing men as part-time soldiers for the local defense of their hometowns. Second, they planned to use the Volkssturm as a means to indoctrinate all German men into willingly and fanatically participating in and sacrificing for the ultimate victory. Moreover, achieving this motivational goal would unify the German Volk—obediently, fanatically, and loyally—behind the leadership of the Party. This would complete the cherished *Gleichschaltung* that the NSDAP had pursued for years as its most fundamental objective.

Today it is certainly difficult to see how Germany could have won the war after mid-1944, but my aim is not to argue that the Nazis' plan was feasible. I merely intend to identify the perceptions that drove decision making in the Third Reich in late 1944 and early 1945 and to show that the strategy was consistent with the Nazi system and its worldview. While I want to show that influential German leaders considered their plan workable, the majority of the book focuses on the precise reasons why the Volkssturm failed to achieve its overall objectives. Among the most salient obstacles to Volkssturm success were the deteriorating military and economic situations, poor civilian morale, Nazi political infighting, and, perhaps most important, the fundamental inaccuracy of the ideological assumptions—both of Allied strength and of German and NSDAP abilities—that guided Nazi thought. Because of the Volkssturm's scope, understanding the reasons behind this organization's existence and performance helps us better grasp the German perspective—at all levels—during the last months of the Third Reich.

Anyone researching the Volkssturm quickly encounters a discouraging fact—its primary sources are scattered and fragmentary. This resulted from several historical factors. Volkssturm administration had national, regional, and local branches; therefore, the remaining documentary evidence is housed in the numerous German archives that serve these levels. Volkssturm records typically reside in the collections of other agencies, largely because the militia's officials held positions in other organizations and kept their Volkssturm files in the offices of these other groups. Moreover, the Volkssturm's scope—it included all men aged sixteen to sixty—touched every public and private entity in Germany, and all generated some paperwork on some aspect of the force. Therefore, Volkssturm primary sources are frequently located in obscure places.

Further complicating research is the fact that German record keeping in late 1944 and early 1945 was poor and uneven. Time and supplies were short, and Volkssturm officials typically had many other duties to perform. Furthermore, much of the paper actually generated on the Volkssturm fell victim to intentional or accidental destruction during the war's closing phase. After the war, the stock of documents continued to decline, since neither the Germans nor the Allied Military Government placed high priority on preserving the full range of Volkssturm records. Fortunately, however, the Volkssturm's national scope created a duplication of effort that helped ensure the survival of primary evidence on virtually every aspect of the force. On the other hand, no single set of Volkssturm documents is comprehensive. Virtually every archive that contains Nazi era materials has some fragmentary files, and relevant material may appear in the collections from almost any agency. This necessitates probing many different archives' holdings and looking in rather unlikely places. For example, perusal of the National Socialist Teachers' Union files led to the discovery of the largest and richest single folder of Volkssturm documents. Ultimately, the most effective approach was simply to examine any documentary collection—NSDAP, military, governmental, or otherwise—dating from the period between the fall of 1944 and the end of the war.

Assembling such a mosaic of sources produced a sufficient evidentiary base but created a rather patchwork appearance for the bibliography and notes. In addition, citations may appear excessive in number or somewhat bloated in specific cases, although they have been rigorously pruned both collectively and individually. Two factors create these impressions. First, information presented in the text is frequently a conclusion pieced together from several sources. Second, labeling a trend as typical or widespread often required citing documents from various individual units or specific localities. Likewise, showing how a national directive was ignored, altered, or implemented at the regional or local level similarly required citing several documents from separate areas or entities. Thus, the nature of the sources tended to mandate dense and frequent citations.

Contemporary events also impacted my research in a curious way. A few months after my dissertation defense in 1990, the two Germanies united. This effectively opened former East German archival collections and necessitated a second archival tour that—given my work and family situations—I could not undertake until 1996. Aside from proving that historians are indeed profoundly affected by history, I mention this as a caveat in connection with using the citations. The notes and bibliography give the preunification locations of documents in the German Federal Archives (Bundesarchiv) because that is where I consulted them. Today much of what I cite as holdings of the Bundesarchiv Koblenz is no longer there. Berlin-Lichterfeld has the NS- and most R-prefixed collections, Lastenausgleichsarchiv Bayreuth has the OstDok collections, and Koblenz has photographs. Thus unification further dispersed the Volkssturm's primary source base.

Working with such a scattered source base also creates an extensive list of institutions and individuals to whom the researcher owes a debt of gratitude. In my work, I received indispensable financial assistance from the University of North Carolina Graduate School and the German Academic Exchange Service (DAAD), while a sabbatical leave from Gardner-Webb University facilitated my postdissertation research in former East German archives. I am boundlessly thankful to the legion of archivists who have aided my work, particularly Richard Boylan, John Taylor, Tim Mulligan, Bill Lewis, Will Mahoney, and Rick Wehmann at the National Archives; Gregor Verlande at the Bundesarchiv Koblenz; and Herr Meyer, Dr. Ringsdorf, and Herr Moritz at Freiburg's Militärarchiv. Heartfelt gratitude also goes to Dr. Brommer, Rheinland-Pfalz LHA Koblenz; Dr. Eichler, Hessisches HStA Wiesbaden; Dr. Faust, Nordrhein-Westfälisches HStA Düsseldorf; Dr. Hermann, Saarländisches LA Saarbrücken; Dr. Hönig, Niedersächisches HStA Hannover; Dr. Lauchs, Bayerisches HStA Munich; Dr. Wehner, LA Sachsen-Anhalt Magdeburg; Dr. Wittern, Brandenburgisches LA Potsdam; Archivar Braunn, Württemburgisches HStA Stuttgart; Archivar Lißner, Thüringisches HStA Weimar; Herr Raab, Badisches GLA Karlsruhe; Volker Viergutz, LA Berlin; Dr. Böhme, StA Bückeburg; Dr. Lent, StA Wolfenbüttel; the late Dr. Karl H. Mistele, StA Bamberg; Dr. Niebuhr, StA Detmold; Dr. Weber, StA Munich; Archivamtmann Friedrich, StA Nürnberg; Archivoberrat Fritsch, StA Amberg; Archivarin Schnorbus, StA Münster; Dr. Ecker, Stadtarchiv Freiburg; Dr. Wisotzky, Stadtarchiv Ratingen (who allowed me to visit on a day when the archive was closed); and Dr. Kalcyk, Deutsches Rotes Kreuz—Suchdienst München. Thanks also to the archivists and staffs of the Institut für Zeitgeschichte, the Deutsche Dienststelle für die Benachrichtigung der nächsten Angehörigen von Gefallenen der ehemaligen deutschen Wehrmacht, the Volksbund Deutsche Kriegsgräberfürsorge, StA Ludwigsburg, Zweigarchiv Schloß Kalkum, and Stadtarchiv Rastatt, who were all so very helpful with my inquiries and/or brief visits.

For generously sending copies of relevant documents and publications, I must acknowledge Frau Ortmanns, Bundesarchiv Zentralnachweisstelle Korneleimünster; Dr. Delbanco, StA Osnabrück; Dr. Moczarski, StA Meiningen; Archivarin Büttner, StA Hamburg; Dr. Ecker, Stadtarchiv Freiburg; Reinhard Schippkus, Stadtarchiv Goch; Senior Archival Officer O. A. Cooke, Canadian National Defence Headquarters' Directorate of History; and Elena Danielson, Hoover Institution. Furthermore, I would also like to express my appreciation for the efforts of the host of archivists who graciously took time to try to locate Volkssturm documents in depositories where there were none. Without their efforts, my research would have been infinitely more frustrating, expensive, and time-consuming.

I owe a very special debt of gratitude to Herr Michel, Sozialabteilung chief of the German Red Cross's Landesverbandstelle in Mainz, for entrusting me with his office's copies of the *Vermißtenbildliste (Pictoral Lists of the Missing in Action)*. The efforts of Heidemarie Daher, Director of the Gedenkstätte/Museum Seelower Höhen, the Bundesarchiv's Martina Caspers and Martina Geilen, Ullsteinbild's Jörg Lampertius, plus Warren W. Odegard, Darrin Weaver, Anthony Le Tissier, Ron Carey, Kasey Hughes, Mike Yelton, and King Photography helped me immensely in locating and procuring Volkssturm photographs and specific information concerning equipment and weaponry. I greatly appreciate John Yelton's taking my very raw geographic information and turning it into polished maps. My thanks also go to Hermann Schelling and Hans Sturm for the openness and honesty with which they answered my queries concerning their personal experiences with the Volkssturm.

Gerhard Weinberg, who has always been most generous with both his encyclopedic expertise and his limited time, has provided invaluable encouragement and assistance since the project's inception. My gratitude also goes to Konrad Jarausch, Josef Anderle, Donald Reid, Joseph Caddell, Samuel Williamson, John Headley, George Taylor, Don Higginbotham, James Leutze, Lewis Bateman, David Grier, Gil Blackburn, Geoffrey Megargee, Perry Biddiscombe, Dennis Showalter, and Michael Briggs, who read and provided valuable suggestions on all or part of this work. For their efforts and patience, I am most appreciative of the librarians and interlibrary loan staffs at both the University of North Carolina and Gardner-Webb University. Likewise, I am indebted to my colleagues in the Social Sciences Department at Gardner-Webb for willingly shouldering the additional burdens created by my sabbatical leave. Thanks go to the Kundel family of Koblenz, and Hermann, Wolf-Dietrich, and Bärbel Schelling for their hospitality during my research trips to Germany and other forms of direct and indirect assistance.

In closing, I want to thank my family, without whom success would be both meaningless and impossible. My parents, Charles and Frances Yelton, have always supported and encouraged my educational pursuits. My three beautiful daughters, Katie, Allyson, and Emily, who though they came along after much of the work was already done, always happily and unknowingly provided me with entertainment, perspective, and diversions. Finally, I cannot overstate the magnitude of the contribution of my wife, Denise. She endured without complaint many long weeks and months alone while I was researching, cheerfully proofread drafts, suffered my frustrations, shared my successes, and generally lifted my spirits on countless occasions. Without her limitless love and support, this book would have been unthinkable. To my family, friends, colleagues, and mentors, I offer my humble thanks for all their contributions to this book. Of course, I alone am wholly responsible for whatever flaws may remain.

Introduction

Following the smashing of German Army Group Center in the summer of 1944, Soviet troops pushed across the German frontier into East Prussia near Fichtenhöhe on August 17.[1] Thus, for the first time since the desultory French raids of 1939, German soil came under enemy occupation. Only this time, further Allied offensives were inevitable, and the Wehrmacht was much weaker relative to its enemies. This situation sparked a sequence of events that culminated in the creation of the German Volkssturm, a compulsory national militia, under the organizational and administrative control of the Nazi Party (NSDAP). This book seeks to provide a comprehensive explanation of this militia and to put it in the broader context of strategy, politics, and morale in the Third Reich during the last months of World War II.

In spite of the national scope and sheer size of the Volkssturm—it sought to enroll all German civilian males between the ages of sixteen and sixty—scholars, especially in the English-speaking world, have largely ignored this force. One reason for this neglect is that historians have tended to view German resistance after the summer of 1944 as nothing more than incoherent and hopeless efforts to protract the death throes of a criminal regime. This view originated in Allied perceptions at the time; one of the charges levied against Nazi defendants at Nuremberg was unnecessarily prolonging the war via the Volkssturm and other measures.[2] With German efforts in this period deemed reactive, improvisational, and therefore generally unworthy of serious attention, scholars—again especially those in the English-speaking world—focused almost exclusively on Allied decision making instead. Certainly, there are substantial numbers of German *"Kriegsende"* works on the events of 1944–1945, but most of these narratives limit their analysis to excoriating the Nazis for bringing destruction on some German locality and for wasting additional lives. Thus they, too, assume Nazi Germany followed only pointless and disjointed impulses in late 1944 and 1945.

This long-standing view fails to address several important questions. Precisely what did Germany's leaders hope to achieve by prolonging the war, and how did they plan to accomplish this? Were the various German efforts in late 1944 and early 1945 really part of no coherent larger pattern? Why, if the war was so clearly lost, did the final conquest of Germany require significant heavy fighting—particularly on the Eastern Front—with casualty rates comparable to those of campaigns earlier in the war?[3] Why was there so little concerted, serious effort by Germany's leaders to negotiate peace and thus try to salvage what they could of their power? Finally, what motivated average Germans either to fight on or to surrender?

For a number of reasons, the German Volkssturm provides an extremely useful window into these issues. It was a national organization and consisted of a cross section of German civilian society, which allows for substantial insight into public opinion. Moreover, evidence suggests that in late 1944 a number of influential German leaders—in both the party and the military—considered a militia to have considerable potential value for the war effort. Thus, a better understanding of the goals and operation of the Volkssturm should clarify a whole range of military, political, morale, and economic issues related to the Third Reich in its final months.

Several works specifically address the Volkssturm, but none do so comprehensively. All focus too narrowly either on the militia's military aspects[4] or exclusively on its political issues.[5] While these works clarify specific parts of the Volkssturm, none furnishes a satisfyingly thorough and contextually accurate explanation of the force's formation, purpose, and performance. Furthermore, all erroneously assume that the Volkssturm was shaped exclusively by the party and that it failed because the NSDAP, solely responsible for all mistakes made during the Third Reich, was inept. No Western scholar acknowledges any strategic purpose for the Volkssturm, apparently simply assuming that there could have been none at this late date. East German interpretations, on the other hand, depict a strategic role for the Volkssturm but saw it—due more to Marxist ideology than to demonstrable fact—as a tool the capitalist elite created to safeguard its material interests.[6]

None of these studies fully explore the impact of National Socialist ideology on the Volkssturm. Nor do they examine the effect of the NSDAP's internal political divisions. Likewise, they neglect the role played by institutions such as the Wehrmacht or party-affiliated organizations (e.g., the SA or Hitler Youth), economic concerns, or public morale. Also, they fail to evaluate how the Volkssturm operated at the regional and local levels, which was the real focus of the militia's activity. Finally, none of them utilize the full range of available sources.

During the last decade, some scholars have turned their attention to aspects of Germany's situation during the war's final phase. While none have directly addressed the Volkssturm, some have addressed issues relevant to the militia. Gerhard Weinberg's latest works, including the massive and magisterial *A World at Arms*, strongly suggest that many of Nazi Germany's leaders continued to hope even into the war's last months that they could salvage some sort of victory—or at least avoid defeat—if they could convince the German people to continue the fight.[7] Eleanor Hancock's *National Socialist Leadership and Total War, 1941–45* and Perry Biddiscombe's *Werwolf! The History of the National Socialist Guerrilla Movement, 1944–1946* generally support this conclusion as well.[8]

Further scholarly interest in issues related to the war's end and—again tangentially—the German Volkssturm, grew out of the *Historikerstreit* (loosely, the "clash of historians") that began in Germany during the late 1980s. This debate touched off considerable discussion, often generating more heat than light, on a range of topics swirling around the core issue of the Holocaust's uniqueness in history.[9] Among the specific questions raised in this connection was whether Germans, particularly in the war's final phase, could also be considered victims of Nazism. This in turn generated an ongoing discussion— quite relevant to the Volkssturm though not addressing it specifically—of the motivational role that National Socialist ideology played in the military. This debate revealed evidence that Nazi ideas, particularly those grafted onto traditional attitudes and perceptions, often proved a strong inspiration for average German soldiers.[10] However, proponents of linking the Wehrmacht and Nazism have also been charged with overstating their case, the most publicly controversial example involving the Hamburger Institut für Sozialforschung's exhibition "War of Extermination: Crimes of the Wehrmacht 1939–1945."[11]

To some extent, the *Historikerstreit* also revitalized the significant and long-running debate between the intentionalist and structuralist-functionalist schools of thought. This controversy originally had focused on the 1930s, Jewish policy and the Holocaust, and the war's early phases. Intentionalists generally argued that Nazi actions grew out of consciously designed programs that were ultimately based on Hitler's interpretation of National Socialist ideological goals. Structuralists-functionalists, on the other hand, argued that Nazi policy formulation was primarily chaotic and incomprehensible, and resulted from internal political clashes generated by the overlapping and competing jurisdictions within the Third Reich's tangled bureaucratic structure.

Several post-*Historikerstreit* works have not only shifted this investigation into Nazi Germany's final months but also begun to synthesize the best of the intentionalist and functionalist schools. They show that while Hitler remained the ultimate arbiter of policy formulation, his subordinates simultaneously held considerable leeway to suggest, modify, and interpret policy options. Because Nazi ideology tended to form the common vocabulary of decision making, the individual most adept at couching plans and programs in this language, displaying zeal, and portraying his efforts as best contributing to Hitler's most cherished goals typically received and maintained the Führer's blessing. This approval, in turn, was essential to the implementation of the subordinate's ideas and to enhancing his power and prestige.[12]

This book seeks to build on these views and to go beyond them to provide a clearer understanding of the Volkssturm and Nazi Germany as World War II neared its end. To accomplish this, it centers upon four major categories of issues: the Volkssturm's strategic purpose, its organizational structure and operation, the preparation of the force to carry out its goals, and its combat performance. The first main cluster of questions (chapters 1 and 2) concerns the Volkssturm's founding in September 1944. Understanding this decision requires placing it in the strategic context faced by Nazi Germany at this time. This not only necessitates examining the actual strategic situation but also requires grasping how National Socialist ideology shaped the Reich leadership's perceptions of contemporary conditions. This investigation will clarify the purpose of the Volkssturm but—in conjunction with chapter 3—also will help illuminate decision making late in the Third Reich. In turn, it will thereby contribute to synthesizing the intentionalist and structuralist-functionalist views.

The second major group of issues (chapters 3–5) furthers the understanding of Nazi Germany's power structure in late 1944–1945 by comparing the theoretical and actual operation of the Volkssturm at the national, regional, and local levels. This involves a detailed discussion of how the interaction between various organizations influenced Volkssturm policy creation and implementation. Martin Bormann's Party Chancellery is sometimes perceived as omnipotent over the Volkssturm, but other NSDAP-affiliated organizations—particularly Heinrich Himmler's SS and police, the Hitler Youth, SA—exerted influence as well. Two non-Party entities, the Wehrmacht and the Reichs Ministry for Armaments and War Production, also played relatively important roles. Finally, there is the significant impact of public morale upon the militia. This section tests the prevailing assumption of Bormann's dominance over the Volkssturm, illustrates the role of ideology in Nazi political infighting, and shows that the political power of the SS was perhaps beginning to wane—at least vis-à-vis the NSDAP.

Also integral to this second section is an unprecedented examination of the Volkssturm at the local level. Here one can see the negative impact of national power struggles and discover how regional and local non-Party entities, particularly the Wehrmacht, industry, and public opinion, frequently exerted influence on the militia, often in ways contrary to the force's official objectives. Finally, this section shows how Volkssturm leaders created the Levy *(Aufgebot)* System for personnel classification as a way to keep Volkssturm training and mobilization from disrupting the war economy, but it also served Bormann's political interests. This Levy System clearly reflected the Third Reich's final military mobilization priorities but also generally proved frustrating for all involved and damaging to morale.

The third group of issues (chapters 6–7) addresses the Volkssturm's preparations for combat and how National Socialist ideology, public opinion, and military and economic concerns affected them. This section emphasizes the immense difficulty—even impossibility—faced in preparing the Volkssturm for combat but also examines the methods employed in the effort to overcome these obstacles. One significant theme is that the public demand that the Volkssturm conform to international legal requirements (to ensure that the Allies treated captured militiamen as prisoners of war, not partisans) often forced the watering down of Nazi ideological goals. The pursuit of legality ultimately affected unit organization, officer selection, and political and military training, as well as how units were equipped, armed, and utilized. It also created an opportunity for the Wehrmacht to expand its role within the force, which—contrary to many officers' postwar assertions[13]—was often extensive.

The fourth and final category of topics (chapters 8–9) concerns the Volkssturm's performance in light of its objectives. While most accounts stress the force's numerous battlefield failures and accept the oversimplified and exculpatory explanations produced immediately after the war by former Wehrmacht commanders,[14] I attempt to account for the full range of factors behind both the Volkssturm's defeats and its more infrequent successes. In particular, it explains why the militia performed better on the Eastern Front than the Western Front and examines not only military factors (e.g., the extent and effectiveness of Wehrmacht involvement in command, control, communication, and logistical issues) but also the perspectives, morale, and motivations of Volkssturm members.

Therefore, while to some a study of the German Volkssturm might seem unneeded, a better understanding of this force gives considerable insight into several significant issues from the war's final, turbulent months. This book clarifies policy formulation and implementation in the late Third Reich and assesses the shifting power relationships among various groups and individuals. It also illustrates the continued importance of Hitler and ideology in Nazi Germany's policy-making process. Moreover, it reveals some interesting information concerning the Wehrmacht's attitude toward the Volkssturm and Nazism in the wake of the July 20 Plot. Furthermore, the book illuminates how local and regional officials implemented and modified national decrees and shows the crippling effects of the NSDAP's internal power struggles. It also identifies the Reich's final mobilization priorities. In another vein, it helps enhance our understanding of the views of average Germans toward the NSDAP and the war in its closing phase. Finally, the Volkssturm provides insight into the Battle of Germany by showing motivations of troops, the role of the militia in combat, and the severe handicaps faced by both the Volkssturm and the Wehrmacht by 1945. Ultimately, because the Volkssturm was so heavily shaped by the perceptions of both Germany's leaders and its people, a better understanding of it significantly enhances our growing knowledge of the Third Reich—rulers and inhabitants—during the maelstrom of World War II's final months.

CHAPTER ONE

Founding the Volkssturm

The German Volkssturm's founding on September 25, 1944, followed a series of disastrous military defeats during the summer that had left Allied armies poised on the Reich's eastern and western borders. Germany tottered psychologically as well, with civilian morale declining due to the enemy advances, increasingly disruptive Allied bombing, and growing fears of revolts by foreign laborers or prisoners. In fact, many Nazis saw the dreaded mythological specter of the "stab in the back" rear its ugly head on July 20, when Hitler was the target of an unsuccessful assassination attempt as part of a failed coup d'état. Facing the prospect of Götterdämmerung, the Reich's political leaders conducted a thorough reevaluation of the war effort that led them to conclude that mastering the desperate situation required the NSDAP to lead a complete military and psychological mobilization of all Germans. As a part of this total-war strategy, Hitler dropped his long-standing opposition and allowed the establishment of the NSDAP-supervised militia ultimately called the German Volkssturm. This chapter and chapter 2 examine this process in detail and illustrate that the Volkssturm, although clearly an improvisation in many of the details of its implementation, was part of a consistent—though ideologically influenced—strategy intended to turn the tide of the war in Germany's favor. This chapter focuses on the course of events surrounding the Volkssturm's founding and illustrates that while the military had long planned on creating a militia to meet home defense contingencies, the NSDAP had done virtually nothing to prepare for raising a national militia, yet Hitler awarded the Party control of this new force.

Even in the war's early phases, Wehrmacht planning for tactical emergencies and for local defense within Germany included creating and deploying militia formations. The field army often used so-called alarm units, which typically included furloughed soldiers, stragglers, units and individuals in transit, and convalescents; but the Army High Command (OKH) had instructed that "even the last German man, regardless of his training or position, is to be enrolled [in the alarm unit] and, in emergencies, to be committed to battle."[1] Alarm units were weak, limited stopgaps with no formal, systematic mechanism for mobilizing civilian men on a broad and/or permanent basis; but they do reveal the Wehrmacht's basic willingness to employ hastily conscripted civilians in combat.

There are other clear examples of Wehrmacht willingness to utilize civilians in more permanent auxiliary formations. During preparations for the invasion of the Soviet Union, the Replacement Army[2] established so-called alarm companies to supplement its local defense and security forces. Each contained up to 150 German men aged forty-five or younger who were fit for—but occupationally exempt from—military service. They lived in the vicinity of, or were employed by, an important installation to which they were assigned to provide security. To prepare these men for their duties, the Replacement Army mandated that each company hold monthly training drills scheduled around its members' work. Armed with rifles and light machine guns provided by the *Wehrkreis* (the Replacement Army's regional commands), alarm company members were identifiable on active duty by regulation field caps and yellow armbands bearing the words *Deutsche Wehrmacht* in black letters. In case of commando raids, sabotage, prisoner-of-war or foreign worker uprisings, or even enemy invasion, alarm companies would mobilize and fight as soldiers under Wehrkreis command.[3]

In 1942, changing home security needs prompted transfer of the alarm companies to police control. They were subsequently expanded, reorganized, and renamed the *Stadtwacht* in urban areas and the *Landwacht* in the countryside. With the diminished threat of attack by enemy land forces and the growing number of foreign workers and prisoners of war in Germany, police (especially rural gendarmes) required augmentation more than did Wehrkreis forces.[4] By mid-1943, the *Stadt- und Landwacht* had developed into a valuable security auxiliary that had apprehended 6,556 prisoners of war (escapees and downed airmen), 12,346 wayward foreign workers, and 1,345 criminals. By year's end, the Stadt- und Landwacht numbered nearly 1 million men and possessed enough Italian weapons, pistols, hunting rifles, and other miscellaneous arms to equip about half its members.[5] As the military situation worsened in the summer of 1944, the Stadt- und Landwacht—its limited firepower notwithstanding—began assuming additional duties such as combating small groups of airborne commandos and spies. Furthermore, Wehrkreis emergency defense plans continued, as with the earlier alarm companies, to call for its use as combat-ready militia units.[6]

Other evidence plainly illustrates the Wehrmacht's intention to expand militia forces should Germany actually be invaded. In September 1942, shortly after the disastrous Anglo-Canadian raid on Dieppe, Wehrmacht High Command (OKW) chief Field Marshal Wilhelm Keitel, authorized the call-up of "all German males . . . for short-term military service" in any area threatened by invasion. Keitel did not specify whether these men would serve in separate militia formations or as auxiliaries in existing army units, but he emphasized they would be legally considered soldiers, would be equipped with helmets, weapons, and armbands by the Wehrkreis, and would be used in combat if needed.[7]

Indeed, as the war situation worsened, the army began actually establishing substantial regional militias. In mid-1943, Major General Adolf Heusinger, chief of the OKH Operations Section, proposed that the eastern Wehrkreise organize and train part-time auxiliary formations to defend fortified areas and cities and to provide rear area security. Though little is known about Heusinger's plan, Hitler, fearing adverse effects on public morale, flatly rejected it.[8] Nonetheless, by February 1944, Wehrkreis XXI (Posen) had established eighteen so-called Grolmann militia battalions consisting of reliable, draftexempt, or deferred German men for use against Polish partisans or, if necessary, the Red Army. Wehrkreis XXI pressed forward with this plan against local NSDAP opposition until the Volkssturm's creation mooted the whole issue.[9]

The Wehrmacht also moved to create similar militia formations in other areas. During July 1944, General Walther Warlimont of the OKW Operations Section, seeking troops to occupy newly constructed positions in the Alpine foothills, ordered the expansion of the largely ceremonial Tirolean *Standschutz* (previously little more than marksmanship clubs) into a militia of about 30,000 men under the supervision of a Major von Reichel.[10] About twenty Standschutz mountain infantry battalions of 1,125 men each existed when the Volkssturm absorbed this organization in late 1944.[11] On September 30, 1944, *Oberbefehlshaber* (OB) West, Field Marshal Gerd von Rundstedt, invoking Keitel's September 1942 order, instructed his town battle commanders *(Kampfkommandanten)* in Germany to enroll "all men capable of bearing arms regardless of age . . . to strengthen [their] defense forces."[12] Clearly, these actions show that the Wehrmacht as a whole perceived that properly organized, trained, and led militia units could effectively contribute to Germany's defense.

While the army broadly favored using militia forces, Hitler and other top NSDAP leaders had typically opposed them. The Reich's political leaders allowed police auxiliaries like the Stadt- und Landwacht or the ethnic German paramilitary "self-defense" forces in occupied or annexed territories to deal with criminals, partisans, or internal unrest; but preparing civilians to combat enemy soldiers was another matter entirely. Top Party leaders not only opposed Heusinger's plan and Wehrkreis XXI's "Grolmann" action but squelched even Party-controlled militia schemes. In late 1941, the Party Chancellery flatly rejected a proposal from Gau Hesse-Nassau to incorporate all armed Nazi units into the framework of the Wehrkreis alarm companies.[13] On July 14, 1943, Swabian *Gauleiter* (NSDAP regional chief) Karl Wahl reported his effort to form in his Gau a so-called *Heimatschutztrupp* of 15,000 to 20,000 loyal Nazis as a means of combating potential internal disorders or Allied attack. This met fierce objections from Party Chancellery chief Martin Bormann and *Reichsführer SS* (RFSS, Reich Leader of the SS), and chief of the German Police Heinrich Himmler, who ultimately thwarted Wahl's plan.[14] Viennese Gauleiter Baldur von Schirach's similar proposal found no more success than did Wahl's.[15]

The national Party leadership's opposition to these Nazi militias sprang from two sources. One was the byzantine political structure of the Third Reich. Militias inside Germany represented a potential avenue for encroachment into police matters, that is, Himmler's domestic power base.[16] Furthermore, Bormann feared that a Gauleiter (e.g., Wahl) could parlay a regional militia into a national organization, thereby giving him a source of authority independent of Party Chancellery (i.e., Bormann's) control. Given these concerns, Himmler and Bormann used their considerable influence to block the creation of Nazi militias prior to the late summer of 1944.

Hitler's personal biases formed the other factor behind Nazi hostility toward militias. With the arrogance of a proud former *Frontkämpfer,* Hitler considered part-time civilian soldiers ineffective in and undisciplined for the rigors of combat. More important, the Führer suspected that creating even a substantial regional militia could damage or even collapse civilian morale. Firmly convinced that Germany's defeat in 1918 had resulted from a disintegration of the home front's will to fight, Hitler refused to contemplate forming a militia under anyone's control for fear that this could prompt history to repeat itself.[17]

In the summer of 1944, however, the political leadership's adamant opposition to militias began to shift as the military situation deteriorated. On June 22, the Red Army initiated the first of a series of massive offensives in White Russia that destroyed German Army Group Center. Lacking sufficient mobile reserves, surprised due to incorrect intelligence reports, hampered by partisans and Hitler's insistence on holding as far east as possible, the Germans could not halt the Soviet drive until it reached the East Prussian border in late August. Subsequent Soviet offensives knocked Finland out of the war, isolated German Army Group North in Courland, and smashed deep into the Balkans. Before Soviet southern advances ended in November, Romania and Bulgaria had defected and Germany had lost most of the Balkans and part of Hungary, which remained a German ally only at gunpoint.[18]

Compounding the Wehrmacht's problems was the opening of the long-awaited "second front" in France. By September 11, Allied forces had broken out of Normandy's difficult hedgerow country, liberated most of France and Belgium, and crossed the German border near the village of Keppeshausen on the Luxembourg border due west of Bitburg.[19] In Italy, Rome had fallen on June 4, and Army Group C's Gothic Line formed the last defensible Italian terrain south of the Po and the Alpine foothills. The other active front, in the Far North, was stable; but after the Finnish armistice, the German Twentieth Army fought on alone.

Although the disastrous summer of 1944 cost the Reich vast expanses of territory, personnel losses were even more catastrophic. Between June 1 and November 30, the army and Waffen SS admitted 1,457,000 casualties; OKH listed 106 divisions as either destroyed or disbanded for replacements. The strength of the field army in the east fell from 2,620,000 in June to 1,920,000 in October; and by mid-December, after herculean efforts to make good these losses, German infantry and panzer divisions were still, on average, one-third understrength.[20] The increasingly effective Allied strategic bombing campaign which tied up personnel on the home front in antiaircraft, civil defense, and repair duties only complicated the manpower problem of shifting troops from civilian to military status.[21]

With war reaching German territory, the Wehrmacht's Replacement Army—1,249,000 men strong at the beginning of October—could augment the field army's strength, but it could not carry out extensive combat tasks and simultaneously replenish the depleted ranks of the field armies.[22] While each of the nineteen Wehrkreise maintained a special combat command structure resembling that of an army corps, their fighting potential was rather low. Most Wehrkreis troops were administrative and logistical personnel; and the most combat-ready men, Replacement and Training cadres, were too valuable to risk except in extreme emergencies. The other Wehrkreis combat component, *Landesschützen* battalions composed of superannuated healthy men aged forty-five to fifty-five and younger men deemed unfit for full combat duty, were of limited value.[23] Of the 336 *Landesschützen* battalions, one-fourth (86) were already serving with the field army, and the rest were often fully occupied in such essential security duties as guarding prisoners of war. Finally, most were badly understrength due to furloughs for essential skilled workers and efforts to comb out replacements for frontline units.[24] Although providing a command and logistical framework for home defense, the Replacement Army was too deeply engaged in enlisting, equipping, and training new recruits, establishing the twenty-five new "Volksgrenadier" divisions ordered in August by Hitler, and performing essential rear area security, logistical, and administrative tasks to contribute much to defending Germany's borders.

Clearly, recovering from the disasters of the summer of 1944 necessitated raising additional manpower for the Wehrmacht. The dilemma facing German political and military leaders in September 1944 was how to balance this with the necessity of maintaining or even increasing production levels. Efforts to replace healthy adult male workers with women, foreigners, and men too young or old for the draft were under way, but this process was complex and time-consuming. The need for troops was immediate.

Colonel General Heinz Guderian, appointed on July 21 as Chief of the Army General Staff—and the commander directly responsible for the Eastern Front—found this situation particularly vexing. Not only had his troops taken the greatest mauling during the summer, Hitler had decided in August to commit the bulk of refitted divisions, particularly the armored ones, to the west. Hitler wanted an offensive in the Ardennes aimed at knocking the Western Allies out of the war.[25] To strengthen the Eastern Front, Guderian first sought to create 100 fortress infantry battalions, supported by an equal number of artillery batteries, to garrison the various fortified zones in eastern Germany. This would, he reasoned, help create a defense in depth that could forestall any further deep penetrations and encirclements by the Red Army. Guderian hoped to tap hitherto unused resources by equipping the batteries with captured artillery and filling the units' ranks with older men classified as only partially fit for field duty.[26]

Formation of Guderian's fortress units began in late July, but Hitler upset OKH planning on September 2 by transferring these fortress troops to the West Wall.[27] Although Guderian—who had no command responsibility on the Western Front—protested vehemently, OKW desperately needed reinforcements to halt the Western Allies' rapid advance.[28] Again facing the need to procure additional troops for the Eastern Front, Guderian, on the suggestion of his Operations Section head, General Walter Wenck, revived Heusinger's 1943 militia proposal. Sometime between September 3 and 6, Guderian proposed forming a Landsturm[29] from eastern German men who, for reasons of occupation, age, or health, were exempt or deferred from military service. These Landsturm units, once organized, trained, and deployed by the eastern Wehrkreise, would substitute for the transferred fortress battalions. Hitler, however, flatly rejected the suggestion.[30]

Desperate for troops and convinced of the utility of a properly prepared militia, Guderian subsequently modified his Landsturm proposal in hopes of overcoming Hitler's preconceptions and fears. Overall command would remain with the Wehrkreise, and military experience would be required for all unit leaders, but to ease the Führer's mind, the SA—whose chief, Wilhelm Schepmann, Guderian considered competent and *"Wehrmachtfreundlich"*—would supervise raising and training the Landsturm. As with so many of the Führer's major decisions, no written record exists of either the proposal or Hitler's response, but Guderian's claim that the Führer approved his modified proposal on or around September 6 seems accurate. Indeed, Goebbels's diary records a meeting with Schepmann on September 8 concerning a proposed SA-led Landsturm.[31] On September 11, OKW apparently referred to a militia in a message which stated that "the highest German leaders have made a radical decision that will win time and above all manpower *[Kräfte]* for the security and defense of the Reich," while a Foreign Office memorandum referred to the founding of a "type of *Landsturm*" comparable to the army-controlled militia that existed in World War I.[32] Finally, in a September 18 teletype to Bormann, East Prussian Gauleiter Erich Koch stated his opposition to the formation of a Wehrkreis-led Landsturm, claiming that only the NSDAP had the necessary authority, leadership, and "ability to inspire" the German people for the coming "holy people's war."[33]

Although Guderian apparently did win Hitler's approval, the army-SA *Landsturm* never came into being. By September 14, Hitler had shifted control of the militia to the NSDAP. On that date Bormann informed his staff that Hitler had decided to create a national, rather than regional, "*Volkswehr*" to be organized by the Gauleiters and employed on security tasks in conjunction with the Wehrkreise. He added that further instructions would be forthcoming from the Party Chancellery and the Replacement Army command; this clearly indicates Bormann and Himmler—not the army—would run this enterprise. By September 18, Bormann had the basic organizational structure in place, and on September 21 Himmler publicly used the name "German Volkssturm" for the first time. On September 25, 1944, Hitler formally announced the Volkssturm's creation to high-ranking officials in a Führer Decree granting Himmler control of military matters and Bormann administrative and organizational issues.[34]

What prompted Hitler's sudden changes of heart, first in dropping his opposition to a militia, then in shifting control of it to the NSDAP? The former seems to have stemmed, at least in part, from the desperate military situation; but his decision to award significant powers to the NSDAP sprang from the broad reassessment of the German war effort that the summer's military disasters and the July 20 Plot had necessitated. Although chapter 2 fully discusses National Socialist perceptions, it should be noted here that for Hitler and other convinced Nazis, July 20 proved that defeatist and traitorous elements in the officer corps and elsewhere had undermined the war effort. Indeed, in the Nazi Weltanschauung, treason and sabotage formed the most logical explanation for how the Reich's enemies—degenerate, mongrelized Aryans (i.e., the Western Allies) and subhuman Slavs (i.e., the Soviets) led by racially inferior Jews— could have inflicted such severe defeats on the biologically superior German Volk.

Furthermore, to ardent Nazis the key to victory was equally obvious: root out the traitors and restore the confidence, morale, and will to resist of the German people, soldier and civilian alike. For the die-hard National Socialist, such a task was not unlike that which faced them in the *Kampfzeit* (the "period of struggle," i.e., the years prior to 1933 when the Party was seeking to gain power in Germany); now as then, only the NSDAP could quickly and effectively mobilize the German people body and soul to meet the racial enemy's threat.[35]

Although the process had already begun by July 20, the NSDAP's role in all but the most technical aspects of the war effort greatly expanded after the assassination attempt. One of the first steps in this process was a purge of the Replacement Army leadership. Its commander, Colonel General Friedrich Fromm, had been implicated in the July 20 Plot; his chief of staff, Count von Stauffenberg, had actually planted the bomb at the Wolf's Lair; and there were plans to use Replacement Army troops to carry out the coup. Around four o'clock on July 20, with the dust from the bomb blast hardly settled, Hitler assigned Himmler the task of restoring the Replacement Army's loyalty and spirit through genuine Nazi leadership.[36] Although at the time this had nothing to do with the creation of a militia, the knowledge that the trusted Himmler would be involved, as either Replacement Army commander or Chief of German Police or both, certainly may have made Hitler look more favorably on the idea when it was later raised. Obviously, Himmler's opposition to militias ended with this appointment, which, coupled with his post as Chief of German Police, assured him a major role in any such force.[37]

Other changes confirmed Hitler's belief that only the NSDAP could master the crisis facing Germany. The Führer assigned another loyal Nazi associate, Propaganda Minister Joseph Goebbels, the task of tackling the Reich's manpower problems as Reich Plenipotentiary for Total War. Armed with sweeping powers to reduce draft exemptions and deferments, Goebbels relied on a small staff and the Gauleiters, a decision that significantly increased these regional officials' mobilization powers.[38] Hitler believed this exemplified the Kampfzeit spirit and would enable Goebbels to eliminate the bureaucratic delay and infighting that had previously characterized German manpower policy. Again, Goebbels's initial enthusiasm for this task buoyed the self-confidence of the Party leadership and may have encouraged Hitler and Bormann to try this approach with the new militia.

Expanding NSDAP influence over the war effort was not confined to the national level. Prior to summer 1944, regional Party officials controlled only civilian matters—morale, evacuation, and recruitment for antiaircraft work, police auxiliaries, and civil defense.[39] This changed in July as Hitler broadened the Gauleiters' powers as Reich Defense Commissars (RVKs) into the area of home defense. He authorized them to assume full executive power over all Reich government branches, including all armed police auxiliary and Party formations, in any region declared an Operational Zone (i.e., any Gau within twenty kilometers of the front). In areas immediately behind the front, the so-called Combat Zone, the military commander's authority remained supreme, but even here Keitel had declared that the army would confine its activities "to purely military tasks."[40]

In particular, one of the Gauleiters' new duties, the so-called People's Levy *(Volksaufgebot)*, seems to have confirmed predictions that the regional bosses would respond energetically to their tasks and would compete with one another to fulfill the Führer's wishes.[41] The People's Levy began on July 13, when East Prussia's Koch took the initiative to mobilize fully one-quarter of his Gau's populace for border defense construction. For Koch, the People's Levy was exclusively a Party task; he even refused military advice in technical matters. Throughout the summer, thousands of Hitler Youth and members of other

Nazi organizations labored alongside East Prussians from all walks of life—as well as foreign forced laborers—constructing antitank ditches, bunkers, and similar defensive works in the so-called East Wall. The Nazi press heralded this endeavor as a spontaneous, though Party-inspired and Party-guided, expression of the East Prussian population's will to defend itself. The apparent success of the People's Levy led Hitler to order its adoption in other frontier areas; on September 1, Hitler instructed Bormann to authorize any Gauleiter to use "all means" within his Gau for constructing necessary fortifications.[42]

Emboldened by their new powers and inspired by Koch's success, independent-minded Gauleiters began not only to prepare fortifications but also to create their own militias in order to man the new defenses. Small SA and Party formations had long existed both within the Stadt- und Landwacht and in separate auxiliaries, called SA Special Purpose Units *(SA Stürme zur besonderen Verwendung)* or Political Leader Squadrons *(Politische Leiter Staffeln)* for emergency use against internal unrest.[43] As the Allied armies approached the borders, some Gauleiters, particularly the fanatic Koch, began to assign these units military duties such as combating partisans, acting as military police, and even securing the newly built defensive fortifications.[44]

During the summer of 1944, many Gauleiters even began expanding their existing armed Party formations into larger militias. By September, Gauleiters in Carinthia, Hamburg, Lower Silesia, Steiermark, Westmark, Westphalia South, Westphalia North, and Württemberg-Hohenzollern—and perhaps elsewhere—had undertaken formation of loyal Nazis into substantial armed units.[45] Koch, who had instructed members of the People's Levy "to bring firearms and ammunition with them," was in the vanguard of this movement.[46] Party officials had also begun enrolling men for militia service in Schleswig-Holstein, East Hannover, and Munich–Upper Bavaria, where Gauleiter Paul Giesler had ordered all males aged eighteen to sixty to sign up at the local Wehrkreis registration offices.[47] These Gauleiters, particularly those in the border regions and perhaps others, all seemed to want a loyal praetorian guard under their command as protection against the threat of internal unrest and Allied invasion.

Clearly, many regional Party leaders had come to favor militias, but similar sentiments could be found among national officials as well. On July 13, a Propaganda Ministry staff member, perhaps inspired by Koch's efforts, suggested that the Party create its own volunteer home guard, with units commanded by veterans and registered through the Wehrkreise. About the same time, Hitler Youth chief of staff Helmuth Möckel was pondering the merits of establishing Hitler Youth "self-protection" units nationwide; and German Labor Front (DAF) head Dr. Robert Ley suggested a DAF-led militia. National Socialist Kriegsopfer Versorgung (NSKOV) chief Hanns Oberlindober unsuccessfully sought to form veterans into *"Landwehr* and *Landsturm* formations" under his command.

Clearly, many Nazi officials had concluded that some type of militia was needed to counter the kind of internal unrest they believed had caused the home front collapse in 1918.[48] This widespread conviction, coupled with the enthusiasm and energy with which national and regional Party officials undertook their new home defense assignments, must have impressed Hitler, steeled his conviction that the NSDAP's fanatical leadership could bring victory, and made him reconsider the idea of a Party-led militia.

While the enthusiastic energy and apparent—as opposed to real—efficiency with which Party officials undertook their new duties must be counted as a major reason in overcoming Hitler's long-standing aversion to militias, Martin Bormann's personal intervention seems to have been the final and decisive factor in Hitler's decision to shift control over the militia from the relatively well-prepared Wehrmacht to the very Party leaders who had stymied earlier militia proposals. Like Hitler, Bormann's vehement opposition to militias had begun to soften because of fears of internal unrest from the large number of foreigners (slave laborers and POWs), concerns about declining public morale, and the reliability of the army in the aftermath of July 20. During August, Bormann had in fact begun moving in the direction of creating a dependable armed force that could counter internal uprisings by launching an effort to arm all Political Leaders.[49] Furthermore, on August 16, Bormann sent each Gauleiter, Reichsleiter, and Unit Leader three copies of the Prussian Landsturm Ordinance of April 21, 1813, with instructions merely indicating the Führer's desire that these men read the document. He did not even request a response.[50] While Bormann's intent is unclear, it seems that at the very least he was fathoming the level of support among Nazis for total war measures, perhaps including a home guard.

Given the fact that during August, militias—both proposed and real—were blossoming like desert flowers after a rain, Bormann must have recognized his two options: gain control of the movement and enhance his power, or oppose the militia and risk having a rival such as Himmler or one or more Gauleiters gain political influence at his expense. Under these circumstances, and with Guderian having convinced Hitler to form a substantial regional militia, Bormann chose the former course of action.

Bormann's reactions during August and September to the militia issue parallel his course of action with the Gauleiters' newly enhanced war powers. As with Wahl's Heimatschutztrupp episode a year earlier, Bormann did not want some Gauleiter parlaying his new duties into an independent position. For example, on August 29 Hitler had granted Hamburg Gauleiter Karl Kaufmann control of the entire fortification effort, including the People's Levy, on Germany's North Sea coast. This gave Kaufmann authority over parts of three Gaue other than his own. On September 1, Hitler, "on the suggestion of the Leader of the Party Chancellery," shifted course and awarded each of the four Gauleiters in the area the responsibility for fortification work inside his own region only. Even more important, he granted the Party Chancellery supervisory powers over all Gauleiters' fortification construction efforts nationwide. Bormann used his considerable personal influence with Hitler to interpose himself between the Führer and the Gauleiters, thus making them dependent on him for their authority in this case.[51] Bormann, a master player in the social Darwinian political world of the Third Reich, effectively repeated this performance with the Volkssturm. While there is no record of what Bormann did to change Hitler's mind about Guderian's Landsturm, the most likely explanation is that Bormann employed ideological arguments to play on the Führer's suspicions, doubts, and prejudices about the war situation while appealing to his faith in the NSDAP's ability to master all difficulties. Bormann must have pointed out that the potential threat of rebellion among prisoners of war and foreign workers showed that Germany's problem was not, as Guderian portrayed it, purely military.[52] Furthermore, such internal threats required a national, as opposed to a regional, response. Bormann probably pointed out that the number of Gauleiter-initiated defense forces proved the Party's zeal, efficiency, and ability to mobilize civilians for the war effort; but that these efforts, like the People's Levy which he now supervised, would be most effective if coordinated nationally by the Party Chancellery.

Most important, Bormann certainly contrasted the Party's obedient enthusiasm with the defeatism and disloyalty that Hitler believed had undermined the Wehrmacht. Guderian's army-controlled Landsturm would, in his view, be infected with pessimism, would lack the will to fight, and thereby might even bring about the collapse of morale Hitler had always dreaded. By contrast, the NSDAP, Bormann argued, had always been sensitive to public morale and could, through its propaganda expertise and inspirational leadership, minimize any potentially negative fallout following the militia's proclamation. Over time, it could even use the new force to educate and indoctrinate German civilians and thus actually strengthen public morale. Furthermore, the NSDAP could overcome what Hitler perceived as the weakness inherent in all militias—poor discipline—by directly instilling its will and devotion to National Socialism in each and every German man, which would improve the force's combat potential. In the wake of the military defeats and July 20, these arguments would have had particular resonance with Hitler. In his view, although the Wehrmacht, particularly Himmler's Replacement Army, could provide technical expertise and advice, only the Party could awaken the fighting spirit of the average German. Although there is no direct evidence as to precisely what Bormann did to convince Hitler to turn the Landsturm into the nationwide, Party-led Volkssturm, it is apparent that his personal influence proved decisive.[53]

The Volkssturm's creation clearly illustrates the decision-making process in the Third Reich. Ideas percolated up from a variety of lower-level regional and national sources but could be thwarted or championed by those in the upper echelons of power. For something to become official policy, however, the Führer's approval was ultimately required. This necessitated that someone who had direct access to Hitler and was adept at explaining how a proposed policy supported National Socialist ideological goals had to endorse the idea, generally for his own benefit. Martin Bormann performed this role perfectly in the case of the Volkssturm.

Whatever the reasoning behind it, Hitler's decision to grant control of the Volkssturm to the Party and not the Wehrmacht was to have far-reaching implications. Since at least Operation Barbarossa, the Wehrmacht had been the Reich's main proponent of militia forces. Its contingency planning included provisions for the temporary mobilization of civilian German males to supplement the Replacement Army's scattered units in local emergencies such as opposing commando raids, combating saboteurs, finding escaped prisoners of war or downed Allied airmen, or controlling unruly foreign workers. Should Allied forces invade Germany, the Wehrmacht had made at least some preparations to use hastily mobilized civilians in combat and by 1944 had organized militia units in some areas. Furthermore, all Wehrkreise had an existing infrastructure, thinly stretched though it had become, to enroll and train the militia.

The NSDAP, on the other hand, had typically displayed a hostile attitude toward militias until the summer of 1944. While willing to accept small-scale police auxiliaries, Hitler, Himmler, and Bormann strongly opposed large militias out of prejudice and concerns for morale or personal political power. While the rapidly deteriorating military situation demonstrated the necessity of creating a mechanism to tap the pool of deferred and exempted civilians, political considerations shaped the decision to entrust the militia to the Party. The July 20 Plot destroyed any confidence the Party leadership might have had in the Wehrmacht's ability to head the war effort and confirmed Nazi suspicions that the Reich's reversals were due to defeatist, traitorous officers. The Reich certainly could not trust such unreliable men with the delicate task of forming a national militia.

On the other hand, regional and local NSDAP leaders had responded to the home defense duties awarded them in the summer of 1944 with energetic confidence, loyalty, and apparent effectiveness. Martin Bormann exploited these attitudes to convince Hitler that an NSDAP-controlled Volkssturm not only would prevent a collapse of morale but also it could be the means through which the Party could infect the entire populace with National Socialist fervor, and thereby kindle a new enthusiasm for the war effort throughout the Reich. While this logic convinced Hitler to end his long-held opposition to militia forces, the decision to award the Volkssturm to the NSDAP and not the army meant that the enterprise would be handicapped from the start by substituting hasty improvisation for preparation and planning.

CHAPTER TWO

"Ein Volk steht auf":
The Volkssturm in National Socialist
Strategy, Ideology, and Propaganda

To understand the Volkssturm and why Hitler awarded control of it to the NSDAP and not the Wehrmacht, one must ascertain what its Nazi founders hoped the force would achieve. This chapter addresses how Hitler and his advisers viewed the war situation in the late summer of 1944; it shows that they thought they could win the war, how they planned to achieve this, and that the Volkssturm had a critically important role to play in their strategy. While in retrospect it is abundantly clear that Germany had no realistic chance of winning the war after September 1944, the leaders of the Third Reich, lacking objectivity and the luxury of hindsight, hoped to turn the tide by creating among all Germans a fanatical will to resist. This would enable them to force the Allies to fight bitterly for every German city, town, and village and thereby turn the war into a protracted stalemate. Such a struggle would maximize Allied casualties and minimize their territorial gain. Eventually, they expected that war-weariness would wear down Allied morale and ultimately collapse the Allied war effort. In effect, they hoped to replay the 1918 "stab in the back" scenario, only this time with the roles being reversed.

For several reasons, National Socialist ideology and propaganda constitute an important part of understanding this strategy and the Volkssturm's central role in it. First, because of the fluidity of political power in the Third Reich, the Führer's minions had to justify their proposals and positions with Hitler—still effectively the system's ultimate power broker—through appeals to supposedly irreproachable and generally held ideological constants. Second, lacking any real blueprint for the Volkssturm, Party leaders tended to look for guidance among their common assumptions and ideals, many of which came from the early years of Nazism. Third, and most important, because the Volkssturm was to be a key means of infusing a new spirit into the faltering war effort, it had to appeal to lofty, inspiring ideals and attempted to do so through various forms of propaganda based on the National Socialist worldview.[1]

Ideology also largely explains why the Party leadership continued to believe Germany could win the war even after the disasters of summer 1944. National Socialists viewed the war as nothing less than a "struggle for existence *[Existenzkampf]*,"[2] a "people's war in which one race and one nation wants to and must annihilate the other."[3] In such a conflict, surrender was not an option, for as Bormann confided to his wife, "Victory for Bolshevism *and Americanism* [my italics] would mean not only the extermination of our race, but also the destruction of everything that its culture and civilization has created."[4] The Party's social Darwinian outlook justified, even demanded, that the Volk harness all its human and material resources in this struggle for survival.

National Socialist beliefs also caused its adherents to shift blame for their reversals away from Hitler and the Party. In 1944, Nazis attributed their defeats to the poor military performance of Germany's former allies, low German morale, or, most important, traitors in the officer corps.[5] Nazis had long feared a replay of the supposed "stab in the back" of 1918 by treasonous and defeatist elements, and events during July 1944 (particularly the July 20 assassination and coup attempt) seemed to validate these suspicions.[6] Ardent Nazis needed scapegoats because they could not admit, without fundamentally challenging the veracity of all National Socialist thought, that supposedly subhuman Jews and Slavs, weak Britons, or mongrel Americans had bested the superior Aryans in battle. Nor could they admit that the Führer and his top NSDAP aides had erred without undermining the Party's overall credibility. Because their ideological preconceptions blinded the Nazis to the real reasons for their reversal of fortune, they could continue to believe in the possibility of German victory.

Finally, and most basically, National Socialists believed that Germany possessed a valuable trump card—its racial superiority. Having already rid Germany of its Jews, the NSDAP planned to immunize the Reich against the possibility of a "stab in the back" by eliminating defeatists and reviving and sustaining the Germans' determination to fight. On the other hand, Nazis reasoned, with the Allied states remaining under Jewish domination, the morale of these degenerate and inferior peoples could be expected to collapse in a long, hard struggle. According to this view, Germany could not lose if the country were properly led and its people sufficiently determined to fight.[7]

The Party had always considered itself the leader, educator, and protector of the superior German people and its culture. As discussed in the preceding chapter, many Nazis concluded in mid-1944 that it was therefore only natural to expand NSDAP involvement in guiding the war effort; and as the Party's role grew, so did some Nazis' faith in victory. In mid-September, Hitler solemnly ordered all Party offices to document their activities carefully so that this "decisive commitment of the NSDAP in the greater German war for freedom will be held safely [in the Party Main Archives] . . . for later historical writing."[8] Many Nazis also confidently remarked that the war had entered "a new phase in our struggle for survival."[9] Perhaps the greatest manifestation of confidence among Nazi officials was the heightened intensity of political power struggles during the second half of 1944, a topic covered in the next chapter. With the Party assuming new powers in directing the war, individual dedicated Nazis wanted to be in a position to claim a share of the credit for Germany's victory.

How, then, did the Reich's leaders intend to win the war at a time when, in retrospect, German defeat seems assured? In late July, Himmler outlined this strategy in a speech to National Socialist Leadership Officers (NSFOs):

> When the Eastern Front is screened off, [and] the enemy in the west and south no longer achieves decisive successes, . . . when the U-boat war takes off again, when the enemy receives further injury to his strength of nerve and war policy through the V-1 and V-2, then one day the moment will come when one of the three great opponents in this war will recognize the war as senseless. At this moment the war is won for us. . . . [But] there are no more miracles. . . . we must earn everything ourselves.[10]

Essentially, the Nazi leadership hoped to defeat the Allies in a contest of willpower, a struggle in which devout National Socialists believed Germans had an inherent biological advantage. With the NSDAP directing the war effort, the Reich would have leadership committed both to continuing the war and to developing among all Germans, civilian or military, an unbreakable, fanatic will to resist Allied conquest. As the Party mobilized the home front physically and psychologically, the military would seek to create a stalemate on all fronts to maximize Allied casualties. Once the major Allied powers were forced to realize the high cost of defeating the Reich, the Nazi leaders expected one or more of them would eventually sue for peace.

Achieving and maintaining this stalemate required the Germans "to conduct their battles in depth."[11] This entailed relying on stoutly defended fortified zones to delay, channel, or prevent enemy breakthroughs and gathering mobile reserves to contain and eliminate any enemy penetrations. Although the strategy was essentially defensive, the Wehrmacht would make every effort to launch counterattacks (e.g., the Ardennes Offensive), while Germany's V-1s, V-2s, new U-boats, and other "miracle weapons" would carry the war to the Allies' homelands and supply lines.[12] The ultimate purpose of all this bitter, sometimes tactically senseless, resistance was to prove that Germany could not be defeated without an immense sacrifice in blood for all the Allies, particularly the British and Americans.[13]

One might logically argue that in late 1944 the Germans merely sought to improve their bargaining position. Although some diplomatic contacts occurred, there were never any official, concerted, serious high-level peace contacts. The most that Hitler ever considered seeking was a temporary truce to facilitate preparations for later renewal of the struggle. Furthermore, even into the war's final weeks, the Führer continued to view anyone (e.g., Himmler) who actively engaged in unauthorized negotiations guilty of high treason.[14] Hitler had no intention of initiating peace talks; Versailles had taught him the danger of seeking peace on terms other than your own. His strategy relied on exploiting the supposed racial, moral, and ideological weaknesses of the Allies to force *them* to beg for an armistice once their will collapsed.

Understanding why Nazis thought the Allies would collapse again depends on ideological preconceptions. Hitler and other ardent Nazis viewed the Allies as an "unnatural coalition" of capitalists and Communists whose inherent conflicts of interest would eventually drive a wedge between them.[15] Some Reich leaders believed German diplomats could strike a deal with Stalin—as in 1939—by exploiting his distrust of the West. Furthermore, these Nazis argued, the Soviets would be likely to negotiate, since they were nearing the end of their manpower reserves and willpower.[16] Other Nazis, including Hitler, believed that since both Great Britain and the United States were supposedly dominated by selfish Jewish leaders, perhaps the Aryan majorities in the West would eventually realize that they had no real interest in dying for the benefit of Jews and Bolsheviks, and would force their governments to end the war.[17]

Hitler himself believed the United States had the weakest resolve among the Big Three. He doubted that the United States could sustain any major national effort and felt confident that American morale would ultimately succumb. The Führer did not "believe that an American could fight like a hero," a weakness he attributed to racial mixing.[18] Furthermore, he thought that Aryan-Americans would ultimately realize that they had no vital stake in the war. He stated in December 1944 that "if America says out, finish, we are giving no more youths for Europe, nothing happens, New York remains New York, Chicago remains Chicago. . . . It changes nothing."[19] Hitler and other Nazis expected that if war-weariness reached a high level, influential American Jews would panic and force the government to seek peace, just as Nazis believed their German counterparts had done in 1918. With the United States out of the war, Britain, they reasoned, would be unable to sustain the effort alone and would soon become discouraged and quit. Germany could then concentrate against the Soviets in a tough battle, which the racially superior Germans would ultimately win.

To spread this perception, Nazi propaganda from late 1944 strongly emphasized evidence of Allied weaknesses and vulnerability. Goebbels and his subordinates stressed the "limited political and material possibilities of our opponents" and repeatedly described every Allied problem as evidence of impending collapse.[20] Disputes between the Allies, invariably portrayed as deep rifts, were especially popular, as were stories featuring Allied setbacks, casualties, shortages, and war-weariness.[21] Anti-Soviet propaganda focused mainly on manpower problems and unrest in the USSR and eastern Europe, with stories on anti-Soviet partisans being common. Western, especially American, morale and economic problems received even more coverage. To demonstrate both the war-weariness and the psychological softness of Americans, the Propaganda Ministry often discussed how shortages of luxury items in the United States lowered civilian morale. Other reports touted the physical and psychological damage inflicted by V-2 rockets in Britain, or how Allied shipping shortages proved U-boat effectiveness and enemy logistical limitations.[22] Finally, German propaganda tried to show that American losses had generated antiwar sentiment at home and in the army.[23] Clearly, the goal was to convince Germans that the Allies, particularly the Americans, could still be beaten.

Through descriptions of alleged Allied atrocities, Nazi propaganda also sought to convince all Germans of the disastrous personal consequences that Allied victory would bring.[24] Although tales of horrors committed by the Red Army were both more frequent and more gruesome, stories of Anglo-American atrocities were also often featured to demonstrate the perceived conspiracy to destroy Germany via hunger, humiliation, racial mixing, and so forth.[25] Such propaganda plainly sought to exacerbate Germans' existing hatred and fear of the Soviets and to create a similiar loathing of the British and Americans.[26]

By creating such a mood, the Nazi leaders hoped to fanaticize the Wehrmacht and the civilian populace, the essential prerequisite to their strategy of prolonged resistance. The war in the east, widely viewed as an all-out "people's war," demonstrated the advantages of a politicized war effort to Germany's leaders, some of whom attributed Soviet success to the Red Army's political indoctrination program. To defeat the Soviets, top Nazis reasoned, Germany would have to motivate its people to fight with equally bitter determination on all fronts.[27] They insisted that Germany's "battle slogan must be revolution against revolution. Fanatical political people's army against the stirred-up hordes of inner Asia."[28] These zealots argued that their plan did not require the creation of a new army but only the strengthening of the numbers, spirit, and determination of the existing one.[29]

On September 16, Hitler explained how this fanaticism was to influence all military operations. "Every bunker, every block of houses in a German city, every German town must become a fortress on which the enemy is either bled to death or in which its defenders are buried beneath [the rubble] in man-to-man combat. . . . There are no more large-scale operations, but only holding the position or destruction."[30] Führer Decrees mandated that commanders of fortified areas, especially cities designated Fortresses *(Festungen),* hold them at all costs and authorized subordinates (even noncommissioned officers or privates) who favored continued resistance to remove from command any superior officer advocating surrender.[31] Army instructional guidelines also sought to encourage fighting to the very last man and last round of ammunition, particularly in towns or cities.[32] Wehrmacht doctrine began to stress that any dogged opposition, no matter how brief or apparently futile in and of itself, would deny the Allies the advantages of mobile warfare—speed and the psychologically demoralizing factor of surprise—and thereby create a strategic stalemate of the sort that existed on the Western Front during World War I.[33]

Nazi propagandists sought to contribute to this goal by creating the idea that a lone, determined German soldier could dramatically affect military operations. Propaganda often featured the heroic exploits of "individual fighters [Einzelkämpfer]" (literally, lone fighters) and stressed how "personal bravery triumphs over mass and matériel."[34] For example, one pamphlet compared the 13,000 man-hours, 15,000 kilograms of steel, and 182,000 Reichsmarks required to build one Soviet T-34 tank with the 1 man-hour, 5 kilograms of steel, and 8 Reichsmarks needed to construct a Panzerfaust, the single-shot antitank rocket capable of destroying most Allied armored vehicles. It concluded by asking the reader, "What does this [using the Panzerfaust] require? An iron heart, a well-aimed shot; do you still believe in the superiority of masses?"[35] An interesting poem took the belief in fanaticism over material still further:

> Ein Holzschwert mit Mut
> Schütz Hab und Gut
> Besser als eine Kanone
> —ohne.[36]

This sort of propaganda aimed at making every individual German feel not only capable of contributing to the Reich's defense but also personally responsible for doing so. Each soldier had to believe that he could make a real difference and that everyone must sacrifice for the greater good. To foster this attitude, German propaganda did not employ bald-faced lies but selectively presented fact and interpretation designed to confirm Nazi preconceptions and deflate Allied and inflate German capabilities.[37] The Allies had numerical superiority, but the Party sought to counter this by tapping what they perceived as Germany's greatest strengths: the superior will, unity, and courage of the master race. All victory required was obedience and loyalty to the NSDAP's leadership and the determination to continue fighting.

Carrying out this essential psychological mobilization took a variety of specific forms. In the military, as discussed in chapter 1, it involved appointing Himmler to command the Replacement Army and allowing the Gauleiters to encroach on military affairs in the hope that they would infuse political zeal and enthusiasm into local defense while simultaneously monitoring the conduct of Wehrmacht field commanders.[38] The proliferation of new formations bearing the title "Volks"—for example, Volksgrenadier Divisions, Volks Artillery Corps, and the Volkssturm—also revealed the increasing ideological influence on the military.

The most extensive program aimed at fanaticizing the Wehrmacht, however, was the expansion of the NSFO program.[39] Originally created in response to the Stalingrad debacle, the NSFOs—which were modeled after the Red Army's commissars—were to "train every soldier in the National Socialist worldview so well that he goes to the front not only as a fully worthy fighter but also as a convinced National Socialist."[40] In a July 1944 speech, Himmler stressed the importance of the program to an NSFO gathering by attributing the army's defeats to its lack of proper "ideological *Ausrichtung*" and "good old soldierly conception of doing one's duty."[41] By successfully educating the troops about National Socialism's goals, the NSFO program would improve Wehrmacht morale and battlefield performance while inoculating the military against defeatism and further anti-Hitler conspiracies. This would be of particular importance on the Western Front, where soldiers were perhaps less likely to see the "true" nature of the war, but where fanatical resistance was no less necessary.

The other main purpose of the expanded NSFO program was to secure the loyalty of the officer corps in the wake of the July 20 Plot. Nazi ideology strongly emphasized the importance of the leader—especially those of junior grade—whose duties, even in the military, went far beyond technical expertise.[42] For Nazis, "there [was] no division between military and spiritual leadership—today's soldiers win with weapons and ideology."[43] An apolitical officer, according to this view, was derelict in his duties and lacked essential leadership qualifications; a German officer should inspire his troops through his military knowledge, his bravery, and his National Socialist convictions. In fact, Hitler even ordered that "the foremost task of the troop leader is the political activation and fanaticization of his troops."[44] Nazis believed that a politicized officer corps would translate into increased Wehrmacht fighting power; as Bormann stated, "Often only a single energetic man suffices to enflame the populace of a town to fanatical resistance."[45]

Because the strategy of fanatical resistance would require not only soldiers but also civilians to withstand immense sacrifices, the Party also planned to put the entire "Volk in the highest moral and material defensive readiness."[46] The task of carrying out this total physical and mental mobilization of the Reich's civilian populace fell primarily upon the German Volkssturm.[47] Militarily, the force could help create "a relentless struggle everywhere that the enemy . . . set foot on German soil," thus assisting the Wehrmacht in containing Allied breakthroughs and airborne assaults and, in turn, considerably slowing the war's pace. Although the Volkssturm could, at best, only "reinforce [not replace] the active strength of our Wehrmacht," Nazi leaders expected it to help convince the Allies that conquering Germany would generate losses for them that would be equivalent to "national suicide."[48]

The Volkssturm's military success, however, depended largely on its ability to mobilize the spirit of the German civilian.[49] To contribute to the Reich's defense, Volkssturm men would have to fight against overwhelming odds as fanatically and unyieldingly as the Japanese were doing in the Pacific War. To accomplish this, Nazis hoped to use the Volkssturm to create among German civilians "a burning enthusiasm like that of a second National Socialist revolution."[50] By using the Volkssturm as a means of indoctrinating all German civilians, particularly those who had previously ignored Nazi propaganda, the Party planned to steel home-front morale for the coming struggle and simultaneously generate the fanatic resistance that its strategy required.[51]

Prominent Nazis believed that only the Party itself had the necessary experience with propaganda and inspirational leadership *(Menschenführung)* that would enable it to win this crucial "battle of the mental-spiritual powers of the will and faith."[52] Furthermore, devout Nazis believed that only the Party, with its zeal and organizational talents, could organize and administer the mobilization effort quickly, efficiently, and with a minimum of bureaucratic delay. Throughout the Reich, regional, county, and town NSDAP officials (the *Gau-*, *Kreis-*, and *Ortsgruppenleiter*, respectively), like Wehrmacht officers, were expected to lead by word *and* deed and to command respect through their personal example of loyalty, bravery, and devotion.[53] These Nazi bosses were supposedly so familiar with the temperaments and attitudes of their charges that they could tailor the propaganda message to reach and inspire each and every German. To these local Nazi officials fell the task of making Germans feel personally responsible for contributing to the Volk's defense in its hour of mortal peril.[54]

Very early on, the Volkssturm leadership decided that the political training needed to motivate its men should be frequent, subtle, and administered in small doses during every training session.[55] Bormann wanted National Socialist indoctrination to permeate all Volkssturm activities, just as the Nazis wanted their ideals to shape the Volkssturm's structure and even the average member's thoughts and deeds. Party leaders also wanted the Volkssturm to reflect their ideology so that average Germans did not merely hear about National Socialism but could consciously experience the positive benefits its leaders believed it offered the German people.

Nazi ideology shaped the Volkssturm in a wide variety of ways, beginning with its very name. Rejecting the existing regional or historical alternatives (e.g., *Landwehr, Heimatschutz, Landsturm, Volkswehr*), Volkssturm founders selected a name that they believed conveyed "the main supporting ideas *[haupttragenden Gedanken]* of the Volkssturm . . . People and Storm."[56] The word *storm*—as in a contemporary propaganda song, "A People Rises Up and the Storm Bursts Forth"[57]—invoked the image of the Volkssturm unleashing the overwhelming power that National Socialists claimed was biologically inherent in the German master race. They believed that "soldiering is in our blood. Soldierly qualities are born in us. It [soldiering] fills all Germans equally whether they serve our Volk in the city or in the country, with weapons or at the work bench. Soldiering is the most characteristic German quality."[58] These Nazis intended to use the Volkssturm to awaken the average German's allegedly superior martial qualities, couple them with the supposedly superior Aryan will, and thus produce the storm of fanatic resistance required by their desperate strategy.

The selection of the word *Volk* symbolizes the most significant impact of Nazi ideology upon the Volkssturm: the efforts to structure the force in such a way as to allow its members to experience the intangible benefits of the *Volksgemeinschaft*. It was precisely this racially defined Volk community, not just the German government or its citizens' property, which the Nazis saw as threatened with destruction. Correspondingly, they sought to use the Volkssturm as a means of bonding the average German's loyalty not to the state or region but to the Volk.

Foremost among the traits that the Nazis wanted the Volkssturm to draw from the idealized Volk was a sense of *Gemeinschaft* (community) that would transcend all divisions based on status, rank, class, age, or occupation and would generate a number of psychological advantages. "Common service [in the Volkssturm] of all age groups of an Ortsgruppe . . . should . . . strengthen the feeling of community and allow all men to grow together in a close local armed community *[Wehrgemeinschaft]*," thus producing cohesive fighting units.[59] Portraying the Volkssturm as an "especially impressive demonstration of the determined will to resist of the German Volk"[60] would not only encourage Germans but simultaneously serve notice to the Allies that the Reich was unified in its determination not to surrender. Furthermore, as the Party recognized from experiences with rationing, Allied bombings, and other hardships, a strong sense of community and shared sacrifice could mitigate any negative sentiment caused by Volkssturm service—so long as all segments of society served equally.[61] Finally, the main goal of "the disappearance of class and rank"[62] in the Volkssturm was to encourage every German man to direct his loyalty exclusively to the Volk and its leadership, the NSDAP. Thus, the Volkssturm can also be seen as an attempt to complete the Gleichschaltung that began on January 30, 1933.[63]

Creating this sense of community required that all men of German blood— ethnic as well as native—serve in the Volkssturm, a stipulation laid out in the initial Führer Decree founding the organization. In addition, politically and racially acceptable volunteers from Nordic countries such as the Netherlands, Norway, Denmark, or Belgium could serve.[64] Bormann even ordered criminals inducted, if Nazi officials judged them sufficiently reformed, so that they could redeem themselves.[65] On the other hand, the Nazis barred from the Volkssturm all Jews and other persons considered "racially inferior" or "unworthy to bear arms" (e.g., men guilty of "crimes damaging to the Volk").[66] The Party wanted the Volkssturm to reflect the true German Volk and to become a shining example of this racial community's positive characteristics. This could occur only if it included all segments of the Volk—not just Party members or volunteers—and excluded those considered biologically unfit.

Bormann did exempt certain Germans from Volkssturm service if he deemed their inclusion detrimental. Members of Germany's princely houses were suspect because of their questionable loyalty, their families' international connections, and their potential to be socially divisive.[67] Bormann particularly sought to exclude Christian influence by forbidding both chaplains and religious services in the force and by barring all clergymen from service.[68] When Dr. Robert Ley (German Labor Front head) urged Bormann to enroll clergymen for unity's sake, the Party Chancellery chief angrily responded that the churches firmly opposed National Socialism, and clergy in the Volkssturm would be a "divisive fungus" who would counter Nazi indoctrination and spread their own "weakening" influence.[69] Bormann even rudely rejected requests for Sunday Volkssturm training exemptions for church organists, sextons, and other lay assistants, sarcastically adding that he had already granted "extensive courtesy" to the churches by exempting the clergy.[70] Bormann and other anti-Christian Nazis saw the Volkssturm as an opportunity to get German men out of the churches not only temporarily—as Volkssturm training sessions occurred on Sunday mornings—but permanently by turning them into fanatic Nazis.[71] If successful, the Volkssturm would unite all Germans in complete loyalty to the NSDAP; allowing clergymen to influence members in any way could undermine the renewed Gleichschaltung.

One of the most important efforts geared toward making the Volkssturm reflect the Volk community was Bormann's insistence that each unit mirror the social composition of its home area. With all members of the community serving, the Party Chancellery chief believed each Volkssturm man would feel a "sense of local pride" and "racial community *[Heimatgebundenheit* and *Volksgemeinschaft]*" that would make him "answer the call to arms gladly."[72] Creating such a social balance required basing Volkssturm units strictly upon members' place of residence. Contrary to Bormann's wishes, a number of German officials sought to base Volkssturm units upon occupation, Party affiliate units, or other criteria. He reacted angrily to these efforts, stating that the Volkssturm was "the opposite of division by occupation or firm, by class or rank," and that "a baker's Volkssturm is nonsense, a contradiction in terms." In Bormann's opinion, the Volkssturm would succeed only if it reflected the community's mystical spirit of unity.[73] Only in the most compelling circumstances was Bormann prepared to tolerate Volkssturm units based on the workplace. He and his supporters genuinely believed that average Volkssturm men could experience the benefits of the racial community—and therefore develop a willingness to defend it—only if their unit was a microcosm of the larger German Volksgemeinschaft.

Also in pursuit of fostering this community spirit within the Volkssturm, the NSDAP made a special effort to ensure that prominent persons did their fair share. For example, business leaders who used their position to excuse themselves from Volkssturm training came in for particularly harsh criticism.[74] Nazi propaganda stressed that the Volkssturm consisted of men of "all occupations and ages"[75] and sought to provide specific illustrations, such as the sixty-eight-year-old retired corps commander (in Poland and France) who volunteered to serve in the ranks of the Volkssturm because he believed that "the general and the worker" should serve side by side.[76] If local notables did not fulfill their obligations, the Party knew rhetoric about unity would ring hollow among the less privileged segments of society.

In hopes of reinforcing bonds between unit commanders and their men, Volkssturm organizers eschewed standard military etiquette. Unit commanders bore the functional title of "unit leader" (e.g., Company Leader) rather than regular rank designations. Enlisted men addressed their commander by his title or with "Heil Hitler," but never with the traditional "Herr" followed by the officer's rank.[77] Some officials even encouraged Volkssturm men to call each other "comrade."[78] To make the unit a living reflection of the strong, harmonious bonds of the mythical Volk community, Party officials (hypocritically and unsuccessfully) commanded unit leaders to set aside all "petty conflicts and jealousies of a personal and organizational nature."[79] Group singing was encouraged not only because it provided a simple means of learning slogans but also because such emotional collective activities engendered unity.[80] While these matters may seem trivial, they were subtle efforts to make the Volkssturm man experience and cherish the benefits of his threatened *Volksgemeinschaft*, something Bormann deemed crucial to the militia's success.

The mass public meeting, long a standard Nazi propaganda tactic, was another means of encouraging and demonstrating Volkssturm solidarity. The first such rally occurred on October 18—the anniversary of the Battle of Leipzig—in Bartenstein, East Prussia, to announce the Volkssturm's formation. Massive Volkssturm oath-taking ceremonies took place nationwide on November 12, the Sunday following the anniversary of the November 9 Beer Hall *Putsch*. These spectacles consisted of parades, speeches by prominent Nazis, and patriotic songs and culminated in the assembled Volkssturm men pledging their loyalty to Hitler.[81] The purpose of such ceremonies, as with the massive Nuremberg Party rallies of the 1930s, was to overawe the individual, encourage personal identification with the Volk and the Party, and allow the Volkssturm man to experience the deep emotional bonds of his community.[82]

The desire to encourage unity led the Party to stress its intention to minimize bureaucratic routine in the Volkssturm, a goal also designed to hasten the militia's establishment. Ideally the Volkssturm would become a fighting organization with "no staffs, no rear echelon, no officer's mess; instead only a single resolute community that is prepared to defend its home to the last breath."[83] In such a Volkssturm no member could shirk his duty with a rear-area job; everyone would share the same responsibilities and dangers. The NSDAP, upon whose structure the Volkssturm was based, supposedly epitomized this spirit of unbureaucratized efficiency and community, and would rally Germany by example just as the Nazis believed they had done during the Kampfzeit.

The effort to make the Volkssturm reflect the broader racial community also helps clarify why Nazis believed that the NSDAP had to control the new force. In their view, only the Party could achieve the objective of "releas[ing] all [the] political, ideological and spiritual powers" of the German people through the Volkssturm.[84] In a broader sense, however, according to National Socialist ideology, true unity was possible only under Party leadership because it alone possessed the ideological understanding necessary to determine the German Volk's best interests. Nazis believed that "National Socialism draws its revolutionary power from the highest worth of the race"; thus, at least in the view of Bormann's influential wing of the Party, the NSDAP was a revolutionary elite that ascertained the will of the Volk, set policies accordingly, and then sought to shape public opinion in favor of the NSDAP's programs.[85] In practical terms this meant Party leaders equated their decisions with the will of the Volk. Therefore, unity within the Volkssturm, as with unity within the Volk, was possible only under Nazi guidance.

Given this view, it is easier to understand why Nazis genuinely believed that the Volkssturm was a "demonstration of the determined will to resist of the German Volk."[86] Although Volkssturm service was mandatory for all civilian men aged sixteen to sixty, Nazi leaders did not consider the Volkssturm to be a form of conscription but instead an "uprising from the idealistic and material power of resistance of the entire Volk."[87] First of all, there was no dichotomy between the Party and the people in Nazi ideology; the Party was simply the vanguard of the Volk. Furthermore, because the Party leaders viewed all military—including Volkssturm—service as a sacred duty expected of all German men, and because they had decided that the Volk's survival was at stake, Germans were obligated to defend the Volk in its hour of mortal peril.[88] Such arguments appealed to the German sense of duty and had resonance both for the convinced Nazi and for average citizens who feared foreign—particularly Soviet—conquest. It also shifted the blame to the Allies for creating the need for the militia. Most important, however, it enabled the Party to portray the Volkssturm as a unifying national—and not just an NSDAP—organization.

As a part of the effort to stress the Volkssturm's popular national character, the Party's massive propaganda campaign emphasized the Volkssturm as part of the German militia tradition. In his speech announcing the Volkssturm, Himmler referred to the War of Liberation's *Landsturm* as the Volkssturm's direct ancestor.[89] Other propaganda recalled Andreas Hofer's Tirolean peasant uprising of 1809 or the *Freikorps* of the early interwar years.[90] This propaganda sought to persuade Germans that the Volkssturm was just another of those popular patriotic movements that arose out of the public's desire to protect the Fatherland and its people in times of danger.

A further Nazi effort to make the Volkssturm reflect idealized characteristics of the Volksgemeinschaft included attempts to encourage among Volkssturm members the Party's interpretation of typical traditional German values. In this connection, the Party Chancellery issued a code of behavior (described by one of its authors as "having the character of a manifesto") for the model Volkssturm man that urged them to be "chivalrous to women, courteous to children, the sick and elderly."[91] Other approved behaviors included "voluntarism and idealism, preparedness, willingness to sacrifice, courage, bravery, toughness and steadfastness."[92] Of course, each Volkssturm man must "remain true to his duty"—as traditional an idea as existed in Germany—or suffer the stigma of being branded a traitor. Propaganda also reminded German men of their masculine duty as protectors when it called them to rally against the enemy "who threatens our freedom and life, wants to rape our women and murder our children."[93] Above all, the Nazis demanded that all Volkssturm members swear, in a formal oath, to remain unconditionally loyal and obedient to Hitler and to "rather die than surrender the freedom and . . . social future of his Volk."[94] Simply put, the ideal Volkssturm man reflected the Party's view of the model German male. He should carry out his orders to the letter, confident in the firm belief that the Party knew what was best, and be willing to sacrifice his very life for the larger good—as determined by the omniscient NSDAP—of the racial community.

To illustrate the value of these ideal traits, Nazi propagandists produced a number of stories based on the experiences—some of which may have been apocryphal—of the first Volkssturm units to enter combat in East Prussia in mid-October.[95] A typical story focused on how an anonymous Volkssturm Einzelkämpfer used the Panzerfaust to destroy two Soviet T-34 tanks, thereby slowing a Soviet thrust southeast of Gumbinnen until German armor arrived to restore the situation. Other propaganda sought to emphasize the particular advantages of Volkssturm men, such as their knowledge of local geography, determination to defend their homes, and loyalty to their neighbors and comrades. Many stories lionized the East Prussian Volkssturm men as World War I veterans who had "left the work of their generation, not in order to lose it, but in order to protect it and restore its old splendor."[96] Such stories, whether factual or not, were intended to prove that the contributions of determined individual Volkssturm men could alter the course of events. They also served to remind Germans that just as a few determined men (i.e., Hitler and the "old fighters" of the NSDAP) had pulled Germany out of its postwar despair, so the Nazis believed that a few heroes, be they in the Party, Volkssturm, or Wehrmacht, could again save Germany by setting an inspirational example of fanatic resistance for their countrymen.

The immediate responsibility for fostering these qualities, as well as military skills, among Volkssturm members fell to the unit leaders, who in turn were themselves to be paragons of National Socialist virtue. Bormann decided early on that unit leader candidates needed "revolutionary drive" in addition to military competence.[97] The Gauleiters generally agreed; some even argued that Volkssturm commanders' Nazi convictions were "more important than their military knowledge."[98] Model unit leaders should be "front-experienced soldiers who are equally political activists."[99] They should reject the Wehrmacht's traditional Prussian methods, that is, those that demanded loyalty based on rigid discipline, tradition, and rank, and instead emulate Adolf Hitler, motivating their men by the force of their Nazi convictions, personality, and actions.[100] Clearly, Volkssturm founders wanted its commanders to employ the Nazi leadership style that had begun to permeate the Wehrmacht officer corps' junior ranks.[101]

Party officials stressed the political qualifications of unit leaders so strongly because they were responsible for the Volkssturm man's primary source of indoctrination, the weekly company training sessions.[102] In addition to military instruction and practice, these meetings generally emphasized the personal and collective ideals and beliefs that the Nazis wanted to encourage in all Germans. Themes included the need for obedience to and faith in Hitler and the Party; the meaning of the Volk community; the danger of world Jewry; German and Allied war aims; and Allied shortages, losses, and morale problems. Propaganda designed for Volkssturm consumption aimed for realism—as the Party saw it—and sought to explain that the situation, although serious, could be mastered if everyone remained calm, resolute, and dutiful.[103]

Volkssturm and NSFO approaches to indoctrination were quite similar; in fact, Volkssturm unit leaders relied heavily on NSFO publications for their instructional material. This is not surprising, since the goals of the Volkssturm unit commander and the NSFO were precisely the same—to motivate every man to want to fight to the death for the sake of the Volk.[104] As Bormann himself put it, Volkssturm leaders should always strive to "mobilize the spiritual powers of the Volkssturm soldiers and increase their fanaticism."[105] Some historians have concluded that "with training time at a premium for the Volkssturm it was sheer stupidity for some of the lower leaders to engage in propaganda."[106] This, however, misses the entire point of the Volkssturm; it was not merely a military effort to raise more troops but a means to motivate Germans, individually and collectively, to sacrifice willingly in defense of the Volk and the Fatherland.

Based on the goals and ideas that shaped the Volkssturm and its idealized portrayal in Nazi propaganda, one must conclude that the Nazis *hoped*—if and when their indoctrination efforts succeeded—to create what might best be termed a people's militia, a hybrid blend of elements from both the traditional militia and the people's army.[107] To understand this apparent paradox, one must first realize that the Nazis considered the entire Wehrmacht to be a people's army. The creation of a politicized military force fighting for the goals of National Socialism and motivated by Nazi ideology had been an NSDAP objective since the Kampfzeit, and this was precisely the goal of the NSFO program.[108] While the Wehrmacht and Waffen SS would remain the Reich's permanent, primary, and most flexible military forces, the Volkssturm, although having the same goals and motivations as the regulars, limited its military tasks to assisting in local defense.[109] Thus, in effect, the Volkssturm formed a militia alongside the Wehrmacht and the Waffen SS within the politicized National Socialist people's army.[110] As with any militia, the Volkssturm was legally organized by the state (i.e., from above), had territorially defined operational limits; would supplement and not replace Wehrmacht forces; and would have conventional local defense as its chief military role.

Yet because it would serve as a militia within a politicized National Socialist people's army, the ideal Volkssturm also resembled a people's army. Although the Reich's leaders intended the Volkssturm to fight conventionally, Nazi rhetoric suggested that if the Party could achieve its goal of fanaticizing German civilians, Volkssturm men might employ guerrilla tactics. Nazi officials repeatedly asserted that the Volkssturm would use *any means* to defend their homes. More specifically, Himmler even claimed that "what the Russians have done in partisan warfare, we can do too" and that the Volkssturm would assure that the Allies never had secure rear areas.[111] Had the Party succeeded in fanaticizing the Volkssturm as thoroughly as it desired, some of its men—with the Party's blessings—would almost certainly have resorted to guerrilla warfare.[112]

The Volkssturm also resembled a people's army in other respects. Administration rested with the NSDAP's regional structure, not the Reich government or Wehrmacht. Volkssturm unit leader selection guidelines placed a premium on political qualifications. The Party expected these men to be inspirational examples of National Socialist faith and conviction; and it depended on the activist political element throughout the Volkssturm for success, at least in its motivational role. Plans called for minimizing administrative bureaucracy in order to adapt to unique local conditions and encouraged relying on local initiative. All these factors clearly show that the Volkssturm's founders wanted its men to be motivated by and to fight for National Socialism's goals.

The effort to incorporate National Socialist ideals into the very structure of the Volkssturm was the most striking similarity to a people's army. The Volkssturm's founders sought to make the force reflect the mythical Volksgemeinschaft by encouraging racial and ideological purity; rejecting class, regional, or other nonracial loyalties; and fostering selfless devotion to the Volk and total obedience to the NSDAP. Through Volkssturm service, Nazis wanted German men in a locality to experience firsthand the bonds and benefits of the larger Volk community and to learn of the mortal threat posed by an enemy victory. Reich leaders believed this would allow each unit to develop into an armed community of men dedicated to the defense of the Volk. If this happened on a sufficiently large scale, the Nazis expected to be able to continue their self-proclaimed people's war indefinitely.

As the militia component of the National Socialist people's army, the German Volkssturm had an important dual purpose in the broad, ideologically based Nazi strategy of 1944–1945. Militarily, the Volkssturm existed to mobilize civilian men to supplement Wehrmacht forces in meeting local contingencies such as destroying isolated Allied mechanized or airborne formations, helping slow or channel Allied breakthroughs, allowing the Wehrmacht to gather its reserves, and providing security against internal threats from traitors, rebellious foreign workers, or prisoners of war. By enabling the Germans to defend any populated area within the Reich, the Volkssturm would, in theory, help render rapid Allied advances almost impossible, thus contributing to the creation of a strategic stalemate by deepening, fortifying, and strengthening the Wehrmacht's fronts. Once the fronts had stabilized and then deadlocked, Allied casualties would mount, and Germany's wonder weapons, including the V-1, V-2, and new U-boats, would further disrupt the Allies' supply lines and home fronts. Eventually, war-weariness would sap the determination of the Allies, probably the United States first and then Great Britain, and their supposedly Jewish-dominated governments would enact a role reversal of the "stab in the back" myth, thus enabling the Reich to dictate the peace terms and achieve the ultimate victory.

The success of the military portion of this strategy, however, depended on the Party's ability to mobilize the entire German Volk psychologically. While the NSDAP launched a number of programs intended to ensure that all Germans developed an iron will, the Volkssturm itself was the most important effort aimed at civilians. In addition to preparing Volkssturm men to fight fanatically, the Party planned to use the force as a means to indoctrinate *all* adult German males, thus helping galvanize the entire civilian populace in the face of additional casualties, reduced rations, destruction of property, evacuations, continued bombings, longer workdays, and the other hardships entailed by the prolonged struggle. Without a secure home front, the Nazis feared that these sacrifices might cause morale—and the entire war effort along with it— to collapse as they believed it had in 1918.

Fundamentally, the entire plan, as with the Gleichschaltung of the 1930s, sought to convince individual Germans to accept unquestioningly that the NSDAP leadership knew what was best for them. In 1944 the Party increasingly revived this view in the hopes of reinvigorating the war effort by making all Germans fanatical political soldiers in the Party-led National Socialist crusade. Although the plan relied on both indoctrination and coercion, its success depended on the Party's ability to win the average German's undivided loyalty. To do this the Party's leaders sought to reemphasize what they perceived as the fundamental strengths of their movement: the methods and ideas of the Kampfzeit and Gleichschaltung.[113] As in the Nazis' idealized view of the Kampfzeit, the dedicated and politically aware Party would employ its activism, will, motivational leadership, and improvisational skill to awaken the German public to the dangers facing the Reich and Volk and lead them to salvation. This was the central element in the Nazi strategy to win the war, and the Volkssturm was to be an important means of bringing this to fruition.

The Volkssturm's founders set both military and political goals for this organization that were inextricably bound both with each other and with the Nazi plan for winning the war. The Volkssturm was not merely a means of *forcing* Germans to continue the fight; its success depended, as did the broader Nazi strategy for victory, on making individual Germans *want* to prefer death in battle over surrender. This was the Party's goal, but its leaders had no real plan to guide them, only rhetoric and vague notions based on National Socialist ideology and mythical interpretations of past experiences. As the following chapters show, these ideological preconceptions, particularly those based on racial ideas, caused the Nazis to distort their assessment of the German and Allied situations in both physical and psychological terms. In large part, because their entire strategy was based on inaccurate ideological assumptions about themselves, the Germans, and the Allied peoples, the Nazis found it nearly impossible to translate the Volkssturm ideal into reality.

CHAPTER THREE

National Administration

Although one of the Volkssturm's loftiest ideological goals was the unification of the German people behind the Nazi Party's leadership, the militia's creation actually widened divisions among the Reich's top officials by sparking a series of power struggles for control of the new force. These clashes, endemic among the vaguely defined and overlapping jurisdictions of the Party and government, were intensified by the Volkssturm's improvised nature and by the desire of many leading Nazis to gain credit for the great mobilization that they hoped would save the Reich—a clear indication that in the fall of 1944 these men did not consider the war irretrievably lost. Eventually, Martin Bormann combined skillful machination, strong positioning, and deft ideological arguments to emerge as the dominant national figure in the Volkssturm. His authority over the militia was never total, however, and other individuals and groups continued to exert significant influence upon it. More important, Bormann's efforts to ensure his domination tended to stifle the spirit of cooperation, dedication, and unity that the Nazis—himself included—believed essential to Volkssturm success. Understanding these power struggles is therefore critical not only to knowing who won them but also to unraveling their important negative effect on the Nazi effort to realize the Volkssturm ideals of unity, loyalty, and fanaticism.

The Führer Decree of September 25 formed the basis for power within the Volkssturm, but in typical Hitlerian fashion, it delineated authority very poorly. The decree awarded Himmler control of Volkssturm military affairs as Replacement Army commander, but by naming SA head Wilhelm Schepmann and National Socialist Motor Corps (NSKK) chief Erwin Kraus as Inspectors for Marksmanship Training and Motor Training, respectively, it also sanctioned potential infringements on Himmler's powers. Bormann (who helped draft the document) received a broader, though no less murkily defined, mandate over the Volkssturm's "political and organizational" aspects. Also, Hitler's order charged the NSDAP structure, which Bormann supervised, with the Volkssturm's "establishment and leadership."[1] Because "organizational" matters could be interpreted to include almost anything, and given the paramount importance attached to political and indoctrinational functions, from the outset Bormann held the greatest potential to dominate the Volkssturm.

The Führer Decree's ambiguity and the social Darwinian nature of the Third Reich's power structure guaranteed a power struggle for control of the Volkssturm. Himmler, Replacement Army Commander, head of the SS, Chief of German Police, and trusted associate of Hitler, obviously rated as Bormann's strongest challenger. In fact, Himmler was apparently quite confident of his position when he publicly boasted on September 21 that "the Führer has given me the command of this Volkssturm."[2] Bormann moved quickly to ensure this did not come to pass by working to confine the Reichsführer's authority to purely military issues. Toward this end, he quickly and correctly insisted that the Führer Decree granted Himmler authority exclusively as Replacement Army Commander, a much weaker position than his other post as head of the SS and police.[3] From the beginning, even in trivial matters, Bormann stood vigilant lest Himmler score points against him. For example, Bormann was convinced that Himmler's nationally broadcast radio address announcing the force on October 18 had created "the completely false impression that the Volkssturm is an SS affair." To counter this he ordered his subordinates to correct any press reports that inflated the Wehrkreis's—and thereby Himmler's—role in the Volkssturm.[4] Moreover, Bormann, who normally avoided public appearances, even demanded that Munich–Upper Bavaria's Gauleiter rearrange the national Volkssturm oath ceremony so that Himmler's keynote address was pared to a brief statement and Bormann appeared prominently on the rostrum with the Reichsführer.[5]

Bormann not only sought to contain Himmler's influence; he frequently encroached upon the latter's Volkssturm military responsibilities. For example, Bormann used his authority as supervisor of fortification construction to direct Volkssturm participation in these plainly military projects.[6] He also involved himself in logistical details; for example, Bormann ordered procurement of Volkssturm winter uniforms and even mandated their appropriate color. In February 1945, he instructed the central German Gauleiters to report their weapons stocks to him and began urging military commanders to expand the use of Volkssturm antitank teams.[7] All these issues clearly fell within Himmler's realm of authority, yet Bormann readily meddled in them.

For his part, Himmler seems to have restricted his clashes with Bormann to defending his SS and police powers, particularly in the occupied territories, against Party encroachments. To prevent the Volkssturm from infringing on police duties inside Germany, Himmler apparently ordered subordinates not to provide police training to the Volkssturm without his or Hitler's written approval.[8] In the Protectorate of Bohemia-Moravia, Himmler and local SS officials at least partially defeated the NSDAP Liaison Office's efforts to amalgamate local SS-controlled police auxiliaries into the Party-commanded Volkssturm. Similarly, Himmler prevented NSDAP officials in the Netherlands from dismantling the SS-led Landwacht in favor of a Party-run Volkssturm. The SS not only thwarted efforts to create a Volkssturm in Slovakia but actually used the opportunity to expand its *Heimatschutz* (police auxiliary) there to include all ethnic German civilian males aged eighteen to sixty. Likewise, in the General Government, Himmler created a police-controlled Stadt- und Landwacht from all German men aged sixteen to sixty, short-circuiting Party efforts to create a Volkssturm there from these very men. To forestall any future expansion of Bormann's Volkssturm authority into occupied territories, Himmler, as military commander, ultimately simply restricted the use of Volkssturm units to the Reich proper.[9] Himmler also used his authority as Reich Commissar for the Strengthening of Germandom to encroach on Bormann's control of personnel issues on at least one occasion. He exempted all men categorized as *Volksliste III* (persons of doubtful German heritage) in the Weichsel and Warthegau areas from Volkssturm service. Clearly, Himmler's power remained greater than Bormann's in what remained of Germany's conquered territories. Inside Germany proper, the Party's position was stronger.

Himmler typically avoided direct conflict with Bormann over the Volkssturm, opting instead to allow his ambitious Volkssturm chief of staff, SS *Obergruppenführer* Gottlob Berger, to conduct the frontal assaults.[10] During late September and October, Berger relentlessly sought to undermine Bormann, particularly on personnel issues. He championed numerous efforts to secure deferrals and exemption from Volkssturm service for certain groups.[11] He also backed several affiliates' attempts to gain permission to form their personnel into segregated units, a situation that would have created independent roles for these organizations within the Volkssturm. Berger hoped to fragment the Volkssturm into autonomous groups that would owe their status to him and thus increase his influence over personnel allocation. In time he hoped to combine an enhanced role in Volkssturm manpower issues with his existing control over Waffen SS recruitment as the foundation for the fulfillment of a cherished personal dream—the creation of the national Manpower Central Office under Berger's own direction.[12]

As a general principle, Bormann, as noted previously, insisted on forming Volkssturm units based on the members' place of residence. Ideologically, allowing particular lists to form their own segregated units would make a mockery of Volkssturm ideals of unity and shared sacrifice. Militarily, these units could prove wasteful of scarce resources and disruptive of the chain of command by giving every official or businessman with such formations veto power over Volkssturm use of his personnel. Politically, and most dangerously from Bormann's own perspective, such units could become hostile blocs within the Volkssturm. Therefore, Bormann could cite military and ideological reasons to demand that Volkssturm units be based on members' place of residence while simultaneously protecting his political base.[13]

Berger's challenges to Bormann's position found support from several willing allies; among the earliest and most determined was SA chief Schepmann. Upset by the cancellation of Guderian's SA-led Landsturm, Schepmann—during a stormy meeting at the Party Chancellery on September 22—had adamantly but unsuccessfully demanded that the SA either control the Volkssturm or be allowed to form its own independent, segregated units within the force.[14] To support his claims, Schepmann pointed out that 82 percent of all SA men had served or were serving in the military—12 percent had become casualties— and that the organization had extensive experience with police auxiliaries like the Stadt- und Landwacht; in teaching basic military skills (i.e., weapons use, signals, first aid, and rudimentary infantry tactics) to civilian volunteers; and in conducting intensive propaganda campaigns.[15] Evidence notwithstanding, Schepmann failed to win over the Party Chancellery, and he angrily took his case directly to Hitler.[16]

Bormann had typically supported Schepmann and the SA, but he could not let this blatant challenge pass. After "long discussions" with Hitler on the night of September 25–26, he convinced the Führer to reject Schepmann's proposal. Once again Bormann persuaded Hitler that an NSDAP-led Volkssturm could unify and fanaticize the German Volk, whereas an SA-controlled force would only intensify rivalry among the affiliated organizations. In addition, Bormann almost certainly conjured up the specter of Ernst Röhm's ambition to turn the SA into a revolutionary people's army, which had led to the blood purge of June 30, 1934.[17] In a classic example of National Socialist decision making, Bormann's combination of ideological arguments, stronger political base, and personal influence with Hitler easily trumped Schepmann's logic and technical competence.

Stung by his rebuff, Schepmann, a relatively weak newcomer to the highest echelon of Nazi power, next conspired with Berger to continue his quest of creating an independent SA role within the Volkssturm. Toward this end, Schepmann first campaigned to have Gau and Kreis Volkssturm chief of staff posts reserved for local SA leaders. Bormann blocked this proposal, arguing that the chain of command required that the Gau- and Kreisleiters—that is, Bormann's subordinates—select the men most qualified for these posts. He added that surely many of these appointments would go to suitable SA officials. He did not, however, note that such an arrangement allowed the Volkssturm to tap the experience and skills of individual SA men while denying the SA any privileges as an organization.[18]

Schepmann next sought to create independent, segregated Volkssturm units from skilled SA personnel (medics, cavalrymen, signalmen, and engineers) and the armed SA Special Purpose Units—the latter being of particular interest to the SA chief. Berger had authorized a similar deal for NSKK chief Erwin Kraus on October 14, which allowed the NSKK to form its personnel into elite motorized combat, transport, repair, and courier units.[19] If successful, this would allow Kraus and Schepmann both to retain control over their personnel and to create for themselves an autonomous political base within the Volkssturm. Of course Bormann found this intolerable and rescinded

Berger's order, stating again in the name of unity that specialist units must be under local Volkssturm command and must include all qualified men regardless of SA or NSKK membership.[20]

Undaunted, the SA chief next convinced Berger to have the SA *Gruppenführer* recognized as "Gau Representatives of the Inspector for Shooting Training," that is, as Schepmann's personal deputies. Once more, the Party Chancellery balked, claiming this would further complicate the cumbersome Volkssturm chain of command and encourage similar demands from other affiliates.[21] Yet again Bormann stood upon ideological arguments for unity to deny the SA an independent institutional position within the Volkssturm. Bormann's determination to eliminate the slightest hint of SA autonomy or authority even led him to forbid the use of SA unit designations (*Standart, Sturmbann*, etc.) in the Volkssturm.[22] By October's end, Schepmann resigned himself to defeat and his subordinate position in the militia.

Although Bormann stoutly opposed any SA or NSKK encroachment upon his powers, he genuinely believed their cooperation was essential to Volkssturm success. Toward this end, Bormann sought to mend fences with Schepmann by assuring him of the SA's prominent role in the Volkssturm and reminding him that it was "on my suggestion" that Hitler named him Inspector for Marksmanship Training.[23] Bormann hoped to placate both Schepmann and Kraus with advisory roles, but he also strongly urged his Party Chancellery Volkssturm staff to include representatives from all the affiliates in their planning sessions. He also encouraged Gau- and Kreisleiters to appoint qualified SA and NSKK men to their Volkssturm staffs.[24] Bormann and his Volkssturm Chief of Staff Wilhelm Friedrichs even urged the affiliates to publicize their Volkssturm contributions; and Schepmann did issue a number of stirring statements designed to show SA cooperation.[25] While desirous of the affiliates' "inspired and willing cooperation," Bormann brooked no challenges to his control of the Volkssturm and granted duties to affiliate members only as individuals, not institutions, and as technical advisers and policy implementers rather than decision makers.[26]

Bormann won an expensive victory, however, particularly in the SA's case. Schepmann's abilities and experience were wasted in his post as Inspector for Marksmanship Training, which allowed him to issue—through Berger's office—nothing more than basic technical bulletins.[27] Although Schepmann cooperated, he was never wholeheartedly enthusiastic, nor did he abandon his efforts to create segregated SA combat units.[28] Bormann thwarted the SA chief's political ambitions, but in doing so he alienated a potentially valuable contributor to the Volkssturm's preparation whose organization had considerable experience in providing rudimentary military training to civilians. This clearly illustrates the negative consequences of the intensely competitive power structure that existed in the Nazi Reich.

Gottlob Berger enlisted a number of other allies in his challenge to Party Chancellery control over Volkssturm personnel issues. During October, he authorized a series of segregated units, wholesale deferments, and exemptions for the personnel of several affiliates and government agencies. He approved the National Socialist German Student Union's request to form "academic legions" and ordered the German Red Cross to set up the Volkssturm's medical service.[29] He also instructed the Reich Traffic Ministry and the Reich Postal Ministry to form their employees into deferred, segregated units. Finally, he negotiated an agreement with the Luftwaffe High Command (OKL) concerning its civilian employees' Volkssturm responsibilities.[30]

While facing no real political challenge from any of these entities, Bormann angrily forbade all these special formations in order to thwart Berger's bid to become arbiter of Volkssturm manpower policy. Yet again Bormann relied upon ideology and unity to safeguard his personal authority.[31] To rein Berger in more permanently, Bormann instructed Friedrichs to appoint a clever and politically aware liaison officer to Himmler's staff to ensure that it followed proper procedure in the future. Next, Bormann vowed to meet with Himmler, who had already given assurances that Berger would restrain himself. On October 26, Himmler and Bormann jointly declared that both Friedrichs and Berger were Volkssturm Chiefs of Staff, the former responsible for organizational and political matters and the latter for military and training concerns.[32] Also on October 26, Friedrichs directly confronted an apparently conciliatory Berger, who agreed to rescind a number of objectionable orders, pledged closer cooperation, and promised to issue important orders only under Himmler's signature and not his own. Berger, however, defended himself against objections to his use of the title "Chief of Staff of the German Volkssturm"—which implied that Berger was Friedrichs's superior—by correctly pointing out that Himmler had given him this exact title.[33]

This truce collapsed within days. Berger circumvented the regular Volkssturm chain of command by directly ordering the Senior SS and Police Commanders (HSSuPF) to exempt all German police personnel from Volkssturm service. Also, he suggested creating segregated units for auxiliaries such as the Stadt- und Landwacht, *Werkschutz* (a factory police that guarded foreign laborers), Postal Police, and Rail Police. Although Bormann agreed to exempt active policemen, he insisted that civilian employees and members had to serve as individuals and that the Stadt- und Landwacht would be absorbed into the Volkssturm and abolished. He also moved to rein Berger in permanently.[34]

Bormann angrily complained that "the organization of the Volkssturm is, as Pg. Berger is obviously still not clear, a concern for which I am in overall control." He insisted that Berger "take his fingers out of my organizational sphere and instead concern himself with the urgent framing [Zimmerung] of the military aspects" of the Volkssturm. Furthermore, he accused Berger of self-aggrandizement, dereliction of his duty to produce meaningful training directives, violation of the established chain of Volkssturm command, and failure to cooperate with the Party Chancellery. Bormann added that Himmler "should have appointed Pg. Jüttner [SS Obergruppenführer Hans Jüttner, Himmler's Replacement Army deputy commander] and not Berger" as his Volkssturm staff chief.[35] On October 31, the feud climaxed when Bormann directly warned Himmler "to understand me correctly: I do not want to mix in your area of responsibility"; but, if Berger continued to ignore proper procedures and neglect Volkssturm training, particularly in modern antitank weapons, the Party Chancellery would be forced to turn to Guderian and OKH for assistance. Ominously, Bormann added, "Once things have started in this direction, it will no longer be possible to change course."[36]

This threat apparently worked, for although Berger remained active in the Volkssturm,[37] he began to confine his and his staff's activity to such purely military tasks as collecting and distributing weapons and equipment, and serving as liaison between the army and Volkssturm officials on mobilization issues. This shift to a more purely military focus is reflected in the composition of Berger's staff, which eventually numbered a dozen army and Waffen SS officers and about thirty civilian employees.[38] In November, Berger replaced his chief assistant, a Colonel Palm, with Colonel Hans Kissel, of whom Friedrichs approved on the grounds of Kissel's competence and willingness to "limit himself to military tasks."[39] Furthermore, under Kissel technical experts headed the staff's three sections (Supply/Organization, Weapons, and Training).[40] While extremely important, these military duties conferred little political power. By successfully confining Berger to these matters, Bormann secured victory over his SS rivals.

Himmler and Berger had accepted their political defeat by mid-December, when the Reichsführer SS commented that the Volkssturm had become an "instrument of power for Bormann . . . and the SS had no interest in it." Nonetheless, Himmler also believed that the Volkssturm would be crucial to German victory, "and therefore [he] wanted his subordinates to cooperate fully with Volkssturm officials."[41] This is hardly a ringing endorsement, and, as noted in the following chapter, such cooperation as existed was neither wholehearted nor spirited. Thus wasteful competition between Berger and Bormann dampened enthusiasm for the Volkssturm among key leaders and considerably handicapped efforts to prepare the force for combat.

Bormann alienated other Nazi leaders in his relentless pursuit of Volkssturm domination. Reich Women's Leader Gertrud Scholtz-Klink offered to set up a Volkssturm women's auxiliary to serve as quartermaster assistants, couriers, clerks, and cooks. Bormann declined the potentially helpful suggestion—even though it was precisely the kind of cooperation he openly claimed to want—lamely citing his concern that women should be kept away from combat.[42] More likely, although Scholtz-Klink herself posed no political threat, Bormann feared that a male rival might exploit this auxiliary to challenge his position. Once again political concerns smothered the kind of genuine Nazi enthusiasm and inventiveness upon which Volkssturm success depended.

Bormann's relations with Propaganda Minister Joseph Goebbels further illustrate the corrosiveness of Volkssturm power struggles. Bormann felt compelled to limit Goebbels's contributions given the latter's long-standing advocacy of a total psychological mobilization and his desire to parlay his position as Reich Plenipotentiary for Total War into complete control of manpower allocations.[43] Therefore, Bormann refused to allow the Propaganda Ministry to provide anything more than technical assistance to the Volkssturm. To Goebbels's chagrin, the Party Chancellery not only set Volkssturm indoctrination guidelines but also used the Gauleiters' staffs—not the regional Reichs Propaganda Offices—to implement them.[44] Thus, Goebbels would be prevented from taking any credit for whatever success the Volkssturm might achieve in generating fanaticism among the German people. As a consequence, the ability and experience of Goebbels and the Propaganda Ministry would largely be forfeited.

Goebbels did find at least one way, albeit a minor one, to get back at Bormann. He formed 1,300 Propaganda Ministry employees into two Levy II battalions, and furthermore declared that these men did not need deferment cards *(Zuteilungskarte)*. This enabled him to defer an additional 1,300 Propaganda Ministry employees, who served as individuals in their regular neighborhood units. He also equipped his two "house battalions" with "flawless new uniforms" and other equipment donated directly to them by the head of the NSKK's Transport Corps "Speer."[45] Goebbels could blatantly violate the letter and spirit of Volkssturm policy because he had the trust of, and personal access to, Hitler, but also because he was Berlin's Gauleiter, a position that empowered him to interpret and implement Volkssturm organizational policy and to grant deferments and permission to form special units. In this case he justified his actions based on the Propaganda Ministry's importance to the war effort, although his primary motivation was to retain control over his employees and perhaps to impress Hitler. Clearly, in this relatively minor case, Bormann was hoisted by his own petard, that is, Party control of the Volkssturm. The incident also shows how Party officials often put petty personal agendas ahead of national interest.

At any rate, just as the conflicts with Berger et al. peaked in late October, yet another rival, Reich Minister for Armaments and War Production Albert Speer, mounted a significant challenge to Bormann's authority. For this, Speer relied on the powerful combination of economic logic and direct access to Hitler.[46] Fearing that Volkssturm training and mobilization could wreak havoc upon the faltering war economy, Speer supported, sometimes with Berger's connivance, the unsuccessful efforts of a number of economic officials and factory managers to gain exemptions or deferrals from Volkssturm service for their personnel.[47] These efforts culminated when Karl Otto Saur, Speer's Technical Department head, proposed organizing Volkssturm units based on the members' place of employment rather than residence to enable factories to coordinate Volkssturm training with work and production schedules. Under Saur's plan, proposed directly to Hitler, Dr. Robert Ley, an early militia proponent, and his German Labor Front (DAF) would assume supervision and administration of the Volkssturm. According to Ley, long both a loyal Nazi and a Bormann critic, Hitler was "enthused" about this suggestion.[48]

Thwarting Saur's plan required Bormann to use his ideological trump card once again; Volkssturm success depended on the Party's unique ability to transcend self-interest. Bormann viewed Saur's plan as a selfish attempt to turn the Volkssturm into a personal security police for factory owners and a scheme to safeguard their manpower. He railed that "business leaders were not politically educated. Many business leaders even believe that under the slogan 'self-responsibility of industry' everything must go according to their wishes." Bormann "objected strongly to this special wish," claiming that "if I were to give in to this request, then we would not have a Volkssturm." Once again Hitler concurred with these ideological arguments and rejected Saur's plan.[49]

Speer subsequently recognized that his goals would be more easily achieved by working with, rather than against, Bormann. Likewise, once Bormann was convinced that Speer and his ministry had ceased threatening his political control, he willingly addressed their legitimate concerns and allowed generous deferrals for workers in essential war production. Furthermore, he promised that some factories' employees could, in exceptional cases and with proper authorization, form segregated units.[50] For his part, Speer made a genuine effort to equip the Volkssturm, but he continued to try to safeguard as much manpower as possible and even claimed that he and *Himmler* worked out deferral details.[51] Furthermore, Hitler, who stated "in all sharpness *[aller Schärfe]*," that the Volkssturm was worthless without weapons in sufficient numbers, apparently supported Speer's efforts to keep the militia from interfering with war production.[52] Ultimately, the Speer-Bormann conflict illustrates two important points: one, Bormann willingly compromised if his rivals acknowledged his political supremacy over the Volkssturm, and, two, Bormann's power had limits.

Another example of the impact of Bormann's tactical decisions in power struggles came with his positions toward the Reich Labor Service (RAD) and Hitler Youth (HJ). Both were allowed significant independence—the RAD from the Volkssturm and the HJ within the Volkssturm—and in both cases Bormann deviated from his opposition to segregated units and his insistence on unity, NSDAP control, and formations based on members' place of residence. Though military concerns played a role, Bormann's generosity toward the RAD and HJ was also politically motivated. These groups' exceptions enhanced Bormann's voice in overall manpower issues at the expense of Gottlob Berger and the SS by giving the Party Chancellery a significant role in allocating Nazi Germany's last reserves: the recruiting class of 1928.

The HJ's uniquely independent status within the Volkssturm shows how political concerns could outweigh ideology with Bormann. According to his own arguments, those sixteen- to nineteen-year-olds obligated to serve should have been enrolled in neighborhood formations; yet Bormann allowed them—apparently and ironically on Himmler's suggestion—to be segregated from older men as the Volkssturm's Levy III.[53] The 1928 recruiting class (boys turning seventeen in 1945) numbered at least 550,000 youths, and Hitler, Bormann, Friedrichs, Himmler, Speer, and Reich Youth Leader Artur Axmann all agreed that their status had to "be decided upon [the basis of] military necessity" because this "last reserve of blood must stand ready as soon as possible."[54]

Indeed, Bormann believed that the HJ was ideologically reliable, and its heavy involvement in premilitary training (basic field skills, marksmanship, physical training)—which dated back to 1942—gave it the experience and infrastructure needed to prepare the youngest Volkssturm members for military service.[55] Therefore, he mandated, with full HJ approval, that all civilian youths aged sixteen to eighteen (i.e., Levy III members) undergo six to eight weeks of basic military training and political indoctrination in the HJ's WE-Lagers (*Wehrertüchtigungslager*, premilitary training camps). In addition, fifteen-year-olds would take four-week introductory courses. During this training, each camp would form a segregated Volkssturm unit under HJ commanders, although they could be used in combat only under absolute emergency conditions.[56] As a result, the HJ controlled the Volkssturm's entire Third Levy.

Militarily this was sensible enough, since it would speed training of the new recruiting class, but Bormann had political motives as well. Granting this special status might win Bormann some goodwill from the HJ leadership, but more important, Levy III brought the WE-Lagers and the 1928 class under Party Chancellery purview. Although the HJ remained fairly autonomous during the final part of the war (another reason Bormann could not simply run roughshod over it as he did the SA), Waffen SS recruiters had successfully built up influence in the WE-Lagers. In many instances the SS had often employed press-gang methods to sway impressionable and vulnerable youths.[57] Indeed, Berger had expressed a desire to "get the younger classes for our Waffen SS."[58] Thus, by creating the Volkssturm's Levy III, Bormann could undermine his SS rival's ambitions.

To further assist in thwarting Berger's goal of procuring the bulk of the 1928 class, Bormann allied with the Wehrmacht just as he had threatened to do in late October. Top generals agreed that this last manpower reserve was "of decisive meaning [and] . . . should by no means be used in combat prematurely," that is, until it was properly trained and assigned experienced officers.[59] Once its share of recruits were fully prepared, the army intended to allocate them entirely to combat formations (65 percent infantry, 20 percent armor, 10 percent engineers, and 5 percent artillery); none were planned for rear-echelon assignments. In support of this arrangement, Bormann forbade, except in cases of sudden airborne assault, combat deployment of any Levy III Volkssturm units. Even in early March, Hitler authorized the evacuation from combat zones of all boys born in 1928 or 1929, including Flak Helpers, to safeguard this last reserve.[60] Although some members of the classes of 1928–1930 did serve in HJ combat units during March and April, on the whole Bormann and the Wehrmacht collaborated to prevent the piecemeal premature commitment of sixteen-year-olds to battle.[61] More important from Bormann's perspective, they kept these youths partially insulated from SS influence within Levy III.

Volkssturm regulations stipulated that upon completion of their WE-Lager instruction, Levy III youths immediately enter the RAD for further military training. All RAD personnel were exempt from Volkssturm service, and although its units could serve in combat as part of the Volkssturm, such arrangements had to be personally approved by RAD leader Konstantin Hierl. In fact, the Labor Service could even withdraw young men from the Volkssturm for its use.[62] Clearly part of the explanation for this unprecedented exemption was, as Hierl argued, the RAD's critical wartime duty in antiaircraft batteries, military construction units, premilitary training (a top priority by fall 1944), and even combat.[63] Another part is political, since keeping the 1928 class together, first in Levy III and then in the RAD, helped preempt Berger's SS recruiting efforts. In addition, Hierl, a former Reichswehr colonel, was on good terms with the Wehrmacht and could be expected to complement Bormann's efforts to ally with the generals against the SS. Finally, and perhaps most important, he was not a political threat.[64]

Bormann's alliance with the generals, HJ, and RAD seems to have at least partially succeeded in the competition with the SS for the class of 1928. In October, Keitel requested the following distributions (numbers in parentheses indicate volunteers):[65]

Branch	Previous Quota	Proposed Quota
Army	350,000 (200,000)	380,000 (200,000)
Navy	40,000 (30,000)	35,000 (30,000)
Luftwaffe	60,000 (45,000)	40,000 (40,000)
Waffen SS	100,000 (100,000)	95,000 (95,000)

While Keitel's proposed army increase came largely at Luftwaffe expense, it also cut the Waffen SS allotment by 5 percent. By mid-February, Hitler had approved Keitel's 95,000-man SS allocation and increased the army's to 412,500 recruits; early in March, he authorized OKW to begin inducting these seventeen-year-olds.[66] Although the army's gains at the SS's expense were only a fraction of the total, the SS share declined (by 5,000 *volunteers*), while the army's grew substantially (by 72,500). Furthermore, of the 87,549 seventeen-year-olds actually inducted by the end of March, the army received 72 percent, whereas the SS claimed only 9 percent—about half its allotted percentage.[67]

Such evidence reveals that SS recruiting power was definitely not unlimited, nor had the Wehrmacht's ability to influence manpower allocations evaporated.[68] This is not what one would expect given the widespread view that SS power grew unchecked into the last days of the Reich. The Volkssturm's HJ premilitary training program played a key role in limiting SS recruiting. Indeed, the SS *Führungsamt* (Leadership Office) admitted that the Volkssturm's Third Levy derailed their plans to train 20,000 Hitler Youths annually in vehicle operation, thus adversely affecting recruitment into the Waffen SS's largely mechanized German divisions.[69] Bormann's control over the Volkssturm almost certainly reduced SS influence in the WE-Lagers, thereby further disrupting its intensive, high-pressure recruiting efforts there. While Bormann's exact role is not clear, it seems that he cobbled together an alliance of the Wehrmacht, HJ, and RAD to use against his formidable rivals Berger, Himmler, and the SS in this case.

Bormann's cooperation with OKW extended beyond the issue of personnel. Keitel, who "place[d] great worth" on OKW participation in the Volkssturm,[70] fully acknowledged Bormann's political control in return for support on the issue of the 1928 recruits and for adherence to the Führer Decree's stipulation that the Volkssturm should only supplement the strength of the existing Wehrmacht. To this latter end, Bormann refused to allow local officials to recall active-duty officers for militia commands or to plunder army supply stocks for Volkssturm equipment.[71] The Party Chancellery and OKW also negotiated a mutually satisfactory agreement authorizing the creation of segregated, Second Levy Volkssturm units for all male Wehrmacht civilian employees, soldiers on long-term work furloughs, and civilian flak personnel (except Flak Helpers).[72]

Although there was cooperation, particularly with OKW, on the Volkssturm, relations with OKH and army operational commanders were not always smooth. Some officers considered the militia nothing more than a source of low-quality troops, a view that clashed with Bormann's belief in the significance of the Volkssturm's motivational propaganda role. This fundamental difference of opinion led to friction between the military and Volkssturm officials in a number of instances.

One such clash grew out of the efforts of Major General Wilhelm Burgdorf, chief of OKH's Personnel Office, to gain more influence over the appointment of Volkssturm unit commanders. In October, the general submitted a list of qualified, inactive army officers, which Bormann forwarded to the Gauleiters with the caveat to consider "only those officers who possess the necessary political vitality."[73] In March, Burgdorf sought to bypass the Party Chancellery altogether by asking Hitler's permission to allow his office to nominate suitable battalion leader candidates directly to the Gauleiters.[74] Even at this late date, Bormann resentfully blocked this intrusion by arguing—as usual—that the proposal would undermine NSDAP control and thereby damage the Volkssturm's critical political-motivational functions.

Other generals also mounted challenges. On October 8, Guderian, without authorization and in a blatant effort to substitute the Volkssturm for his defunct Landsturm, ordered eastern Gauleiters to organize 103 Volkssturm units along the lines of army fortress battalions and to turn them over to OKH to replace the units transferred to the west.[75] Bormann blocked Guderian's initial effort—as well as the general's attempts on January 14 and 16 to gain control of all Volkssturm units in eastern Germany—as detrimental to Party control in this region.[76] Similarly, OB West Rundstedt, fearing a potential Allied airborne assault on the Rhine bridges, unsuccessfully sought command of all auxiliary forces, including the Volkssturm, within the jurisdictions of Wehrkreise VI (Münster), XII (Wiesbaden), and V (Stuttgart).[77] Finally, in February 1945, Army Group North commander Field Marshal Ferdinand Schörner failed to convince Hitler to give him control of the entire Volkssturm in his area.[78]

In most cases such proposals made sense militarily, but Bormann successfully opposed them, ultimately issuing instructions refusing to allow the army to induct Volkssturm personnel, as either units or individuals, directly into its ranks without express authorization. Bormann feared the army, if allowed carte blanche, would merely cannibalize Volkssturm units for replacements and labor. Furthermore, he believed that the generals failed to recognize the importance of the Volkssturm's psychological and propaganda role.[79] He insisted that the Volkssturm retain its separate identity, even under Wehrmacht command, and feared that morale would suffer irreparable damage if everyone considered the force nothing more than a second-rate militia. Moreover, if the Volkssturm became a purely military force, the justification for Bormann's authority, the Party's ability to carry out the political-motivational function, would be severely diminished, if not eliminated outright.

Yet, as shown earlier, Bormann did not attempt to exclude Wehrmacht influence, and he fully acknowledged the need for Volkssturm units to serve under army operational command. For example, when Guderian requested the mobilization of eastern Volkssturm units through proper channels instead of seeking control over the entire apparatus, he had no problem procuring fresh battalions for specific tasks.[80] Rundstedt's proposal was eventually settled by allowing the Wehrkreise to assume command of all military forces in its region, but only when an enemy air landing had actually begun. This compromise apparently considerably cooled Rundstedt's initial ardor over the potential of the Volkssturm, again proving how Bormann's insistence on domination stifled his rivals' enthusiasm and willingness to cooperate.[81]

Nonetheless, far from excluding the Wehrmacht from the Volkssturm—as Keitel asserted at Nuremberg[82]—Bormann welcomed the generals' involvement so long as they acknowledged his political control and confined themselves to military matters or supporting his initiatives. He realized that army participation would help improve the Volkssturm's potential while simultaneously diminishing Himmler's importance in the force. Although lacking any officially sanctioned role, many generals were keenly interested in developing and exploiting the Volkssturm's military potential and did so through their technical and logistical assistance, their operational supervision of active Volkssturm units, and, when possible, their personal political efforts. In the aftermath of July 20, the Volkssturm shows that the generals could—and did—still participate in national policy making, but only in cooperation with significant political figures like Martin Bormann.

During October 1944, the Volkssturm began to take shape in the crucible of this series of intense power struggles. Martin Bormann, assisted by his diligent, creative, loyal, and obedient Party Chancellery staff (who drafted most of the orders issued under their boss's name), emerged the victor in these clashes for a variety of reasons. The first factor was Bormann's influence with Hitler, which enabled him to help draft the Führer Decree that established the Volkssturm and set the initial division of authority. With responsibility for organizational and political issues, Bormann could allocate decision-making power within the Volkssturm, thus permitting him to expand the Party Chancellery's and its allies' positions while restricting his adversaries' roles.[83] Conversely, the Führer Decree dealt Bormann's opponents a weak hand. Speer, Ley, and Goebbels received no role whatsoever, except for the last man's position as Gauleiter. Schepmann and Kraus were de facto subordinates of Himmler within the militia; and Himmler's realm of training and logistics conveyed little clout but a great deal of difficult responsibility, which in any case had to be shared with the Wehrmacht. No one else was even mentioned. Finally, the Führer Decree entrusted Bormann with what many Nazis viewed as the Volkssturm's top priority—political indoctrination—which, if successful in creating a groundswell of fanatical resistance, would position Bormann as the savior of the Reich, even possible heir to Hitler.

A second major factor that helped Bormann was the NSDAP's political position. Bormann could much more readily portray the Party as the obvious choice to lead the Volkssturm given its long-standing image as the leadership elite of the German people. No other Nazi entity could claim to be as broadly based, as experienced in motivational leadership or as well organized through-out Germany. On the other hand, the affiliates could be portrayed as divisive. Even Himmler's SS, often seen as having eclipsed the Party by the late stages of the Third Reich, was clearly unable to defeat Bormann and the NSDAP within Germany on Volkssturm-related issues.

A third reason was Bormann's ability to control personnel matters. The Führer Decree did not specifically award this duty to the Party Chancellery, but it seemed to fall naturally in Bormann's administrative and organizational bailiwick. Figures great and small challenged Bormann over personnel issues, indicating that indeed this issue involved domination of the Volkssturm. Had the affiliates and other special interests gained the right to maintain their own units, the Volkssturm would have been nothing more than a collection of private armies. Bormann's ultimate victory in preserving a unified NSDAP chain of command greatly enhanced his power by granting him significant influence over all manpower allocation issues. Anyone seeking exemptions, deferments, or permission to form segregated units had to curry the Party Chancellery's favor. Most important, Bormann's control of Volkssturm personnel issues enabled him to exert influence, in conjunction with the army, on recruitment and conscription allocations through Levy III's control of the 1928 recruiting class, the Reich's last major military manpower prize.

A fourth main ingredient in Bormann's victory was his own character. His sense of personal responsibility, coupled with his ideological motivations and adroitness in crafting ideological arguments, ruthless determination, and lust for power made him a formidable and successful competitor in the Third Reich's last great round of power struggles. From the very start he tenaciously insisted that "the Volkssturm is a Party matter"; and excepting Himmler's military capacity as Replacement Army Commander, only he and Hitler had authority to issue orders to it. He even privately referred to the organization as "my Volkssturm."[84] Bormann took an extremely active and direct interest in even the most minute details—he personally made decisions concerning specifics of deferments, etiquette, insignia, unit designation, uniform color, unit flags, stationery, rubber stamps, and other matters.[85] While the Volkssturm needed such energetic leadership, Bormann centralized the decision-making process, even in trivial matters, in his own hands; although this approach was justified in some cases, it generally proved detrimental in the long run by stifling zeal and initiative at the local level and overburdening regional and local Volkssturm officials—a subject addressed in the following chapter.

Bormann's control of the ideological high ground, coupled with his close relationship with and regular access to Hitler, further strengthened his bid for Volkssturm dominance. He had convinced the Führer that the Volkssturm could rekindle the indomitable spirit of the Kampfzeit if everyone, including government agencies, industrialists, and the affiliates, would obediently unite behind NSDAP leadership. In this way, Bormann, Hitler's trusted Party deputy, could portray his motives as unselfish while tarring his rivals with the brush of factionalism, defeatism, and heresy against sacred Nazi principles. While Bormann may well have used these arguments as cynical rationalizations of his power, it seems that he genuinely believed that Volkssturm success depended on his personal leadership.

Despite Bermann's strong position, his control of the Volkssturm was never total and existed only at the sufferance of Adolf Hitler. The Führer kept his subordinates dependent on him for their positions through perpetual competition for authority, and Bormann was no exception. Schepmann, Guderian, Saur and Ley, Schörner, and Burgdorf each challenged Bormann's control of the Volkssturm by appealing directly to Hitler; and because some of these proposals initially won favor with the Führer, Bormann was forced to defend his position again and again. Also, Hitler's support of Speer's view that the Volkssturm should not be allowed to reduce weapons production obliged Bormann to increase munitions worker deferments by 20 percent.[86] In one instance, Hitler, on OB West's request, ordered Bormann to make a recalcitrant Gauleiter transfer ten Volkssturm battalions to army command.[87] Although Adolf Hitler was not the man he was during the Reich's earlier years, these cases illustrate that national power in the Volkssturm, including Bormann's, still ultimately depended on him.

Bormann's control was also circumscribed by the fact that Himmler retained command of Volkssturm military matters and might have made more of his authority had he chosen to do so. In addition, Bormann's authority was weak in regions, such as occupied areas, where Party influence was weak. Because of their members' particular skills, the RAD and HJ—and to a much lesser extent the German Red Cross, NSKK, and even portions of the SA—retained a degree of independence within the Volkssturm. OKW and OKH, through their operational control of Volkssturm units, technical and logistical assets, and the desperate military situation, influenced decisions concerning the Volkssturm. Likewise, Speer could impact decisions that affected personnel classification and deferral within the Volkssturm in the name of essential war production. Although Bormann was its dominant figure, many entities and individuals affected various aspects of Volkssturm policy decisions.

Bormann's largely, though not totally, successful drive to control the Volkssturm was not merely political and personal but also ideological. He adhered to a commonly held Nazi belief: Volkssturm success required a truly selfless national effort, and this necessitated that the national leadership set an example of sacrifice and unity. Therefore, Bormann wanted and solicited, as well as demanded and coerced, the cooperation of all sorts of groups.[88] In seeking to create this unity, however, Bormann required subordination from his colleagues as a price for their participation. Although he successfully denied his rivals like Himmler, Berger, and Schepmann a political base within the Volks-sturm, Bormann's victory was costly. The power struggles that led to Bormann's domination also caused poor coordination, false starts, wasteful delays, and du-plication of effort during the first crucial weeks of the Volkssturm's existence.

Furthermore, although Bormann's defeated rivals worked for the Volks-sturm's success in narrow, specialized matters, they were not inspirational leaders either for their subordinates or for the German people. Ironically, Bormann's efforts to enforce the *Führerprinzip* (Führer Principle) robbed the Volkssturm of the one thing the Nazi leadership believed it needed most: en-thusiastic, dedicated, selfless, diligent leaders whose force of personality and National Socialist convictions could motivate the average individual to want to obey his superiors' orders faithfully and blindly. Therefore, the behavior of the Volkssturm's founders was plainly counterproductive to the goals they had established for this militia.

CHAPTER FOUR

Local Administration

Nazi leaders assumed Party control of the Volkssturm would provide three advantages at the regional and local levels. The first was that Gau and Kreis officials, theoretically granted extensive freedom to improvise, would be able to tailor the Volkssturm to meet diverse and changing circumstances in their areas and tap into hitherto underutilized resources. Second, the official view held that these regional and local Party bosses would compete against one another to create the most effective units and highly motivated Volkssturm men. However, Bormann's efforts to exclude his rivals' influence and to deny any Gauleiter the chance to build a national reputation for effective leadership led to overcentralized policy making. This restricted Gau and Kreis officials' independence, stifled local initiative, demoralized the overworked and often underqualified local Volkssturm officials, and generally diminished chances for achieving the very goals set by the national leadership.

The third perceived advantage was the Party's ability to inspire and unify all Germans in a fanatical defense of the Reich. In reality, competition rather than cooperation characterized Volkssturm national leadership, and local and regional officials often mimicked their superiors. Organizations that failed to secure an institutional role in the Volkssturm nationally generally carried on their struggle in the Gaue and Kreise, thereby reducing the cooperation considered essential. Many Party officials, instead of providing inspirational leadership, often pursued selfish personal interests instead. Those Nazis, mostly some of the Gau and Kreis Chiefs of Staff or HJ officials, who worked diligently for Volkssturm success generally found the Wehrmacht more help than either the Party or its affiliates. Ultimately, control of the Volkssturm by Gau and Kreis NSDAP officials, perceived as its greatest strength, ironically turned out to be a major weakness.

The Führer Decree of September 25 gave the impression that the real locus of Volkssturm activity would be the regional level. It charged the Reich's forty-two Gauleiters with "establishment and leadership of the German Volkssturm in their Gaue."[1] This apparently authorized a Gauleiter—who was in theory answerable only to Hitler[2]—to issue whatever orders he deemed necessary to ensure that his Volkssturm was properly organized, trained, and equipped. Furthermore, only the Gauleiter, Himmler, or Hitler could activate his region's Volkssturm for training, labor, or combat duty.[3] Having responsibility for these areas, however, was not the same as controlling them. In practice a Gauleiter had to report to Friedrichs's or Berger's staffs on

Volkssturm issues. Party control of the new force provided the bedrock of Bormann's dominance over the Volkssturm, but it also created an opportunity for Gauleiters to increase their independence from the Party Chancellery and enhance their personal reputations. They could also grant rivals, like the SA or SS, institutional roles within their regions' Volkssturm. Therefore, Bormann sought to ensure that all officials, particularly the Gauleiters, merely implemented his—rather than set their own—Volkssturm policies.

Bormann successfully restricted the Gauleiters' prerogatives in a number of areas.[4] He rejected the sensible suggestion that a Reich Defense Commissar, a non-Party position held by the Gauleiters, be appointed as liaison for each Wehrkreis. Since each Wehrkreis included parts of several Gaue, this would elevate the status of some Gauleiters and, in Bormann's view, allow the ambitious among them to enhance their power and autonomy at his expense.[5] While on paper the Gauleiters controlled personnel matters, Bormann issued twenty-one "Implementation Instructions" that detailed precise personnel procedures on Levy assignments and segregated unit formation. This left the Gauleiters only the authority to apply Bormann's guidelines to specific circumstances.[6] Some ignored Party Chancellery personnel policies, but usually for their own personal gain (e.g., forming *Gauleitung*—the Gauleiter's staff—employees into segregated Levy II units or incorporating their existing militias into the Volkssturm as privileged formations) rather than for reasons of accommodating unique local circumstances.[7] Still others cooperated with Bormann merely to resist encroachment on their powers from outside the NSDAP or to strike a blow against a rival.[8] While more willing to tolerate deviations from Gauleiters than the affiliates, Bormann's actions clearly reveal his intent to circumscribe his NSDAP subordinates' decision-making authority, thus enhancing his own, in the critical area of Volkssturm personnel policy.

Bormann curtailed Gauleiter independence in other ways. For instance, all fortification work done by the Volkssturm or People's Levy officially fell under Party Chancellery supervision.[9] Even in the most minute details, Bormann kept the Gauleiters on a short leash; the Party Chancellery even issued instructions standardizing Volkssturm nomenclature, including specifications for rubber stamps, flags, and so on, and chastized any recalcitrants.[10] In an action that reveals one of Bormann's main concerns, he rejected several Gauleiters' plans for local public collection of old uniforms for Volkssturm use or programs in which militia members could exchange cloth or rags for a finished uniform. Yet, in the winter of 1944–1945, Bormann approved a national collection drive for these very items.[11] Obviously, he wanted credit for himself and feared that his NSDAP underlings might gain too much attention with their own successful regional efforts.

Some Party Chancellery limitations on Gauleiter efforts, however, were motivated by pragmatic as well as political concerns. Early on, the Party Chancellery insisted that weapons and equipment distribution had to be nationally centralized to ensure that top priority went to Volkssturm units nearest the front.[12] Some Gauleiters, however, sought to arm and outfit their own special formations through a variety of unofficial channels, even including purchasing on the black market.[13] Other Gauleiters sought to commandeer supplies from Wehrmacht stocks or to divert goods or factory capacity from army to Volkssturm use.[14]

Naturally, these actions generated loud protests from the military. By mid-February 1945, Keitel claimed that rogue Volkssturm procurement was disrupting army logistics. The Army Administration Office even complained that requisitions of uniforms had reached the point where, if they continued, "the soldiers themselves will have to be sent back to the barracks this summer with [only] an armband."[15] Bormann and Berger responded with a series of rather ineffective orders demanding that local officials end unauthorized procurement but reassuring them that active-duty Volkssturm units would be supplied from a central arsenal.[16] National weapons and equipment distribution was a sensible plan designed to conserve scarce supplies, but it also contributed to Bormann's political objectives by allowing him to meddle in Himmler's sphere and by making the Gauleiters even more dependent on him.

Another critical area where Bormann curtailed Gauleiter freedom of action came in selecting Gau Volkssturm Chiefs of Staff *(Gaustabsführer)*. While the Gauleiter was the titular commander of his region's Volkssturm, most regular administrative chores fell to a staff typically consisting of divisions handling clothing and equipment, personnel, registration, training, weapons, administration and organization, medical issues, communications, and perhaps Wehrmacht liaison and/or indoctrination. Although some staffs included army officers as training or logistics advisers, the bulk of posts went to SA, NSKK (for transportation matters), SS, or HJ leaders or men from the Gauleiters' own Party staff.[17]

Heading these staffs was a Gau Chief of Staff, a difficult job that required interpreting, reconciling, and implementing the frequently vague and conflicting orders and requests received from national Volkssturm officials, the Gauleiter, and anyone else affected by the force. Further complicating their assignment was the fact that the Gaustabsführer had no authority to issue orders on his own, particularly to the Kreisleiters, but was nonetheless charged with supervising virtually all aspects of his region's Volkssturm.[18] In effect, responsibility for the Gau's Volkssturm rested on the Gaustabsführer's shoulders despite his lack of real power.

As Bormann desired, this made each Gaustabsführer dependent on him. To further ensure this, the Party Chancellery could veto any of the Gauleiter's nominees for this post. Bormann instructed the Gauleiters to select a "believing, fanatic, and therefore convinced National Socialist, front-proven leader of troops, and proper organizer."[19] Also, he demanded that each nominee have

World War II combat experience and skill in modern infantry weapons, specifically antitank weapons like the *Panzerfaust* and *Panzerschreck* rocket launchers.[20] Bormann wanted the Gaustabsführer to be combat-experienced motivational leaders, not merely former staff officers or the Gauleiter's political cronies. There was also an unwritten qualification: Bormann wanted men who would loyally and obediently implement his orders, thus tacitly restricting the Gauleiter's independence to set or circumvent Volkssturm policy.

Bormann carefully scrutinized the Gaustabsführer nominees, unhesitatingly rejecting candidates he deemed lacking in either political or military attributes. He vetoed four candidates and expressed reservations—some quite strong—about a further seven who nonetheless may have ultimately served as Gaustabsführer. His most common objection was insufficient recent combat experience, particularly on the Eastern Front and/or in the infantry, although age and, in one instance, the fact that the nominee had too many other duties also aroused Bormann's opposition.[21] Additionally, the Party Chancellery chief, arguing that the Volkssturm should supplement, not weaken, the Wehrmacht, flatly denied at least four Gauleiters' requests to recall a loyal longtime associate from active military duty.[22]

By screening the nominees, Bormann could ensure that the Gaustabsführer were militarily competent Nazis and also demonstrate to them that their new jobs ultimately depended on his approval. To reinforce the idea that the Gaustabsführer were subordinates of the Party Chancellery, Bormann ordered all of them to meet with him in Berlin on October 24 and again on December 8. Although there was certainly enough confusion about the Volkssturm to warrant these meetings, Bormann seems to have used them to impress upon the Gaustabsführer that they should look to him for guidance.[23]

Bormann's objections did not automatically eliminate candidates from chief of staff appointments. For example, Bormann rejected Schleswig-Holstein Gauleiter Heinrich Lohse's first nominee because of his lack of recent infantry experience. He raised the same doubts about the second candidate but allowed him to take the position after concluding he might indeed be the best man available.[24] Although in early October Bormann opposed Swabian Gauleiter Karl Wahl's nominee, Hans Geisser (who had also headed the ill-fated Heimatschutztrupp of 1943), he remained in this post in March.[25] Furthermore, Wahl, when asked to name a new candidate, replied that he was carefully weighing the qualifications of all candidates but had not found a more suitable man. He added with obvious relish that "no Gauleiter was happier" to hear of the Volkssturm's creation and

> it should be known to the Party Chancellery that the formation of the Volkssturm is in no way something new for my Gau, where long ago on my own initiative I worked on this issue, but nevertheless found no sym-

pathy among my superiors. Thirty-six thousand men were already organizationally enrolled [in the *Heimatschutztrupp*] and formed up exactly as it is to be expanded today.[26]

Locating an ideal candidate was not simple, but it seems that the Gauleiters tried—although in some cases reluctantly and under pressure[27]—to locate men who met Bormann's high political and military standards. Examination of the forty-one identifiable Gaustabsführer reveals that all had solid political qualifications.[28] Each was a Party member, and of the twenty-six for whom the date of enrollment could be fixed, all but three had joined before 1933. All held significant regional Party office—twenty-two were high-ranking SA leaders (seventeen as *Oberführer* or higher). Thirteen others were from the Party structure: four *Gauorganisationsleiter*, three Kreisleiters, an Ortsgruppenleiter, and five men from miscellaneous Gau staff offices. HJ, SS, and NSKK leaders placed two men each. Clearly, Bormann's demand that nominees have proven National Socialist records was an important consideration in the selection process.

These men were, however, not merely Gauleiter lackeys. Although nothing is known about the military experience of four identifiable Gaustabsführer, the others had fairly extensive service records. In terms of highest rank attained, there were two generals (one of whom was a general of the police and SS *Gruppenführer*), two lieutenant colonels, nine majors, ten captains (including one man listed as "battalion leader" who may have held higher rank), nine first and four second lieutenants (including two men simply listed as "officer," who may have held higher rank), and one sergeant; one additional man's rank was not listed, though he had some experience. Of these men, at least thirty-five had served in World War II—twenty-three on the Eastern Front and primarily as infantry commanders. Of the thirty-one listing military decorations, all had won the Iron Cross Second Class, twenty-three the Iron Cross First Class, four the German Cross in Gold, and six the Knight's Cross (Ritterkreuz), Nazi Germany's highest military award.[29] Eleven held various Assault Badges, and sixteen had earned Wound Badges. In fact, wounds may have ended the active military careers of several of these officers: Salzburg Gaustabsführer, HJ leader, and former captain Adolf Neutatz had lost an arm fighting in Russia; and in Thuringia, SA *Standartenführer* and Lieutenant Colonel Georg Feig lay wounded in a hospital when he was nominated in October.[30]

This evidence strongly suggests that Gaustabsführer selection followed Party Chancellery guidelines. Politically, the average appointee was a loyal and dedicated National Socialist who had proven his leadership in the NSDAP or one of the affiliates. Militarily, he had been a combat field commander—often in the ideological war in the East—as opposed to a staff officer.[31] Ideally, he was the epitome of National Socialist leadership—a man who did not issue orders for others to execute but personally led his men in the accomplishment of their tasks. The expertise of these Gaustabsführer was tactical: carrying out a superior's orders, inspirational leadership of men in combat, improvisation under adverse conditions, or perhaps training troops. While this might help with some aspects of their new job, such nominees were not required to have the kind of organizational (i.e., staff) experience needed to establish and administer the Volkssturm efficiently.[32] Bormann insisted that the Gauleiters place higher priority on ideological factors than bureaucratic and technical expertise, and it seems the Gauleiters implemented these demands, which, of course, worked to the Volkssturm's detriment to some degree.

Bormann's efforts to ensure the Gaustabsführer met his specifications clearly fit National Socialist ideological notions but equally plainly served his own personal agenda. Lower-level combat commanders were accustomed to adhering to a fixed chain of command, and the Führerprinzip likewise encouraged—at least on paper—obedience of Nazi officials to their superiors. Thus Bormann could further rein in the Gauleiters' independence and ensure that none of them could gain personal credit for Volkssturm successes. Finally, through vigilant supervision and a steady stream of detailed instructions on all matters, the Party Chancellery could help ensure that its rivals could not carve out a power base for themselves at the Gau level. Bormann never totally dominated the Gauleiters or their chiefs of staff—they could and did defy him on all sorts of issues—but he was effectively able to exert control over "his" Volkssturm even at the regional level.

Like the Gauleiters, Kreisleiters and their Volkssturm Chiefs of Staff *(Kreisstabsführer)*—the Volkssturm's third and lowest administrative level—possessed significant responsibility to implement though not formulate policy.[33] Charged with the "leadership, enlistment, formation and organization of the Volkssturm" in his area, the Kreisleiter initially was expected to enroll all civilian males, assign them to the proper Levy, organize units, and appoint company commanders. Once units were duly constituted, the Kreisleiter was then responsible for such administrative and training tasks as distributing equipment, paying for miscellaneous expenses (office supplies, instructional materials, rental of meeting halls, train tickets for Volkssturm travel, etc.), overseeing political and military instruction of the Volkssturm, enforcing discipline, and supervising subordinates.[34] Bormann considered the Kreisleiters to be the "most important Political Leaders below the Party Chancellery itself" because they had regular, close contact with individual Germans. Thus their energy and enthusiasm could yield immediate dividends in their local Volkssturm.[35]

Although the Kreisleiter's authority, by Bormann's design, was primarily executive, the Kreis was somewhat remote from direct Party Chancellery supervision. As a result, some officials used this independence to pursue their own interests. For example, Karlsruhe's Kreisleiter defied orders by forming his own staff into a special Shock Troop Kreisleitung and allowed city government employees to do the same. Both units were well equipped and formed the Kreisleiter's personal deferred reserve.[36] Treuburg's (East Prussia) Kreisleiter flouted several orders by combining his six Volkssturm battalions into a regiment (officially, the Volkssturm's largest unit was the battalion), by naming himself regimental commander (Kreisleiters were to have no unit commands), and by swelling his "regiment's" ranks with large numbers of invalids who clearly should have been exempt. Apparently his aim was to impress Gauleiter Koch with his diligence.[37]

Not all Kreisleiters deviated from policy for personal gain; some simply sought to adapt the Volkssturm to specific local circumstances, purportedly a benefit of Party control.[38] For example, rather than organizing his units on the prescribed Ortsgruppen structure, the Kreisleiter of rural Schönlanke (Pomerania) based his formations on towns with good road connections so as to speed mobilization of men living in scattered farming communities.[39]

These officials, however, could not ignore national directives with impunity, even for legitimate reasons, as demonstrated by a series of incidents in Kreis Vilshofen (Gau Bayreuth). Here, the local Kreisstabsführer, SA *Hauptsturmführer* and former First Lieutenant Hans Schedlbauer, initiated a number of programs designed to make his units more effective, but his efforts were negated by decisions made at higher levels. First, he organized his nine Volkssturm battalions into a regiment under his command and, in hopes of increasing the combat potential of his troops, had each battalion place its healthiest veterans in an elite assault platoon and the members of the Landwacht in a reserve platoon.[40] Orders from Berlin forced him to abandon this plan by forbidding the Kreisstabsführer any independent command authority, banning elite units (particularly for the Stadt- und Landwacht), and mandating strict adherence to members' place of residence as the criterion for unit assignments. Also, Schedlbauer made Levy assignments quickly and energetically only to have Bormann's subsequent directives force him to reallocate virtually everyone.[41] Finally, he discovered that confiscating hunting weapons, done to facilitate marksmanship training, was forbidden.[42] Logically, Schedlbauer's enthusiasm diminished quickly, an illustration of why Kreis officials often showed initiative only when it promised personal rewards.

To assist in Volkssturm management, each Kreisleiter was authorized to have a staff and a Kreisstabsführer. The staffs varied considerably in composition, but most had sections for training, transportation, medical matters, weapons and equipment, organization, and finances, and many later added police and army liaison.[43] Understandably, populous Kreise, particularly cities, had the more sophisticated arrangements.[44] Although duties primarily involved preparing the Volkssturm for service, the Kreis Staff continued to handle paperwork—particularly concerning personnel issues—once its units were on active duty under Wehrmacht command.[45]

With more than 800 Kreise in Germany, the Party Chancellery could not hope to supervise every Kreisstabsführer closely; this would fall to Gau officials (another reason for Bormann's keen interest in Gau chiefs of staff). The best Bormann could do was set criteria for this post and scrutinize the qualifications of a sampling of the Kreisleiters' nominees.[46] As with their Gau counterparts, the Kreisstabsführer were to be dedicated National Socialists with recent military experience who would loyally and enthusiastically implement policies set at the national level.

Insufficient documentation renders comprehensive conclusions about the Kreisstabsführer impossible; but surviving evidence—primarily from Gau Bayreuth[47]—suggests that the Kreisleiters attempted to follow established Party Chancellery criteria. In the main, Bayreuth's Kreisstabsführer had substantial recent military experience and had demonstrated political ability within the Kreis, though understandably their records in both categories were less impressive than those of the Gaustabsführer.

Of the thirty-one identifiable Gau Bayreuth Kreisstabsführer, virtually all had the desired political qualifications. Fourteen were SA leaders, six came from Kreis NSDAP Staffs, three held both SA and Kreisleitung Staff posts, three were HJ leaders, one was an NSKK commander, and one a retired police official (three men provided no information)—a breakdown strikingly similar to that of the Gaustabsführer. All were, of course, Party members, although only three were true "Old Fighters." Two-thirds joined in or after 1930, eleven after January 30, 1933.

More surprisingly, these Kreisstabsführer had military experience to complement their political backgrounds. Twenty-five had served in World War II (at least seventeen on the Eastern Front), and sixteen of those had seen duty in both world wars. Four of the remaining five had experience only in World War I, while the fifth man had served, but records provided no further details. Like their Gau counterparts, many of Bayreuth's Kreisstabsführer had earned combat decorations (three German Crosses in Gold, fourteen Iron Crosses First Class, twenty-one Iron Crosses Second Class, eleven Wound Badges, and eight Assault Badges). The overwhelming majority of these men had attained battalion- or company-level commissions (four majors, three battalion commanders, eight captains, three first and five second lieutenants) with six NCOs (three sergeants and three corporals), a police colonel, and one unknown forming the remainder. Also eight had Freikorps experience, a paramilitary qualification the Nazis may have deemed particularly useful for Volkssturm officials.

Examined individually, two-thirds of Bayreuth's Kreisstabsführer had clearly demonstrated the kind of military abilities demanded by the Party Chancellery. Of the remaining third, four had extensive combat records (three with decorations) in World War I but only limited frontline experience in the opening campaigns of World War II and/or rear-area tasks such as commanding *Landesschützen,* coastal artillery, or prisoner-of-war camp units. Nonetheless, they might have been deemed the most qualified men available. Only six of the Kreisstabsführer possessed questionable military records, that is, a combination of low ranks, no decorations, and limited recent military experience. Of the six, three did have Freikorps backgrounds, but five were SA officials, and five had joined the NSDAP before 1933, which suggests a premium on political qualifications. The clearest case of this came with Selb's Kreisstabsführer, whose military experience consisted of four years in World War I at a rank no higher than corporal (but who could have openly criticized that?), and a brief stint as a Luftwaffe technical inspector. He was, however, a long-serving and relatively high-ranking SA officer *(Obersturmbannführer).*

Kreis chiefs obviously lacked the Gaustabsführer's qualifications, but the pool of bona fide Nazi military heroes must have been somewhat limited and unevenly distributed by late 1944. In fact, given the dominant image of local Volkssturm officials as inept political hacks, it is surprising that so many of them had legitimate military credentials. Although there is no evidence suggesting the Party Chancellery scrutinized all nominees, it does seem that the Kreisleiters took seriously Bormann's orders to select Kreisstabsführer who were both experienced front commanders and convinced Nazis.

Although the Kreis was the lowest level of Party officialdom with any Volkssturm authority, Bormann wanted to base units on the Ortsgruppen (and even Blocks and Cells, where feasible) in order to cement NSDAP domination over the force still further.[48] Many Ortsgruppe officials did in fact participate in establishing the Volkssturm in their areas, primarily in preparing lists of potential members from card files of the Party, Resident Registration Offices, and rationing agencies and from the knowledge of the block and cell leaders. Ortsgruppe staffs also enrolled volunteers and screened out the obviously disabled.[49] After the initial registration, the Ortsgruppe updated unit rosters by adding those who moved into the area or forwarding records of anyone who left, a daunting challenge particularly in 1945's great refugee floods.[50]

Some Nazis wanted to expand the Ortsgruppenleiters' Volkssturm role. Erich Koch believed Ortsgruppenleiters were the Volksgemeinschaft's natural leaders and should control this "popular uprising."[51] Ley suggested that since Volkssturm companies would be based on the Ortsgruppen, the Ortsgruppenleiter should nominate company and subordinate commanders. Bormann rejected this, stating that company officer selection was the Kreisleiter's prerogative because the Volkssturm's tactical unit was the Kreis-based battalion. Furthermore, Bormann must also have realized that maintaining centralized (i.e., his) control of the Volkssturm would be impossible if the thousands of Ortsgruppenleiters had extensive decision-making powers.[52]

In some areas, however, Kreisleiters chose to delegate considerable authority to their Ortsgruppenleiters. Because the Volkssturm primarily trained in companies, that is, at the Ortsgruppen level, many Ortsgruppenleiters were deeply involved in Volkssturm military and political instruction.[53] While no one could object to these activities, in many areas Ortsgruppenleiters wielded considerably more authority than Bormann intended them to have, often assuming command of units or nominating commanders precisely as Ley had suggested, and in some cases making Levy assignments or handling other unauthorized duties.[54]

A more serious example of how local Nazi officials' behavior undermined not only established policies but also the very goals and ideals of the Volkssturm occurred when they evaded service in the force. Bormann had warned that lower-echelon Party leaders must set the example of sacrifice and could not expect special treatment. Only those with requisite military skills could hold command posts; and Bormann expected Political (and affiliate) Leaders to serve in regular Levy I units unless their occupation had been classified as essential or there was no one to assume their Party duties.[55] Many local NSDAP officials fell far short of Bormann's standards, however. For example, virtually all Gau Bayreuth's Kreisleiters kept Political Leader Squadrons as a part of their independent (and no doubt deferred) Kreis Staff Companies. Some Ortsgruppenleiters here even claimed total exemption from Volkssturm service or insisted that their Party rank entitled them to militia command positions.[56]

Such problems were not limited to Gau Bayreuth. Segregated Political Leader units existed in the Lower Danube and Berlin Gaue; Hessen-Nassau's Political Leaders not only had their own unit but also served in Levy II, doubly violating Bormann's orders.[57] East Prussian NSDAP officials were so reluctant to serve that the Fourth Army chief of staff remarked in exasperation, "Why doesn't the Party leadership report to the Volkssturm?"[58] Some Gau Cologne-Aachen Nazis enrolled in the Volkssturm for the sole purpose of claiming exemption from regular military service obligations—even though no such exemptions existed.[59] Clearly, Bormann was mistaken in his basic assumption that regional and local Party leaders would set the example of fanaticism and sacrifice needed to inspire the German people to fight to the bitter end. In reality, many local Party officials were more interested in keeping themselves and their associates and employees out of the Volkssturm and were sufficiently distant from the Party Chancellery to get away with such blatant violations. The real damage caused by such antics was the destruction of any hope that Germans would rally behind the Party and fight fanatically, which of course was the Volkssturm's basic purpose. If NSDAP leaders could not put the German Volk's interests ahead of their own, how could they expect the average citizen to do so?

The attitudes and actions of the affiliated organizations, particularly the SA, NSKK, and SS, at the regional and local levels further reveal the Nazis' inability to cooperate and sacrifice. SA leaders publicly claimed extensive Volkssturm involvement, and SA (and NSKK) men did figure prominently on Gau and Kreis Volkssturm staffs.[60] As per the Führer Decree, the SA was heavily involved in Volkssturm training, especially marksmanship; in fact, Berger adopted SA training methods as the Volkssturm's national standard, and the SA added riflery courses to accommodate Volkssturm demand. Regional SA leaders were so busy with Volkssturm training that Schepmann canceled the monthly Gruppenführer meeting in December.[61] Surviving SA Group records reveal a heavy SA presence in Volkssturm training all over Germany;[62] some SA *Standarte* even ordered all their members to volunteer for Volkssturm service.[63]

Yet SA participation gave neither power nor prestige; and national, regional, and local leaders frequently expressed their dissatisfaction in a variety of ways. Some complained that militarily qualified SA men had been ignored for Volkssturm commands,[64] while others used their Volkssturm offices to circumvent explicit restrictions on SA influence. Many SA Special Purpose Units or other formations were simply absorbed into the Volkssturm intact, usually as a segregated elite formation.[65] Hessen-Nassau's chief of staff, SA Standartenführer Kurt Schädlich not only kept SA units separate within the Volkssturm but allowed them to remain under SA command at all times, something Bormann had expressly forbidden.[66] Saxony's Gaustabsführer, SA *Brigadeführer* Artur Rabe, also defied Bormann by instructing Kreisleiters to appoint the local SA Standartenführer as their Kreis staff chiefs.[67] SA formations often—though not always—lent the Volkssturm supplies but insisted that these remained SA property and fretted that the NSDAP might not replace depleted stocks of even trivial items like paper targets or pellet gun ammunition.[68] Overall, the SA's willingness to cooperate was tempered by a selfishness toward its possessions and personnel and a desire to enhance its own position within the local Volkssturm.

Similarly, local and regional NSKK leaders sought to use their legitimate role in forming and training motorized formations to expand their Volkssturm authority. The sparse surviving evidence shows that Party Chancellery instructions specifically barring NSKK control of mobile units and mandating inclusion of qualified personnel from outside the NSKK were regularly—though not entirely—ignored.[69] Many local NSKK officials simply attempted to designate their formations as Volkssturm motorized courier and transportation units; they incorporated suitable outsiders only if absolutely necessary, and then only in small numbers and at the lowest ranks. Frequently, NSKK leaders were automatically appointed to command motorized units regardless of their military experience.[70] As some of their SA counterparts had done with their special formations, regional NSKK leaders in Thuringia, Moselland, and Bayreuth even ordered that all mobile unit commanders should be NSKK leaders.[71] Although Volkssturm motorized units amounted to little, the NSKK's behavior confirms the trend toward selfishness rather than sacrifice among Nazi entities.

Local branches of even the minor affiliates, such as the National Socialist Flyers Corps (NSFK), successfully pursued their own agendas within the Volkssturm. Munich–Upper Bavarian Gauleiter Giesler granted, no doubt on NSFK request, deferments to all its personnel.[72] In East Prussia, NSFK *Oberführer* Ewald Oppermann's Volkssturm Night Attack Squadron consisted of his personnel and a few training and sport planes. They literally never got off the ground due to fuel shortages, but the unit enabled the men to avoid serving in infantry combat.[73] In a similar vein, the chief test pilot at the Dessau Junkers factory requested Himmler's permission—and fifty fighter planes—to form a Volkssturm pursuit squadron from his fellow test pilots. Although this man stated what may have been a genuine burning desire to smite the aerial foe, it is just as likely that he wanted to avoid the less glamorous task of Volkssturm infantry training—while impressing the Reichsführer with his zeal.[74]

Not surprisingly given Himmler's feud with Bormann, relations between the Volkssturm and SS and police officials sometimes proved less than cooperative at the local levels. Regional SS leaders, like so many others, sought to form their Volkssturm-liable personnel into segregated units under SS control and to secure command posts for their leaders.[75] Although active-duty police were exempt from Volkssturm service, auxiliary personnel were not, and regional police officials proved reluctant to give them up. Many sought to form their Werkschutz (an auxiliary designed to guard foreign workers in individual factories) members into segregated Levy II units, or simply claimed the right to recall Werkschutz men from Volkssturm duty.[76] Similar disputes arose over the Stadt- und Landwacht, which was scheduled to disband once the Volkssturm was on its feet, and police authorities typically worked to ensure that these local auxiliaries became segregated Volkssturm units as well.[77] One police commander, SS Obergruppenführer Martin (HSSuPF Main), was so angered at losing his Stadt- und Landwacht that he refused to turn over the former auxiliary's weapons to the Volkssturm and banned his subordinates from providing basic security training to the militia.[78] This hardly epitomized the comradeship touted in Nazi propaganda.

On the other hand, in some places police-Volkssturm cooperation did exist. Police granted Volkssturm authorities access to lists of local inhabitants in order to draw up initial membership rosters. Station houses served as enrollment centers for men who had recently moved into the area.[79] Police also assisted in forcing recalcitrant Volkssturm members to report for duty and training;[80] and individual low-ranking police officers volunteered their help in training local Volkssturm units.[81] Like so many others, police officials were not opposed to the Volkssturm in principle, but when its practices began to disrupt the performance of their duties, affect their personnel, or infringe upon their prerogatives, some actively obstructed the Volkssturm's efforts in pursuit of their own interests.

In contrast to the aforementioned groups, some Party affiliates' regional branches did provide the desired example of cooperation. Gau Essen's DAF office instructed subordinates to assist leaders of factory-based Volkssturm units in training and political indoctrination sessions.[82] In neighboring Gau Düsseldorf, the top DAF official ordered his Kreis officials to support the Volkssturm in word and deed by donating all its spare uniforms and to work, as he was doing, to locate supplies, available factory capability, and spare fuel to produce Volkssturm goods. He added that "we don't have time to wait for central instructions, it depends much more on the ability of every individual fanatic National Socialist to improvise." Most important, he urged all DAF members to set a good example by serving as assigned in the Volkssturm.[83] This was not the situation everywhere, as Gau Bayreuth's DAF officials directly contradicted Bormann by successfully seeking special consideration for command appointments in Second Levy—and therefore deferred—factory units.[84]

The National Socialist Women's Organization proved another of the few affiliated groups to adopt some of the official spirit of cooperation, sacrifice, and improvisation. Bayreuth's branch restored old uniforms to fieldworthiness, while the Schwansee (Kreis München-Ost) group made caps for all Volkssturm men who could furnish the necessary cloth.[85] Kreis Oberlahn-Usingen's (Hessen-Nassau) local *Frauenschaft* operated a veritable factory producing packs, bread bags, caps, and leggings for any Volkssturm man providing the required raw materials.[86]

As one might expect given their privileged positions, local RAD and HJ branches also worked well with the Volkssturm. Although as jealously protective of their personnel—even in individual cases—as any officials, local RAD leaders willingly assisted by providing trainers or surplus uniforms.[87] Similarly, the HJ, with its role in providing premilitary training to fifteen- and sixteen-year-olds, enjoyed sweeping Levy III deferrals for its adult personnel. It could even recall HJ leaders from active duty with the People's Levy, the Replacement Army, or even the field army if they were needed for training duties.[88] With these extensive favors, local HJ units were naturally favorably disposed toward the Volkssturm.[89]

In fact, the daunting, high-priority challenge of enrolling and training the class of 1928—over 550,000 youths—in less than six months probably justified HJ privileges.[90] The four- to six-week WE-Lager course consisted of physical training, weapons instruction (which now included antitank weapons for the first time), rudimentary infantry tactics, and a strong dose of political indoctrination. Although these boys could be trained in shifts, the WE-Lagers also had to stage refresher courses for all previous graduates still in civilian life, instruct members of the 1925–1927 classes who had health exemptions from army but not Volkssturm service, provide specialized training for 48,000 navy and air force recruits, and prepare the 1929 class beginning in early 1945. All of this necessitated a major expansion of WE-Lager facilities.[91] For example, HJ Region 22 (Bayreuth) alone planned a total of fifty-nine camps, each with a capacity of at least 60 youths.[92] To assist, the Replacement Army, Waffen SS, and Wehrmacht were called upon to do their utmost to provide trainers and supplies.[93]

The HJ had less than two months to ready the necessary camps, but it made a genuine effort to meet its deadlines. For example, with Organization Todt's help, Harburg's (Swabia) HJ commander added a third camp and doubled his barracks capacity, although he had trouble procuring weapons. A week before 400 recruits were scheduled to arrive, he had only thirteen rifles and one light machine gun available.[94] Finding instructors was also difficult despite the HJ's carte blanche on recalling personnel; and their quality (all supposedly were former military men) was mixed though generally adequate.[95] Once training began, HJ officials remained busy sending the police to ensure that all boys attended their required courses.[96] Of all the major affiliates, the HJ worked the hardest for Volkssturm success and was least involved in the petty bickering that characterized the attitudes toward the Volkssturm of SS, SA, and NSKK officials.

The reasons for this cooperation are obvious—the HJ, as an organization, had a task of clear national urgency within the Volkssturm, that is, training the Reich's last group of fresh recruits. No other affiliate had comparable privileges and independence; therefore, it is not surprising that the HJ, locally and nationally, put this degree of effort into the Volkssturm. Relatively speaking, all Party-affiliated groups put a level of interest into the Volkssturm that was proportional to the credit their organization could expect in return. The Frauenschaft or DAF cooperated in hopes of improving their status in the Nazi hierarchy; but the SA, NSKK, or SS (and the police) saw little to be gained from participating in the Volkssturm on Bormann's terms. Some individual members of these groups willingly cooperated, but the majority maintained a primary loyalty to their organization and showed little interest in making sacrifices unless Volkssturm rules could be bent to their affiliate's gain. The inability of Party and affiliate officials to substitute unity for self-interest proved to be a prime obstacle to Volkssturm success.

Although the Wehrmacht had no control over inactive Volkssturm units, it worked harder than any of the affiliates—possibly excepting the HJ—to make the militia succeed. Local military men had two avenues by which they could influence the Volkssturm. One was the fact that the army was the only source for technical advice and equipment; the other was that all active Volkssturm units came under the command of the nearest Wehrmacht combat officer.[97]

The military made a serious effort to provide the Volkssturm with what equipment it could spare, although shortages of matériel curtailed generosity, and the Gauleiters rarely thought the army was doing enough.[98] In terms of technical advice and instruction, the military, especially the Replacement Army, worked closely with Volkssturm officials. Himmler ordered all Wehrkreise to assist Volkssturm training, and they seem to have complied as fully as the circumstances allowed.[99] Army officer and noncommissioned officer schools helped train Volkssturm leaders, and many Replacement Army formations furnished instructors for area Volkssturm units.[100] As the main providers of training and advice, army officers could gain considerable influence with their locality's Volkssturm.

The necessity of incorporating Volkssturm units into the army's tactical defense plans also enabled Wehrmacht officers, particularly town commanders, to gain some control over these formations. Officially, only Hitler, Himmler, or the Gauleiter could mobilize Volkssturm units; but this proved impractical in meeting the kind of fluid tactical situations precipitated by enemy assaults.[101] Thus, the army and Party developed early-warning systems to speed alerting and mobilizing all rear-area troops. Where these systems existed, town commanders could activate Volkssturm units automatically by sounding the proper warnings.[102] Based on this authority, the officer could often integrate the Volkssturm into his defense plans as he saw fit, even to the point of breaking up militia units and dispersing their personnel among his regular Wehrmacht units.[103]

A local army commander's ability to shape the Volkssturm obviously depended on NSDAP collaboration that was not always forthcoming. East Prussia's Koch was the worst offender, even reportedly forbidding his Volkssturm subordinates from having any contact with the army.[104] Gauleiters Otto Hellmuth (Mainfranken) and Wilhelm Murr (Württemberg-Hohenzollern) also had serious disputes with the Wehrmacht over the use of Volkssturm personnel.[105] Local NSDAP officials in such diverse places as Kreise Westerburg (Hessen-Nassau), Leslau (Wartheland), and Prenzlau (Brandenburg) and other eastern Ortsgruppen also caused problems by refusing to work with the army in tactical planning and joint training exercises.[106] To some degree NSDAP intransigence is understandable. The Volkssturm was the only armed formation under local officials' command, and these officials jealously guarded their powers over it, fearing the army would negate their motivational efforts or simply break up units for replacements. Whatever the logic, it should have been clear that successful local defense required close coordination of all available resources.

Indeed, many Party officials did recognize the value of effective Wehrmacht-Volkssturm collaboration. Some Gau and Kreis Staffs established good relations with the army quite early and even included officers as military advisers and liaisons.[107] For their part, the Wehrkreise worked particularly hard to maintain cooperative working relationships with Kreis-level Volkssturm officials; and several Wehrkreise included Volkssturm commanders in their local defense conferences.[108] The widespread existence of early-warning systems confirms cooperative efforts in many areas.[109] The fifteenth Army Rear Area Command found itself in a position where it could attempt disciplinary action against recalcitrant Party leaders, Bürgermeisters, and Volkssturm unit leaders.[110] Even in East Prussia, Fourth Army commander Hossbach commented, "I must expressly state that the lower offices of the Volkssturm in East Prussia [as opposed to the Gauleiter], in realistic recognition of their possibilities and their abilities, worked in the closest cooperation with the officers and troops of my army."[111] Likewise, many local Party officials elsewhere realized that without army assistance they lacked the resources and expertise to make the Volkssturm succeed.[112]

Whatever the Wehrmacht's degree of local influence on the militia, the NSDAP dominated Volkssturm policy formulation and implementation at every level. On paper, the Gau- and Kreisleiters wielded sweeping powers, yet in practice three factors limited their authority and ability: Bormann's attempts to maintain his control over the Volkssturm, a lack of cooperation among Nazi organizations, and the fact that most of these men were simply not qualified to organize and lead the Volkssturm given its scope and their lack of planning and preparation.

Bormann's desire to dominate the Volkssturm led to micromanagement and overcentralization of authority. He did not trust the very subordinates, the Gauleiters, upon whom he relied to run the Volkssturm and sought to prevent any of them from using the force to enhance their reputations. Bormann counted on the Gaustabsführer, who had no independent authority and were in part dependent on him for their positions, to implement his detailed instructions. Although he successfully prevented anyone from usurping Party Chancellery powers, this overly centralized control led to delays, confusion, duplication of effort, and despair on the part of local officials. Furthermore, it stifled the initiative that Bormann hoped would allow Gau and Kreis Volkssturm officials to tap locally available resources fully and efficiently. What local initiative existed was generally either thwarted by national decrees demanding standardization, frustrated by a lack of equipment, or directed toward placating some special personal or organizational interest.

Furthermore, the Volkssturm's regional and local strata were permeated by the same divisiveness that characterized the national level. Organizational and personal rivalries rent the force, quite often precisely mirroring national divisions. Party leaders expected affiliates to participate in the Volkssturm as obedient subordinates, while affiliate officials often sought to try to circumvent directives that reduced their organization's influence or prestige. Predictably, the most fully cooperative affiliates, the HJ and the RAD, also had the most advantageous positions concerning the Volkssturm. On the other hand, the SA, NSKK, SS, and even the police willingly assisted the Volkssturm only as long as their organizations were not inconvenienced or when there was something at stake that was deemed valuable, such as command positions or segregated units. In some areas various Party organizations worked selflessly, but on the whole, regional and local Nazis cooperated with each other no better than did their overlords in Berlin.

Further handicapping the Volkssturm at the local level was the quality of its Nazi leaders. As has been well documented by others, the Nazi Party suffered from a lack of competent local officials, particularly as the war progressed.[113] In all fairness, in addition to being unqualified, local Party officials were badly overworked and their offices understaffed by 1944. Many Volkssturm officials held not one but several other Party jobs, and for most, the militia was a secondary or tertiary priority at best. By this stage in the war, communications were often poor—Vilshofen's Schedlbauer apologetically and exasperatedly lamented that it took the post at least a week to arrive from his outlying Ortsgruppen—which further handicapped all efforts.[114] Even under the best of circumstances, however, some Gauleiters and many Kreis- and Ortsgruppenleiters were poor administrators. Most had very little ability to manage the overwhelming responsibility of forming a home defense force virtually from scratch. Even more important, many of the Party's Political Leaders lacked the courage and motivation even to perform their basic duties in the Volkssturm, much less serve as examples of bravery and sacrifice to the average German.

In such a situation, the abilities of the area's Chief of Staff were crucial. Although it is impossible to assess the talents of all these men, it does seem that the Gau- and Kreisleiters tried to appoint men with some military ability and experience to these posts. It is not clear whether many of them possessed any real organizational, logistical, or administrative competence, but evidence suggests at least some of them conscientiously attempted to make the Volkssturm viable. In the final analysis, the key factor that a local Volkssturm official needed was a willingness to allow the Wehrmacht to participate in the Volkssturm. For many, particularly the Gauleiters, this was a bitter pill they refused to swallow; for others, particularly at the Kreis and lower levels, the realization that they lacked the skills, resources, and time to turn civilians into an effective defense force made army assistance most welcome.

In the long run, Bormann's Volkssturm dream was sabotaged by the very system and men he trusted to make the vision into reality. He, in his zeal to exclude his rivals, handicapped his own efforts by holding the reins of power so tightly that he stifled any initiative and enthusiasm for the Volkssturm that his regional and local subordinates might display. Likewise, lower-level Nazis often demonstrated a counterproductive selfishness of both a personal and institutional nature. Other local officials unwittingly undermined the Volkssturm by their own incompetence. The wisest among them recognized the impossibility of their situation and turned over many of their powers to the Wehrmacht, the only organization with even a chance to have made the force useful on a large scale. Rather than generating fanaticism and efficiency, the ill-defined and highly competitive Nazi administrative structure proved ineffective in the Volkssturm's case. The Volkssturm was conceived as an expression of the National Socialist will to resist; it is fittingly ironic that the negative features of the Nazi political system helped strangle enthusiasm for the Volkssturm both nationally and locally.

CHAPTER FIVE
The Aufgebot System: Personnel Classification

In order to reduce the inevitable economic impact of Volkssturm mobilizations, the militia's founders devised a complex, four-tiered Levy (Aufgebot) System designed to categorize members according to age, health, and, most important, occupation. This Levy System adhered to the basic guidelines and priorities utilized for army conscription and succeeded to some degree in protecting personnel in those economic sectors deemed most critical—mining, transportation/communications, heavy industry, and government. To achieve this, however, the Levy System shifted the burden of service to sectors considered less immediately important—agriculture, light industry, banking and insurance, commerce, tourism, and professionals. In terms of technical ability and job type, the system shielded considerably more miners and skilled heavy industrial workers from active duty than it did unskilled and semiskilled workers and men in white-collar occupations. Overall, the Levy System did work as designed; however, it was cumbersome and generated considerable tedious work for Volkssturm officials. Furthermore, the difficulty of finding adult males in occupations that everyone could agree were superfluous, coupled with the impact of institutional political concerns and the occasional arbitrariness of NSDAP administration, meant that the Levy System—by its very nature—ran counter to the ideological proclamation that all Germans would sacrifice equally in the Volkssturm.

The Levy System seemed quite simple on paper. Levy IV contained all men healthy enough to perform security but not combat duties. Levy III, the so-called HJ Levy, consisted of the few remaining civilian males of the 1925–1927 recruiting classes plus all sixteen-year-olds (the 1928 class entered in 1944; 1929 followed in 1945).[1] Levies I and II contained all other civilian men aged twenty to sixty who met the minimal health standards set for combat service. First Levy units, which could be activated for duty anywhere inside their home Gau, contained men who could be mobilized for approximately six weeks "without endangering the home front's essential functions." Second Levy units served only in their home Kreis and included men with jobs deemed absolutely essential, for example, in war production, utilities, food processing and distribution, communications, or transportation.[2] In practice, these apparently simple assignments, particularly for Levies I and II, proved the most time-consuming, divisive, and intractable problem faced by local Volkssturm officials.

Bormann, although proclaiming a desire to make the Levy System "flexible" enough to meet all economic needs,[3] also knew it gave him considerable political leverage. The system forced everyone in the Third Reich's fiercely competitive labor market to negotiate with the Party Chancellery over deferral quotas for their personnel.[4] Berger recognized this significant power and sought to undermine Bormann by proposing the sensible, simpler alternative of a three-levy Volkssturm with one for the HJ, one for the Stadt- und Landwacht, and the other for everyone else. This would have eliminated the complicated occupational classification process but still met ideological demands for broad social-economic representation. Bormann saw a twofold political threat inherent in this proposal: first, the Stadt- und Landwacht levy could become a Trojan horse for Berger and Himmler's influence; second, eliminating Levy II occupational deferrals would diminish the Party Chancellery's role in manpower issues. It would also tend to focus Volkssturm activity in the Kreise, making central control more difficult. Therefore, Bormann vetoed Berger's plan, though of course he employed only economic arguments in doing so.[5] One could certainly conclude that the political advantages conferred by the Levy System were equally—if not more so—important to Bormann than the officially stated economic justifications.

Once established, Bormann fully exploited his influence over personnel issues through a series of detailed Implementation Instructions *(Ausführungsbestimmungen)*, many of which addressed the crucial, thorny issue of where to draw the line between the First and Second Levies. In preparing these edicts, Bormann gladly redressed many of the grievances of any official willing to recognize the Party Chancellery's political control over the militia. For example, Bormann was enraged by Reich Postal Minister Ohnesorge's collaborative effort with Berger to procure deferrals and segregated units for *Reichspost* employees; but once Ohnesorge acknowledged Party Chancellery authority, Bormann guaranteed deferrals for 30 percent of male postal employees and granted permission to form segregated Levy II Postal Police units.[6] More strikingly, once Speer ceased open efforts to undermine Bormann, he received guidelines for forming "factory-affiliated units," a very generous 70 percent deferral rate for industries under his ministry's supervision, and a voice for factory managers in assigning deferrals to their own employees. All of this deviated from basic stated Volkssturm principles and contradicted earlier orders.[7] The deals struck to produce these Implementation Instructions—which Bormann issued "in cooperation" with the officials responsible for supervising the relevant economic sector— clearly reveal that political and economic pragmatism often outweighed ideological calls for unity when it came to the Levy System.[8]

Bormann's Implementation Instructions also show that the Party Chancellery, not the Gauleiters, determined personnel policy.[9] Nowhere was this clearer than in the Fifth Implementation Instructions, which included a detailed, eleven-page list of the specific transportation jobs granted automatic deferral![10] Bormann left regional and local officials only the power to interpret and implement Party Chancellery instructions through the Gau and Kreis Commissions. These draft boards, created to scrutinize army occupational deferrals by Goebbels's total-war efforts, consisted of local representatives of the Wehrkreis, NSDAP, Labor Ministry, Reich Ministry for Armaments and War Production, and various other governmental economic offices. At the Gau- or Kreisleiter's pleasure, they either reviewed all individual Volkssturm deferral cases or, as was more typical, examined random or representative ones.[11] Most of the gargantuan task of quickly classifying the more than 12.5 million potential Volkssturm members fell to the Kreis Commissions, which were chaired by the Kreisleiter or his chief of staff.[12] As discussed in chapter 4, however, in some areas Ortsgruppenleiters made the initial Levy assignments, a blatant contravention of Bormann's orders.

In October 1944, local Nazi officials zealously attacked the first step in the Volkssturm assignment process, registering potential members.[13] Ortsgruppen officials—in some cases even before the Volkssturm was publicly announced—compiled rosters from a variety of sources, including Resident Registration Office records, Party card files, and information gathered at mandatory enlistment meetings. Ration coupon lists, particularly for food, proved accurate, complete, and thereby quite a valuable source for locating liable men.[14] All German males, native and ethnic, between ages sixteen and sixty had to register; and healthy older men could volunteer, as could Nordic men (e.g., Norwegians, Danes, Dutch) who passed a police screening for political and racial acceptability.[15] Bormann even ordered the induction of criminals—if Nazi officials deemed them sufficiently reformed—so that they could redeem themselves.[16] Exemption from Volkssturm service was limited to active Wehrmacht, RAD, police, and—because of their work in repairing bomb damage—Organisation Todt and Technical Emergency Aid *(Technische Nothilfe)* personnel.[17] As discussed in chapter 2, any man considered racially or politically suspect was specifically barred.[18]

Levy assignments began during the registration process as local HJ officials simply enrolled in Levy III all males born in 1925 or afterward.[19] Registration lists of men born prior to 1925 were submitted to Kreisleiter-approved doctors who—in conjunction with Party officials—determined the physical fitness of the men one Ortsgruppe at a time.[20] Those with chronic illnesses, such as serious stomach disorders, insulin-dependent diabetes, and serious heart ailments, or who were categorized as over 70 percent disabled were fully exempted, although they could volunteer for clerical or advisory duty.[21] The other men deemed by the doctors to be fit only for limited security duty were then enrolled in Levy IV.[22]

Levy IV classification procedures generated substantial confusion and abuse. Officially, Volkssturm doctors were under orders to apply the "strictest standards" and limit Levy IV status to men with permanent disabilities.[23] Indeed, some physicians conscientiously ensured that their Levy I and II men were physically fit; a few were even unnecessarily stingy with health deferments.[24] Other doctors, confused about Levy IV qualifications, granted too many men this special status. Still others were apathetic toward their task and performed only cursory physicals; some even relied solely on medical records rather than actual examinations.[25]

Shoddy screening, coupled with low morale and efforts to avoid duty, resulted in a "flood" of men seeking Levy IV assignments well into 1945.[26] Further complicating matters was the fact that officials occasionally mixed men from all levies in the same units, ultimately necessitating complete reexamination of everyone.[27] Employers' and supervisors' accidental and intentional efforts to use Levy IV to protect their personnel from Volkssturm service only added to the confusion.[28] Some devious managers tried to shield their entire labor force by filling their Levy I quotas with unhealthy employees—who would later be shifted to Levy IV—so that they could reserve allotted deferrals for physically fit workers.[29] Such maneuvers increased the suspicion with which Volkssturm officials viewed any Levy IV assignment requests and thus exacerbated problems generated by the classification process.

Confusion and abuse regarding medical screening paled in comparison to difficulties surrounding Levy II deferrals. Officially, everyone was a member of the First Levy until issued a Z-Card (Zuteilungskarte, or deferral card);[30] and although variations existed, it seems that assigning Z-Cards generally proceeded as follows. For businesses, the Gau or Kreis Commissions (usually the latter), cooperating with the entities responsible for supervising that segment of the economy (the Reich Ministry for Armaments and War Production for most factories, the local Economic Chamber for banks, the Kreis Craftworkers Society for craftsmen, etc.), used Bormann's Implementation Instructions to establish a deferral quota for each firm based on the number of male employees required to serve in Levies I and II and on the firm's importance to the war economy. Then the supervisory agency allowed firms to nominate individuals for deferral. The supervisory agency checked the individual cards, corrected any problems, and sent the cards to the Kreis or Gau for a final inspection. Once completed, the Z-Cards went into a special file at the Ortsgruppe Volkssturm office.[31]

Governmental offices followed a similar, but simpler, procedure. The Gau Commission, after consulting relevant Party Chancellery orders and personnel lists, set the deferral quota for the agency's branches and issued the cards to the office chief, who nominated individuals he wanted deferred. He then returned the cards to the Gau Commission, which checked them and deposited them with the proper Ortsgruppe.[32] Although some conscientious commissions sought to evaluate the relative importance of each individual's job, this was not typical procedure.[33]

To simplify Volkssturm classification and limit disputes, many Gaue and Kreise chose—with Party Chancellery blessing—to utilize the same deferment criteria employed in the Wehrmacht conscription process. As a general rule, essential workers designated "key employee" *(Schlüsselkraft)* or possessing double military exemptions were automatically assigned to Levy II. Other "essential workers" *(Fachkräfte)* were deferred according to their specific job's priority.[34] Both employers and the Party and government agencies assigned to oversee the various segments of the economy—especially the Reich Ministry for Armaments and War Production regional Armaments Commands *(Rüstungskommando)* and Armaments Inspectorates *(Rüstungsinspektionen)*—played major roles in determining who met deferral criteria and in establishing Z-Card quotas for individual factories.[35] Also, managers could select which of their Levy I employees would be activated first, though they were held personally responsible for any abuses or irregularities in Volkssturm classification involving their personnel. Finally, employers had to receive notification before any worker could be mobilized into the Volkssturm.[36] Although evidence is sparse, it seems that the DAF also assisted in Levy assignments in some localities.[37] Ultimately, local Nazi officials ran the process, although employers, the Reich Ministry for Armaments and War Production, and other government agencies could influence Volkssturm personnel classification.[38]

While the NSDAP loudly proclaimed that its self-professed unbureaucratic style and efficiency would overcome any organizational difficulties,[39] the Levy System's complexity quickly destroyed this myth. Local officials were often badly confused about even the most basic and unambiguous issues. Youths who should have been in Levy III ended up mobilized in Levy I units.[40] Men explicitly exempted by national decree, such as clergymen or ethnic Poles, wound up in some Volkssturm units—occasionally in substantial numbers.[41] Perhaps the oddest violation occurred when police forced a half-Jewish former concentration camp inmate to enlist in his Berlin Ortsgruppe's unit![42]

Compounding this confusion was the attitude that "it is better to do something than to do nothing."[43] Bursts of unplanned and misguided Nazi zeal naturally spawned additional problems. Overly enthusiastic *Kreisstabsführer*, often bidding to impress their superiors, simply assigned too many men to Levy I, in some cases 85 or even 100 percent of their total number of healthy adult Volkssturm men.[44] Others erred in the opposite direction, as did Pfulgriesheim's (near Strassburg) Ortsgruppenleiter, who put all his men into Levy II because he thought they, as farmers, were essential to the war effort.[45] Some deviated from policy in an attempt to make their Levy I units more combatworthy by assigning men to them based on relative youth and fitness rather than economic considerations.[46]

Aside from misunderstandings and/or overzealousness, Kreis Volkssturm leaders frequently lacked the requisite economic knowledge and personal tact, a situation less than surprising given Bormann's insistence on having fanatical Nazis in these key positions. In spite of their public appeals for cooperation,[47] many Gau- and Kreisstabsführer tended to adopt an adversarial attitude toward employers. Some even used their classification powers to conduct vendettas against personal or political opponents.[48] Such attitudes did nothing to reduce economic dislocations caused by Volkssturm mobilizations, but they did damage Party credibility and undermine appeals for unity.

Although local Volkssturm officials were poorly prepared to balance the pressure from Party superiors to maximize Levy I enrollment with that from employers to broaden deferrals, their task was complicated by conflicting guidelines. For example, Kreis Lüdinghausen officials wanted younger farmers in Levy I because of ideological reasons, but the Reich Nutrition Estate and the State Peasants' Leader ordered them deferred because of their productive farms.[49] In other instances, local officials simply had to proceed without guidance because directives could not address every possible classification issue. For example, Volkssturm officials in the Augsburg area had to work out a way to defer fifteen- and sixteen-year-old apprentices' WE-Lager training until factory managers dependent on these young laborers could make arrangements for replacing them.[50]

Further complicating matters was the fact that classification was a continual process whose difficulty often prompted local officials to procrastinate.[51] Bombing damage, shortages of skilled labor, new production orders, employers' shifting needs, and supply irregularities often altered the priority attached to individual workers.[52] As a result, managers naturally felt compelled to try to protect their personnel—either individually or in groups—as thoroughly as possible.

Furthermore, large influxes or exoduses of refugees from bombed cities, frontline regions, or enemy-occupied territories often forced wide-ranging reevaluations of Z-Card quotas and reorganization of existing units.[53] All newly arriving male refugees had to be classified; and although they were required by law to register voluntarily for military and/or industrial and Volkssturm service within two days of arrival at their new residence,[54] officials often had to track these men down (again, often using ration coupon applications), find out where they were working, and then assign them to the proper Levy.[55] Finally, acts of war could force officials to redo the entire classification process, as happened in Magdeburg when a January bombing raid destroyed the entire file of deferral records.[56]

All of this generated frustration on the part of overworked Kreis Volkssturm officials, who resented the extra effort and difficulty they found in meeting Levy I quotas.[57] Some Party officials complicated things by mobilizing key workers who had Z-Cards or refusing to recognize legitimate authorization for segregated Levy II factory units.[58] A few officials became so disgusted with the Levy System that they simply branded all complaints about it as sloth or fraud, refused to entertain further deferment requests, or even ignored classification guidelines altogether and filled mobilization quotas however they pleased.[59] Even those who attempted to do their jobs conscientiously complained that ferreting out abuses only won them more enemies and made their work more difficult.[60] The complexity of operating the Levy System often simply overwhelmed underqualified and overworked Kreis officials.

Moreover, employers were hardly cooperative. Few willingly released any of their German workers—even temporarily—for Volkssturm service. For example, when Bayreuth's Kreisleiter activated a Levy I unit, he received deferment requests from the employers of 150 of the unit's 267 members.[61] Business and government officials typically complained that losing any of their employees would jeopardize militarily essential production or services or would disrupt their security or civil defense efforts.[62] To protect their workforce, some managers even resorted to illegal means such as counting subcontractors' employees in their own deferral quotas, seeking Z-Cards from neighboring Armaments Commands when rejected by their own, putting only their oldest, worst, and/or unhealthiest employees in Levy I, or simply resorting to fraud.[63] Some employers tried to argue that their deferred personnel were exempt from Volkssturm service altogether or refused to release workers who had received mobilization orders.[64] Although few employers went to such lengths, virtually all of them tried everything available to maximize their number of deferred employees. Speer himself encouraged this by instructing subordinates to support the Volkssturm only until it began to impact production negatively.[65]

Given the impossibly strained German labor situation of late 1944, no scheme could have eliminated all economic disruptions created by the Volkssturm. In fact, the Levy System never sought to eliminate but only to reduce the impact on war production; and problems notwithstanding, the system as a whole seems to have generally functioned toward that pragmatic end. Obviously, one cannot separate the Volkssturm's impact from that caused by loss of territory, Allied bombing, transportation disruption, Wehrmacht conscription, casualties, shortages, and so forth. One can, however, ascertain which sectors of the economy bore the greatest burdens of Volkssturm mobilization. Examination of national directives on deferrals, local correspondence on implementing those directives, and statistical evidence reveals that the Levy System generally adhered to the Wehrmacht's mobilization and deferral priorities, thereby exacerbating existing economic difficulties rather than generating new ones.

Statistical data suggest that the economic sectors most burdened by Volkssturm service were banking/insurance, trade/professions, tourism, and agriculture, while mining, government, and transportation/communication enjoyed more extensive protection (see the appendix, Table 1). This pattern closely mirrors that of Wehrmacht mobilization (see appendix, Tables 2 and 3), since Volkssturm service fell most heavily on those sectors with the lowest priority for army draft deferrals. Precisely those sectors best endowed with Wehrmacht deferrals were also best shielded by the Volkssturm Levy System.[66] Thus officials seem to have applied, as instructed, existing conscription priorities in assigning Volkssturm personnel.

The age structure of those missing in action (MIAs) from the various economic sectors (Table 4) generally confirms that sectors with extensive army deferrals also successfully procured Z-Cards for their draft-age workers.[67] Draft-age men in transportation/communication, government, and to a lesser extent manufacturing are underrepresented among MIAs; those from agriculture, trade/professions, and tourism are overrepresented. The overrepresentation of draft-age miners is an anomaly resulting from this sector's exceptionally large draft-age population (mining enterprises still had to allocate 30 percent of their men to the First Levy); the underrepresentation of banking/insurance springs from its extraordinarily small number of draft-age men. Because both anomalies result from army conscription priorities, they actually confirm the general trend.

Further age breakdowns reveal that Volkssturm service typically fell more heavily upon men near or above the upper age limits for military service (typically forty-five to forty-eight) than under it. Men of draft age are noticeably underrepresented among Volkssturm MIAs (Tables 5 and 21), with nearly 62 percent being age forty-five or older; although certain "elite" Levy I units were supposed to, and apparently did, contain the youngest available personnel.[68] The few extant complete unit records also show the tendency to grant a greater proportion of Z-Cards to draft-age men (Table 6), who obviously had Wehrmacht deferrals, too. Ortsgruppen records of Levy assignments (Table 7) also generally support the contention that men above draft age often filled Levy I quotas in order to defer younger men deemed more economically valuable.[69] All of this points toward the Levy System's heavy reliance on Wehrmacht conscription priorities and procedures.

MIA data broken down by job skill (Table 8) also show the similarity of the Levy System priorities to those of the regular draft machinery. Among specific job types, farmers, white-collar employees, and professionals formed nearly half of the Volkssturm MIAs, whereas unskilled and semiskilled workers—who could not have been an extremely large proportion of German civilian men in late 1944—constituted an additional fifth. Conversely, skilled workers and master craftsmen appear underrepresented at only approximately one-quarter of total MIAs.[70]

No sector, or individual factory, was completely immune from Levy I duty (the most generous deferral quota was about 70 percent). To maximize deferrals for skilled workers in priority sectors—heavy industry, mining, or transportation/communication—the burden of First Levy service had to be shifted onto others in those sectors. This meant low Z-Card priority for semiskilled or unskilled laborers (e.g., maintenance personnel) and all types of workers in light industry or craft work (e.g., food processing, printing, textiles or wood products; see Tables 9–11 and 12–13). The understandable tendency to shield skilled workers at the expense of employees deemed less immediately critical also appeared in specific firms' Levy assignments. For example, Augsburg's Keller and Knappich Machine Factory divided its 535 Z-Cards among its 655 German men (an amazingly high deferral rate of 82 percent, indicative of high-priority production), with skilled workers and Werkschutz personnel receiving preference (Table 14).[71]

Such shifting is plainly evident elsewhere. In transportation/communication, semiskilled and unskilled workers in trucking and postal services and white-collar postal employees were sacrificed to protect skilled railway workers (Table 15). To maximize Z-Card allotments in other critical areas, authorities reduced them in areas such as construction and, to a lesser extent, forestry and light industry (see Tables 9–13 and 16–17).[72] Craftsmen also bore some additional burden (see the Rötz platoon in Table 18) but were not grossly overrepresented in the statistics, apparently because both the Reich Ministry for Armaments and War Production and the Gau Economic Chamber's Crafts Office guarded artisans engaged in essential war work.[73]

Data from Levy I Volkssturm units also illustrate how protecting skilled factory workers meant—insofar as possible—filling mobilization quotas with other personnel. Among MIAs from the Levy I Volkssturm special purpose battalions (Battalions *zur besondere Verwendung* [zbV]), skilled factory workers, miners, and government employees were underrepresented, while white-collar employees and professionals and construction workers were overrepresented (see Tables 11a–b). Because several of these units came from urban areas (e.g., Hamburg, Würzburg, Bayreuth), manufacturing occupations were overrepresented and agriculture underrepresented by national—but not local—standards. Complete rosters listing members' occupations exist for only a few other units, but these further confirm (Table 18) that the Levy System, as designed, safeguarded skilled factory workers at almost everyone else's expense.

There are several reasons why skilled workers in mining, heavy industry, or transportation/communication received more extensive deferral from Volkssturm duty. Foremost is the fact that the Levy System was designed to minimize disruption in sectors considered the most critical to the Reich's war economy. Additionally, political factors played a role as powerful economic officials such as Speer and Reich Traffic Minister Julius Dorpmüller used their influence to guard their manpower.[74] Evidence of this lies in the substantial concessions these men gained from Bormann: 70 percent Z-Card quotas, automatic deferrals for all men engaged in certain occupations (particularly in transportation/communication), and the participation of local transportation and Reich Ministry for Armaments and War Production officials in setting Levy quotas for individual firms.[75] In particular, Speer's Armaments Commands often, though not always, proved sympathetic and able champions of factory efforts to keep skilled workers, regardless of the number employed, out of Levy I.[76]

Speer and Dorpmüller also procured extensive permission to form segregated Levy II "factory" units; after some initial resistance from local Volkssturm officials, these formations became a relatively common means of meshing training and work schedules, particularly for railway employees.[77] Although many factory units were legitimate,[78] this apparently ideal compromise between the Volkssturm and economic interests generated problems. Some managers abused the factory units in an effort to exempt themselves and their employees from Volkssturm duty altogether.[79] The situation became so bad that Friedrichs ultimately had to issue precise regulations governing factory units, chastise offending managers, and even dissolve the most egregious violators' units.[80] Overall, though, the existence of segregated factory units reveals the Volkssturm structure's willingness to accommodate genuine economic concerns—so long as they did not threaten NSDAP control of the militia.

Further evidence of Speer's political clout and his skillful use of the powerful argument of economic necessity came in early 1945 as Volkssturm mobilizations and training intensified in the wake of the Soviet winter offensive. Acting on industrial leaders' complaints that Volkssturm activity was crippling the German war economy,[81] Speer won Hitler's approval for the Armaments Emergency Program. This sheltered from mobilization into the Wehrmacht, People's Levy, or Volkssturm all essential workers engaged in producing two-way radios, generators, trucks, ships, and most basic weapons.[82] Speer also procured Volkssturm deferrals for all actively employed miners and virtual exemptions for oil-drilling and refinery workers.[83] The Armaments Emergency Program provided extensive protection for eligible munitions workers; for example, almost 80 percent of the employees (2,713 of 3,410) of Augsburg's fifty-five firms covered by the program were shielded from Volkssturm mobilization.[84] In fact, many managers whose firms were not covered begged to be included in this attractive arrangement.[85] Besides evidencing Speer's political clout and the limits to Bormann's powers, the program also stands as the Nazi leadership's tacit admission that the Volkssturm could have a disastrous impact on critical segments of the war economy.

In spite of the relatively extensive consideration which the Levy System afforded the manufacturing, mining, and transportation/communication sectors, there were loud, frequent, and unquestionably legitimate complaints about Volkssturm-spawned disruptions in these sectors. They began in the borderlands in 1944 and spread throughout Germany in 1945.[86] Managers believed that Volkssturm training overtaxed their workers physically, thereby reducing productivity and increasing absenteeism. They blamed mobilizations for making it difficult to supervise foreign workers properly, hindering essential repairs and maintenance, reducing the number of males entering training programs, and threatening their ability to shift workers from lower- to higher-priority jobs.[87] Surviving evidence chronicles local interruptions and delays in telephone, telegraph, mail, and courier services and more widespread disruptions of such things as public transportation and unloading rail cars, all of which had to continue day in and day out.[88] Obviously, if Volkssturm activity negatively affected these well-protected areas, it must have been even more widely and seriously disruptive in lower-priority sectors such as forestry/wood products or agriculture.[89]

Ultimately, given the lack of superfluous German male labor, any mobilization or extraoccupational activity was bound to have an impact. For example, Swabia's Armaments Commission reported its labor pool was so shallow that no more than one Volkssturm battalion could be mobilized, and it for no more than two weeks, without undermining production.[90] Therefore, it is safe to assume that even though skilled workers in priority sectors were often deferred from early mobilization, substantial numbers of them were activated (see Tables 1, 7–9, and 10–11), and the loss of these men must have significantly handicapped production in specific areas. Furthermore, it is abundantly clear that the Volkssturm not only produced disruptions but also generated tension between economic leaders and Party officials, yet another obstacle toward fostering unity.

While the Volkssturm spawned problems, some undoubtedly severe, in manufacturing, transportation/communication, and mining, the real burden of Levy I service fell on areas considered less essential to the war effort. White-collar employees and professionals (the largest single MIA contingent; see Table 8) formed one such group, but the impact was unevenly spread among them (see Table 19). For example, government employees (12.54 percent of the entire German male workforce and primarily white-collar) are clearly underrepresented at just under 7 percent of all Volkssturm MIAs (see Table 8)— and with teachers removed, this figure drops to under 5 percent (Table 19). In the civil service, deferral quotas ran as high as 70 percent, although 30 to 50 percent was more common. Tax collectors, officials engaged in the prosecution and punishment of crimes, mint employees, munitions factory inspectors, anyone with double military deferral, higher-ranking officials (who had a voice in handing out the Z-Cards), and those involved with supervising or planning some aspect of the war economy were generally well protected.[91] Also a number of segregated Levy II units composed solely of civil servants existed despite orders banning this practice.[92]

Civilian Wehrmacht and police employees are strikingly underrepresented (see Table 14) due to their extensive deferrals,[93] the formation of segregated Levy II units, and the simple fact that local military and police officials did not prove very cooperative with the Volkssturm when it came to their civilian personnel.[94] Similarly, full-time NSDAP employees are also grossly underrepresented in Levy I. In Ortsgruppen Meinau and Lingolsheim (Kreis Strassburg), nearly two-thirds (63 percent) of Party officials and members had Z-Cards,[95] thus putting the lie to Bormann's claim that the Party formed the vanguard of the Volkssturm.

On the other hand, remaining types of government employees served in the Volkssturm at levels comparable to their overall numbers in the population (see Table 20). In fact, mobilizations caused significant problems for local and regional government activities,[96] particularly education. Educators were grossly overrepresented among MIAs at 1.84 percent of the total (1.88 percent for western Levy I special purpose battalions).[97] Only medical, technical, and propaganda-oriented school faculties, or researchers deemed essential to the war effort had extensive safeguards; all other institutions had to make do with skeletal staffs.[98] For example, almost three-quarters of Kreis Goslar's fifty-one male teachers were in Levy I. Also, teachers were grossly overrepresented in the Rastatt and Werne First Levy companies, constituting 6.1 percent of each.[99] Obviously, with such low deferral priority for educators, the Volkssturm further weakened Nazi Germany's already bankrupt educational system.[100]

Among nongovernment white-collar occupations, office workers, middle- and lower-level supervisors, and certain professionals frequently served in Levy I. Those working in the banking or insurance sectors had low deferral quotas (30 and 10 percent, respectively, the latter the lowest percentage of any economic sector), and men from these occupations were represented in the Volkssturm at more than double their share of the general workforce (1.28 percent to 0.6 percent; see appendix Tables 1 and 2). The same held true for the trade/professional and tourism sectors, although the latter was not entirely white-collar. Merchants had only a 30 percent deferral rate, but employees of retail establishments selling coal, drugs, ironware, textiles, household items, and tobacco had Z-Card priority among this group.[101]

The Volkssturm also mobilized significant numbers of professionals, who constituted over 15 percent of all white-collar MIAs and nearly 4 percent of the total Volkssturm MIAs (Table 13). As a result, professional services, such as medicine and dentistry (particularly doctors in private practice), experienced significant disruption.[102] Furthermore, even prior to mobilization the Volkssturm placed heavy demands on doctors' time by forcing them to conduct physicals and train medics. Mobilizations could seriously threaten health services, particularly in small towns with only one doctor, although the Office for People's Health tried to minimize damages.[103] For example, the branch in Bayreuth intervened with the *Gaustabsführer* to gain a deferral for the only doctor in Waischenfeld, who had landed in Levy I because of a dispute with the *Kreisstabsführer* over the use of his office building.[104]

White-collar employees in manufacturing were also likely to serve in Levy I; although, as in the civil service, technical or top management personnel were almost invariably deferred. In fact, technicians—especially those in mathematics, physics, ballistics, or high-frequency technology or others officially classified by the Wehrmacht as researchers—received automatic deferrals and could only be mobilized with approval from the Reich Research Council's Planning Office.[105] The Levy I contingent at Helmuth Sachse's Kempten factory, for example, contained only 2 managers and 1 technician (a draftsman) but twenty lower-level office workers. Only 15 office workers held deferrals, whereas 27 managers (including the factory's top 2 men) and 6 technicians did.[106] Similarly, at Augsburg's

Keller and Knappich factory, only 2 of 16 managers and 16 of 95 technicians served in Levy I.[107] At Wankel Research Workshops in Lindau, the 3 top managers (including the owner) and 10 technicians received almost half of the firm's alloted Z-Cards, while no other white-collar employees gained deferrals.[108] In some factories, shop floor supervisors were not well protected; 15 of 38 of Sachse's and 6 of 7 of Lindau's Michel Werke floor supervisors served in Levy I. On the other hand, Keller and Knappich's higher Z-Card allotment enabled them to defer 28 of their 32 low-level supervisors.[109]

Even more than with white-collar employees/professionals, agriculture contributed a disproportionate share of men for Volkssturm duty. This was in spite of Bormann's establishment of a generous 70 percent deferral quota for farmers, skilled food-processing workers and managers, and Gau and Kreis Farm and Nutrition Office employees.[110] Nonetheless, MIA lists show that farmers were significantly overrepresented (see Tables 1 and 8). In part, this resulted from geography, since Volkssturm mobilizations were more extensive in eastern than western Germany. Still, indications strongly suggest that Volkssturm mobilization seriously disrupted German agriculture. Activation of East Prussian units in late 1944 reduced milk production and delivery and delayed the grain harvest so badly that entire Volkssturm formations had to be diverted to farm work.[111] Peasants' Leaders in Westphalia and Bayreuth both reported that food supplies were endangered because too many farmers had been activated in Levy I units.[112]

Complicating the problem was the mobilization of food-processing workers, theoretically protected but nonetheless well represented among Volkssturm MIAs (see Tables 9–11 and 12–13).[113] As with doctors, however, mobilization of a single individual (e.g., a village's only baker) could cause severe local difficulties.[114] In early 1945, many officials recognized that Germany would face a serious food crisis if farmers and other agricultural workers were not released from active Volkssturm duty. As early as January, Bormann ordered deferrals for skilled repair personnel in tractor garages or food-processing firms,[115] but the real crisis loomed as spring planting time approached. By March, Bormann ordered, on the Reich Nutrition Minister's insistence, that all farmers be released from active Volkssturm duty and exempted from mobilizations except in areas under immediate enemy threat. Even here they should be used primarily to evacuate foodstuffs.[116] Gau Peasants' Leaders immediately began pushing to get farmers out of Volkssturm service; in some areas they had to be replaced by industrial workers.[117] Such was the Third Reich's manpower dilemma.

In addition to disruptions caused by mobilization, Volkssturm training also interrupted agricultural work. Rural units, particularly in the east, had to gather their members from a relatively widely dispersed population, and travel to and from meetings took much more time out of a farmer's day than a city dweller's.[118] Even during winter, farmers—especially those with dairy herds or other livestock—did not have days off; and many had foreign laborers who required close supervision. All this ensured that the Volkssturm held the potential to interrupt agriculture as much as or more than any other segment of the economy.

Why, then, were so many farmers assigned to Levy I in the first place? One answer is ideological: Nazis considered farmers the pillar of the Volk, and some wanted them in the forefront of the movement to save Germany.[119] A second, more prevalent, factor is that many mobilizations, especially in the east, occurred during the dead of winter, when it seemed that farmers were relatively idle compared with other workers and could be spared for a few weeks.[120] A third reason is that many of the German men still in agriculture in 1944 were over the draft age (see Table 3); therefore, they formed a large pool of available manpower, particularly in the more rural eastern Gaue. Fourth, with the eastern provinces being rather heavily agricultural, the Volkssturm's greater role on the Eastern Front meant more impact on food production.

The final reason was political. Many Volkssturm officials saw farmers as the easiest targets for mobilization because they were self-employed. Village Peasants' Leaders were supposed to protect farmers' interests, but evidence from Gau Bayreuth suggests that many of these officials served in Levy I themselves.[121] Gau Peasants' Leaders offices did try to shield agricultural personnel but seem to have limited their efforts to specific cases such as securing individual Z-Cards for a town's only miller, an extremely productive farmer who also trained agricultural apprentices, or a man responsible for testing milk quality.[122] Thus it seems that agricultural officials were politically too weak to shield many farmers from Volkssturm mobilizations.

Clearly, the Volkssturm negatively affected agriculture; but assessing the Volkssturm's precise overall economic impact is impossible. One can only conclude that the Volkssturm had a widespread but uneven effect. Disruptions were certainly greater in the east than in the west; more severe in services, forestry, or light industry than in heavy industry, government, transportation, or mining; and greater in medicine, education, and the traditional civil service than in criminal justice or the Party. As the war situation deteriorated, government and NSDAP officials recognized the negative cost of Volkssturm mobilizations.[123] Even Bormann admitted the detrimental economic impact— tacitly in decrees releasing farmers, hospital workers, and others from duty (at least until fighting forced their places of employment to shut down) and explicitly by forbidding unnecessary mobilizations.[124]

Given the strained nature of the economy and labor situation, mobilization of just a few men, or even a single individual, could cause inordinate upheaval for a factory or community. One manager claimed, perhaps exaggeratedly, that mobilization of his Levy I German workers (30 percent, or forty-one men, in this instance) would cut production by half, and the loss of even ten men would cause "serious problems."[125] Certainly, losing Waischenfeld's only doctor would have made getting health care difficult in this rather isolated town. Although the impact of such specific cases would have been purely local, they give an impression of just how disruptive large-scale Volkssturm mobilizations must have been.

The Volkssturm did not cause the German war economy to collapse, but it did exacerbate the effects of bombing, loss of territory and resources, and other strains on production. Volksturm mobilizations, even on a small scale, could create bottlenecks or shortages of specific items. Volkssturm training interfered with certain types of work that had to be conducted seven days a week, and it helped exhaust and demoralize workers by depriving them of their last hours of leisure and relaxation. Also, time spent by officials implementing the confusing and complicated Levy System might have been more fruitfully utilized on other tasks. Finally, Bormann's efforts to impose order on this unwieldy system resulted in a rigid, centrally controlled assignment procedure ill suited to meeting Germany's rapidly changing economic needs in late 1944 and 1945.

The Levy System sought to balance war industry's requirements with Germany's need for more troops and Nazi efforts to motivate the populace. On paper, the idea seemed logical; if one involved employers, the NSDAP and the existing military draft classification apparatus, then Volkssturm training and mobilization would not unduly disrupt the economy. In a general sense, the system worked by protecting those groups that Bormann and top economic and manpower officials wanted to exempt. Skilled industrial labor, technicians, miners, transportation and communications personnel, certain government employees, NSDAP officials, and high-level managers and plant owners were not generally assigned to the Volkssturm's First Levy. To compensate for these deferrals, those in tourism, education, agriculture, certain professions, construction, and light industry, as well as office workers and semiskilled and unskilled laborers of all types had to be assigned in inordinately large numbers to Levy I. Some groups were simply considered more essential to the war economy than others, and therefore they were given greater deferral from Volkssturm service just as they had been given protection against conscription into the Wehrmacht.

There was another, more political, reason that some groups fared better than others. The Levy System, managed by Kreis and Ortsgruppen officials, constantly generated immense amounts of complicated and confusing work that had to be done over and over as men moved or were drafted, as the importance of their jobs changed, or as their health declined. For the often overworked and/or incompetent local Party bosses, the Levy System was frequently an overwhelming task, and they often simply did what was the most expedient for them. For most, this meant applying Bormann's rules rigidly; for others, Volkssturm classification and mobilization provided a means of conducting personal vendettas. As a result of all this, the majority of deviations from Bormann's guidelines resulted not from a clever exploitation of a unique local situation but from personal self-interest.

Under such conditions, a man's Levy II status sometimes depended more on the ability and political clout of the agency that supervised his occupation than on the importance of his work. The Reich Ministry for Armaments and War Production, well organized and politically powerful both nationally and locally, was able to defend very well the personnel it chose to guard. If the Volkssturm drafted a key employee of an important factory, the plant manager could appeal to the local Armaments Command, which could intervene to get the man released from duty. A similar situation existed for all the other groups granted extensive protection. On the other hand, mobilized farmers often had no one to intercede on their behalf because they were self-employed and their local Peasants' Leaders often lacked political power or were themselves among the first mobilized. Furthermore, at least during the winter, farmers were considered expendable. Bluntly stated, in assigning men to Levy I, local Nazi bosses had two concerns: either ensure the man's job was not deemed essential or make sure that neither he nor his employer could make trouble over his assignment.

Neither course fit well with the Volkssturm ideal of a unified racial community fully, selflessly, and harmoniously mobilizing for its own defense. Just as with the members of the Party and its affiliated organizations, economic leaders also proved unwilling to sacrifice for the Volkssturm's success. Many refused to set the desired example for their employees and rarely took a cooperative attitude toward Volkssturm officials—a feeling that was often mutual. Managers typically wanted to hang on to all their employees and spent considerably more time trying to procure additional Z-Cards than locating new workers or reducing the number of men needed. Far from being a capitalist tool, as asserted by Marxist scholars, the Volkssturm was the bane of many factory and office owners' and managers' lives during the closing months of the war. They clearly did not want it and worked either to minimize its impacts or even to sabotage its efforts.

From a purely economic standpoint, the Volkssturm Levy System met its basic goal of mobilizing men while limiting the damage done to war production. Although the Volkssturm complicated matters, caused disruptions, and overburdened the existing draft machinery at a time when conscription officials should have been focused on making the complicated shifts necessary to release men for Wehrmacht service, it did not cause Germany's war economy to collapse. But in seeking to achieve its economic aim, the Levy System violated the Volkssturm's fundamental motivational principle—that people would fight for the Volk once they saw it transcended distinctions of class, occupation, or rank. The existence of deferrals made it impossible to believe that the burden of self-defense was shared equally. Rather than contributing to the creation of a sense of unity, the Volkssturm Levy System—intended to satisfy pragmatic economic and political concerns—undermined the hope that Germans could work together in a selfless manner. Therefore, from an ideological standpoint, the Levy System failed disastrously.

Himmler announcing the formation of the German Volkssturm to the German public via radio on October 18, 1944. The date (the anniversary of the Battle of Leipzig) and the location (Bartenstein, East Prussia) of the speech were intended to conjure up positive images of the War of Liberation and its militia, the *Landsturm*. (BA-KO Bild 146/87/128/10)

SA chief Wilhelm Schepmann at a marksmanship competition. Schepmann believed the SA's experience justified a greater role for him and his organization in the Volkssturm. When he was denied this, his participation in the militia was neither extensive nor enthusiastic. (BA-KO Bild 146/79/107/12)

Munich Volkssturm men take their oath on the "Blutfahne" that accompanied Hitler in the ill-fated Beer Hall Putsch in 1923. Bormann specifically ordered this program rearranged so that he would play as significant a role as his rival Himmler. (BA-KO Bild 146/74/121/20A)

Berlin Volkssturm unit on parade during the nationwide Volkssturm oath-taking ceremonies on November 12, 1944. Weapons were borrowed for this event and returned immediately afterward. These parades aimed at showing the Volkssturm's size and the German Volk's determination to resist the Allied invaders. (BA-KO Bild 146/71/33/15)

An East Prussian Volkssturm unit heads off for duty in October 1944. The Nazis found that photos such as these did not raise morale but instead generated concerns that men attired in civilian clothing would be treated—that is, shot—as partisans if captured. (BA-KO Bild 146/74/120/24A)

The wide variety of civilian, Party, and military clothing worn by these thirteen Seelow Volkssturm men gives them the appearance more of representatives attending some sort of local interagency meeting than a military unit. (Museum/Gedenkstätte Seelower Höhen)

A battalion leader (left) confers with one of his company leaders. The unit served somewhere in the east in 1945, probably in Brandenburg either on the Oder-Neisse Line—perhaps as part of a Battalion zbV—or in one of the positions behind it. Note the wound badge on the company leader's tunic, evidence that he, like many of his comrades, had previous military experience. (W. Darrin Weaver Sr. This photo and the others credited to W. Darrin Weaver Sr. are from the company leader's personal collection and have never before been published.)

Contrast the *Kompanieführer*'s standard-issue army uniform (left) with those worn by his subordinates. Many commanders had uniforms from their previous military service, while their men had to take whatever was issued—Luftwaffe clothing in this case. (W. Darrin Weaver Sr.)

Paperwork, the bane of a Volkssturm unit commander's existence, had to be maintained on active duty as well, despite the minimal staff and equipment at his disposal. (W. Darrin Weaver Sr.)

Levy III Hitler Youth participate in a sand table exercise. Such indoor alternatives often had to substitute for outdoor training during the winter months. (BA–KO Bild 146/76/35/3)

In a typical Nazi propaganda photo, a Hitler Youth receives Panzerfaust instruction from a highly decorated combat veteran. The boy's disciplined unit comrades look on attentively. (BA-KO Bild 146/74/139/39)

A more realistic view of HJ training shows a Luftwaffe officer demonstrating the Panzerfaust to a somewhat motley group of boys whose expressions range from interested to amused to somewhat fearful. (BA-KO Bild 146/74/167/6a)

Volkssturm unit leaders observe a demonstration of magnetic antitank charges. The utility of such a weapon for elderly Volkssturm men seems rather questionable. (BA-KO Bild 146/71/33/9)

A Volkssturm man has just fired a Panzerfaust: note the backblast that made the weapon dangerous for the uninitiated. The man's comrades in the background probably did not have this opportunity, for although the Panzerfaust was the Volkssturm's most widely available weapon, there were not enough to allow for extensive live firing in training. (BA-KO Bild 146/73/1/35)

Volkssturm men digging an antitank ditch somewhere in eastern Germany. Use of militia personnel for such fatigue duties became so widespread that Bormann had to restrict it out of concern for essential economic activities. (BA-KO Bild ADN 23A GX 1939 293 J31 397)

At a railway underpass in Berlin, Volkssturm men construct a roadblock. This ubiquitous Volkssturm activity was often ridiculed, then as it is now, as militarily worthless. While such obstacles were often meaningless if incomplete or undefended, they illustrate how Nazi strategy sought—by whatever means available—to turn the war into a static struggle of attrition. (BA-KO Bild ADN ZBA GX 1939 293 J31 385)

In Festung Königsberg, two Volkssturm leaders man a former aircraft machine gun converted for infantry use. Such improvisations were common in the effort to equip the Volkssturm for combat. (BA-KO Bild ADN ZBA GX 1939 293 J28 805)

Volkssturm troops at the entrance to their bunker somewhere on the Eastern Front, probably along the Oder or Neisse. Note that the bunker is properly placed on the reverse slope of a ridgeline as part of a static position. (W. Darrin Weaver Sr.)

Gallows humor. Members of a company or battalion staff clown for the camera while on active duty on the Eastern Front as a unit commander "disciplines" a "surrendering" subordinate. Such situations were hardly joking matters for many Volkssturm men in 1945, however. (W. Darrin Weaver Sr.)

An active Volkssturm unit constructing bunkers in a forest, probably between Berlin and the Oder River or behind the Oder-Neisse Line. Note they all wear Luftwaffe uniforms, but only one member of the ten-man squad has a rifle. (W. Darrin Weaver Sr.)

A Volkssturm patrol somewhere in eastern Germany, probably Brandenburg. Note that only one man is armed. Volkssturm troops often lacked even the most basic weapons. (W. Darrin Weaver Sr.)

This picture from a position in the Oder-Neisse area shows a Volkssturm rifleman armed with a civilian hunting piece. Officials forbade such firearms, but some were apparently used given the desperate situation. (W. Darrin Weaver Sr.)

Silesian Volkssturm men wearing Slovak army helmets and manning a German machine gun (MG 42) await the Red Army's advance. As this photo illustrates, Volkssturm men were equipped with whatever was available. (BA-KO Bild ADN ZBA GX 1939 293 J28 898)

A Volkssturm position directly on the bank of the Oder River at Frankfurt (note the Stadtbrücke in the right background). The platoon leader at left holds—apparently for the camera's benefit—a Volksgewehr model VG 1-5 automatic assault rifle. Numerous Volkssturm units fought, some quite well, along the Oder in the spring of 1945. (BA-KO Bild ADN ZBA GX 1939 293 J28 732)

Volkssturm troops on the outskirts of Festung Küstrin armed with rifles and Panzerfaust antitank rockets. Of the 900 Volkssturm men in action here, 782 became casualties. (BA-KO Bild ADN ZBA GX 1939 293 J28 875)

Although Hitler Youth troops formed a minority of the Volkssturm units sent into combat, and there were orders to keep them out of the front lines until they could be trained and committed as part of Wehrmacht or SS formations, HJ boys played a notable role in defending Berlin and the Oder. This bicycle-mounted HJ antitank team is in Frankfurt am Oder. Volkssturm laborers look on from the right side of the street. (Ullstein Bild)

In April 1945, a lone Volkssturm man armed with a *Panzerschreck* (a German bazooka) awaits Soviet armor east of Berlin. Many Berlin Volkssturm units were deployed well east of the city in an effort to hold the Oder Front. (BA-KO Bild 146/85/92/29)

Men from a Moselland Volkssturm unit ready their machine gun for action in a West Wall bunker in late 1944. They were among the first western Volkssturm men deployed. (BA-KO Bild 146/79/49/3a)

The Ludendorff Railway Bridge at Remagen as seen from the Erpeler Ley tunnel on the eastern side. Many of Remagen's Volkssturm men either did not report for duty or hid here in the tunnel rather than fighting. The Remagen Volkssturm's failure to hinder the U.S. Ninth Armored Division greatly aided the American capture of the bridge on March 7, 1945. (National Archives)

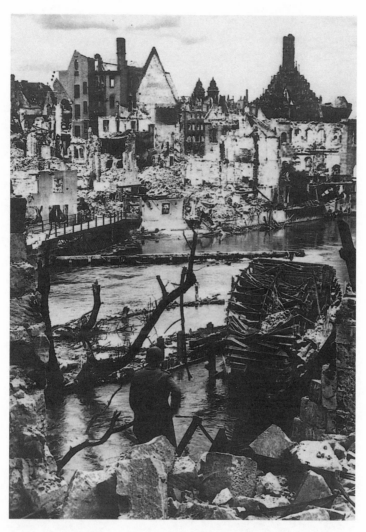

Heavy bombing did immense damage to German cities, and subsequent evacuations often wreaked havoc on urban Volkssturm units. It also created ideal terrain that enabled Volkssturm and Hitler Youth personnel to contribute to the heavy fighting here in Nuremberg in mid–April 1945. (National Archives)

An image typical of the western Volkssturm. Two elderly POWs, one of whom seems clearly relieved to be safely out of combat and in the hands of British troops. (Provenance unknown)

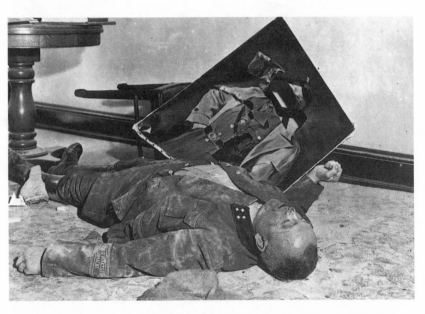

Another common perception of the western Volkssturm. The U.S. War Office's official caption to this photo of a dead battalion leader/Nazi fanatic in Leipzig read: "He committed suicide rather than face U.S. Army troops." Volkssturm resistance in Leipzig, however, was actually quite bitter. (National Archives)

A less widely publicized image of the Volkssturm. U.S. 89th Infantry Division troops crossing the Rhine at Saint Goar. The official caption to this rather well-known picture states that "the lead was flying around like hail." It does not state, as do unit records, that much of the German resistance here was provided by Volkssturm men. (National Archives)

Another lesser-known image of Volkssturm activity. Volkssturm men under SS supervision participated in the massacre of these political prisoners near Gardelegen. The concentration camp inmates were herded into a large barn that was set on fire, and the SS and Volkssturm guards shot anyone who tried to flee. (National Archives)

CHAPTER SIX

Partisans or Combatants?
The Volkssturm's Legal Identity

As Bormann, Himmler, and their associates began organizing the Volkssturm, they elected to pattern the force after basic elements of standard Wehrmacht infantry practice. While this seems innocuous and natural enough, it posed significant and unforeseen implications for the National Socialist plan to create a Party-led and Party-inspired people's militia that would fight fanatically for the preservation of the German Volk and Nazism. In essence, the decision to adhere to a regular army model meant that the Volkssturm would become a more traditional militia than what the Party intended.

Time concerns provided one reason for deciding to pursue a standard military model; it was a ready-made and generally familiar pattern. A second factor was that the Party had no alternative plan and no experience with raising and operating any type of military forces, partisans included. Nor was there any extensive recent German tradition of guerrilla warfare against regular forces on which to build. Finally and most important, the German public showed clear, firm opposition to serving in any sort of force that might be viewed as a partisan organization. With Nazis strongly emphasizing the Volkssturm's motivational function, such widespread concerns could not be ignored, particularly in the force's early stages. Ultimately, the public's mood demanded that the Volkssturm conform to international legal requirements governing militias because Germans wanted assurances that its members would have combatant status. The decision to meet this public demand, in turn, profoundly influenced virtually all aspects of Volkssturm organization, particularly its intended duties, leadership selection, logistical arrangements, and unit structure.

Himmler publicly announced the Volkssturm's founding via radio on the evening of October 18, 1944, the anniversary of the victory over Napoleon at Leipzig during the War of Liberation. Planners wanted to link the Volkssturm with the romanticized popular notions about the Landwehr and Landsturm militias of that war. In his speech, the Reichsführer stressed this but also sounded what would become a Nazi propaganda standard—the Volkssturm was nothing more than the Party's response to the German Volk community's desire to join in the armed defense of the Fatherland.[1] The Nazis hoped to convince Germans that the Volkssturm was not being forced upon them but was merely the NSDAP reacting to widespread grassroots sentiment favoring the creation of a militia.

89

Morale reports concerning public reaction to the Volkssturm's debut reveal this as a lie. Few Germans wanted the force, and, in fact, promulgating the Führer Decree on the Volkssturm lowered morale in many areas.[2] Expressions of support existed but were scattered and typically qualified and tentative (e.g., a militia might be useful against rebellious foreign laborers or prisoners of war, though not Allied troops).[3] While negative comments were plainly numerous and widespread, the degree, distribution, and depth of positive sentiment are impossible to ascertain, in part because the very agencies responsible for maintaining morale or supervising the Volkssturm filed many of the reports containing favorable comments.[4] It seems certain, however, that most Germans took the Volkssturm announcement stoically, as just another burden to bear.[5] The kind of fanatic enthusiasm the Nazis hoped to generate was quite rare. Certainly, the German public was not clamoring for the creation of a militia in October 1944.

The reasons behind the cool reception are clear. Morale in mid-October was already low because of the summer's disasters. Moreover, the Soviets had just opened an offensive in East Prussia, and the American seizure of Aachen, the first major city in the Reich to come under ground assault, was imminent. Against this background, the Volkssturm seemed more a sign of desperation than salvation, and most believed avoiding defeat would require much more than forming a home guard. Some argued that there were plenty of young soldiers and Reich Labor Service men remaining on the home front who should be sent into combat before the old and infirm were. Workers grumbled that the Volkssturm would take the last of their free time. Many other Germans doubted the Party's abilities and expressed preference for Wehrmacht control of the militia.[6]

The most salient element of public reaction was fear that the Allies would consider the Volkssturm an illegal partisan organization. Many Germans— apparently quite aware of their own country's historically brutal reaction to partisan activity—stated they would not serve as guerrillas. They feared that the Allies would execute them if captured and would exact reprisals against civilians.[7] Indeed, this had been standard German policy during the Franco-Prussian War, World War I, and particularly the current war; there was no reason to expect Allied treatment of Nazi partisans would be less brutal.[8]

Volkssturm leaders recognized the force would fail unless they could overcome the public's anxiety. While indoctrination might ultimately convince German men that Allied treatment of a conquered Germany would be so harsh that avoiding defeat necessitated any and all sacrifices, they first had to be convinced to serve in the Volkssturm. Otherwise, they would not be fully exposed to the Party's view of the gravity and meaning of the war. Nor could they experience the mystical bonding with their Volk comrades that the Nazis hoped the Volkssturm would provide. Reich leaders launched a major effort to secure international legal recognition of the Volkssturm in order to dispel Germans' fears that the force was a guerrilla movement.[9]

The first step toward legal recognition was sounding out Allied opinion. Toward this end, the German Foreign Office contacted British Undersecretary for Foreign Affairs George Hall. The Nazis had reason for concern because in 1940 they had loudly denounced the British Home Guard as an illegal guerrilla movement and threatened to treat its members accordingly.[10] In spite of this precedent, Britain—soon followed by the United States—assured the Germans in early November that as long as the militia acted in accordance with international law, they would consider Volkssturm men legal combatants.[11] In late October, the Wehrmacht made a blatant bid for French recognition by reversing earlier policy. It ordered German troops to treat all members of the French Forces of the Interior as regular soldiers so long as they wore either a uniform or the standard tricolor armband bearing the cross of Lorraine.[12] It is not known whether the Germans bothered extending similar feelers to the Soviets.

International legal recognition necessitated that the Volkssturm adhere to the Hague Regulations' four stipulations on militias: militiamen had to carry their arms openly, wear uniforms or other recognizable marks identifying them as soldiers, observe the rules of warfare, and operate under a specified chain of command. Furthermore, designated commanders had to bear responsibility for their subordinates' actions.[13] Simply put, they must not be partisans employing guerrilla tactics. Examination of the Volkssturm's organizational preparations reveals extensive efforts to adhere closely to these guidelines.

Despite some initial confusion spawned by propaganda rhetoric, the Volkssturm's assigned duties fit well within the constraints of international law. As part of the overall strategy of deepening the front against enemy breakthroughs, the Volkssturm performed three rather mundane tactical roles typically assigned to garrison troops or militiamen: rear-area security, labor, and, most important, the static defense of towns and fortified zones.[14]

In its rear-area security role, the Volkssturm functioned much like the Stadt- und Landwacht, which was ultimately dissolved and its men taken into the militia. Volkssturm men played a major role in the Airborne and Armor Warning Services, an observation system intended to sound the alarm in the event of sudden Allied armored penetrations or airborne assaults.[15] They also located and apprehended deserters, escapees, downed airmen, and infiltrators, a potentially dangerous task. Volkssturm men also maintained order and searched for survivors after air raids, directed traffic, patrolled evacuated towns, provided security for and preserved order in refugee columns, and guarded economically valuable objects (including stranded trains, a common late war problem) and POW camps. They often enforced curfews on foreign workers and guarded (and even helped conduct security sweeps in) their camps and work details and escorted—with Hitler's express authorization to employ deadly force—columns of evacuated concentration or POW camp inmates.[16] These police auxiliary duties did occasionally lead to Volkssturm involvement in atrocities, including the summary execution of accused deserters and traitors[17] and the massacre of concentration camp inmates. In fact, some prisoners reportedly despised being guarded by Volkssturm men, who frequently, in their nervousness, treated their charges harshly and shot anyone remotely suspected of trying to escape.[18] Nonetheless, such incidents were relatively isolated and did not bring the legality of the Volkssturm as a whole into question.

The Volkssturm's other noncombat duty, as laborers, was thoroughly innocuous from a legal standpoint. Volkssturm men evacuated supplies, harvested crops, repaired roads and railroads, cleared snow and rubble, broke up river ice, cut trees, loaded and unloaded trains and barges, and—throughout the Reich—constructed roadblocks and other defensive positions.[19] The Volkssturm effectively replaced the People's Levy as ready labor; in fact, army and Party officials eventually so abused the situation that Bormann, out of fear for disrupting essential economic activity, had to restrict use of inactive militiamen in work details.[20] Clearly, however, none of these tasks could undermine the Volkssturm's legal standing in any way.

In combat, Volkssturm assignments typically consisted of assisting the Wehrmacht with the static defense of fortifications and towns. Tactical training to carry out these tasks called for nothing more unorthodox than setting ambushes, utilizing surprise, and conducting local counterattacks. All operations were to be coordinated with, and under the command of, regular formations, and they provided little opportunity for officially sanctioned guerrilla warfare. The only possible exception came with special mobile formations—Hunting Teams *(Jagdkommandos)* and Tank Hunting Teams *(Panzerjagdkommandos)*—or Demolition Teams *(Sprengkommandos)*, which existed to perform specific skilled tasks. These units primarily functioned to give Volkssturm formations greater tactical mobility and flexibility, but they conceivably could have conducted hit-and-run raids in the enemy's rear areas.[21] Although the possibility existed that if the Volkssturm met its motivational goals, it might adopt guerrilla tactics on individual members' or units' initiative, until a broad segment of the German public was willing to engage in and support a partisan struggle, the force was designed and structured to follow the basic rules of warfare as a legal militia.

Volkssturm organizers also painstakingly addressed Hague Regulations requiring combatants to wear uniforms or an emblem that would distinguish them as combatants. Initially, Himmler and Bormann very pragmatically decided that the supply situation required Volkssturm men to provide their own clothing. To fulfill legal obligations, members would wear a standard armband bearing the words *German Volkssturm—Wehrmacht* and carry a standard pay-book. There was even considerable debate over how to design the armband so as to maximize its visibility.[22] Armbands and paybooks were, however, not enough to assuage fears that Allied, especially Soviet, troops would execute Germans caught fighting in civilian clothing.[23] Furthermore, as Bormann realized, neither armbands nor fiery fanaticism would keep Volkssturm men warm in the rapidly approaching winter. Therefore, Volkssturm officials decided to attempt to clothe its members in field gray uniforms.[24] For similar legal reasons, these officials balked at issuing shotguns or other unorthodox weapons, preferring military firearms instead, even though this curtailed available weapons stocks.[25] Given the impossibility of providing all Volkssturm men with a uniform or a standard weapon, the decision to attempt this suggests the lengths to which Nazi leaders would go to satisfy Germans on the issue of legality.

The most important step in organizing a legal militia was creating a regular chain of command with designated officers who were responsible for their men and their unit's actions. Bormann had a rough outline set by September 27, and the structure was completed within six weeks. The command system spelled out command responsibility at all levels from Bormann and Himmler down to individual squad leaders.[26] Another critical step in this process came when Himmler and Bormann decided that active Volkssturm units would be under the nearest Wehrmacht formation's control. Any regular officer, regardless of rank, had full authority over the active Volkssturm personnel attached to his unit, thereby effectively incorporating them into the army for the duration of their service.[27] This not only contributed to assuring legality but also improved tactical and logistical cooperation and accelerated the trend of employing regular army practices in the Volkssturm.

In mid-November, the release of a set table of organization and equipment (TO&E) for Volkssturm battalions marked another step in standardizing the chain of command. Bormann rejected the option of designating Volkssturm units with Party terminology (e.g., *Standart, Sturm,* or *Sturmbann*) and instead utilized traditional military unit names. He also assigned each formation a numerical designation as in the Wehrmacht rather than allowing local officials to choose their own names (e.g., Freikorps Sauerland, or *Gausturm* Ruhr).[28] While developing the chain of command in this manner obviously served Bormann's political ambitions (as noted earlier, he believed using terms such as *Sturmbann* would suggest SA control), it also further standardized the Volkssturm along military lines and enhanced its claim to combatant status.

Volkssturm unit structure resembled common German infantry practices in more than nomenclature. From the largest formation (battalion) down to the smallest (squad), Volkssturm unit TO&Es were similar to their Wehrmacht counterpart in structure, size, and theoretical equipment allocations. For example, Volkssturm unit TO&Es followed the army's basic triangular structure at the platoon, company, and battalion echelons. Even at the squad level, army influence is evident; both army and Volkssturm squads had, at least on paper, their own light machine gun to maximize integral firepower. Again like their regular counterparts, Volkssturm battalions had antitank and infantry support weapons and engineering, medical, logistical, and administrative components.[29] With Volkssturm units based on the Party's Kreise and Ortsgruppen, which varied greatly in population, rigid adherence to any TO&E was impossible;[30] nonetheless, the tables helped establish a fixed organizational template and delineate a precise chain of command.

Volkssturm officials took the TO&E seriously, expending considerable effort to provide each unit with the proper support elements. For example, each battalion was to have an aid station with its own doctor in order to gather casualties, provide them with first aid, and, if necessary, pass them on to field or civilian hospitals for more extensive treatment. Medically qualified civilians and Party affiliate personnel staffed these units, and their existence probably helped ease members' natural trepidation about being wounded in combat.[31] To direct fortification and obstacle building, demolitions, or mine laying, the battalion TO&E authorized an engineer platoon drawn from local members of Technical Emergency Aid, veterans with relevant experience, or other qualified men such as miners or construction workers.[32]

Volkssturm battalions also included much the same type of administrative and logistical personnel—cooks, clerks, ordnance men, and craftsmen—as one would find in a comparable Wehrmacht unit. Their numbers, however, were kept to a minimum due to the perception that a Volkssturm unit's needs in these areas were relatively limited.[33] Party officials handled supply and administrative matters until the unit was activated, and then the Wehrmacht entity commanding the militia formation took care of most of these functions. These administrative, maintenance, and logistical personnel did handle essential duties; but they are also further evidence of the Volkssturm's reliance on the Wehrmacht model and of the concern over legal issues. Bormann even refused to allow the formation of an official women's auxiliary to assist in logistical and administrative tasks because he feared that putting women in an official role would create the image of a partisan force.[34]

Aside from a smaller administrative and logistical tail, the only other significant variation from standard German infantry practice was that Volkssturm companies contained heavy support weapons (machine guns and mortars), while the army placed these at battalion level.[35] This deviation resulted from the tactical needs of local defense and the way in which Volkssturm units were raised. A battalion might contain companies from several towns, and if the unit's heavy support weapons were all in one company—that is, in one town—other formations, and thereby towns, would have only light weapons. So to accommodate local defense needs, the Volkssturm's military raison d'être, heavy weapons were maintained at a lower level than in the regular army.

Orthodox German military practices also clearly influenced special Volkssturm units. Motorized formations, the most significant noninfantry units, existed not to conduct hit-and-run raids but to improve mobility and communications, increase mobilization speed, and handle logistical tasks. Motorized unit personnel (including leaders) generally consisted of NSKK men and qualified civilians, but assignment to these units depended more on party connections or technical skills as drivers or mechanics than on personal fanaticism. Moreover, training consisted of map reading, march discipline, security, camouflage, and courier skills; guerrilla tactics were conspicuous only by their absence.

Gau- or Kreisleiters, who controlled vehicular transport, generally preferred to concentrate it into companies or battalions rather than dispersing it, although individual units could have bicycles, horse carts, and motorcycles.[36] Mobile combat units (e.g., the aforementioned Hunting Teams) did exist, but they were primarily bicycle mounted, organized like regular formations, and served merely as rapid response teams for the local commander.[37] Volkssturm leaders do not seem to have viewed their mobile units as a means to enable volunteer fanatics to disrupt the enemy's rear areas.

Although other improvised Volkssturm formations existed, they were not partisan units but attempts to improve local defensive capabilities or to allow someone to retain control over his personnel. In many areas, officials redesignated the old Political Leader Squadrons or SA Special Purpose Units as select Volkssturm alarm units; but they usually remained the Kreisleiter's personal showpiece, his ready reserve against civil unrest or sudden enemy attacks, or merely enabled his employees and/or cronies to avoid more onerous duties. Furthermore, they were generally organized as standard Volkssturm companies and battalions and did nothing to prepare for guerrilla warfare.[38] The best example of this is Gau South Westphalia's "Freikorps Sauerland," which predated the Volkssturm but was amalgamated into the Gau's First Levy as several elite volunteer battalions.[39] Some areas formed special Tank Hunting Teams (often from HJ personnel) designed and trained to ambush enemy armored vehicles; but such units seem to have neither worked behind Allied lines nor carried out typical guerrilla operations such as sabotage of supply routes or harassment of occupation forces.[40]

A German partisan force, the Werewolf, did exist, but it was distinct from the Volkssturm and never enjoyed either Hitler's or Bormann's full support, although the Wehrmacht did provide some assistance. Created under SS auspices at the suggestion of *Obergruppenführer* Richard Hildebrand, chief of the SS Race and Settlement Main Office, these guerrillas occasionally disguised themselves as Volkssturm members, but there was no official connection between the two organizations.[41] Although some officers, notably the fanatic Field Marshal Ferdinand Schörner, wanted the Volkssturm to undertake extensive "partisan-style" warfare in the enemy's rear areas, nothing came of this.[42] Finally, Freikorps Adolf Hitler, launched in the spring of 1945, consisted of fanatic Nazi volunteers organized into small antitank teams. They may have carried out some minor partisan operations, but as with the Werewolf, they were not associated with the Volkssturm in any official way, although some individuals served in both organizations.[43]

With a standard organizational structure and a corresponding chain of command in place, the Volkssturm needed a system of military justice to ensure that commanding officers could indeed control their men. The Party Chancellery began work on such a code within a week of drafting the Führer Decree on the Volkssturm, an indication of its importance. However, the Chancellery did not complete and promulgate the code until February and March 1945.[44] During the interim, the regular Wehrmacht justice system governed Volkssturm troops on active duty.[45] For inactive Volkssturm units, where the only real offenses were insubordination or failure to attend training sessions, police could arrest recalcitrants under the authority of laws against undermining the war effort. Typically, however, coercion was employed against only the most chronic violators.[46] Furthermore, in some areas unit leaders took it upon themselves to punish slackers, while some local Party officials withheld ration cards from men who had not enrolled and/or participated in the Volkssturm. They also threatened reprisals against the families—especially those who had been evacuated—of men who shirked training duties.[47] The special Volkssturm courts, founded in February and March, provided the Volkssturm with a complete and unified legal system. Supposedly they enforced a less stringent code of military discipline than the Wehrmacht's and could try infractions that occurred in training as well as on active duty. It is, however, doubtful that the Volkssturm's legal apparatus accomplished much at this late date.

Being subject to military law, whether the Volkssturm or the Wehrmacht version, helped guarantee the average militiaman all the protections accorded regular soldiers under international law, but it also made him subject to punishments for infractions. Although the Volkssturm might not treat unexcused absences from training as harshly as the Wehrmacht handled being absent without leave, both were criminal offenses. Once an individual was on active duty, however, infractions or dereliction of duty were serious, even capital, offenses. During the last weeks of the war, numerous Volkssturm deserters found that the Party, police, SS, and army considered theirs a crime worthy of the harshest penalty.[48] For the Party, placing the Volkssturm under the military legal system doubly aided achievement of its objectives. First by ensuring recognition as a lawful militia, it reduced one of the public's greatest fears and encouraged participation in the force. Second, it gave the Party a legal means to coerce those Germans who still had reservations into either serving as ordered or risking punishment.

With the Volkssturm command structure established, the next pressing task was selecting unit leaders. As stated in chapter 2, the Volkssturm's Nazi founders believed that success depended upon the zeal, bravery, and unbureaucratic style of loyal Party activists who could inspire their subordinates to fight fanatically in defense of their homes and Volk. Unit leaders, particularly company and battalion commanders, were therefore critical to the Volkssturm not only because they would lead it in battle but also because they had the responsibility of training, indoctrinating, and motivating their men. Therefore, as with Gau and Kreis Chiefs of Staff, Bormann insisted that local officials select unit leaders with both military skills and political qualifications. Symbolically, Bormann rejected using traditional rank titles, opting instead simply to call Volkssturm commanders battalion, company, platoon, or squad leaders. He did order that these men wear black collar patches adorned with a varying number of silver pips to indicate their rank and thus make them identifiable as commanders.[49]

Bormann insisted that Volkssturm unit leader selection should proceed according to the same criteria he had established for the Gau- and Kreisstabsführer. For all Volkssturm leadership positions, he wanted nominees who were "believing, fanatical, and convinced National Socialists, front-proven leaders, and proper organizers," with a basic familiarity with modern weapons, particularly machine guns and antitank weapons. They should be chosen according to their qualifications, not Party or army ranks.[50] He wanted leaders who could motivate their men and who would constantly strive to "educate [their men] to hate the enemy fanatically."[51] Bormann welcomed the use of former military officers who possessed the requisite political aptitude and enthusiasm, particularly if they had served on the Eastern Front, where reality and Nazi ideological views on war meshed closely. He even allowed OKH's Personnel Office to provide lists of suitable retired officers to the Gauleiters; but, as with the Gau- and Kreisstabsführer, he would not allow active officers to be recalled from duty for Volkssturm use.[52] Bormann wanted Volkssturm commanders to lead by their military and political example, and to try to foster camaraderie and fanaticism among their men. He believed that only men with leadership experience in Germany's political *and* military struggles could truly achieve this goal.[53]

This was the ideal; but what sort of men actually led Volkssturm units? A common perception is they were totally incompetent "draft dodging friends" of the local Nazi boss, but is this view accurate?[54] Indeed, some officials proclaimed that unit leaders' Nazi convictions were "more important than their military knowledge,"[55] but how widespread was this attitude? As with all Volkssturm records, unit commander information is sketchy, but sufficient evidence exists in unit and local Party records—particularly Bayreuth's Gaustabsführer's files, the most extensive surviving files of any Volkssturm entity[56]—and in the Red Cross MIA lists to provide some supportable conclusions concerning Volkssturm leaders' age and occupational, political, and military profiles.

Concerning age, Volkssturm leaders tended to be older men—forty-five to fifty-two years old—particularly at the higher levels (see appendix, Tables 21 and 22). In 1944, the Wehrmacht's severe shortage of field- and company-grade officers meant that the only ex-officers at home were superannuated or graded unfit for service, often due to wounds. Therefore, the age profile indicates that local officials were indeed trying to locate the available experienced men.[57] With approximately 80 percent of identifiable MIA officers and Bayreuth company leaders and over 90 percent of Bayreuth battalion leaders over the upper age limit of the draft (generally age forty-five), it certainly appears few Volkssturm leaders were young, fit men who had used Party contacts and exemptions to avoid military service.[58]

The Volkssturm leaders' occupational profile was apparently dominated by office workers, supervisors and managers, professionals, and government employees and officials. Although farmers did not appear as frequently among its leaders as in the ranks, they were fairly well represented in some areas. On the other hand, workers of all sorts were severely underrepresented.[59] Of the 71 leaders identified in the Red Cross MIA lists, 50 (70.4 percent) came from the white-collar occupations mentioned previously, 10 were farmers, and only 8 were blue-collar workers. Among the 128 company leaders in Gau Bayreuth for whom records listed occupational information, 90 (70.3 percent) held white-collar jobs; the remainder consisted of 20 farmers, 6 master craftsmen, 3 retirees, and 9 blue-collar workers. Of the 54 Bayreuth battalion leaders with identifiable occupations, all held white-collar positions save for a lone farmer.

The dominance of white-collar and professional occupations among Volkssturm leaders is further confirmed by individual unit records. Of the 21 officers in Battalion 24/29 (Unterlüß, Kreis Celle), 18 held white-collar jobs, while the proportion among unit leaders in the First Company of Rastatt's VII Battalion was 13 of 18.[60] Fifteen of 18 company and battalion leaders in Kreis Villingen held managerial, office, government, or professional positions; in nearby Triberg and St. Georgen, 6 of the 8 battalion and company leaders held similar jobs.[61] All 8 Bergheim area company leaders and all 5 in Ortsgruppe Bremen-Walle worked in white-collar occupations.[62] Finally, among company leader nominees in Ortsgruppen Bad Freienwalde, Ladeburg, Finow, Strausberg/West, and Strausberg (Kreis Eberswalde-Oberbarnim), 28 of 41 held white-collar jobs.[63] Comparable profiles existed among leaders in other areas.[64]

Substantial numbers of owners, top-echelon managers, directors, and others in high positions could be found among Volkssturm unit leadership.[65] For example, of the 21 men commanding at or above platoon level in the Unterlüß battalion, almost half were higher-echelon managers or supervisors.[66] Teachers and education officials formed another overrepresented group among Volkssturm leaders, constituting just under 18 percent of the identifiable Bayreuth company leaders (23 of 128). From a different perspective, 45.1 percent of the

male teachers in the Goslar area held some sort of Volkssturm command; figures for the Salzgitter and Wolfenbüttel regions were 43.5 percent and 26.5 percent, respectively.[67] One Volkssturm battalion commander's remark that most
of his colleagues were "popular and trustworthy personalities . . . who were in
close contact and good standing with the local populace" seems indeed accurate for many units.[68] Although workers and farmers could and did gain appointments, as in all militias, community prominence greatly enhanced one's
chances of gaining Volkssturm command.

Although social position played a role, the crucial factors in appointing
Volkssturm commanders were, as Bormann ordered, political and military
qualifications. Therefore, an extremely high proportion of unit leaders, particularly at company and battalion levels, were members of the NSDAP or its
affiliates. Gau Bayreuth records identify 173 of 416 (41.6 percent) battalion
leaders and only 97 of 682 (14.22 percent) company leaders as Party or affiliate members. Political information on most of these men, particularly company commanders, is very much incomplete and uneven from Kreis to Kreis.
When examining the individual Kreise that reported more thoroughly (though
again not completely), proportions rise dramatically (see Tables 23–24), and
records from other areas confirm this trend. For example, all the leaders in
Detmold's First Company were NSDAP members, as were all but one of the
battalion, company, and platoon leaders in Unterlüß's Battalion 24/29. Nearly
one-third—7 of 22—of the unit leaders in the Oberesch (Saarland) Company
were not Party members, but all these were squad leaders, the lowest Volkssturm command.[69] In Kreis Eberswalde-Oberbarnim, at least 36 of 41 company leader nominees were Party, SA, or NSKK members, as were all 8 platoon
leaders in Ortsgruppen Buchholz and Eschenbach in Kreis Pankow (Berlin).[70]
This evidence suggests that Party or affiliate membership was virtually a prerequisite for Volkssturm commands, particularly battalion and company leaders, that is, those having indoctrinational responsibilities.[71]

Many Volkssturm commanders, in fact, also held NSDAP, SA, SS, or
NSKK leadership posts (see again appendix Tables 23–24). As mentioned elsewhere, NSKK officials led most Volkssturm motorized formations; and, in Gau
Munich–Upper Bavaria, there was even a German Volkssturm Leader Reserve
consisting of SA officers available for unit commander duty.[72] The 4 battalion
and 8 company leaders identified from Kreis Lüdinghausen documents included
the Kreisleiter, 2 members of his staff, an Ortsgruppenleiter, 3 SA officers, and
an SA NCO. Information from other areas suggests a similar pattern.[73] Preva-
lence of Party and affiliate officials in Volkssturm leadership positions resulted
from three basic reasons. One, the ideological goals of the Volkssturm, as set by
Bormann, required activists to hold these posts. Two, these men had personal
contacts with the nominating officials. Three, the Party's rather generous draft
exemptions meant that they had relatively fit men available.

That so many unit commanders had Party backgrounds is no surprise—
Volkssturm leaders have always been portrayed this way. The military background of these men is what has generally been ignored, and a surprisingly
high proportion of Volkssturm commanders had military experience, many as
officers or NCOs. Of the 416 battalion leaders in Gau Bayreuth (see Table 25),
records indicate that at least 51.2 percent (and probably more) had some military experience: 176 (42.1 percent) as company or battalion officers, 35 as
NCOs, 2 with purely logistical or administrative military experience, and 1 with
a background in the police.[74] Among the 682 company leaders (see Table 26)
were 61 former officers, 96 ex-NCOs, and a further 14 men with unspecified
military experience (a total of 25.1 percent). Again, these records are incomplete, particularly for company leaders; examining the Kreise that provided
the most information suggests much higher actual proportions of militarily
experienced men (see Table 26).

Other evidence further confirms this trend. Army instructors at the first
national battalion leader training course at Grafenwöhr recalled that many
participants had sound military credentials.[75] Also several officials from eastern areas reported nearly all their company and battalion leaders were former
frontline army officers, many of whom had recent experience and had been
released from duty because of wounds.[76] For example, the platoon leaders in
Ortsgruppen Buchholz and Eschenbach consisted of 6 former lieutenants and
2 NCOs, while all 10 of Ortsgruppe Brieske's (Kreis Calau) platoon and company leaders had military experience, primarily in World War I, with all but 1
having combat decorations.[77] Thirty-two of 41 company leader nominees identified in Kreis Eberswalde-Oberbarnim records were veterans, again primarily of World War I.[78]

Similar evidence can also be found in the western regions. Of Kreis Celle's
62 company leaders, all but 1 had military experience, 27 as captains or lieutenants and 34 as NCOs. The Unterlüß battalion leader was a retired officer
with a thirty-eight-year career (1906–1944); and although only 4 of the 21 platoon, company, and battalion leaders in this unit had been in World War II,
all had three or more years of military service. Fully half boasted ten or more
years.[79] Similarly, all the Oberesch Company's leaders had military experience, and although none had been officers, 8, including the company leader
(who was also the Ortsgruppenleiter), had served as NCOs in the current
war.[80] Likewise, all platoon and squad leaders in Battalion 19/XVI's Second Company (Munich) were veterans.[81] Even in segregated factory units,
where one might expect rank in the firm would have determined unit command appointments, leaders seem to have had military qualifications as
well. Of the 89 battalion and company leaders and adjutants in the fourteen
Nuremberg Railway Directorate battalions, 48 were former officers and 36
were ex-NCOs.[82]

Contrary to the prevailing image, evidence points to the conclusion that there was indeed a genuine effort, as with the Gau and Kreis Chiefs of Staff, to locate Volkssturm leaders with both political and military qualifications. At the very minimum, 27.8 percent of Gau Bayreuth's battalion leaders had both Party and military experience. In fact, the Danzig Gauleitung, unable to find sufficient numbers of militarily experienced men, even ran newspaper and radio advertisements urging former officers to volunteer for Volkssturm duty, while Kreis Teltow ordered that it would screen for possible promotion all former officers who were in its Volkssturm units, but not in command positions.[83]

Not only did local Volkssturm officials actively seek men with military backgrounds; they seem to have assigned men to command units at a level commensurate with their earlier military experience. Note the higher numbers of former officers commanding battalions and the greater number of ex-NCOs leading companies in Gau Bayreuth (see Tables 25–26).[84] This suggests that local officials heeded Bormann's instructions to appoint unit leaders with both military and political qualifications.

Furthermore, Volkssturm unit leadership reveals something about the degree to which Nazism had penetrated the Wehrmacht officer corps. Although fragmentary evidence makes speculation on precise percentages risky, it is clear that a substantial number of the former lieutenants, captains, and majors who were at home in late 1944 and early 1945 were—or had been—fairly active in the NSDAP in some capacity.[85] It was precisely these types of men—National Socialist activists with combat command experience, particularly in the East— whom the Nazis considered ideal candidates for Volkssturm commands. Indeed, they seem to have found considerable numbers of these men, many of whom had left service due to wounds, available to lead Volkssturm units. In fact, the ideal Volkssturm officer was socially, politically, and in other ways a carbon copy of the prototypical Wehrmacht junior officer, yet another indication of how the Volkssturm patterned itself after the regular armed forces.[86]

Finally, appointing ex-officers with proven National Socialist credentials to Volkssturm commands was a logical step toward attaining the force's overall objectives. By locating commanders who knew how to organize, train, administer, and lead standard military units, the NSDAP could improve combat effectiveness and simultaneously ease public trepidation about Volkssturm members' legal status. Furthermore, for the Volkssturm to help create a bitter, stalemated war where Allied troops would have to pay dearly for every German village and town, local units had to be willing to fight against overwhelming odds. This demanded unit commanders who were militarily competent, inspirational leaders who could motivate their men to the point of fanaticism. Nazis believed the best-qualified men for this job were Party activists who had led troops in combat, and they seem to have appointed substantial numbers of such men to Volkssturm commands.

Procuring leaders with the desired political and military qualifications did not necessarily yield the anticipated benefits, however. Damning evidence of Volkssturm unit leaders' poor quality comes from training course performance evaluations. Of 81 participants in a Gau Bayreuth battalion and company leader class, trainers scored 20 (24.7 percent) men as unfit and a further 32 (39.5 percent) as substandard. Two-thirds were thus deemed less than fully competent.[87] In another course, participants' grades were, on the whole, substandard in the critical areas of issuing orders, general knowledge, and decisiveness (their worst category) and merely average in the less significant areas of marksmanship (their best category) and physical fitness.[88]

Volkssturm officials at all levels soon realized that the unit leadership corps was far less than ideal. Bormann himself lamented that many unit leaders were not fully qualified in either the political or the military sense.[89] Some Party leaders even complained that too many Volkssturm leaders were merely old soldiers who lacked the political zeal and motivational powers that the force so desperately needed.[90] Furthermore, locating a man with impeccable military and political qualifications was no guarantee that he would be a good leader in battle. He might be physically unable to stand the rigors of combat, or his military training might even lead him to conclude that resistance was useless.[91] For example, a Kreis Gnesen (Wartheland) battalion leader—Party member, former major, and Knight's Cross holder—fled with his family as the Red Army approached because he was fully cognizant of his unit's unpreparedness to fight.[92]

The main reason for the low overall quality of Volkssturm leaders was that the pool of potential officers was virtually gone. In a desperate effort to replenish its ranks after the summer disasters, the field army had recalled practically anyone even marginally fit for command, yet it remained 10,499 officers short of full strength in mid-October.[93] Any ex-officers not reactivated were either superannuated, not physically fit, or otherwise unsuited. Furthermore, the Volkssturm required at least half a million leaders, just over double the nearly 240,000 officers in the combat divisions in mid-1944! Even after excluding squad leaders, the Volkssturm still needed around 175,000 commanders at the platoon level or above.[94] Given this situation—and the immense difficulty of their task—it is no shock that many Volkssturm leaders were ill suited to lead a combat unit; what is in fact surprising is that many of these men had fairly extensive military backgrounds to complement their prominent political and social positions.

Another reason for Volkssturm leaders' poor quality was morale. Simply put, few men wanted the extensive workload, stress, and responsibilities. Although the NSDAP professed the Volkssturm would operate with a minimum of bureaucratic routine, in practice this was not the case. Aside from training and combat responsibilities, unit leaders, particularly at the company level, faced an ever-increasing administrative burden. A battalion or company leader had to prepare and update records—in triplicate—on each unit member; keep track of all items from weapons to dog tags issued to individual Volkssturm men; send regular reports to a range of officials on his unit's training, personnel, and equipment; plan training and propaganda sessions; authorize men to miss such meetings; correspond with members' employers on training and mobilization schedules; assist in punishing those who did not attend Volkssturm functions; keep up with miscellaneous expenditures; rent meeting halls; try to procure equipment, uniforms, and other supplies; and attend a variety of meetings, all while trying to train and motivate his men, maintain liaison with local army authorities, and prepare mobilization and defense plans for his unit and locality.[95] All this, of course, had to be done in his spare time with whatever limited official and volunteer assistance he could muster.[96] Once called into active duty, the unit leader's administrative tasks did not lessen; he was expected to continue to file standard military reports on all types of personnel, logistical, and operational issues, keep a unit war diary, ensure his men were properly paid, and write all types of orders.[97]

With such a heavy load of paperwork—and a minimal staff—many unit leaders, who also held civilian jobs, complained that they had insufficient time to devote to training their men. This bureaucracy's development directly contradicted Nazi ideals, but it resulted from legitimate needs and—moreover—from the effort to make the force a legal militia. Bureaucracy was the inevitable result of trying to standardize the Volkssturm, regularize its procedures, supervise its activities, and make it mesh with the Wehrmacht administrative and logistical structure, all of which helped the force meet the legal requirements for militias. In return, however, the ever-mounting demands of Volkssturm bureaucratic routines overburdened and demoralized unit leaders,[98] the very men whom the Nazis deemed so crucial to realizing the force's political and military potential. According to its Nazi architects, the Volkssturm's military success hinged upon its members' morale. They publicly proclaimed the Volkssturm would motivate the German people to a zealous defense of their homes, Reich, and Volk; privately, they admitted that without such fanaticism, their strategy would fail.

Essentially, the Volkssturm was as much about morale as local defense because, in the minds of Nazi leaders, the two were inextricably linked. Therefore, when the German public greeted the Volkssturm's proclamation with fairly widespread reluctance and outright disapproval, its leaders knew that they had to make the force more palatable. They recognized the average German's greatest concern was that the Allies would treat the Volkssturm as a partisan force. Germans assumed that captured Volkssturm men would be executed, so there was little reason to serve unless one was already fanatic enough to risk this fate. The Volkssturm's leaders recognized that they could not simply force Germans to fight nor rely solely on volunteers; they would have to make the organization appeal to a broad segment of German civilians. To convince Germans to serve, Volkssturm leaders had to gain legal recognition for the force by standardizing a large number of its organizational and administrative practices along military lines.

Although there were other considerations involved in many of the decisions, the concern for making the Volkssturm a legal militia is evident throughout. Unit TO&Es were clearly patterned after the Wehrmacht's, even though these were often not applicable to the local variations inherent in the Volkssturm. The Volkssturm's assignments were those typically assigned to militias and auxiliary troops. Its legal system, although influenced by Nazi ideals of camaraderie and community, was basically a simplified version of the Wehrmacht's; and even more important, the Volkssturm was subject to the Wehrmacht's legal system for most of its existence. In many other ways, large and small, the Volkssturm copied standard military practices. In part this was simply an expedient, but in many cases standardizing and regularizing the Volkssturm was part of a conscious effort to avoid having the Allies brand the force an illegal partisan organization.

The efforts to make the Volkssturm a recognized legal militia generated unintended compromises of the force's basic ideals. First of all, as the following chapters will demonstrate, they reduced Party control by enabling the Wehrmacht to increase its influence over the force. Second, standardization efforts resulted in an increasing amount of paperwork and bureaucratic routine, something the Party had proclaimed it could avoid. Third, and more important, the burden of this red tape fell upon the overaged and often underqualified shoulders of the unit leaders, which in turn had the effect of ruining the morale of the very men expected to turn average German civilians into fanatic combat troops. As with the political struggles for the control of the militia, the Nazis' behavior proved counterproductive to the very goals they had established for the Volkssturm.

CHAPTER SEVEN

Preparing for Battle

The decision to make the Volkssturm a legal militia not only shaped organizational issues but also profoundly affected decisions concerning weaponry, equipment, uniforms, and training. Adherence to international law in these areas made the Volkssturm ever more dependent on the Wehrmacht because it was the only institution with the skill, experience, and resources required to prepare a legal traditional militia for battle. Ultimately, this created a paradoxical situation—at least from the Nazi viewpoint—where NSDAP motivational efforts were generally ineffective and even counterproductive, while Wehrmacht instructional, technical, and/or logistical involvement not only boosted the recipient units' combat potential but also raised morale. Thus, making the Volkssturm a legal militia further moved the force away from the original Nazi idea of creating a fanatic people's militia. In the final analysis, however, despite strenuous efforts by the Party and army, adequately preparing the Volkssturm on a national scale proved well beyond the capabilities of any and all Nazi German institutions.

As happened with so many aspects of the Volkssturm, Berger and Bormann clashed over training priorities. Berger argued for a focus on marksmanship, while Bormann—again meddling in Himmler's sphere, although with some logic—insisted on stressing antitank training.[1] By early November, Berger relented and emphasized antitank weapons and tactics (including obstacle and fortification construction and defense) in his decree on fundamental Volkssturm training priorities. Other instructional emphases included infantry weapons use (e.g., small arms, machine guns, and hand grenades) and tactical training in street fighting, signals, camouflage, ambushes, patrols, reconnaissance, counterattacks, and defending against airborne landings. Training to quell internal unrest was also mentioned, although it never became a high priority. Finally, Berger's order set March 31, 1945, as the completion date for all Volkssturm unit training.[2]

Establishing these objectives proved easier than meeting them. With Allied armies already on German soil, Volkssturm training had to be done quickly and efficiently; but the men—by definition engaged in important occupations—could train only on Sundays or in the evenings. Furthermore, to allow workers at least some pretense of leisure time, officials restricted Sunday training sessions to a maximum of six hours and weekday meetings to two hours.[3] This—coupled with the March 31 deadline—created an impossible situation, particularly in border regions.

Training, military or indoctrinational, fell primarily to Kreis officials and battalion and company leaders, who could turn to a variety of sources for assistance. For help with riflery, the SA provided equipment, skilled instructors, and courses for both teachers and trainees.[4] The NSKK organized transportation units and taught couriers, mechanics, and drivers.[5] Police in some areas provided purely technical assistance in weapons training, but they generally refused to incorporate the Volkssturm fully into the internal security apparatus or even to prepare it for such duties.[6] As noted earlier, this instance of Himmler and his subordinates on blocking Party encroachment into their police powers clearly shows the negative impact of national-level turf wars. Ultimately, however, for the Volkssturm to become an effective legal militia, its training had to be based on standard military practices, something that only the Wehrmacht could provide. To help, Himmler ordered the entire Replacement Army to cooperate as fully as their regular duties would allow. Field army units in the frontline Gaue also provided their assistance.[7] In the long run, the great majority of the Volkssturm's effective training came from the army.

Initial Replacement Army efforts focused on a series of ten- to fourteen-day training courses for battalion and company leaders, the largest of which occurred at the Grafenwöhr Training Grounds. During these crash courses, the army provided participants with lodging, food, equipment, and clothing. Although some political indoctrination occurred, the courses focused heavily on understanding—and how to teach—the basics of weapons use and local defense tactics.[8] Replacement Army involvement in Volkssturm training rapidly expanded as the Wehrkreise soon began providing all sorts of skilled trainers to conduct courses at regular Sunday unit sessions. To stretch the pool of available instructors, the Replacement Army created mobile training teams and utilized furloughed or convalescing soldiers with special skills.[9] Besides basic infantry weapons and tactical instruction, the army taught specialist courses for Volkssturm unit leaders, signalmen, field cooks, ordnance sergeants, paymasters, and mechanics and provided specific instruction in everything from chemical to antipartisan warfare.[10] By far the most significant, frequent, and widespread courses—particularly after the successful Soviet January offensive—addressed antitank weapons and tactics. Replacement Army formations staged over 1,400 such courses in Gau Bayreuth alone.[11] The military also supplied much valuable instructional literature for unit leaders, including pamphlets specifically addressing Volkssturm training concerns.[12]

As is evident from training plans—which vary considerably because instruction occurred primarily at the company level—Volkssturm preparation developed into a rudimentary version of regular infantry training. Fostering individual weapons skills, particularly use and maintenance of rifles, machine guns, hand grenades, and the Panzerfaust (a single-shot, rocket-propelled antitank grenade), formed a common first goal. As unit members gained familiarity with their weapons, commanders often shifted emphasis toward terrain use and rudimentary unit tactics, typically defending towns, strongpoints, and roadblocks. When the men grasped these basics, the unit began learning more complex tactics like counterattacking, reconnaissance, antiaircraft defense, night combat, and street or forest fighting.[13]

Eventually, some Volkssturm formations conducted full-scale mobilization and combat drills in conjunction with army and/or other locally available units in order to test warning systems, response time, and overall local defense capability.[14] In several Gaue, officials also activated Levy I units for extended periods of intensive training prior to placing them at Wehrmacht disposal.[15] Overall, Volkssturm military training focused on teaching the fundamentals of local defense by an infantry unit; there was little, if any, specific training for riot control or quelling revolts, and nothing on guerrilla operations.[16]

Volkssturm officials adopted a number of methods intended to facilitate quick, effective instruction. To make outdoor instruction (i.e., Sunday sessions) more efficient and varied, unit commanders often divided their men into small groups and rotated them through a series of stations, each devoted to a different topic.[17] Similarly, unit leaders often separated their men according to proficiency, particularly in basic marksmanship, and allowed those with previous military service to move into more advanced and specialized training (e.g., machine guns) while the beginners received more basic instruction.[18] In East Prussia, Gauleiter Koch took this even further by ignoring orders and assigning militarily experienced men to Levy I and others to Levy II.[19] Gau and Kreis officials urged unit leaders to maximize training time by planning sessions thoroughly and using even the time spent marching to and from the training grounds for propaganda songs or speeches and reviews or lectures.[20] Training was to be streamlined, thoroughly practical, and designed to maximize hands-on weapons and tactical experience. Ideally, there would be no close-order drill—public parades necessitated some of this—or calisthenics.[21]

In order to free up precious Sunday outdoor training time, Volkssturm leaders could hold additional sessions—generally indoors—one evening during the week or during factory work stoppages.[22] Topics for these meetings tended toward propaganda but also included sand table exercises and military lectures.[23] Evening training also commonly featured army training films such as *Sharpshooting, Panzerfaust,* or *The Battle for Dobrowski: All-Around Defense* designed to demonstrate techniques and tactics that Volkssturm units could practice later.[24] There was even a series of special films prepared exclusively for Volkssturm use.[25]

In spite of every effort, however, the Volkssturm generally failed to meet its training objectives. One problem was the sheer enormity of the task; even under ideal conditions, Volkssturm units would receive no more than the equivalent of a week to ten days of full-time training, hardly enough to create effective soldiers.[26] Also, Allied advances cut short training in border regions, while problems in organizing units and making Levy assignments delayed training everywhere.[27] Winter weather curtailed outdoor instruction, and indoor sessions proved a poor substitute. Even locating space for indoor meetings, particularly in heavily bombed cities, proved unexpectedly challenging.[28] Finally, despite the Replacement Army's best efforts—nearly 27,000 Volkssturm men, about half of them unit commanders, took part in army training courses in Gau Bayreuth alone—there were simply too few skilled instructors to meet the Volkssturm's massive needs.[29]

As if these problems were not enough to handicap adequate Volkssturm preparation, weapons shortages and poor morale provided additional obstacles. Although the Wehrmacht agreed to supply any unit under its command, it could not meet the Volkssturm's estimated minimal logistical needs of 4 million rifles, 250,000 machine guns, and 25,000 mortars.[30] In October 1944, the Wehrmacht itself was short more than 714,000 rifles, 85,000 machine guns, and 2,900 mortars,[31] and was rearming even regular infantry divisions with captured firearms and artillery.[32] With production of the standard German infantry carbine fixed at approximately 186,000 monthly, Speer admitted that "nobody could supply them [the Volkssturm] with weapons."[33]

Initially many Volkssturm officials expected to have free rein to arm their units from any locally available sources, including military warehouses and new production.[34] However, to ensure available supplies went where most urgently needed and to prevent Volkssturm interference with the Wehrmacht's supply flow, Berger's office—backed by the Party Chancellery, Reich Ministry for Armaments and War Production, and OKW—became the national clearinghouse for Volkssturm equipment collection and distribution. Gaue could gather and keep weapons from Party, police auxiliary, and other internal public and private sources, but procuring arms and equipment directly from the Wehrmacht or munitions factories was forbidden.[35] Regional and local Volkssturm leaders frequently ignored this order, often in search of equipment for their own personal elite units. During February, OKH's Quartermaster Section responded by establishing a Volkssturm Equipment Group to assist Berger with logistical matters and to try to eliminate unauthorized diversion of military goods to Volkssturm use.[36] Ultimately Bormann, on Hitler's instructions, had to order the Gauleiters to turn over to the army all the fieldworthy weapons collected for inactive Volkssturm units and to refrain from trying to get more except through official channels.[37]

Certain Volkssturm officials resorted to even more drastic measures in their quest for arms and equipment. Some, including Hamburg Gauleiter Kaufmann, sought to use personal political contacts to garner assistance in arming their Volkssturm men.[38] Koch even concocted an elaborate—and bizarre— scheme to buy supplies for East Prussian Volkssturm units on the Italian black market. He even authorized purchasing from anti-German partisans![39] Speer's Armaments Staff Italy, which controlled military procurement there, exposed and quashed Koch's plot. It agreed to devote 250 million lire (compared with 400 million for the Wehrmacht) for Volkssturm clothing and equipment purchases from legitimate Italian manufacturers, but it also stipulated that Berger's staff would allocate the purchased items.[40] This enterprise collapsed, however, due to transportation difficulties and a dearth of hard currency.[41]

While there were severe equipment shortages, there was no lack of effort to supply the Volkssturm. In November and December, Hitler personally allocated 13,000 carbines, 1,000 machine guns, 680 mortars, and the necessary ammunition for them from current production; but this was only a small fraction of even the border Gaue needs.[42] By the end of January 1945, Himmler's staff had collected over 40,500 rifles, nearly 2,900 machine guns, and 400,000 Panzerfäuste, but by this time weapons needs had increased as well.[43] German weapons were preferable but simply unavailable, so Volkssturm units often received what remained of stocks of foreign—often Italian—arms seized earlier in the war.[44] Although officials preferred to issue all members of a unit with the same type of weapons, this could not always be done. Worse still, replenishing the limited ammunition stocks for these captured weapons was often impossible; in fact, even production of German ammunition was declining due to the loss of facilities.[45]

Officials tried other ways to increase Volkssturm armament. Some absurd suggestions, such as collecting daggers or conducting police sweeps to find weapons hidden by prisoners of war and foreign workers, were apparently never implemented.[46] A more realistic recommendation, collecting publicly and privately held firearms—including hunting pieces—hit several snags.[47] Institutional owners sometimes proved uncooperative; for example, police officials frequently refused to hand over Stadt- und Landwacht arms and equipment even though the Volkssturm had absorbed its personnel and duties. Also, some local Party and affiliate leaders simply ignored Bormann's orders to donate weapons and supplies.[48] Uncooperativeness notwithstanding, publicly and privately owned weapons were insufficient to meet even a substantial fraction of total needs. Furthermore, officials considered providing Volkssturm men with a motley array of firearms, particularly nonmilitary weapons like shotguns, detrimental to the Volkssturm's legal combatant status.[49]

On the other hand, some individuals displayed the sort of inventiveness that the Volkssturm was intended to generate by offering ways to create new weapons from untapped local resources. Some Volkssturm officials had surplus Luftwaffe airplane machine guns converted for ground use, while others had spare flare pistols reworked to fire small grenades.[50] One engineer offered to build a simple wooden mortar he had invented while serving in the trenches during World War I.[51] Some Volkssturm leaders urged producing homemade land mines, Molotov cocktails, or other explosives.[52] Speer even suggested issuing Volkssturm units quantities of three-pronged nails for scattering on roads to puncture the tires of Allied supply vehicles.[53] Ultimately, however, many of these programs were quashed by national officials who were concerned that issuing Volkssturm units unorthodox weaponry—particularly the nails, which would have to be spread clandestinely behind Allied lines—would make them appear, to either the Allies or their own members, to be partisans.[54]

Berger's office sought to meet the need for standard military equipment without diminishing production through the extensive mobilization of crafts-men and small workshops to produce inexpensive weapons specifically de-signed for Volkssturm use. The most ambitious of these programs involved the so-called People's Rifles (*Volksgewehre*), simplified versions of standard firearms that could, in theory, be produced in approximately one-fourth the time in "the smallest locksmith's shop" or with voluntary factory overtime.[55] Hitler approved manufacture of the People's Rifle on October 12 and person-ally examined prototypes a few weeks later.[56] Production was decentralized, but firms working on People's Rifles in each Gau reported to a single leading firm, which in turn answered to the national program coordinator, Walther of Zella-Mehlis.[57]

The program began well, with a Luftwaffe donation of 245,000 obsolete machine gun replacement barrels, and Berger's staff placing an optimistic order of 50,000 units for the Volkssturm national arsenal at Zeesen.[58] Eventually, the program grew to include five authorized rifle models, a carbine, a pistol, an automatic rifle, and a submachine gun. All the simplified designs appeared rather crude, and they varied greatly in quality, with some reportedly a greater danger to the firer than to the target, and others, particularly Gustloff's assault rifle, the VG1-5, proving quite effective.[59] In spite of their simplicity and the emphasis given the People's Rifle program, production never met its monthly target of 100,000 rifles, and few ever reached Volkssturm units due to supply and manufacturing difficulties.[60] Similar fates met the concrete "People's Hand Grenade" and a proposed single-shot flamethrower.[61]

The Panzerfaust, which one Gaustabsführer even called the "main weapon of the Volkssturm man," proved the only weapon that the force consistently possessed in adequate numbers.[62] Production of this antitank rocket steadily rose to a peak in March 1945 of 1 million units, more than enough to meet the Wehrmacht's needs. In fact, by mid-February the Zeesen arsenal had a reserve of nearly 400,000.[63] Although the Panzerfaust was effective and available, its main problem was that when fired it spewed a backblast of flame and hot gases from the rear of its pipelike launcher tube. This eliminated recoil but posed a fatal danger for anyone—including the operator—negligent or ignorant enough to stand directly behind the tube during firing. Training accidents involving Panzerfäuste injured several men and created a fear of the weapon that could only be dispelled by proper instruction and live firing.[64] Unfortunately for the Volkssturm, there were not enough of these weapons to allow for extensive practice firing.[65]

Weapons and ammunition shortages of all types remained a chronic, insolvable problem for the Volkssturm. On February 10, for example, the Zeesen national arsenal reported that it could arm no more than five battalions per frontline Gau.[66] Furthermore, the centralized distribution system, though militarily sound, deprived inactive Volkssturm units, particularly those in interior areas, of weapons for training use. Issuing captured weapons with unreplenishable ammunition stocks similarly curtailed marksmanship practice.[67] In response, some Gau officials cheerfully encouraged units lacking firearms or ammunition to forgo the rifle range and work on other aspects of combat training using dummy or unloaded weapons. They also insisted that even unarmed Volkssturm men could perform valuable battlefield services as guides, scouts, or laborers or by scavenging weapons![68]

Lacking the real things, Volkssturm leaders attempted to muddle through with pellet guns on scaled-down ranges and improvised nonexploding hand and Panzerfaust grenades.[69] Other units practiced marksmanship with small-bore rifles or privately owned firearms and ammunition; some even expended a portion of their live rifle and Panzerfaust rounds to prepare their men.[70] Despite these efforts, weapons and ammunition shortages severely hampered Volkssturm training. For example, Linz am Rhein's company reported on March 7, 1945— the very day U.S. troops crossed the Rhine at nearby Remagen—that it had finally procured enough weapons to begin training in earnest, although it was far from combat ready.[71] In some units members fired a maximum of only three or four training rounds each; even where units could practice live firing, results were frequently discouraging.[72] In other instances army personnel actually had to provide recently mobilized Volkssturm troops with both weapons and instruction in their use.[73]

Clothing the Volkssturm proved to be as thorny, complex, and intractable a problem as did arming it. With an eye on satisfying both the Hague Regulations and the German public, the NSDAP launched valiant efforts to provide each Volkssturm man with some type of uniform. Officials procured surplus garments from the Wehrmacht, police, Reichsbahn, border guards, Reichspost, SA, NSKK, RAD, SS, HJ, DAF, and any other conceivable source—even zookeepers and streetcar conductors![74] Captured foreign or obsolete German uniforms were also utilized.[75] As with weapons, however, available clothing stocks were inadequate. In part, this was simply the result of shortages and declining textile production, but it also resulted from the reluctance of officials to follow Himmler's and Bormann's orders to surrender their sometimes abundant clothing supplies.[76] Furthermore, Volkssturm men disliked brown Party uniforms because they feared anyone wearing them would be taken for a Soviet and shot by Germans or taken for a Nazi and shot by the Soviets.[77] In response, Bormann had ordered that all uniforms slated for Volkssturm use be dyed field gray, but insufficient factory capacity and dyestuff shortages ultimately rendered this impossible.[78]

Recognizing the inability of existing textile and garment production to meet Volkssturm clothing needs,[79] Nazi officials sought supplementary sources. The Party mobilized and funded independent craftsmen, the NS Women's Organization, and the League of German Girls in a substantial "home work" *(Heimarbeit)* effort to produce and repair leather and cloth items for Volkssturm use.[80] One enterprising battalion leader organized local shoemakers, tailors, blacksmiths, and harness workers to supply his unit, only to have his efforts thwarted by lack of raw materials.[81] To raise both clothing and a sense of community, the Party launched a national "People's Sacrifice" *(Volksopfer)* collection drive in January 1945.[82] A heavy propaganda barrage aimed specifically at encouraging donations from members of the police, the military, the Party and affiliates, and the families of men killed in action accompanied the campaign.[83] Indeed, the psychological and material response to the Volksopfer reportedly exceeded those of earlier collections.[84] Kreis Cologne gathered uniforms for 1,185 men, Siegkreis took in 701 uniforms and 499 army tunics, and Gau Bayreuth netted over 38,000 complete uniforms and 200,000 miscellaneous equipment items.[85] Success, however, was reduced by repair, cleaning, and distribution problems, and the Volksopfer ultimately fell well short of Volkssturm clothing needs.[86] Despite the numerous improvisations, many Volkssturm men served in civilian attire, in some instances even without armbands, paybooks, or identification tags.[87]

Volkssturm logistical problems also extended to other types of equipment. Motorized units, authorized to requisition privately owned trucks to augment their NSKK vehicles, could rarely get them because their owners—often with backing from the Reich Ministry for Armaments and War Production—cited pressing economic grounds for retaining them. Procuring fuel posed another common problem.[88] Furthermore, Wehrmacht units sometimes confiscated the civilian vehicles that the Volkssturm had successfully earmarked for its use.[89] Courier motorcycles also had to come from private owners, and many units launched efforts to procure—through requisitioning, donation, purchase, rental, or loan—bicycles as substitutes.[90] The Replacement Army promised wagons and horses, but there were never enough available, and few farmers willingly parted at any price with their remaining vehicles or animals.[91] Many active Volkssturm units lacked full field kitchens and had to resort to scavenging cookware and utensils from bomb-damaged buildings or procuring military and civilian supplies that could not be evacuated.[92] Shortages of medical and first aid items were also common.[93] Some officials even complained of insufficient propaganda materials, although thanks to Party funding, office supplies were generally adequate.[94] Overall the Volkssturm experienced shortages of virtually every necessity because of the strained war economy, transportation problems, and inadequate preparation.

There were, however, some individual exceptions to the generally poor state of Volkssturm unit training and equipment. The Johannisburg (East Prussia) Levy I Battalion was fairly well trained and fully armed with Italian rifles, forty-eight Russian light machine guns, 400 Panzerfäuste, six bazookas, and four light antitank guns.[95] More typically, all the members of a North Westphalian Volkssturm company entered service with uniforms and paybooks, but no Panzerfäuste, and only a few rifles, and no one had fired more than three practice rounds.[96] In other areas, Volkssturm units had neither sufficient equipment nor training. A Cologne battalion had only a handful of Danish and Italian rifles until it received a shipment of Panzerfäuste, but they were of limited use, since only the battalion leader knew how to operate them.[97] Although some Volkssturm units, due to the efforts of their commanders, Kreis officials, or local army units, were fairly well prepared when mobilized, the vast majority lacked proper training, weapons, uniforms, and equipment.

Volkssturm formations also suffered from low morale. Although the initial announcement of the Volkssturm's creation generally further depressed the public's already pessimistic outlook,[98] there were indications that the organization, given proper leadership and determination, had the potential for a degree of success. Some men did volunteer; for example, Kreis Ennepe-Ruhr reported 463 of them.[99] Furthermore, government and Party officials in areas from Westphalia and Baden to Stettin and the Sudetenland reported elements of strong support for the new organization.[100]

Part of this was due to a general improvement in morale during late 1944 that resulted from the stabilization of the German fronts and the Ardennes Counteroffensive. Furthermore, with the help of propaganda, public confidence in the Volkssturm increased slightly. Stories of the East Prussian Volkssturm's role in stopping Soviet offensives near Gumbinnen demonstrated the force's potential military value.[101] Also during the fall many units, some adequately equipped, began productive training.[102] Oath-taking ceremonies, the largest, most widespread of Volkssturm rallies, and other public events reportedly boosted morale and confidence for some (the majority, in fact, if contemporary reports are accurate), though not all.[103] Breslau's Propaganda Office even declared that the 20,000-man Volkssturm assembly and parade on October 19 was "the strongest morale-building moment in our Gau during the entire war."[104] Hoping to expand on these successes, Volkssturm units, accompanied by Party and Wehrmacht personnel, staged repeat performances in later regional and local rallies throughout Germany.[105] In fact, the Volkssturm became the primary focus of Kreis-level propaganda during late 1944.[106]

While large marches and rallies might provide visible demonstrations of the Volkssturm's size and strength and could boost members' morale and a sense of unity, indoctrination within each unit remained the key component of motivational efforts. Bormann instructed local officials to saturate each Volkssturm meeting with subtle propaganda explaining and demonstrating the Volksgemeinschaft's benefits and making clear the mortal peril posed by the Allies.[107] To accomplish this, unit commanders employed an array of methods generally borrowed from NSFO materials, the most common being brief lectures during Sunday training sessions and longer propaganda speeches and/ or films on weekday evenings. Some units staged rather popular *Bierabends* to build camaraderie.[108] Singing patriotic songs was another means used to heighten a sense of community.[109] During late 1944 and 1945, the Propaganda Ministry's weekly newsreel, *Deutsche Wochenschau*, frequently featured the Volkssturm in order to emphasize to all Germans the official version of its training, unity, and spirit.[110] Berger's staff, the Party Chancellery, and the Propaganda Ministry also devoted considerable attention to such motivational issues as procuring flags for all battalions, issuing lists of inspiring reading, and discussing (though never creating) special Volkssturm decorations for bravery.[111]

The basic aim of propaganda in the Volkssturm was to encourage fanaticism by explaining the National Socialist view of the war and the Volkssturm's role in winning it. A common theme was the "Jewish-International enemy" (in both Soviet and Anglo-American guises) and its plans to destroy not just the NSDAP but the entire German people.[112] In support of this claim, the Nazis publicized and exaggerated atrocities committed by Allied troops and portrayed how the Volkssturm, by forcing the Allies to fight for every foot of German soil, could convince the enemy to abandon its sinister designs.[113] This frequently involved highlighting the combat exploits of Party officials or individual Volkssturm men—such as Knight's Cross recipient battalion leader Ernst Tiburzy, who knocked out five Soviet tanks in Königsberg, or Hitler Youth Günther Nowak of Hindenburg (Upper Silesia), who reportedly destroyed nine—to show that leadership and individual bravery and fanaticism could master apparently hopeless situations.[114] Nazi propaganda also sought to appeal to traditional patriotism and to calm fears about legality by proclaiming the Volkssturm just another chapter in Germany's long militia tradition.[115] All this was not merely a cynical Nazi attempt to manipulate Germans into a desperate effort to prolong their hegemony; it was also a sincere effort to convince Germans that each one of them would suffer in defeat, and each and every one must do his or her utmost to prevent that fate.

Volkssturm propaganda generally not only failed but also often backfired. For example, atrocity stories tended to worsen fears that the Allies would execute Volkssturm prisoners.[116] Likewise, many people interpreted Nazi rhetoric about the Volkssturm fighting with all available weapons and methods as a call for a guerrilla struggle.[117] Others took the analogy between Napoleonic era militias and the Volkssturm too literally by believing that the latter would also be armed with swords, pikes, muskets, scythes, and pitchforks.[118] Public marches and rallies and films and photographs of Volkssturm units carrying weapons that in reality had only been temporarily borrowed for the sake of the camera seriously compromised the Party's dwindling credibility.[119] Similarly, NSDAP officials blatantly and knowingly lied when they assured Germans that the Volkssturm was issued captured weapons only for training purposes, and once mobilized for active duty, the men would receive German arms.[120]

Propaganda efforts based on lies or gross distortions were doomed to fail because everyone could see the reality of the Volkssturm for him- or herself; but not all motivational efforts miscarried. Organized and thorough training sessions, particularly those conducted with army participation, and receiving adequate weapons and uniforms proved the best tonics for Volkssturm morale. Reports evaluating unit leader training courses reveal that where the hosting army units seemed interested in helping the Volkssturm officers, participants' morale improved, and they frequently displayed genuine interest in learning about weapons use (particularly antitank weapons) and participating in practical training exercises. Furthermore, the positive attitude of these commanders tended to carry over to their unit's members once they returned home.[121] On the other hand, disorganized courses, apathetic instructors, and cold, shabby barracks typically generated pessimism among even previously enthusiastic Volkssturm commanders.[122]

Evidence suggests that many average Volkssturm men displayed a similar willingness, even eagerness, to participate in well-organized practical training.[123] In fact, one Berlin Volkssturm man took it upon himself to procure rifles and instructors from the Replacement Army when his unit leaders hesitated to commence weapons training.[124] The success of Freikorps Sauerland—which received top priority for equipment in Gau Westphalia-South—in raising fourteen new volunteer battalions after October 18 proved there were Germans willing to serve if properly armed and clothed.[125] Like their leaders, however, Volkssturm men expressed a distinct aversion to training sessions that were poorly led, overly theoretical, or seemed to waste their time.[126] More detrimental still was the inability to provide units with adequate quantities of weapons, which propaganda officials quickly and perceptively noted was the key to improving and maintaining Volkssturm morale.[127]

By mid-January, with the Eastern Front crumbling and the Ardennes Offensive collapsed, morale began a steep, permanent decline. Confidence in the Volkssturm particularly faltered as it became apparent that, contrary to Nazi promises, all German men were not shouldering an equal burden of service. Workers often grumbled that while they wasted their last hours of free time at often pointless Volkssturm meetings, their bosses used economic excuses to avoid duty altogether.[128] Some older Volkssturm men and their wives argued that young RAD, Wehrmacht, or Organisation Todt men in rear-echelon jobs should be sent to the front before their grandfathers were.[129] Volkssturm men commonly expressed a preference to serve, if they must, in the Wehrmacht because they simply had no faith in the ability of the local Party bosses (whom they also frequently accused of shirking Volkssturm duties) or their unit leaders.[130] The Levy System, its abuses, and the sloth and selfishness of many Party officials meant Volkssturm unity remained only a mythical ideal.

Even more detrimental to morale was the growing realization that the Party had lied about its ability to arm and equip the Volkssturm. A direct, intimate, and crucial connection existed between a Volkssturm unit's logistical situation and its morale—the longer a unit went without weapons and clothing in quantities sufficient for training purposes, the lower morale fell. Many units had only a few old weapons and little ammunition; and Nazi propaganda notwithstanding, Volkssturm members knew that they could neither train nor fight unarmed.[131] Furthermore, the lack of suitable uniforms and shoes or boots also caused morale to plummet as fast as the temperatures. Clothing and footwear were scarce for civilians, and most men, particularly in cities, were unwilling to ruin what they had by crawling around in the mud or snow at Volkssturm training. They were even less enthused by the prospect of serving on active duty in civilian attire and risking being viewed as partisans.[132] Volkssturm men also resented that elite Nazi units (for example, SA or NSKK formations) received better equipment than did regular personnel.[133] Under these conditions, Volkssturm units' public appearances began to highlight the stark contrast between the propaganda image and reality.[134]

Nazi propaganda did ultimately become slightly more realistic in 1945 as it began stressing the Volksopfer's success or the efficacy of the Panzerfaust, the one weapon units had in adequate numbers.[135] Nonetheless, the initial willingness of some Volkssturm men to train and fight disintegrated—except in isolated instances[136]—as they realized they would never be trained, armed, or equipped properly, even though they would be expected to fight as if they were. This attitude was impervious to propaganda and could only be altered by something the Third Reich, particularly the NSDAP, could not provide: adequate equipment and weapons for all Volkssturm units, both active and in training.

Complaining about Levy assignments or equipment shortages may have been a safe way to express more deeply rooted opposition, but most disgruntled members expressed low morale only passively—typically in the form of absenteeism, which became rampant by early 1945. For example, one Munich company leader reported that on any given Sunday, 30 to 50 percent of his men would be absent without proper excuses.[137] Many men indeed worked Sundays, and legitimate requests for releasing them from training were common, but significant numbers of men abused the situation to avoid duties they considered pointless.[138] Other Volkssturm men feigned sickness or exaggerated the extent of their illnesses to avoid weekly training.[139] As absenteeism grew, chances of motivating or training the Volkssturm declined sharply.

Other Germans expressed their lack of confidence in the Volkssturm through humor. In one joke a company leader discovers that so many of his men were absent from training because "some are at confirmation class, the rest are collecting their pensions." Others combined disdain for endless reports of secret weapons with opinions on the Volkssturm: the latest miracle weapon was a supersensitive listening device for all German cemeteries. If it detected any slight breathing, the corpse would be exhumed and enrolled in the local Volkssturm. Also in this genre was the quip that all now knew what the V-2 and V-3 were—the V-2s were sixteen-year-old Volkssturmers, and the V-3s were the sixty-year-olds.[140]

While many Germans expressed their dissatisfaction with the Volkssturm by quietly avoiding duty or by ridiculing the force in private, very few undertook open opposition. In other words, while mood *(Stimmung)* might be poor, behavior *(Haltung)* remained acceptably obedient, with only isolated exceptions. Officials expressed concern that leftist or Alsatian Volkssturm men might use their weapons against the Germans, but little came of this.[141] Austrian resistance groups infiltrated Volkssturm units, and a few actually fought against Germans troops in the war's last days.[142] Within Germany proper, anti-Volkssturm posters and/or pamphlets turned up in Zwiesel, Aurich, Anzing (Kreis Ebersberg), Munich, and elsewhere.[143] In certain areas, a few individuals sought to encourage others to avoid Volkssturm duty.[144] Some Volkssturm unit leaders collaborated with resistance officials in sabotaging their town's defense plans; but by and large, active resistance within the Volkssturm proved atypical and insignificant.[145] For example, while resistance fighters of the so-called *Freiheitsaktion Bayern* within Munich and Penzburg Volkssturm units participated in local uprisings against Nazi control on April 28, 1945, other Volkssturm men remained loyal to the Nazi regime and fought against them.[146]

On the whole, the Volkssturm did not attain its goal of motivating Germans to fight fanatically, a colossal failure for an organization whose success was predicated on making Germans want to bear arms. Indeed, it seems that at least during November and December there existed a significant core of men willing to serve in the Volkssturm, if it could be properly equipped. It might have made more sense to identify these men and build Volkssturm combat units from them; this certainly would have been more feasible from a logistical standpoint. Where the Nazis made their mistake was in believing that speeches, rallies, songs, and other propaganda alone could improve morale, and that outfitting a nationwide local defense force could be improvised at a time when the regular army suffered serious shortages of basic equipment and industrial production was declining.

Furthermore, the propaganda designed to fanaticize Volkssturm men was hardly new, and much actually proved counterproductive. Nazi leaders failed to realize that the best way to raise Volkssturm morale was to provide its members with proper military training, weapons, equipment, and—particularly as winter weather worsened—uniforms and footwear. No kind or amount of propaganda could alter the fact that unarmed men, regardless of their fanaticism, could not stop the Allied armies. The clumsy efforts and blatant lies aimed at hiding the Volkssturm's inadequate armament frequently destroyed any remaining trust average men had in the NSDAP.

As the Party's Volkssturm officials, particularly at lower levels, found themselves confronted with insurmountable logistical and training problems, they increasingly turned to the Wehrmacht for aid. This assistance carried an unanticipated cost, however, for although the Wehrmacht never posed a threat to NSDAP political control, it did come to dominate Volkssturm military issues. Through its ability to equip, clothe, and train at least a portion—though certainly not all—of the units, the army also controlled the only means of improving a Volkssturm man's fighting spirit. Ironically given Bormann and associates' assumptions, it was ultimately the Wehrmacht, not the NSDAP, that held the key to making the Volkssturm succeed in both its military and motivational roles. Therefore, from an objective viewpoint, enhancing the Wehrmacht's, and reducing the NSDAP's, role in organizing and preparing the Volkssturm would have been sensible.

Bormann and other Nazis apparently never realized this, nor did they recognize how they had unwittingly created this situation by altering the Volkssturm's intended nature when they decided to make it a legal militia. Originally their aim was to create a fanatic people's militia, fighting obediently under NSDAP leadership. This required restoring the public's will by indoctrinating all German civilian men through the Volkssturm; however, achieving this first required overcoming doubts about the Volkssturm's legality. By structuring Volkssturm training and equipment (as well as organization, duties, chain of command, and legal system) along standard military lines, the NSDAP partially overcame public trepidation but also unintentionally transformed the force into a traditional militia.

Furthermore, the decision to make the Volkssturm a legal militia ultimately caused Party motivational efforts to miscarry, largely due to logistical issues. The average German quickly recognized that the NSDAP was woefully unprepared to lead and equip its new creation. On the other hand, all could plainly see that the Wehrmacht was in a much better position to make a legal militia work, insofar as that was possible in late 1944. As a result, Germans came to credit Wehrmacht involvement for any Volkssturm successes and to blame the NSDAP for the many failures. Rather than building widespread support for the Nazi regime, the ill-equipped, ill-trained Volkssturm considerably weakened it.

CHAPTER EIGHT

Defending the Reich's Eastern Front

Most assessments of Volkssturm combat performance have focused on the militia's frequent failures; but the record was not entirely negative, particularly on the Eastern Front. Explaining why units succeeded in some areas but failed miserably in many others is critical to a full understanding of the force. This involves assessing military factors such as preparation, logistics, or intelligence, as well as circumstances or simple luck, good or bad. Overall, however, the most important elements contributing to a Volkssturm unit's success or failure were its members' morale and the degree of support it received from the Wehrmacht prior to and during combat.

In the east, the Volkssturm largely served as Guderian's *Landsturm* would have, that is, an auxiliary performing whatever duties the Wehrmacht assigned it. In this role, the Volkssturm handled a wide range of seemingly mundane tasks (some of which were quite dangerous) designed to release field army and Replacement Army troops for other purposes. The most common was constructing fortifications both purely locally and on a regional scale, often in conjunction with POWs, foreign workers, or other nonmilitary personnel.[1] The army also frequently employed Volkssturm men as a convenient source of labor for logistical or other rear-echelon tasks.[2] In some areas, particularly East Prussia and Wartheland, Volkssturm personnel assisted evacuations by escorting refugees or removing economically valuable goods from endangered areas.[3] The Volkssturm also proved useful as a police auxiliary to round up downed airmen, track infiltrators and spies, and fight partisans. Although the feared mass uprisings of foreign workers never materialized, Volkssturm men did assist in keeping check on them. The militia also guarded POWs and located escapees of all types.[4] Units also helped catch deserters, guarded key installations against sabotage, and patrolled evacuated areas.[5]

While such duties helped the war effort, the Volkssturm's primary function was combat, particularly local defense. On the Eastern Front from October to January, however, Volkssturm troops chiefly performed security occupation duties in the area's extensive fortification zones—precisely the task Guderian had originally proposed for his Landsturm. With the Soviet winter offensive's onset in mid-January, Volkssturm units continued in this role but increasingly fought in their local defense capacity as well. Once the German front stabilized on the Oder and Neisse Rivers, and in the isolated Fortress cities *(Festungen)* all over eastern Germany, the Wehrmacht came to rely more and more on the Volkssturm and other ad hoc units to substitute for its depleted infantry battalions—even in the front lines—something for which the force was neither intended nor prepared. In essence, the Wehrmacht utilized the Volkssturm on the Eastern Front however it saw fit both at the front and in the rear, much as it employed its Landesschützen or other low-quality infantry units.

The Volkssturm's baptism of fire came in East Prussia, where fanatic Gauleiter Koch had energetically begun raising units in September to secure the extensive fortified zones constructed during the previous summer by the People's Levy. On October 7 at Memel, the Volkssturm's first battle confirmed the force's potential in this security occupation role. Here, two lightly armed companies clad only in civilian clothes with green armbands took heavy casualties, but they helped hold Memel's defensive perimeter against weak Soviet probes until regular troops arrived to stabilize the front.[6] This first action showed that even ill-prepared Volkssturm units could hold fortified positions until relieved by regular troops and thus boosted confidence in the militia's capability as a security occupation force.

The East Prussian Volkssturm further demonstrated its potential when a Red Army thrust began on October 16 and temporarily captured Goldap and Ebensrode. In the push, Soviet troops mauled at least four of the twenty-two poorly equipped and largely unsupervised (i.e., Party-controlled, not army-controlled) Volkssturm battalions on duty here. Other units, however, fought adequately around Treuburg, Gumbinnen, and along the Angerapp River. Their bitter holding action helped sap Soviet momentum and bought time until German mobile reserves could arrive.[7] After the enemy offensive was halted, Volkssturm units remained in the front, enabling Fourth Army to muster its reserves for a successful counterattack that restored the front to its previous position.[8] Overall, the army rated Volkssturm performance as adequate, despite its high casualties.[9]

These apparent Volkssturm successes prompted both OKH and the NSDAP to expand the militia's role in eastern Germany's fortified areas. Koch mobilized an additional eighty-five Levy I combat and labor (i.e., armed and unarmed, respectively) battalions and instructed all remaining formations to prepare for local defense.[10] Although Koch feared that military influence would undermine his personal authority and the Volkssturm's spirit, many of his subordinates, including some in the Gauleitung and most—though not all—Kreisleiters and unit leaders, welcomed greater Wehrmacht involvement.[11] And generally, the Wehrmacht was plainly anxious to become more involved with the Volkssturm in the east.

During November, Wehrmacht-Volkssturm relations improved as army units in East Prussia began establishing liaisons with Kreisleiters, ascertaining the exact strength and dispositions of Volkssturm units, improving the militia's tactical deployments, and incorporating them into the army's defense plans and chain of command. They also worked to coordinate and direct construction and occupation of fortifications and to improve Volkssturm training, logistical arrangements, and armament.[12] Greater use of Volkssturm personnel freed regulars from such duties as maintaining security patrols and coastal watches, guarding bridges wired for demolition, harvesting crops, escorting refugee columns, and evacuating foodstuffs and other valuable goods.[13] To boost morale, the Party and the Wehrmacht integrated active militia units into the military postal system and opened rest and recreation centers for them.[14] By the end of 1944, army and corps commanders had full tactical and logistical control of every Volkssturm battalion engaged in eastern security occupations; in many instances, they had stationed regular troops nearby to provide control and support.[15] By December, army officers believed that, despite persistent deficiencies in equipment, training, and coordination, "the Volkssturm was actually in condition to support local defense" and had helped AOK 4 expand its reserves.[16]

Army interest in the Volkssturm was not confined to East Prussia. As mentioned earlier, Guderian even unsuccessfully attempted to gain control over the entire eastern Volkssturm, but he nonetheless found the Party leaders generally imposed no real restrictions on his use of the militia. Guderian gained authorization to mobilize substantial numbers of battalions for large-scale security occupations in Austria, Silesia, Pomerania, Danzig-West Prussia, and Wartheland, as well as in East Prussia. He even secured permission to enlist suitable Volkssturm personnel into new army fortress artillery batteries.[17] By mid-January, at least 176 Levy I combat battalions (plus several labor units and special mobile squadrons)—around 90,000 men—manned fortified rear-area positions all over the eastern Reich. Supporting them were either regular formations (mainly in East Prussia, the only Gau then directly on the fighting front) or "Gneisenau" units—police and infantry, artillery, and mechanized instructional units from the region's Wehrkreise.[18] Furthermore, numerous inactive Volkssturm units stood in varying degrees of readiness to defend their hometowns.

The Soviets' successful winter offensive—launched on January 13, 1945—clearly exposed Volkssturm deficiencies in the security occupation role.[19] Although some units were adequately prepared and fought vigorously, the fortified positions did little to slow the Red Army's mechanized advance except in parts of East Prussia. Moreover, Volkssturm casualty rates ran as high as 70 to 80 percent.[20] Some formations panicked, fled, or were shattered by enemy attacks.[21] Soviet progress frequently outflanked defenses, as in Pomerania, where the Red Army surprised and mauled many of the sixty hastily prepared Volkssturm battalions there by taking them in the flank and rear.[22] Similarly, Soviet attacks in March overran Volkssturm units in Austrian border fortifications and—isolated acts of bravery notwithstanding—quickly collapsed the position.[23]

On the other hand, Volkssturm formations fought hard and successfully at Deutsch Eylau, Labiau, Herndorf, and Faulhöden and along the Deime and Pregel Rivers.[24] Volkssturm units also effectively held quieter areas of the front, which freed regulars to launch counterattacks elsewhere.[25] Volkssturm troops themselves even participated in small, successful tactical offensives, including a daring motorized raid led by Königsberg's Kreisleiter that recaptured Neuhausen airfield.[26] The East Prussian Volkssturm's success, however, came at a tremendous price—its members constitute nearly a quarter of all Volkssturm MIAs—and in spite of their best efforts the Wehrmacht could only hold several isolated pockets, the largest around Königsberg.

As the Soviet winter offensive swept westward, more and more Volkssturm units came into action in a local defense role, their raison d'être. Bormann had always envisioned Volkssturm units stanching enemy mechanized exploitations by turning every city or crossroads village into a fanatically defended fortress. Indeed, eastern German units had begun defensive preparations at varying levels of intensity throughout late 1944. Getting units organized, equipped, and trained formed a major part of this effort, as did establishing Armor Warning Services *(Panzerwarndienste)*. These were networks of observation and communication posts designed to alert all rear-area forces to the enemy's approach. Volkssturm troops had also begun constructing and manning local defense fortifications, mainly roadblocks, trenches, and antitank ditches.[27] Some local military, Party, and Volkssturm officials also established liaisons to coordinate all defense efforts and to include all available troops in comprehensive regional defense plans.[28] In some areas, particularly in Gau Mark Brandenburg, Volkssturm units moved to maximize their combat potential by assigning adequately trained men to armed battle groups and putting the others in work detachments.[29]

Despite the effort, local defense preparations in eastern Germany generally proved inadequate. Where unsupported Volkssturm units faced the Soviets, as frequently happened in smaller towns and rural areas, chances for successful defense were virtually nil. Volkssturm men resented being sacrificed as rear guards for retreating regulars and often either went home or followed the army out of town.[30] In unevacuated areas, many Volkssturm men refused to deploy for battle and instead escorted their families westward.[31] Unsupported, poorly trained, ill-equipped Volkssturm units, often defending incomplete or poorly placed and badly constructed positions, quickly disintegrated—especially if surprised—under Soviet attack. Even when Volkssturm men put up a determined resistance, as happened at Hindenburg (Upper Silesia), they could not protect their flanks. Volkssturm units also could not fight long without army combat and logistical backing, nor could they typically retreat as coherent units.[32]

There were, however, exceptions to the Volkssturm's general failure in local defense. The Nakel (West Prussia) unit held at the Netze River long enough to enable townsfolk to evacuate safely.[33] Similarly, Volkssturm resistance in Rosenberg (Upper Silesia) enabled refugee columns to cross the Oder and to buy time for Wehrkreis VIII to reinforce its defenses at the river.[34] At Bahn, Bublitz, Fiddichow (all in Pomerania), Forst (Brandenburg), and Fürstenfeld (Austria), fierce if brief Volkssturm resistance stopped Red Army advances long enough for nearby regulars to form new defensive lines.[35]

The best example of Volkssturm local defense success occurred in Pyritz in southwestern Pomerania. Just before dawn on February 2, Pyritz's Volkssturm Battalion II, an HJ antitank team, and an antiaircraft battery rebuffed the weak vanguard of the 12th Guards Tank Corps. Regrouping and calling in air and artillery support, the 12th Guards mounted a ferocious combined-arms assault supported by up to eighty tanks. The Germans initially lost two-thirds of Pyritz, but they successfully counterattacked and, reinforced on February 4 by a battalion-sized alarm unit, held the Soviets at bay until the 4th SS Police Division arrived on February 7. During this battle, the Pyritz force—commanded by a Luftwaffe colonel named Weiss—destroyed at least twenty Soviet tanks and inflicted heavy casualties. This victory enabled the Germans to build a new defensive line, preserve land contact with eastern Pomerania, and strengthen defenses along the lower Oder and helped buy time to prepare a counteroffensive called Operation *Sonnenwende* (which was ultimately unsuccessful).[36]

Relatively effective Volkssturm combat performances also occurred in the cities designated Fortresses. The German command intended these fortified cities to hold out even if surrounded in order to increase the enemy's casualties, tie down his troops, deny him convenient lines of communication and supply, anchor new defensive lines, and—once cut off—serve as bases of operations in the enemy's rear.[37] In Fortresses, the Volkssturm's initial assignment combined local defense and security occupation by supporting available military and police units in preventing a Soviet coup de main. As a siege progressed, the Volkssturm typically grew in importance as an infantry combat force and labor pool. Once surrounded, everyone in the Fortress came under military command, and the Volkssturm became the only significant source of replacements.[38] Therefore, successful Fortress defense depended on the commander's determination (Nazis tended to stress this as the only factor that mattered), thorough logistical preparations, close party-army cooperation, and full utilization of the Volkssturm.

The most significant Volkssturm contribution to Fortress defense occurred in Breslau.[39] There Volkssturm battalions, a third of the city's original garrison, and a substantial portion of its artillery crews helped blunt initial Soviet probes in late January and remained in the front lines until the siege ended on May 6. Here NSDAP-Wehrmacht relations, though initially rocky, improved dramatically over time, due largely to the desperate situation and Breslau's cooperative Kreisstabsführer, SA Obergruppenführer Otto Herzog, himself a former army officer.[40] Party-army collaboration yielded significant benefits for Breslau's Volkssturm. With a clearly delineated chain of command, Volkssturm battalions came under direct supervision and control of Wehrmacht officers, which boosted the militia's combat value. Also to maximize their potential, the army often assigned Volkssturm units to relatively quiet sectors or left them near their homes (as per the Party's basic organizational principle) to take advantage of the men's familiarity with the area. Furthermore, the military supported and supplied Volkssturm units relatively well and expended considerable effort to improve their training, even establishing a special instructional battalion for this purpose.

Herzog also deviated from standard Volkssturm policy in the pursuit of improved combat effectiveness. He allowed the army to help screen unit leaders for competence. As a result, Volkssturm battalion leader quality improved to the point that some were even entrusted with commanding regular troops. Also violating standard policy, Herzog reassigned Breslau's 15,000 Volkssturm men according to their military training and fitness. Older and less fit men served in the ten construction battalions, which did yeoman service in building defenses, maintaining communications, and running the supply system. Younger, healthier, and better-trained men filled the twenty-six combat (including two HJ) battalions, which often performed well even in complicated street-fighting situations. Ultimately, the extensive army backing helped ensure that Volkssturm morale, though shaken by Soviet attacks in early April, never collapsed; and Breslau's Volkssturm units generally fought well throughout the siege.[41]

Although Breslau provided the clearest example,[42] Volkssturm successes occurred in other Fortress cities. Königsberg's battalions distinguished themselves, some even participating in the crucial offensive actions in Metgethen and Samland aimed at keeping the port open. Other units handled thankless but essential rear-area duties.[43] The Volkssturm contingent in the Pomeranian port city of Kolberg fought well during early March despite suffering nearly 60 percent casualties.[44] Volkssturm resistance in Fortresses Danzig, Gotenhafen, Thorn, Schneidemühl, Graudenz, Glogau, Frankfurt am Oder, and Küstrin also merited positive comments.[45] Finally, substantial numbers of Volkssturm men served well in several Fortresses' artillery units, most notably at Elbing near Danzig.[46]

Increased utilization of Volkssturm men in Fortresses foreshadowed a growing reliance on the force all along the Eastern Front. While continuing to perform rear-area tasks, security occupations, and local defense, Volkssturm formations increasingly served as frontline infantry in 1945. Depleted army formations regularly cannibalized Volkssturm units, using the fit men to replenish their ranks and employing the remainder as labor.[47] This posed a threat to Volkssturm autonomy and identity, and Bormann reacted by forbidding the practice, although it apparently continued. He did allow induction of Volkssturm men who met standards on age, health, and occupation so long as their home and workplace had been overrun by the enemy. Bormann also authorized allotting limited numbers of Volkssturm men to flesh out training cadres in newly formed "Cadet" regiments.[48]

Bormann also authorized using a limited number of Volkssturm battalions outside their home Gau.[49] The primary example of this came in mid-January when Berger ordered each of the nineteen Gaue then not on the front lines to dispatch a Volkssturm special purpose battalion to reinforce defenses in Wartheland, particularly Fortress Posen. Gaue Berlin and Brandenburg also sent units.[50] Hastily mobilized, ill prepared, and following vague orders unsuited to the very fluid situation, the first special purpose units were simply consumed in the maelstrom. For example, near Zielenzig, advancing Soviet armor surprised and annihilated three such units while they were still in their troop trains.[51]

Special purpose battalions arriving in early February, however, played an important part, along with local Volkssturm units, in stabilizing the Eastern Front along the Oder and Neisse Rivers. Despite Ninth Army commander General Theodor Busse's postwar claims to the contrary,[52] documents show Volkssturm units served extensively as frontline infantry. In early February, Volkssturm members constituted half of Ninth Army's 52,000 men; and Army Group Vistula reported at least forty-seven Volkssturm battalions on combat duty.[53] These units' exact deployments are also significant. XL Panzer Corps' February 7 situation map shows at least fourteen—of its seventeen total—Volkssturm battalions in the front lines. Two even held a small bridgehead on the Oder's east bank at Crossen, the corps' most exposed position. Other frontline formations consisted mainly of alarm units, police, Replacement Army, and other stopgap infantry; regular units formed tactical reserves just behind the front.[54] Similarly, on March 23, Army Group Vistula—then reportedly withdrawing and demobilizing Volkssturm units—still listed at least twenty-one of twenty-eight total Volkssturm battalions holding a wide variety of the most forward positions and representing approximately one-fifth of the Army Group's frontline units. The other 80 percent still consisted of such low-quality infantry as flak crews without guns, police, and alarm units and Replacement Army units. Again regular formations remained in tactical reserve.[55]

Volkssturm—and other substitute infantry—units faced a difficult task on the Oder. Lacking infantry training, mobility, experience, firepower, fitness, and communications, and occupying substantial defensive frontages (up to eight kilometers), Oder Volkssturm units relied on the costly tactic of pinning down Soviet patrols with infantry weapons—often only small arms—and then counterattacking with all available men.[56] Realistically, all they could hope to achieve was to block weak probes, delay and channel more substantial attacks until the regular army units held in tactical reserve could react, and provide a covering screen if conditions necessitated withdrawal.

Not surprisingly, many Volkssturm units proved inadequate in this role, but some fought well.[57] Volkssturm units helped contain Soviet bridgeheads at Lauban and Kienitz until reserves counterattacked and restored the front.[58] Volkssturm special purpose battalions from Schleswig-Holstein, Mainfranken, Hessen-Nassau, Franconia, and Hamburg reportedly did excellent work, even conducting successful reconnaissance missions behind Soviet lines. Units near Frankfurt am Oder even took part in at least one limited counterattack.[59] Armed and trained under OKH supervision, thirty-two Brandenburg battalions mobilized on February 9 and repelled heavy Soviet attacks at Forst and Guben ten days later. With army reinforcements, they defended the Neisse River for two months.[60] In every case these units served under the control and supervision of regular units, which provided the Volkssturm with the instructional, logistical, tactical, and command support essential to battlefield success.[61]

Wehrmacht reliance on the Volkssturm as substitute infantry increased still further after the massive Soviet offensive against the Oder-Neisse position began on April 16. Volkssturm units here often fought bravely and inflicted heavy losses on the Soviet attackers, but they could not hold due to the Germans' lack of reserves.[62] Intent on keeping the Soviets as far east as possible, Hitler authorized sending Berlin Volkssturm battalions and some 6,000 boys in HJ antitank teams as reinforcements to defend the Seelow Heights and other positions behind the Oder. Although fierce fighting here generated heavy casualties for both sides, these improvisations only delayed but could not halt the Soviets.[63] Furthermore, much like their special purpose battalion comrades at Zielenzig, many hastily dispatched Volkssturm units were dispersed by air attacks (against which they had no protection) or quickly overrun before they reached their assigned positions.[64]

The decision to fight at the Oder also upset Berlin's defense preparations to some extent.[65] The Berlin Volkssturm not only lost a substantial proportion of its better-equipped battalions, but Hitler also required it to turn over weapons to help arm thirty battalions of Luftwaffe and naval personnel.[66] In spite of these reductions, Volkssturm units still constituted about half of Berlin's defense force; but what remained were generally poorly trained and ill equipped.[67] In fact, one officer reported his zone's Volkssturm units had fifteen different rifle and ten different machine gun models.[68]

On the positive side, however, army-Volkssturm relations in Berlin had been largely cordial since defense preparations commenced in late January.[69] Since then, Party-army efforts had improved fortification construction efforts, logistical arrangements, and Volkssturm unit and leader training—particularly in antitank and street-fighting tactics.[70] As in Breslau, the Party and army had reorganized units to create battleworthy formations, scrutinized unit leader appointees for competence, replaced those found lacking with able former officers, and attempted to assign men to familiar geographic areas.[71] Some units also received a stiffening of police to increase their combat potential.[72] Wehrkreis officials even sought to ensure that rear-echelon soldiers treated Volkssturm men respectfully.[73] These efforts led Berlin's military commanders to report on April 15 that the Volkssturm was willing and somewhat able to fight.[74]

Several Berlin Volkssturm battalions did indeed contribute to the city's bitter, if futile, defense by holding the Teltow Canal, protecting quiet sectors, and ambushing Soviet reconnaissance patrols and in street fighting.[75] As always, however, Volkssturm units were brittle and usually poorly supplied, frequently reduced to procuring essential items by scavenging the battlefield, looting warehouses, or begging from sympathetic civilians.[76] Many Volkssturm men recognized the futility of the struggle and either never reported for duty or threw away their armbands, paybooks, and equipment (if indeed they had any) and went home when they tired of fighting or ran out of ammunition or other necessary supplies.[77]

Hitler Youth military exploits in Berlin—and indeed throughout Germany—have been highly publicized, overshadowing the fact that they were only a fraction of the capital's substantial Volkssturm contingent. The fanatic HJ defense of the Pickelsdorfer bridges over the Havel did delay Soviet encirclement of the city for two days and was one of the most important Volkssturm successes in Berlin. HJ forces also fought, primarily in antitank teams, in other areas of Berlin and in the defenses west of the Oder.[78] Similarly, an HJ antitank unit was instrumental at Pyritz, and the two Breslau HJ battalions were among the Fortress's most effective troops.[79] Viennese HJ units also performed well, even launching successful counterattacks.[80] HJ boys saw action in other locations, although not all fought fanatically or even well.[81] However, according to MIA lists, Levy III accounted for only 3.22 percent (188 of 5,835) of the sample of eastern Volkssturm MIAs, indicating that—as per official policy—eastern HJ units were generally kept out of combat whenever possible until the war's final battles.[82]

For its minimal strategic contributions to eastern Germany's defense, the Volkssturm paid an extremely high price. There are no reliable statistics on total Volkssturm casualties, but 30,390 Volkssturm men were listed by the Red Cross as MIAs on the Eastern Front (Table 27 in the appendix has a breakdown by Gau). Also, U.S. intelligence sources estimated casualty rates for Volkssturm units often ran about 35 percent killed and wounded; about 20 percent were missing.[83] Specific units' statistics confirm the heavy casualty rates: a 900-man Küstrin contingent lost all but 118 members in two months, while a 600-man Goldap battalion lost half its complement in one week.[84] High casualties resulted from inherent weaknesses but also from the fact that the

Soviets considered Volkssturm units easy targets and often chose to attack them. Whatever the rates or reasons, heavy Volkssturm losses certainly depressed civilian morale.[85]

Although every Volkssturm unit's experiences differed, some common factors help explain why certain units succeeded in combat when the vast majority failed. The ingredients most critical to Volkssturm success were proper cooperation and coordination between Volkssturm, NSDAP, and Wehrmacht officials both prior to and during battle, and adequate morale among the members themselves. Where these conditions existed, the Volkssturm occasionally succeeded; where they did not, it invariably failed.

Frequently, the blame for poor cooperation is laid at the feet of NSDAP officials who jealously guarded their powers. Indeed, this was a problem even into the final days of the war despite mounting evidence that Volkssturm success required extensive Wehrmacht involvement.[86] Even in East Prussia, where NSDAP-army relations were good at the Kreis level, obstinately uncooperative Gauleiter Erich Koch insisted on shifting units without consulting or informing the army.[87] In areas not directly on the front lines, Party officials possessed considerable control over defensive preparations, and many protected their Volkssturm powers tenaciously.[88] In the General Government, where the SS and police controlled the Volkssturm, the Wehrkreis did not receive strength and armament reports on the militia until January 17, at which time some units were already under attack![89] In part, Nazi officials were simply reluctant to give up the only military force under their control, but many distrusted the officer corps and viewed army influence as a threat to their plans to fanaticize Volkssturm members. Ironically, however, Party efforts to restrict Wehrmacht involvement were doubly counterproductive, hurting both military preparation and morale.

A portion of the blame, however, for poor Volkssturm-army cooperation must also fall on the Wehrmacht. Some field army officers' tentativeness about using the militia resulted in Volkssturm units receiving confusing or conflicting orders or being left dangerously uninformed about the battlefield movements of both friendly and hostile troops.[90] Worse still for the Volkssturm, the Wehrkreise typically emphasized maintaining training schedules over preparing defenses.[91] Poor liaison resulted in Wehrkreise VIII (Silesia) and XXI (Wartheland), for example, relying heavily on Volkssturm units in their contingency plans despite lacking knowledge of their armament, strength, or capabilities. Such ignorance frequently resulted in officers assigning Volkssturm troops unrealistic tasks; for example, Wartheland battalions in the B-1 Position defended—with limited support—fronts averaging *twenty-four kilometers* apiece.[92] In such poorly backed static positions, a Volkssturm unit might hold but still be destroyed because the unit on its flank collapsed, as happened with Battalion Braunsberg II at Ebersbach,[93] or because its flanks were never covered, as at Hindenburg. Furthermore, Volkssturm formations, untrained in open warfare and withdrawal techniques, often disintegrated if forced to retreat.[94]

Repercussions of poor planning and inadequate NSDAP-Wehrmacht coordination manifested themselves in other ways. Weapons shortages plagued most Volkssturm units, particularly those mobilized hastily under emergency conditions.[95] Some units had adequate Panzerfaust supplies but lacked the firepower needed to deal with the infantry that accompanied Soviet armor.[96] Ammunition shortages, exacerbated by the bewildering variety of foreign weapons issued to the Volkssturm, were endemic, and resupply was virtually impossible in combat.[97] The Wehrmacht armed some units adequately upon mobilization, usually with foreign weapons, but the men then had to be trained in their use and maintenance literally while marching to their positions. Panzerfaust accidents resulting from poor training also proved common in Volkssturm units.[98] Finally, the Volkssturm often received inferior supplies, as illustrated by the newly activated battalion that found, to its horror, that its recently issued machine gun ammunition and hand grenades were mere blanks.[99]

Other logistical problems and shortages generated by poor Party and army preparations also negatively affected combat performance. The inadequate clothing and footwear of many Volkssturm troops seriously threatened health and morale in the bitter winter weather, particularly for older men.[100] Volkssturm units often lacked field kitchens and had to rely on immobile cooking facilities in nearby towns, which made victualing extremely difficult in combat and impossible in withdrawals. In fact, many Volkssturm battalions received much of their sustenance from charity or foraging.[101]

Another Volkssturm deficiency was its lack of intelligence-gathering and communications capability. Early warning of the Red Army's approach was crucial to mobilization, but rapid Soviet advances often disrupted the civilian telephone network, the Volkssturm's primary communications tool.[102] Frequently, Red Army soldiers reached positions before their defenders did, which enabled the Soviets to surprise the unfortunate Volkssturm units in the open and destroy them. The unanticipated arrival of Soviet forces could prevent bridge demolitions or the closing of roadblocks or otherwise disrupt carefully orchestrated mobilization plans and defensive tactics.[103] Lacking solid information on enemy whereabouts, Volkssturm units frequently panicked and dissolved or stuck rigidly to orders that directed them either into the teeth of the Soviet assault or into untenable or tactically useless positions.

Geography complicated mobilization as well. Rural battalions gathered members from a wide area, which not only meant slow assembly but also transformed local defense into the less than inspiring task of protecting a town miles away from one's own village and farm. Furthermore, shifting some units outside their Kreis or even Gau also complicated mobilization and further violated the official Volkssturm spirit, which postulated that Germans—and especially farmers—would fight better if they were defending their own turf.[104]

The Volkssturm also suffered from weaknesses inherent in all militias: relatively small units, poor training, aged personnel, inexperienced leaders, low firepower, and limited resources. Alone, Volkssturm units, lacking communications and intelligence-gathering ability, were virtually blind on the battlefield; and the Soviets could always outflank, surround, and destroy unsupported units. Only the army could provide the weapons, supplies, training, coordination, and guidance required to make a unit battleworthy. Most important, only the army could provide the command, logistical, and combat support that Volkssturm units needed to fight effectively. Even Hitler recognized Volkssturm units' brittleness; after the January disasters, he ordered them used in conjunction with regular troops whenever possible.[105]

Close cooperation with the army did not guarantee success but could improve its chances. Wehrmacht commanders and troops in East Prussia, Pyritz, Breslau, and elsewhere worked to recognize the specific capabilities and weaknesses of attached Volkssturm units and to tailor their assignments accordingly. Being under a regular unit's supervision provided Volkssturm commanders with guidance, access to heavy weapons, logistical support, communications equipment, and battlefield intelligence, none of which a Volkssturm unit could provide for itself. The Wehrmacht also furnished much-needed training, which—coupled with the other forms of assistance—boosted confidence and morale. Most important, as evident from the battle at Pyritz, the military had to provide reserves to support, reinforce, and relieve any Volkssturm unit that successfully resisted.

Relatively functional Wehrmacht-Volkssturm relations existed in the east largely because of the army's desperate need for additional manpower there. Guderian and subordinates concluded, given Hitler's August 1944 decision to earmark most of Germany's available replacements to the west, that they could use a militia to substitute for their transferred fortress infantry units. Indeed, in East Prussia and the Fortresses the Volkssturm proved adequate in this role when properly supplied and supported. Likewise, the Volkssturm, if adequately assisted, could make tactical contributions in local defense. Later, as heavy losses forced the eastern armies to begin using the Volkssturm as a substitute for frontline infantry, performance declined as expectations increased, but the Volkssturm was not markedly worse than the other ersatz infantry available on the Eastern Front in 1945.

Although precise determination of the total number of Volkssturm men who actually served is impossible, evidence suggests substantial mobilizations in the east. Approximately 175,000 Volkssturm men nationwide served long enough under army command for their personnel records to be deposited at the Wehrmacht Information Bureau.[106] Moreover, at least 139 eastern Volkssturm battalions (approximately 70,000 men) received Field Postal Numbers, indicating long-term service and full incorporation into the Wehrmacht administrative structure. Red Cross MIA lists mention Volkssturm formations from nearly 3,000 eastern communities, suggesting extensive short-term employment of the area's Volkssturm.[107] With East Prussians constituting 30 percent of all eastern Volkssturm MIAs and an estimated 200,000 men serving in East Prussia in January 1945, one can estimate that upwards of 650,000 Volkssturm men saw action on the Eastern Front.[108]

Encouraging this widespread combat use of the Volkssturm on the Eastern Front was the fact that the Wehrmacht had no aversion to employing poorly trained, ill-equipped men as infantry in an emergency situation. Furthermore, the low quality of contemporary Soviet infantry also encouraged using Volkssturm formations. By 1945, immense casualties had forced the Soviets to utilize—particularly in rifle divisions—the very old and very young, the unfit and infirm, and other low-quality recruits. Furthermore, these men were hastily trained, if at all, and poorly equipped.[109] This supported Wehrmacht commanders' beliefs that Volkssturm men, particularly if adequately supported, could hold their own.

The psychological factor of desperation, which grew as the Soviets neared, also encouraged Wehrmacht-Volkssturm cooperation. Improved collaboration partially sprang from the field army's complete right of command over areas immediately behind the front, which enabled them to overrule recalcitrant Nazis. It also resulted from regular combat units' constant need for replacements. Perhaps most important, improved relations grew from the desperate desire of many Gau- and Kreis-level officials to keep their areas—and themselves—from falling to the Soviets' not so tender mercies.

Desperation was particularly pronounced in the cities designated Fortresses, where the military situation demanded close coordination and full utilization of resources. Here, Nazi leaders more willingly surrendered authority and worked more diligently both to improve the Volkssturm's fighting potential and to set the oft-touted example of inspirational leadership.[110] For its part, the army took active interest in developing Volkssturm potential—it was typically the only source of additional manpower and often totaled a substantial proportion of available troops—by providing it with supplies, weapons, training, and supervision. The army also sought to match Volkssturm duties to its abilities. Although Party-army cooperation was frequently a marriage born of desperation, it was essential to Volkssturm success and was relatively widespread in eastern Germany.

Army support gave Volkssturm units at least a chance for adequate battlefield performance and survival, which in turn boosted morale, the other critical component of Volkssturm success. The vast majority of men who recognized their unit's weaknesses and knew their chances in battle were poor refused to report for duty at mobilization or deserted soon thereafter. For example, in one sector of Austrian border defenses, all but 25 of 1,727 men left their posts without orders before the Soviets arrived.[111] In unevacuated areas, Volkssturm men frequently refused to serve or quickly returned home out of concern for their families and possessions.[112] The personal example exhibited by local Party officials—so strongly emphasized by Nazi propaganda—could have a positive impact on morale if they served bravely, which many did;[113] but when Party bosses fled, as also happened regularly, Volkssturm men saw no reason not to do the same.[114] Finally, a substantial percentage of Wartheland's Volkssturm and a lesser proportion in West Prussia and elsewhere were "germanized" Poles and ethnic Germans resettled from other areas of eastern Europe. Contrary to Nazi racial ideology, these men had no desire to fight for the Reich in the Volkssturm.[115]

Although Wehrmacht involvement was generally beneficial, the army's view of the Volkssturm men as expendable auxiliaries could generate negative consequences. Some officers mobilized Volkssturm troops for menial rear-area tasks without the slightest concern for the disruption caused in civilian jobs or militia training. Although army units did supply Volkssturm personnel attached to them, they frequently gave only what was unneeded, unwanted, or could not be evacuated.[116] In combat, the army often left Volkssturm units alone as rear guards, which usually caused Volkssturm morale—and typically the unit along with it—to disintegrate.[117] Frequently, relations between soldiers and Volkssturm men were less than cordial, with regulars contemptuously ridiculing members as "grandpas" (Opas) and making them the butt of jokes.[118] In some cases, the army refused to treat Volkssturm men in its hospitals, refused to provide them proper supplies or quarters while in transit, or was otherwise indifferent to active Volkssturm personnel.[119]

Despite low morale,[120] a will to fight was fairly widespread among eastern Volkssturm units. In part, this resulted from Wehrmacht assistance, but another significant factor motivating eastern Volkssturm men and their Nazi supervisors was simply their fear of the Soviets. Although in some areas the Red Army just sent home unarmed Volkssturm men who had not resisted (propaganda leaflets often promised this) or released them earlier than other POWs, most Germans did not believe this was standard procedure.[121] As noted earlier, many Germans expected the Allies would execute Volkssturm prisoners—particularly those captured in civilian clothes—as partisans; but there was good reason for this notion to persist in the east. Soviet troops and Czech and Polish partisans did occasionally kill, mutilate, or otherwise mistreat Volkssturm prisoners, typically mistaking them for Werewolves or Nazi officials.[122] Being older and less healthy, Volkssturm prisoners almost certainly had higher death rates than other POWs, yet another reason for fearing Soviet captivity.[123] Rather than surrendering when surrounded, Volkssturm men often preferred to try to break out or to infiltrate individually back to friendly lines.[124] In fact, some Königsberg Volkssturm men continued to resist even after the city's commander capitulated.[125]

The choices facing an eastern Volkssturm man were not attractive. If he tried to avoid duty, particularly in Fortresses, where there were few places to hide, he risked execution for desertion.[126] Surrender meant an uncertain but reportedly brutal fate through either immediate execution or harsh conditions in a POW camp. The third option, reporting for duty and following orders, though unpleasant, at least gave some chance of survival, particularly if regular troops supported his unit.

The eastern Volkssturm's social composition also helps explain its willingness to fight. Over half (50.65 percent; see appendix Table 2) of eastern Volkssturm MIAs were farmers, shopkeepers, or white-collar personnel, the very groups most overrepresented in the NSDAP in eastern Germany.[127] This does not necessarily mean that most eastern Volkssturm men were fanatic Nazis, but they may well have been more accepting of National Socialist views on the nature of the war and Soviet aims. Certainly to many eastern Germans, particularly farmers or Party members, it must have seemed plausible enough—particularly after the first highly publicized Soviet atrocities against civilians—that the Bolsheviks did indeed want to eradicate all Germans. At the very least, eastern farm owners and middle-class men expected they had much to lose by a Soviet victory and were willing to take up arms to try to protect their families and property so long as they thought their effort might stand a chance of even temporary success.[128]

Furthermore, the average eastern German Volkssturm man was not—contrary to conventional wisdom—a fanatic Hitler Youth but an aging man born and raised during the Wilhelmine era. With nearly two-thirds of eastern MIAs (62.74 percent) over 45—the average age was 47.1 (see appendix Table 15)—it would seem that traditional values of patriotism and duty, a long-standing distrust of and distaste for their Slavic neighbors, and a desire to protect family and possessions against the feared Bolsheviks would have been stronger motivation for these men than any yearning to safeguard the National Socialists' New Order.[129]

The NSDAP failed in its effort to use the Volkssturm to fanaticize all Germans, but by heightening existing fears of Slavic and Bolshevik domination and by building on traditional attitudes, it helped increase willingness to fight the Red Army. To the average Volkssturm man in eastern Germany, the war appeared to fit the Nazis' propaganda description: a brutally total people's war in which surrender would be tantamount to national suicide. Most Volkssturm men in eastern Germany fought not out of fanaticism but out of fear and desperation, and because they saw few options.[130] In essence, their interests seemed to mesh best with the continuation of a National Socialist regime, no matter how they might view it.

This willingness to fight did not always translate into battlefield success—that required army assistance. The Wehrmacht on the Eastern Front believed the situation was serious enough to warrant using ill-prepared civilian soldiers to bolster their infantry-starved front lines, an attitude that led them to seek control of Volkssturm units and to try to improve their fighting abilities. This often steeled the resolve of Volkssturm men and helped them to succeed in combat. Volkssturm resistance at Pyritz was a tactical victory given strategic meaning by the timely arrival of 4th SS Division; the equally tenacious Volkssturm defense of Hindenburg was futile because no reinforcements arrived. A purely tactical force, the Volkssturm depended on the Wehrmacht to translate local successes into strategic victories. By January 1945, the Wehrmacht was no longer able to do this consistently, thereby rendering futile the sometimes valiant, sometimes minimal, efforts of an auxiliary force like the Volkssturm.

CHAPTER NINE

Defending the Reich's Western Front

There were many similarities between the Volkssturm in eastern and western Germany. Its basic structure, purpose, and duties were constant, and on both Eastern and Western Fronts the force's combat deployment followed a similar pattern—initially security occupation of fortified areas but later shifting more to local defense and substituting for frontline infantry. Also, although the Volkssturm failed everywhere in a strategic sense, it could and did achieve tactical victories where army assistance and higher than average morale coincided. Despite these similarities, the Volkssturm's record against the Soviets is glaringly better, a situation that stemmed from two factors. First, western Volkssturm men generally lacked any strong desire to resist the Anglo-American forces. Second, the Wehrmacht on the Western Front took less extensive interest in the Volkssturm and devoted less attention to it than did eastern commanders.

Initially, Field Marshal Gerd von Rundstedt (chief of OB West) viewed the Volkssturm with some enthusiasm. He believed, like his eastern counterpart Guderian, that a militia could help deepen German defenses—particularly in local tasks such as securing Rhine bridges. Certainly, he saw the need for this in the wake of the Allied mechanized sweep across France or the airborne seizure of Dutch bridges during Operation Market-Garden.[1] Rundstedt's interest diminished, however, on discovering that the Volkssturm would be neither Wehrkreis-controlled nor ready for immediate use. He did retain hope that the force could eventually be used in quiet sectors and in rear-area security occupations of fortifications like the West Wall.[2]

Compounding Rundstedt's disillusionment was the Volkssturm's western debut at Metz, which contrasted unfavorably with the positive reports from East Prussia. The Metz Volkssturm battalion—two SA Special Purpose Companies, a company of railroad employees, and a company of Metz's German citizens[3]—was adequately, though lightly, armed and equipped, but it had absolutely no infantry combat training. Poor NSDAP-army liaison left Metz's military commander with "exaggerated estimations about the combat value of Volkssturm battalions," and he sent the unit into the front lines about November 10.[4] With the city surrounded, most of the men, particularly the Metz citizens, had no desire to perish in a hopeless struggle and deserted at the first opportunity. The few diehards—possibly SA men—who remained on duty fought as part of the garrisons of two of the city's forts.[5] Efforts to rally Volkssturm units elsewhere in Lorraine and in Alsace, where many viewed the Allies as liberators rather than enemies, fared no better.[6]

After these initial disasters, OB West abandoned any ambitious plans for the Volkssturm—a stark contrast to the attitude at OKH—and tended from this point onward to leave utilization and coordination of the militia to lower-level commanders. Thus, on November 22 it would be Army Group G—desperate for troops with which to stabilize its front along the Saar River and in Alsace-Lorraine—that initiated what became the Western Front's most strategically successful Volkssturm deployment. The Army Group requested a complete mobilization of all area units; but with the Volkssturm here barely organized, much less trained or equipped, Baden Gaustabsführer Reinhard Burst—Knight's Cross recipient and former regimental commander—wisely suggested employing only a limited number of Levy I units in security occupation of fortifications in relatively quiet West Wall sectors.[7] With OB West's approval, the Army Group implemented Burst's proposal in both the Upper Rhine and Saar regions. This fulfilled Hitler's orders to garrison all West Wall bunkers, released some regular personnel for other duty, and enabled the Army Group to begin training, equipping, and integrating these Volkssturm units into its defense plans.[8]

Although Volkssturm units served throughout the West Wall,[9] the main focus of activity remained in the southern sectors, where by the end of November nineteen Gau Westmark battalions—many virtually unarmed—occupied rearward portions of the West Wall in the Saarland and Lorraine.[10] Plans called for keeping these units out of combat until they were better prepared, but American advances in early December forced Battalion Saarbrücken 1 into combat near Ensdorf. This unit's poor performance shattered remaining illusions about existing Volkssturm capabilities.[11] In response, commanders redoubled efforts to improve the force by tightening liaison with local Party officials, providing supplies, assigning regular troops to support and train Volkssturm units (particularly those stationed near the front), and attaching instructors and supervisory officers to Volkssturm-occupied sectors.[12]

In Gau Westmark, better Volkssturm-Wehrmacht cooperation began yielding benefits in early 1945. In January, Volkssturm units participated in Army Group G's offensive, Operation North Wind, in Alsace-Lorraine. Some units even constituted part of the force covering the complicated withdrawal of the 10th SS and 21st Panzer Divisions at the close of that effort.[13] The Westmark Volkssturm's real test began with renewed American attacks in the Saar Basin during February and March 1945. Some formations—for example, Trier's "Porta Negra" Battalion—simply collapsed when surprised by American troops.[14] Typically, such poorly performing units had only recently been mobilized, were unsatisfactorily organized, were generally unsupported by the army, were inadequately trained, lacked proper logistical arrangements—particularly victualing—and suffered chronically low morale.[15]

On the other hand, Volkssturm troops fought well at Hamm, Serrig, Saar-brücken, Saarburg, Forbach, and elsewhere along the Saar River.[16] Some even continued fighting while surrounded, which allowed regular formations to withdraw.[17] Typically those Volkssturm units that fought adequately had been on duty longer and were decently trained (at least in defending fortifications), passably equipped, and better integrated into the army's command and logistical systems.[18] In many cases, these units had regular troops, NCOs, and even officers attached who both discouraged desertion—sometimes via coercion—and supervised them in combat. Furthermore, fighting from the West Wall's well-constructed, camouflaged bunkers—a task for which they had trained—probably boosted Volkssturm confidence to a degree.[19] Finally, Westmark Gaustabsführer Karl Caspary, ex-lieutenant and veteran of both world wars, had maintained good relations with the army.[20] This facilitated extensive, long-term field army support and supervision that—as in East Prussia—proved crucial to adequate Volkssturm performance.

Volkssturm deployments were even more extensive along the Upper Rhine. In fact, the German army stationed there became so dependent on the militia that it was jokingly known as the Nineteenth "Volkssturm" Army.[21] Volkssturm units began mobilizing here in late November as a security occupation force to ensure that the Allies' rapid advance through northern Alsace did not carry them across the Rhine. Beginning on November 27, Heinrich Himmler himself commanded the grandly titled Army Group Upper Rhine. In reality this was a weak collection of local Volkssturm units (first companies and later battalions), remnants of field divisions, small SS formations, Luftwaffe troops, and police units.[22] Realizing its dependence on the Volkssturm, Army Group Upper Rhine worked diligently to improve the militia's training, equipment, and morale.[23] By early January, active Volkssturm battalions here were adequately armed; some even had heavy machine guns and medium mortars.[24]

To overcome problems imposed by limitations on individual Volkssturm men's terms of active service, Army Group Upper Rhine and Gaue Baden and Württemberg developed personnel rotation systems.[25] Württemberg battalions (in another example of deploying Volkssturm units outside their home Gau) shifted as complete units, first to the Swiss border for four weeks' training with AOK 24, and then to the Upper Rhine for a month. Baden's Volkssturm rotated in companies, with each serving a nine-week tour of active duty. To ensure that no Baden battalion was completely green, every three weeks each battalion demobilized one company's personnel, who turned their equipment, uniforms, footwear, weapons, and supplies over to the replacements. Having Baden's battalions on active duty permanently enabled the Army Group to standardize the unit's structure along military lines. This, however, meant raising the units only in the more populous Kreise.[26] While the rotation system sought to balance economic and military concerns, the mobilizations—

over 12,000 men at any given time in 1945—had a fairly broad negative impact on area economic activity.[27]

These Volkssturm units saw their security occupation duties on the Upper Rhine end in early February as Franco-American assaults eliminated the Colmar Pocket. Army Group G reassumed control of the Upper Rhine on January 24 and planned to replace Volkssturm and other scratch units there with the AOK 19 regulars withdrawing from Alsace. The massive Allied push to and across the central and Lower Rhine—plus the collapse of the Eastern Front—however, repeatedly demanded the transfer of army units from the stable front in Baden.[28] In turn, this forced AOK 19 to rely even more heavily on the Volkssturm for combat troops.[29] As early as February 1, Volkssturm battalions formed 40 percent of XVIII SS Army Corps' frontline infantry.[30] By early April, nearly two-thirds (20 of 31) of the army's frontline battalions were Volkssturm, with an additional three militia battalions in reserve.[31] As on the Oder, Upper Rhine Volkssturm battalions served as substitutes for regular infantry in the main line of resistance (even conducting patrols on the Alsatian bank), while the Wehrmacht combat formations with counterattack capability formed tactical reserves.[32] The army also relied heavily on the Volkssturm to flesh out its engineer units and rear echelon, for example, as cooks, paymasters, and smiths.[33]

Keenly aware of its dependence on Volkssturm troops, AOK 19 made determined efforts to improve their combat potential.[34] It established a permanent liaison with Baden's Gauleitung to ensure NSDAP cooperation.[35] To simplify the chain of command and improve military supervision of all non-Wehrmacht troops, the army reorganized all its miscellaneous units into Upper Rhine Grenadier Regiments and further standardized battalion organization. As done elsewhere, it also established a system for removing incompetent Volkssturm leaders.[36] Wherever possible, AOK 19 provided its militia units with artillery support and reserves.[37] To offset inevitable losses from sickness and enemy action, plug gaps while units were rotated out of service, and increase training opportunities, the Army and Gau Baden set up Volkssturm replacement and training companies.[38] Fearing possible desertion, dereliction of duty, or even potential subversion or espionage, AOK 19 instructed subordinate commanders to punish active militiamen for any infractions and to purge their Volkssturm personnel of any Alsatians.[39]

Furthermore, to develop fallback positions, AOK 19 planned an extensive deployment of Levy II units in fortifications along both the border and the crestline of the hilly Black Forest.[40] Several army staffs supervised the Volkssturm units slated to improve and man these defenses; and Gaustabsführer Burst ordered each of the twenty-eight battalions assigned to the Black Forest Border Position to set up a headquarters there, lay out fire plans, and conduct Sunday training in their assigned sectors. All other armed Volkssturm units were to prepare for local defense of their hometowns.[41] For its part, AOK 19 instructed each town's military commander to establish immediate, permanent liaison with the local Party headquarters and to do everything possible to supervise, coordinate, and improve his area's Volkssturm units.[42] Despite these efforts, Party-army relations at the lowest levels were not always smooth, and AOK 19 simply could not adequately arm, uniform, supply, or train all the region's Volkssturm units, particularly the Levy II battalions slated for deployment in the unfinished Black Forest positions or in local defense.[43]

The Nineteenth Army's extensive preparations deterred a direct assault, but on March 29 the French First Army's Rhine crossings at Speyer and Germersheim flanked the army's defenses. The French advance forced AOK 19 to abandon its prepared positions and rehearsed tactics, thus putting its Volkssturm units at a distinct disadvantage. Further complicating matters was Württemberg Gauleiter Murr's effort—ultimately squelched by Hitler himself—to withhold promised Volkssturm reinforcements for use in his own Gau.[44] Finally, AOK 19, lacking reserves and regular troops, faced a hopeless struggle that prompted widespread desertion and led some Volkssturm units to surrender quickly, as happened at Lichtenau and Balzhofen.[45]

None of this is surprising; AOK 19's commanders themselves harbored no illusions about Volkssturm combat capabilities.[46] What is interesting is how well a number of Volkssturm units did, especially considering that they lacked extensive support from regular troops and were fighting a fluid defensive action for which they had not trained extensively. Resistance from outnumbered Volkssturm battalions and antitank teams in the Pforzheim-Ettlingen-Rastatt area prevented the French from quickly rolling up the army's entire Rhine front, while other units fought well at Offenburg, Zell, and elsewhere.[47]

This performance resulted from the fact that Volkssturm units on the Upper Rhine had long been under army supervision, and their armament, training, self-confidence, and capabilities had improved as a result.[48] Furthermore, being fully integrated into the army's defensive plans, Volkssturm men were as well supplied, supported, and supervised as anyone in the Army.[49] Although certain Party officials caused problems, Baden Gaustabsführer Burst worked closely with AOK 19 in preparing his Volkssturm for combat. All of this combined to enable Volkssturm units to handle a large portion of the Upper Rhine's defense, freeing regular units for use elsewhere and thus accomplishing the western Volkssturm's most strategically significant feat.

The Wehrmacht also used Volkssturm battalions to substitute for regular frontline infantry elsewhere along the Rhine. Initially, Wehrkreis XII planned only to employ Volkssturm units from Gaue Moselland and Hesse-Nassau's river towns to guard bridges; but by March 1945 the U.S. Third Army's rapid advance forced deployment of these Volkssturm units—along with whatever training personnel and antiaircraft gunners (both with and without their artillery) were available—to defend the central Rhine's entire eastern bank.[50] As on other river lines, Volkssturm formations typically manned forward positions, while the few available regulars formed reserves for counterattacking at crucial points.[51] These thinly distributed and poorly trained, equipped, and led Volkssturm units often lacked both support by regulars and enthusiasm for their task; and many surrendered quickly.[52] In the Rhine Gorge, however, Volkssturm units put up fierce resistance at Rhens, Boppard, St. Goarshausen, and Kaub against the U.S. 89th and 87th Infantry Divisions' crossing attempts.[53] Lacking adequate support—particularly readily available reserves— these units inflicted casualties on the assaulting units, but their best efforts only temporarily contained the American bridgeheads.

Some Volkssturm units on the Lower Rhine also performed adequately as frontline infantry. Battalion 38/20—a Levy I unit from the Isselburg-Anholt area in Gau Westphalia North—initially mobilized in November for three weeks' training and then served during the winter as a security occupation force constructing field fortifications and drilling to combat armored or airborne attacks.[54] Around March 1, the unit left its Gau to enter the front along the Rhine at Dornick (between Rees and Emmerich in Gau Essen). Battalion 38/ 20's commanding unit, 6th Parachute Division, reinforced it with a platoon of veterans to increase its combat effectiveness.[55] The Volkssturm unit demonstrated its capabilities by conducting nocturnal reconnaissance patrols on the Rhine's west bank, manning listening and observation posts, laying mines, directing artillery fire, and providing its own limited mortar and antiaircraft machine gun support.[56] One German officer even remarked that the battalion's men were "high standard personnel" who were "imbued with the best intentions and a sense of duty."[57] The unit was fairly well supplied and armed, although with the usually eclectic mix of German, Italian, Czech, Austrian, and French weapons. Based on the number of reports it generated, the battalion was soundly incorporated into the First Parachute Army's bureaucracy and chain of command.[58]

Battalion 38/20's actual combat performance is unknown. There was fierce fighting in the area, however, as several—though not all—Volkssturm units supporting German paratroop and infantry formations fought hard against the Allied combined ground and airborne assault.[59] Battalion 38/20 apparently mounted some local counterattacks but was forced to retreat by the Canadian 9th Infantry Brigade moving up from Rees in the last days of March.[60] Despite the paucity of information concerning its behavior under fire, the unit had all the ingredients necessary for adequate Volkssturm performance: support and supervision from regular troops, satisfactory training and equipment, and a will to fight. Unfortunately for the Germans, Battalion 38/20 was the rare exception rather than the general rule.

Although some western Volkssturm units served in security occupations or as frontline infantry, the majority that saw action did so in a variety of local defense capacities either alone or under command of rear-echelon formations. In this capacity, active-duty Volkssturm troops also provided convenient labor for evacuations or fatigue duties such as repairing roads and railways, unloading trains and barges, or even sorting captured enemy equipment.[61] Furthermore, Volkssturm men secured important installations, directed traffic, searched for escapees or deserters,[62] protected evacuated or bombed areas against looting,[63] kept tabs on foreign workers,[64] and guarded prisoner-of-war or concentration camp inmates both in their camps and in transit.[65] A unique police contingency plan for combating internal unrest even included deploying a few selected Volkssturm units.[66]

Such tasks were, however, secondary to the Volkssturm's basic combat role: static defense of the members' hometown. Most units' tactical planning consisted primarily of defending roadblocks constructed by the men themselves or with occasional assistance from army engineers. Typically, units placed these obstacles at town entrances and exits, overpasses, defiles, or other points that Allied troops could not easily bypass. Rehearsing closing and defending these roadblocks, as well as mobilization drills, often formed the essence of many units' tactical training.[67] Not all Volkssturm units relied exclusively on static defensive methods, however. Some created small, relatively well-armed, and mobile (vehicle or bicycle) Hunting Teams to locate, harass, and ambush enemy airborne troops or armored vehicles.[68] Where specialized personnel were available, there might be Volkssturm engineers to prepare bridges for demolition or to lay mines.[69] In larger towns and cities, Volkssturm men also served as infantry protection for flak guns, frequently the Germans' main antitank and artillery support in 1945.[70] Finally, because of their familiarity with local geography, Volkssturm personnel frequently served in reconnaissance teams, as guides, and in the Armor and Air Landing Warning Services.[71]

In some instances the Wehrmacht sought to minimize Volkssturm weaknesses by combining local defense with security occupations of fallback positions. This occurred along the Erft River—the one natural obstacle between the Roer (where American troops were bogged down in the winter of 1944–1945) and Rhine Rivers. Army Group B planned to halt any Allied penetration of the Roer front along the Erft, or, failing in that, to use the Erft as a blocking position that would cover withdrawal across the Rhine. Construction and occupation of the Erft position fell to local Wehrkreis and Volkssturm units, with the latter performing two key roles. One was defending roadblocks on approaches to the Erft River and Canal, which would buy time to allow engineers to destroy bridges. The other was helping Replacement Army and field army troops hold the main line of resistance on the wooded heights east of the

Erft.[72] To raise Volkssturm combat potential, the Wehrkreis established clear defensive plans, directed fortification construction, conducted training courses, laid minefields, and organized heavy weapons support.[73]

NSDAP-Wehrmacht relations in the Erft area were also good, partly because it was close enough to the front to enable AOK 15 to issue orders to civilian officials and to punish the blatantly uncooperative. With extensive control over all local defense assets, town commanders could use the Volkssturm as they saw fit. Many chose to put the best militiamen into fully armed Hunting Teams, mix others into regular army alarm units, and employ the remainder as laborers or as spotters for the Armor and Air Landing Warning Services. In exchange for full army control, area Volkssturm personnel were better trained and had more effective defense and mobilization preparations and greater firepower.[74]

Despite these efforts, the Erft position did little to slow the American advance. One problem was the lack of regular formations available to defend it.[75] Also, Volkssturm units west of the Erft refused to sacrifice themselves—as was typical—as a delaying force. Consequently, most American units reported no difficulty in crossing the river and canal; and they found that most Volkssturm men, particularly those left largely on their own, only sought an opportunity to surrender safely.[76] On the other hand, in the main line of resistance some units fought well. On March 1, U.S. troops encountered stiff resistance precisely at the Bergheim unit's assigned sector and were soon hit by regular infantrymen, armor, and artillery (retiring remnants of 363rd Volksgrenadier and 9th Panzer Divisions) who either reinforced or relieved the Volkssturm men. The Americans cleared the area only late on March 2 after taking relatively heavy casualties.[77]

Bergheim illustrates how Volkssturm local defense success required immediate support from regular units. There are other examples as well. On April 1, Volkssturm units blunted the British advance near Ibbenbüren, which enabled troops from an NCO school and an antiaircraft unit to hold the town until April 4. This facilitated First Parachute Army's withdrawal to the Weser River and also allowed the Germans to evacuate a large supply depot.[78] At Crailsheim on April 6, a few Volkssturm men supported by an antiaircraft unit put up just enough resistance to allow 17th SS Panzergrenadier Division to counterattack and not only retake the town but also stall the American advance in the area and force a pitched battle that lasted nearly two weeks.[79] On the other hand, on Bremen's outskirts, at Kempten, Kicklingen, and Passau, Volkssturm-HJ troops effectively held up Allied forces but lacked the Wehrmacht support needed to give their resistance any real meaning.[80]

Generally, however, the western Volkssturm performed abysmally in local defense. Nowhere are the reasons for—and potential strategic consequences of—such failures better illustrated than at Remagen. The town's Volkssturm battalion was commanded by an SA *Hauptsturmführer* with Eastern Front experience, but inadequate Party-army cooperation had left it untrained, lightly armed, and ill informed. The fluid military situation, an ambiguous chain of command, and the lack of a detailed defense plan only further confused Remagen's defenders, which aside from the Volkssturm consisted of a platoon of convalescents and a few superannuated engineers. With remnants of defeated combat formations streaming back across the Rhine via the Ludendorff Railway Bridge, many of the town's demoralized Volkssturm men decided either simply not to report for duty or to follow the regulars across the river, where they hid in the Erpeler Ley railway tunnel. As a result, on March 7, U.S. 9th Armored Division troops faced no resistance until they reached the intact bridge itself, which they quickly seized.[81] Had the town's Volkssturm offered any resistance, it might have won the time engineers needed to destroy the bridge.

Although the strategic consequences of Remagen's Volkssturm failure were atypical, the reasons behind it were not. Among the most critical ingredients that were totally lacking among Remagen's Volkssturm men was a willingness to fight. Indeed, the will to resist was often lacking in the west; and where it did exist, it typically sprang from local factors rather than the more general and widespread concerns that motivated eastern Volkssturm men to fight the Soviets.

One element that contributed to some Volkssturm units' willingness to fight was opposing French troops. Long-standing animosity may have inspired some Volkssturm men in Baden and Württemberg to resist the French advance in 1945. Furthermore, propaganda from both world wars portrayed French soldiers—particularly the colonials—as looters, rapists, and murderers. Some Badenese and Württemberger Volkssturm men may have believed their resistance would protect their homes and families against such a fate. Volkssturm men also may have feared the traditional French enemy would treat them harshly in revenge for the German occupation.[82] Indeed, although Germans could not have known it, the French did send all captured Volkssturm men— whether or not they had fought—to POW camps and held them there longer than did the other Western Allies.[83] The fear, hatred, and desperation felt by Volkssturm men fighting the French was not comparable to that of their compatriots facing the Soviets, but it seems that the traditional enmity between France and Germany played some role in encouraging Volkssturm resistance in southwestern Germany.

As on the Eastern Front, fear constituted another motivation for western Volkssturm men to fight. In the west, however, it was not so much fear of the enemy but fear of execution for desertion. In the Lower Franconian town of Lohr am Main, six citizens were hanged for defeatism as American troops closed on the town, a spectacle that encouraged the town's Volkssturm to assist regular troops in fighting the 14th Armored Division for more than a day before being overwhelmed.[84] Similarly, Volkssturm men tended to fight when SS troops were nearby, as many Germans believed—with good reason—that they executed slackers unhesitatingly.[85] Examples of Volkssturm-SS resistance occurred well into April in such places as Soltau, near Bremen,[86] and along the Neckar and Jagst Rivers.[87] In Nuremberg over 1,000 Volkssturm men— including Karl Holz, acting Gauleiter of Franconia, who died in the battle— plus SS, RAD, HJ, and army troops engaged U.S. troops in bitter fighting for five days in mid-April.[88]

Executing deserters was not an SS monopoly. It was common knowledge that army officers also could and would use deadly force against men deemed derelict in their duties.[89] AOK 19, like all German units in 1945, maintained patrols behind the front to catch deserters; but its commander, General Erich Brandenberger, reinforced them. He also warned that every German should realize that the army would take the "sharpest measures" (i.e., execution) against anyone—including Volkssturm men fleeing their positions—who tried to undermine defense efforts.[90]

In many instances, the presence of a fanatic military commander coerced and/or inspired Volkssturm men into fighting, sometimes bitterly and well. At Aschaffenburg, the Volkssturm blunted the initial American assault on March 25 and participated, both in combat and in the rear areas, in the vicious ten-day struggle for that small city. Why? Partly because the fanatical *Kampfkommandant*, a Major Lamberth, unblinkingly used the harshest measures to maintain obedience.[91] Such examples supported the well-publicized threats of reprisals against deserters and defeatists,[92] and convinced numerous Volkssturm men that their safest option was to risk honorable death in battle over execution at the hands of a drumhead court-martial. Obviously, it was not only because of military assistance that Volkssturm troops tended to fight harder under Wehrmacht command.

Indeed, Nazi fanaticism among Volkssturm men themselves accounts for some resistance in western Germany. As the war wound down and the impossibility of arming the entire Volkssturm became increasingly clear, some NSDAP officials provided the available weapons to units of handpicked loyalists.[93] In some instances these hard-core Nazi units fought well, even conducting sophisticated ambushes,[94] and in one case raiding an American supply depot.[95] Elsewhere fanatics represented little more than a nuisance to the Allied advance, although they caused considerable consternation for individual soldiers.[96]

A more common source of fanaticism was the Hitler Youth, whose resistance in such places as Nuremberg, Leipzig, Diesdorf (west of Magdeburg), Kirchborchen, Aschaffenburg, Zeven, along the Jagst and Neckar, and elsewhere caused some American units to cite HJ fanaticism as "one of the stumbling blocks in mopping up operations."[97] HJ boys were certainly more prone to fanaticism than the average Volkssturm man, but they were also easy to coerce. There is no way to gauge how many of them actually fought; but the Red Cross listed 43 Levy III youths among the 590 western Volkssturm MIAs, a proportion more than double that for the eastern Gaue (7.3 percent compared with 3.2 percent) but still well under Levy III's 10 percent share of the total Volkssturm. Also, there is substantial evidence that HJ units were frequently evacuated rather than employed in combat, and where HJ units fought, they often did so due to poor evacuation procedures rather than pure fanaticism.[98] Indeed, most western Volkssturm men who saw combat were not teenage fanatics.[99]

Western Volkssturm troops also tended to fight better in urban areas (e.g., Nuremberg, Cologne, Würzburg, Aschaffenburg, Bonn), although not on the scale seen in eastern Fortresses.[100] In part this was simply due to the larger populations, which meant there were—numerically, though not necessarily proportionally—more fanatics in one place. Furthermore, many cities had been heavily bombed, and this not only created favorable defensive terrain but also gave some remaining inhabitants a motive to fight. This may have played a role at Würzburg, which experienced its first devastating raid only two weeks before the arrival of American troops, and where Volkssturm troops were involved in four days of heavy fighting. Bombing does not seem to have prompted more Volkssturm men to report for duty (in fact, evacuations caused by bombings severely diminished Volkssturm size in Ulm and Wittlich), but in some places it does seem to have stiffened the spine of those who did.[101]

Among the most extensive, bitter, and surprising instances of Volkssturm resistance against the Western Allies occurred in April in Halle, Merseburg, Leipzig, Greiz, Zwickau, and other central German cities. Here SS, army, Volkssturm, Luftwaffe, flak, RAD, and HJ units engaged U.S. forces in bitter house-to-house battles. Why Volkssturm units in these areas were willing to fight so fiercely at this late date is not clear, but coercion, military assistance, and morale seem again significant. SS troops were in the area, and the army, wanting to make a stand here, had provided local Volkssturm battalions with clothing, weapons, and support.[102] Determined *Kampfkommandanten*, especially in Leipzig, probably played a major part in coercing and encouraging resistance as well. The personal example of Halle-Merseburg Gauleiter Albrecht Eggeling, one of only two Gauleiters killed in battle (Franconia's Karl Holz was the other), may have been inspirational to some. Certainly, his actions demonstrated an NSDAP presence advocating and coercing resistance until the very end.[103] Finally, some Volkssturm men may have believed they were helping Berlin's defense by securing the rear and flank of General Walther Wenck's Twelfth Army, the last faint hope for relieving the besieged capital.[104]

Perceptions of increased Volkssturm resistance in the war's final stage may also have resulted, in part, from the increasingly common Wehrmacht practice of using the militia as a source of replacements. Many army units simply mustered the local Volkssturm, enrolled younger, healthy men, and sent others home.[105] Often these new recruits lacked complete uniforms or army documentation, and Allied troops may have simply assumed all men in combat wearing unorthodox clothing were fighting as members of a Volkssturm unit. By April, the lines between Volkssturm and Wehrmacht had become quite blurred.

Just as Volkssturm successes sprang from many factors, so, too, did its much more numerous combat failures. The widespread incidence of poor Party-army cooperation resulting from personality clashes, organizational disputes, and confusion generated by the fluid military situation meant that western Volkssturm units were chronically ill trained and poorly equipped.[106] As in the east, some active western militiamen had to beg, borrow, and scavenge to meet their logistical needs.[107] Volkssturm units, lacking communications and intelligence-gathering capabilities, were often surprised by rapid Allied advances and thrown into confusion when circumstances forced abandonment of their defensive plans.[108] Other Volkssturm formations that tried to resist found that the Western Allies, like the Soviets, often concentrated against them because of their weakness.[109] Volkssturm units were also handicapped by their poor training, their limited firepower and ammunition, and the fact that alone they could never protect their flanks no matter how well they fought.[110]

Generally, however, the most common ingredient in the western Volkssturm's poor overall performance was low morale. Even some reasonably well-equipped men sought to avoid combat by discarding their weapons or refusing to accept ammunition.[111] Desertion and failure to report for duty were rampant, and in some places, unit leaders or town officials simply disbanded units on their own authority.[112] In Backnang, Augsburg, and elsewhere, town officials, Volkssturm men, or average citizens made arrangements to surrender their town peacefully to Allied troops. Others hung out white flags, opened roadblocks, or sought to prevent demolition of bridges, waterworks, or other essential infrastructure.[113] By spring 1945, most western Germans had little desire to fight, and some even willingly risked their lives to bring peace to their locality.[114]

Determinants of morale are innumerable and idiosyncratic, but there are common influences that encouraged defeatism in western Germany in 1945. The local military situation had considerable impact. Seeing Wehrmacht troops retreating in disorder usually convinced even stouthearted Volkssturm men of the futility of resistance. Similarly, Volkssturm men often felt betrayed when army units withdrew unexpectedly or failed to provide them with food, supplies, or orders, even though confusion—particularly in the war's last weeks—was frequently to blame. Nonetheless, western Volkssturm men usually surrendered if they thought they were being sacrificed merely to cover the regulars' retreat. Shortages of weapons, equipment, supplies, and even armbands and paybooks, coupled with the inadequate training common to virtually all inactive Volkssturm units, only added to the despair.[115]

Further depressing morale was the stark contrast between the Volkssturm's general condition and that of the Allies. Germans viewed the Western Allies as overwhelmingly well supplied and equipped, with complete control of the air and such a preponderance of artillery that they could respond even to isolated sniper fire with devastating air strikes and artillery barrages. Furthermore, Allied personnel seemed well-trained, fit young men and, at least in the American case, part of extensive manpower reserves. One army lieutenant summed up the general sense of hopelessness: "The Americans have pushed from the Channel coast to Altenplos [near Bayreuth]; now we are supposed to stop them here?"[116]

Lenient British, Canadian, and American treatment of Volkssturm captives also encouraged surrender. Unlike the Soviets (and to a lesser extent the French), the Americans, British, and Canadians, because of their pragmatic desire to avoid having to keep every adult German male as a prisoner of war, gave Volkssturm men an attractive alternative to futile resistance. Typically, unarmed Volkssturm men who had not resisted could go home, and counterintelligence officers later screened out the Nazi officials and potential Werewolves among them.[117] On the other hand, if a Volkssturm unit chose to fight, the Americans and British frequently called in artillery or air bombardment to convince the town to surrender.[118] It did not take long for word of these tactics to spread,[119] and many Volkssturm units preferred surrender to risking death and/or destruction of their homes in the final moments of a war clearly lost.[120] This held particularly true in relatively undamaged areas, that is, those towns and villages Bormann wanted the militia to turn into fortresses. Furthermore, many Volkssturm men came to realize that surrendering after resistance meant an unpleasant and potentially lengthy stay in prisoner-of-war camps.[121]

While the behavior of some Soviet troops lent credence to Nazi assertions about the war's life-or-death significance, Anglo-American treatment of Volkssturm men disproved propaganda claims that the Western Allies wanted to destroy the German people. In the west, once it became evident that the war was lost, many Germans concluded their national future would be better served by allowing the Western powers, rather than the Soviets, to occupy as much of the country as possible.[122] Therefore, it was not only futile but also foolish—from both an individual and a national perspective—to resist the Americans and British.

Another factor that shaped western Volkssturm morale was Nazi officials' behavior. Despite the claims of their propaganda, Party bosses were often not selfless, energetic men who led by example. As mentioned, Halle-Merseburg's Eggeling and Franconia's Holz were the only Gauleiters who remained at their posts until the bitter end. Many other officials simply fled without fighting, and some even used Volkssturm men to evacuate their personal property.[123] In some cases, Party officials abused their power by assigning personal enemies to the first Volkssturm units mobilized or using harshly coercive measures against men—or their families—who did not report for Volkssturm duty.[124] Such selfish, cowardly, and abusive behavior violated both the lofty ideals espoused by Nazi propaganda and the traditional sense of patriotism and duty that most Volkssturm men respected.[125] The result was widespread resentment and bitterness toward NSDAP, SS, and SA officials and, by default, the Volkssturm.[126]

In the final analysis, the widespread absence of a will to fight contributed mightily to the western Volkssturm's overall failure. As with their eastern counterparts, there is no accurate measure of how many Volkssturm men saw action on the Western Front, but the Allies took, however briefly, upwards of 1 million Volkssturm men prisoner by the war's end.[127] Only a small proportion of them actually fought, though. MIA lists show only nineteen battalions (fewer than 12,000 men) served long enough to acquire Field Postal Numbers; and the lists name only 590 men from thirty-four battalions and 246 communities as having ended up as MIAs. Thus, it would be surprising if the total number of Volkssturm men committed to combat for an extended period of time in the west exceeded 150,000—although this is little more than a guess.[128] The number who may have fought briefly in local defense is impossible to determine, although it would almost certainly be greater given that this was the western Volkssturm's most commonly performed duty.

Numbers aside, the Volkssturm did contribute to the western Reich's defense in some ways. By helping hold the West Wall and Upper Rhine, it released regulars for use elsewhere. By serving as local defense forces, construction gangs, and police auxiliaries, the Volkssturm reduced army rear-echelon manpower needs and thereby released soldiers for combat duty. It also enabled strained army service and training units to concentrate on their essential instructional, communications, and logistical duties. The Volkssturm constructed innumerable field fortifications and roadblocks, which, if defended, could potentially hinder Allied advances.[129] Such work could indeed be dangerous, as Volkssturm labor parties were favorite targets for bored American artillerymen and fighter-bomber pilots.[130] Finally, a small minority of western Volkssturm units fought adequately, a few even quite well.

As on the Eastern Front, western Volkssturm success hinged upon Wehrmacht assistance before and during combat, both to enable the militia to fight and to give their local victories strategic meaning. OB West and OKH viewed the Volkssturm differently, however. Both considered the force useful, but OKH, desperate for manpower, tended to work hard to control Volkssturm units and improve and employ them on a large scale. OB West, until 1945 better supplied with reserves and defending a front that was both shorter and largely outside of Germany, took less interest in the Volkssturm. Unlike Guderian, OB West never seriously challenged Party control of the Volkssturm. Generally it considered the force useful only for local defense, and therefore left its use and improvement to local commanders. In turn, these officers, particularly if faced with uncooperative NSDAP officials, sometimes lacked the time, will, or material, personnel, or political resources needed to make the Volkssturm effective in a significant way.[131]

Whereas OKH mobilized groups of Volkssturm units simultaneously and made some coordinated efforts to integrate them into their defensive plans and to prepare them to perform prearranged tasks, western commanders tended to activate Volkssturm battalions as needed, singly or in small groups. Except in the West Wall's Saar and Upper Rhine sectors, western commanders tended to view and use the Volkssturm as a tactical stopgap; eastern commanders viewed the Volkssturm as an operational-level resource. As 1945 progressed, officers on the Western Front threw Volkssturm troops into the line as units or individuals with increasing frequency and simply expected them to perform as seasoned infantrymen. Given time, support, and guidance, Volkssturm units could do this, as shown by Battalions 38/20 and by some of the units on the Upper Rhine; but by 1945, time was a luxury. Therefore, it is little wonder that Volkssturm men, thrust into combat situations with little preparation and/ or guidance from either the Party or the army, surrendered in droves. Western commanders, particularly early on, had an unrealistic view of individual Volkssturm unit capabilities and never fully appreciated the degree of assistance required to make the units effective. As a result, the army provided the militia with less support in the west than the east, one of the two main reasons for the western Volkssturm's poorer performance.

The other major reason for the western Volkssturm's failure was poor morale. This resulted from inadequate training, poor armament, lack of Wehrmacht support, the military situation, and the view that there was less to fear from defeat and occupation by the Western Allies than from continuing the war. The Nazis' loud proclamations that the Volkssturm would change this attitude and make all Germans want to fight fanatically against any enemy clearly failed miserably in the Reich's western Gaue. Because the Volkssturm did not attain its psychological goal, it usually either did not fight or fought briefly with little vigor unless the Wehrmacht took the Volkssturm unit under its wing. The western Volkssturm was not a total failure militarily; but as a means to inspire Germans to fanatic resistance—the Nazis' primary goal—it clearly fell far short of its objective.

Conclusion

When World War II ended in Europe in May 1945, the German Volkssturm perished along with the Nazi regime that had created it. The militia had existed as part of a strategy intended to save Nazi Germany by creating a bloody and prolonged defense of the Fatherland that would sap Allied morale. The Volkssturm's role in this strategy was both to mobilize more men and to fanaticize the German home front. Clearly, the Volkssturm failed to achieve either goal. This failure sprang from many causes: poor planning, political infighting, conflicting and contradictory objectives, weapons and equipment shortages, lack of training, poor morale, and a whole host of other problems.

Given that the German Volkssturm was so clearly a failure, just what historical value does examining its brief and unsuccessful existence yield? This study has sought to illuminate the Volkssturm's purpose, structure, composition, preparation, and performance, but it has also sought to use the militia as a source of insight into four significant broader issues concerning Nazi Germany's last chaotic year. First, the Volkssturm helps clarify why the Third Reich's leaders continued fighting—without any serious contemplation of negotiations—a war they had clearly lost by late 1944. Second, the Volkssturm also illuminates how the Third Reich's complex and tangled power structure reached and implemented policy decisions (i.e., the intentionalist-functionalist debate) during the twilight of its existence. Third, the Volkssturm reveals average Germans' attitudes and behavior during the war's concluding months and how their opinions and actions influenced Nazi decision making. Finally, the Volkssturm provides a very clear view of why the Nazi leadership's plans failed.

In grasping why Nazi leaders insisted on continuing the war, one must begin with a simple point: they believed Germany could still win. One might assume that by late 1944 rational statesmen would have reassessed their desperate situation with an eye toward immediately pursuing negotiations. But when one factors the Nazi leadership's worldview into the assessment—as historical accuracy demands—one can see that Hitler and his associates did begin reassessing their situation, but they rejected the idea of negotiations. By agreeing to create a militia, a step top Nazis had vehemently opposed earlier, the Reich leaders showed their willingness to recognize and adapt to unfavorable circumstances. Although negotiations seem logical to us, Nazis did not consider them a viable option. One of the most basic National Socialist beliefs was that human existence was a social Darwinian struggle between peoples. Wars were winner-take-all affairs; losers ceased to exist as a nation. Allied demands for unconditional surrender and the Morgenthau Plan merely confirmed what the Nazis thought obvious about Allied war aims—they wanted to destroy the German Volk completely. In such a conflict, requesting negotiations—particularly from a position of weakness—seemed tantamount to surrender. If anyone needed concrete proof of this, Versailles provided the perfect example to many Nazis.

The "stab in the back" legend also heavily influenced Nazi thinking in late summer 1944. Nazis viewed the July 20 Plot as a narrowly averted attempt by a new generation of traitors to repeat the dastardly acts of 1918. Furthermore, to National Socialists the plot also clearly exposed treason in the officer corps and thereby explained Germany's battlefield reversals. Admitting the truth—that supposedly degenerate Aryans or subhuman Slavs had militarily bested Germany—would have required Nazis to abandon their worldview's racial cornerstone. Thus, ideological notions predisposed Nazis to look for what Germany had done wrong, to correct the mistakes, and to renew—not end—the fight.

Indeed, National Socialist ideology also gave its adherents hope for regaining the initiative. According to convinced Nazis, Germany's biological superiority remained their ultimate advantage. To capitalize fully on this, however, the German people needed to develop—at the front and at home—a unified, fanatic determination to continue the struggle regardless of its cost. The war had to be turned into a contest of wills, which meant that the Germans had to minimize Allied territorial gain and maximize enemy casualties. Nazis reasoned that in a long and brutal struggle, the morally soft Americans, the exhausted British, or the bloodied and inferior Soviets would give up either piecemeal or en masse. Here again is the omnipresent notion of a "stab in the back"—only this time it would be the Allies who would lose because of a collapse in morale. After all, these Nazis reasoned, this time—unlike in 1918—Jews dominated only the Allied governments.

The Nazi strategy harkened back to World War I in another way; it essentially called for replicating the kind of bloody stalemate that reigned on that war's Western Front. To achieve this, Germany would have to deepen its fronts with fixed and fortified positions that could deny the Allies the type of devastating mechanized breakthroughs and exploitations that they had executed in the summer of 1944. This required raising additional manpower quickly; therefore, the Reich's leaders—after some discussion—agreed to create a militia.

Intense debate, however, erupted over the scope and role of this proposed militia. Guderian wanted the force simply to raise additional troops for the replacement-hungry Eastern Front. On the other hand, Martin Bormann envisioned broader goals. From a pragmatic perspective, he argued that a national militia could help turn every inhabited place in Germany into a fortress and thus make the entire country part of the new strategy's defense in depth. This type of militia would also have a deterrent effect against potential uprisings by Germany's foreign workers. Furthermore, it could provide sixteen- and seventeen-year-old youths with basic military instruction before they enlisted in the armed forces, thereby speeding the training process for new recruits without sacrificing quality of preparation.

Most important, Bormann also employed ideologically compelling arguments in favor of a national militia. It could be used to indoctrinate German men and thereby kindle the fanaticism deemed essential for a prolonged war effort. This motivational objective, in turn, would require that the NSDAP dominate the new militia. Not only did the Party have practical propaganda experience, but Nazi ideology held that only the Party could understand the true needs of the people, only it could craft and implement policies for the good of the nation, and only it could inspire Germans to support these programs fully. Overall, Nazis believed that only the NSDAP could successfully lead the German Volk. In addition, the NSDAP considered itself uniquely able to tackle difficult tasks with minimal red tape and debate. In theory, when Nazi authorities gave subordinates a task, these underlings would compete with one another in an unfettered effort to achieve their goal quickly and thoroughly. Thus, Bormann's ideological argument went, through competition, zeal, and loyalty, the Party would be able to build a militia sooner and better than could the military's more traditional bureaucratic methods.

Furthermore, Bormann argued that a national militia under NSDAP leadership would be ready to fight, whereas an army-led regional militia might be demoralized. Just as the NSDAP had risen from the ashes of World War I— as its propaganda so fondly and frequently proclaimed—to save Germany from its internal and external enemies in the Kampfzeit, its leaders believed they could stage a repeat performance in late 1944. Thus, when one examines the ideological perceptions involved, Nazi leaders did not consider their militia to have been a desperate and improvised gamble. To them it was a natural, coherent, and logical response to difficult circumstances and was firmly grounded in what they perceived as valid historical lessons and specific German and National Socialist strengths.

Ultimately, because Bormann's ideological arguments carried the day with Hitler, the German Volkssturm developed a twofold strategic purpose. Because of its military role, the Volkssturm resembled a traditional militia in some respects. It would mobilize auxiliary troops to assist the Wehrmacht in deepening the fighting front. Also, the force could man fortified positions, provide rear-area security (against advancing enemy troops or rebellious foreign workers), or serve as a ready reserve of armed and trained men for the local defense of all German villages, towns, and cities. Furthermore, the Volkssturm resembled a traditional militia because its troops would serve only for limited time periods and only in their home areas, would perform normal military tasks, and would only supplement, and not replace, the Wehrmacht.

For the militia to carry out its combat duties, its Nazi founders reasoned that members would need both fanaticism and obedience. Due to this motivational objective, the Volkssturm also resembled a politicized people's army in its emphasis on indoctrination, officer selection criteria, rules on membership, and a number of other aspects. The overall intent was to make the force reflect positive elements of the romanticized *Volksgemeinschaft*, and thereby make average German men more aware of this community's benefits. This, in turn, was intended to make them more willing to sacrifice for its defense. As these measures created the desired fanaticism, the Nazis hoped that the militia would develop into a thoroughly spontaneous movement under NSDAP supervision, a further reflection of the Nazis' ideal Volk community. If this motivational effort succeeded, Nazis believed the Volkssturm would unleash the German people's supposedly inherent military capabilities in a violent burst of fanatic rage against the invader. Therefore, its Nazi architects gave this new force the ideologically charged name German Volkssturm. Given the blend of ideological (i.e., people's army) and traditional militia influences, the Volkssturm is therefore best described as a hybrid National Socialist "people's militia." The Volkssturm was—as with other Nazi endeavors—an attempt to graft revolutionary ideas onto traditional ones in order to benefit from both.

The creation of the German Volkssturm as a people's militia also reveals a considerable amount about the Third Reich's power structure during its last months. Overall, one of the most striking things about the force is how it shows the heavy influence of ideology, and not merely opportunism and power, on decision making at the national level in the later Third Reich. Given ideology's powerful impact on policy formulation, it is not surprising that in the Volkssturm's case, Adolf Hitler clearly appears as the Reich's supreme arbiter and distributor of power. While day-to-day executive and administrative tasks fell to his subordinates and their organizations, the Führer had the final word on all key national decisions. Ideas and initiatives constantly bubbled up from a variety of sources, but none became policy without the Führer's approval. Hitler's opposition prevented establishment of a large-scale militia prior to fall 1944; and once he had authorized its creation, control of the militia depended on his continued favor. The Führer—at Bormann's urging—shifted control of the Landsturm from OKH, the SA, and Wehrkreise to the NSDAP. Only Bormann's strenuous personal intervention prevented rivals like Schepmann, Ley, or Speer from convincing Hitler to shift control again, this time away from the Party. Although the stress of twelve years of leading Germany had taken its toll on the Führer, Adolf Hitler continued to hold the reins of German authority in late 1944.

This leads to a second point concerning Nazi Germany's power structure. Success in winning and retaining Hitler's favor—and thereby in winning and retaining power and influence—depended on the skillful employment of ideological arguments. Martin Bormann, often portrayed as consumed with personal ambition, could not have succeeded in the competitive world of Nazi politics without an adept grasp of National Socialist ideology and the ability to convince the ultimate authority on orthodoxy—Hitler—of his unwavering fidelity to the movement's goals. Indeed, any substantial political achievement in the Third Reich required more than ambition and cunning. It required the ability to convince the Führer that one's aims and methods would further the cause of National Socialism and the good of the German Volk. While plainly a ruthless opportunist, Bormann—as indicated by his actions concerning the Volkssturm—was to some degree also a National Socialist true believer. At the very least he was consistently able to portray himself as such to Hitler.

Indeed, it was primarily the ideological appeal of Bormann's vision of a people's militia that interested Hitler. The Volkssturm offered more than a way to raise auxiliary troops; it even offered more than a way to motivate them to fight. It offered a means to achieve what was arguably Nazism's highest goal—completion of the Gleichschaltung. Through the Volkssturm, Bormann promised to translate and transmit National Socialist ideas to the mass of Germans and to unite them behind the NSDAP once and for all. Thus Bormann's Volkssturm, if successful, would yield benefits not only on the battlefield but after the final victory as well. Such an accomplishment would position Martin Bormann high in the pantheon of Nazi heroes, both as one of Germany's military saviors and as the man responsible for finally convincing the masses to follow National Socialism wholeheartedly. Surely, Bormann and his rivals must have recognized that such a feat could win him the ultimate prize: designation as Hitler's successor. In this light, the intensity of the power struggles over Volkssturm control becomes clearer and strongly suggests the Nazi leaders' continued belief in their chances for victory.

A third issue concerning the Reich's structure is that basic power relationships were fundamentally shifting in late 1944. Historians generally agree that Heinrich Himmler and the SS continued their steady acquisition of power even into 1945. An examination of the Volkssturm, however, suggests that the NSDAP was beginning to gain at SS expense. Clearly, Bormann was able to defeat Himmler on a number of Volkssturm-related issues, most prominently gaining control of the force itself. There were other significant triumphs; for example, Bormann curtailed Waffen SS recruiting ambitions and won control from Himmler of the nearly 1-million-member Stadt- und Landwacht. On the other hand, the SS preserved its authority over police auxiliaries—and even expanded some of them—in the occupied territories. This suggests the SS power base was centered outside Germany, and as these areas shrunk, so, too, did SS authority. The NSDAP's star followed an inverse path; it took on a relatively greater role as the Reich became more limited to Germany itself.

The Volkssturm also shows that NSDAP influence, while growing, was not unlimited either. A variety of agencies and individuals opposed—sometimes successfully—Bormann and the Party's domination of the Volkssturm. Some challenges came from NSDAP-affiliated organizations like the SA, but the most effective were from two non-Party entities. One was Albert Speer's Reichs Ministry for Armaments and War Production, which successfully used economic arguments to force concessions from Bormann. The other was the Wehrmacht, whose leverage sprang from its essential technical expertise. Whereas Speer enjoyed prestige at the highest levels, the Wehrmacht's national political clout was more circumscribed—though not eliminated (e.g., it gained recruits from the class of 1928 at SS expense)—after July 20. Army influence increased, however, as one moved farther down the Volkssturm chain of command. As these examples show, pragmatism retained significant force of argument in the Third Reich, particularly at the lower levels, where policies had to be implemented. Nationally, ideology tended to hold the upper hand. Speer or the generals typically gained their wishes concerning the Volkssturm only when they worked with, rather than against, Bormann and the NSDAP.

Close examination of the Wehrmacht's role in the Volkssturm reveals that Keitel lied on the witness stand at Nuremberg when he claimed that the army had nothing to do with the militia. Indeed, Wehrmacht influence in the Third Reich was not as completely and thoroughly tarnished after July 20, 1944, as the generals' postwar memoirs typically claimed. The military was intimately involved with the Volkssturm from its inception and, if anything, worked to expand army participation. Also, the Volkssturm unit leader corps suggests that there were substantial numbers of older former officers—many of whom were World War I veterans—who had been actively involved in the NSDAP or its affiliates. All of this indicates that while the Wehrmacht may not have been the National Socialist People's Army called for in the NSDAP party program, it was hardly aloof from or firmly opposed to Nazism. Even at this late date in the war, close links existed between the Party and army in many ways.

Finally, examining the Volkssturm reveals a fourth point concerning Nazi Germany's political system; there was an ideological basis behind the tangled, shifting, and unorthodox power structure. Hitler and other Nazis seem to have believed that competition spawned efficiency—or at least quick results. Thus, the Volkssturm was structured to set Himmler, Bormann, Schepmann, the Gauleiters, and other subordinates competing among themselves to gain Hitler's favor. The Nazi logic—if such an oxymoron existed—was that this would force them to demonstrate their creativity and commitment and would produce results much more quickly than in a restrained and impersonal bureaucratic system. Ideology further held that loyalty to the German Volk,

National Socialism, and the Führer would provide the unifying theme in all this competition.

Because of all these factors concerning the Reich's power structure, the Volkssturm suggests the merit of synthesizing the structuralist-functionalist and intentionalist historiographical perspectives. In this synthesis, one must acknowledge the role of Hitler and National Socialist ideology, as well as the significance of power politics, opportunism, and pragmatism. The Volkssturm's example clearly validates the structuralist-functionalist description of the polycentric Nazi power structure. Examining the shifting power relations among the competing entities—bewildering at best and impossible at worst—is plainly essential to understanding the day-to-day exercise of authority. Furthermore, as the Levy System's operation or Volkssturm unit training plainly illustrates, the farther one moved from the Führer's inner circle, the more policy implementation was determined by power relationships and practical concerns rather than ideology.

On the other hand, there is considerable evidence from the Volkssturm to confirm aspects of the intentionalist interpretation. Hitler remained at the pinnacle of this system, and National Socialist (i.e., Hitler's) ideology lay to a substantial—though varying—extent behind all national decisions. Ultimately, all major policy decisions had to be justified to the Führer based on how they fit Nazi goals. Even the confusing structure itself, with its intense competition, can be seen as originating in National Socialist ideology.

Studying the Volkssturm also clearly exposes the problems generated by the National Socialist approach to government. Among the most serious of the many factors that frustrated the grand designs behind the Volkssturm were the very power struggles, rivalries, and personality clashes spawned by the Third Reich's social Darwinian structure. The Volkssturm did not unify contentious national leaders in productive competition; it only intensified bickering as Nazi paladins jousted with one another for the honor of—and credit for—guiding a program intended to win the war. Although Bormann ultimately won the struggle, his was a Pyrrhic victory. The resentful and uncooperative attitudes of the losers—particularly Himmler, Berger, and Schepmann—poisoned relationships between Volkssturm and other officials even to the lowest levels. Rather than creating harmony, the Volkssturm intensified the NSDAP's inherent fragmentation and ensured that the very men on whom the force depended for its fanatic leadership had little incentive to participate fully and selflessly. If Party activists themselves could not cooperate in the face of mortal perils, there was little hope that the Volkssturm could rally all Germans to do so.

The divisiveness of Bormann's quest for Volkssturm dominance is clearly apparent with the Levy System. It also shows the craftiness of Bormann's tactics. To justify the existence of deferrals, he could cite the desire to balance economic needs with the need to maximize the number of militia units available in any Gau. On the other hand, deferrals gave him considerable influence over almost the entire civilian manpower pool. Levy III also existed for a valid reason—to hasten the preparation of Germany's next class of recruits—and Bormann used this rationale to justify special exemptions and privileges over this group for the RAD and HJ. This, however, also enhanced Bormann's political position by securing allies against the SS, but it alienated those groups to which he denied such extraordinary consideration. Furthermore, Bormann's partnership with the HJ, RAD, and Wehrmacht allowed him to influence the distribution of the critically important 1928 recruiting class—the Reich's last immediately available reserve of military manpower. Bormann apparently used this leverage in the army's favor to undermine his main personal rivals, Himmler, Berger, and the SS. None of this seems conducive to the unity that the Volkssturm was supposed to generate.

Finally and most important, Bormann's desire to cement his political control led him to centralize, standardize, and bureaucratize the Volkssturm to the point where he personally dominated decision making on most significant—and many insignificant—issues. Denying rival organizations any regional political beachheads inside the Volkssturm required Bormann to ensure that the Party apparatus—his power base—administered the militia. Simultaneously, though, Bormann had to prevent his nominal subordinates, the Gauleiters, from using the militia to enhance their résumés significantly or to become independent of Party Chancellery control. Therefore, Bormann sought to dominate decision making. The unforeseen result of these efforts, however, was to stifle the local initiative and enthusiasm that the Nazis proclaimed essential to Volkssturm effectiveness.

Compounding the negative consequences of the Nazi power structure were the constraints imposed on the Volkssturm by the war economy. Not only was output falling in all key categories, but the Volkssturm sought to mobilize workers essential to war production. To minimize disruption, Bormann and his staff created the Levy System. This cumbersome approach required review of each individual Volkssturm member's health and economic significance, which increased centralization, bureaucracy, and complexity. It also overburdened local officials. Moreover, the Levy System strained the regular conscription system to some degree because both systems relied on the same personnel and procedures.

In the final analysis, the Levy System enhanced Bormann's power but yielded little other benefit. The Levy System did successfully minimize Volkssturm impact on sectors deemed critical to the war effort, but it imposed heavy burdens on those activities with lower priority. While Volkssturm leaders anticipated some of this economic disruption, there was an unexpected problem. The Levy System tended to favor groups and individuals who were politically well connected and also created the often justified impression that local Nazi bosses made assignments arbitrarily or on personal and/or political grounds. This did irreparable damage to Nazi claims that all Germans served in the force equally, undermined the remaining credibility of the Party, and thereby dimmed any hope of the Volkssturm achieving its ideological and motivational objectives.

Indeed, the Volkssturm's motivational role made the attitudes of average Germans critical to Volkssturm success. Immediately upon the Volkssturm's promulgation, however, the Nazis' indoctrinational efforts encountered a serious problem in this area. Germans, apparently well aware of their military's historically brutal treatment of partisans, generally demanded that the Volkssturm conform to international legal standards. Otherwise, they expected the Allies would execute captured Volkssturm men and exact reprisals against civilians just as German armies had long done in response to guerrilla activity. Hopeful that their indoctrination efforts would eventually eliminate such fears, the Nazis willingly compromised in order to get Germans simply to attend militia meetings. Thus, officials launched a massive effort to make the Volkssturm fit international law. This included attaching active militia units to Wehrmacht commands and seeking to provide all members with uniforms, armbands, paybooks, a regular chain of command, standard unit organization, and a judicial system. All these efforts were accompanied by extensive publicity stressing this evidence of Volkssturm legality to the German public.

Some historians have portrayed the Volkssturm as primarily an instrument of control—even terror—intended to keep the German people harnessed against their will to the war effort.[1] The Volkssturm did have this effect in some areas—particularly in the desperate days of 1945—but it was not the Nazis' primary intention. The goal was to use the Volkssturm as a means of encouraging Germans' full and willing support of the Nazi leadership and the war effort. The Third Reich's leaders had always envisioned a nation where the people would wholeheartedly accept National Socialist ideas, and they knew coercion and terror alone could not achieve this. To maximize public participation—and thereby guarantee full exposure to Nazi indoctrination efforts—the Party made extensive efforts to accommodate public concerns about the militia. This suggests that Germans were not simply and wholly coerced and manipulated by the Nazis, at least in the Volkssturm's case.

Although the Volkssturm's leaders deemed legal recognition essential, the effort to achieve it generated significant unanticipated consequences. It increased logistical demands immensely and accelerated the trend toward greater standardization, bureaucratic routine, and central control. Pursuing legal recognition also created a larger role in the force for the Wehrmacht, since it was the only institution in the Reich with the expertise and equipment needed even to begin building an effective militia. However, the pursuit of legal status and reliance on the army turned the Volkssturm away from the original Nazi people's militia ideal and more toward a traditional militia model.

Wehrmacht influence with Volkssturm units ultimately grew to the point that in many areas the Party's role became secondary, irrelevant, or even counterproductive due largely to local public opinion. Volkssturm morale proved generally impervious to Nazi indoctrination, none of which was new in content or form at this stage of the war. On the other hand, Volkssturm morale responded well to practical measures such as properly organized and relevant military training, receiving adequate stocks of weapons and supplies, and cooperation from regular troops. The Party could provide none of this, and average Germans plainly knew it. Therefore, the supposedly discredited Wehrmacht, not the NSDAP, proved the only institution capable of motivating Germans to fight. In fact, where Volkssturm troops fought well, they typically did so because regular units had taken an interest in improving their combat potential and had closely supported them in battle.

Aside from Wehrmacht assistance, fear provided the other factor that led to a willingness to fight among Volkssturm men. Sometimes this fear resulted from threats of punishment by German military or political officials, but fear of the enemy proved the most potent motivating factor. This held particularly true in eastern Germany, where Nazi propaganda meshed well with widely held perceptions about the war against the Soviet Union. To eastern Germans—especially the older farmers and middle-class men who formed the majority of this region's Volkssturm—the war indeed seemed to fit the Nazi description of a brutal people's struggle. Germany had to use all available means to defeat and destroy the Bolsheviks, or the barbaric Communists would crush the German nation and enslave its people. To heighten eastern Germans' sense that their Fatherland was in danger, Nazi propaganda could easily play on the widespread fear of Communism, traditional ethnic chauvinism, and notions of patriotism, honor, and duty. In many instances this prompted those living in the Red Army's path to serve dutifully in the Volkssturm.

Indeed, western Germans shared the Nazi assessment of the stakes involved in the war on the Eastern Front. Bormann and associates hoped to use the Volkssturm to convince them that the war against the Western Allies was no different. With the exception of a tiny fanatic minority, however, Germans never considered their individual, national, or cultural survival to be threatened by the Western Allies. In some instances in southwestern Germany, traditional hostility toward France apparently intensified Volkssturm resistance against French troops; and in isolated cases, resentment of Allied bombing may have motivated some to take up arms. But at least as far as the Volkssturm was concerned, the British and Americans wisely distinguished between those who supported the Nazis (i.e., actually fought in the militia) and those who did not, and appeared to treat the latter with leniency. Ultimately, then, defeat and occupation by the Western Allies simply did not hold the same personal or collective horror for Germans as did losing to the Soviets. As Germans began to realize that the war was lost, many saw no sense in resisting the Western Allies' advance; it would be better to let the Americans and British get as far east as possible. As shown by events in mid-1945, Germans, if they had to lose the war, overwhelmingly preferred surrendering to the British or Americans. For the average German, the Volkssturm and Nazi propaganda could not change the entrenched perception that the consequences of defeat in the West were simply less severe.

The Volkssturm's typically poor performance—even in the east—clearly suggests that the Nazi Gleichschaltung remained incomplete. National Socialism simply did not command the fanatic loyalty of a majority of Germans by 1945. Where Nazi ideology reflected widely held traditional attitudes—as in eastern Germany—the Party could make progress toward its objectives. When goals diverged too greatly from public opinion—as in western Germany—the Party's success was limited. Few Germans had so wholeheartedly committed themselves to the movement that they were willing to follow it into death. These fanatics did exist, but they were a tiny minority even among Party officials. Of the forty-two Gauleiters, only two fought to the death—ironically, both against the Americans—while the other forty chose to flee. Most Germans had at some point found something about the Nazis that they could support, but by 1945 only in areas threatened by Soviet occupation was there a widespread sense that risking death to preserve NSDAP rule was preferable to surrender. And even here the motivation was more fear of the Soviets than support for Nazism.

Attitudes go far toward explaining why the Volkssturm performed better in the east than in the west; but in neither area did it meet expectations. Weapons, ammunition, uniforms, and other essential supplies were simply not available for even a significant fraction of the Volkssturm. Without weapons, units could not train adequately, much less hold their own in battle against a well-equipped foe. Because of their age, insufficient rations, inadequate clothing, and bitter winter weather, Volkssturm men were prone to sickness. This put them at an even greater disadvantage in combat—especially against the younger and better equipped soldiers of the Western armies. Although the Party apparently made extensive efforts to appoint militarily experienced men to Volkssturm commands, unit leaders were always overworked, sometimes underqualified, and generally inadequately trained in modern warfare. To complicate their formidable task still further, they lacked reliable communications equipment with which to control their own troops in battle or to cooperate with nearby German formations. Finally, the largest Volkssturm unit, the battalion, was a purely tactical formation too weak to survive long on the battlefield without proper support. Not surprisingly, inadequate military preparations often destroyed any will to fight among Volkssturm men, even in eastern Germany.

Only Wehrmacht assistance could increase Volkssturm combat potential and morale. In their postwar writings, many army officers squarely blamed Party officials for all Volkssturm failures; and, indeed, certain regional and local NSDAP bosses obstructed even legitimate Wehrmacht involvement with their militia. On the other hand, numerous examples of good Party-army relations existed, such as the efforts of Baden Gaustabsführer Burst, Westmark's Caspary, or Breslau Kreisstabsführer Herzog. Furthermore, the Wehrmacht's view of the militia as an expendable, second-rate auxiliary sometimes hurt Volkssturm morale, especially when military men callously ordered militia units to sacrifice themselves to cover their own withdrawal. Some army officers, particularly on the Western Front, also tended to expect the Volkssturm to fight as well as a regular formation even without proper preparation or assistance. Ultimately, Volkssturm military failure grew primarily from the inability of the collapsing war economy to equip and arm the force properly, from low morale, and from the weakened Wehrmacht's inability to provide the required support and guidance both prior to and during battle.

Some have suggested that the Volkssturm's failure proves that part-time civilian soldiers have no place in modern warfare. Yugoslav and Soviet partisans certainly provide extensive evidence to the contrary. Furthermore, the British Home Guard—a traditional militia—made a number of contributions, albeit unglamorous ones, to Britain's defense. Also Soviet Workers' Battalions distinguished themselves at Leningrad and Stalingrad despite their unpreparedness.[2] Critics often ignore the fact that under the right conditions the Volkssturm contributed to the Reich's war effort. At Pyritz and Crailsheim, the Volkssturm showed it could delay Allied mechanized advances long enough for regular troops to form new defensive lines. In East Prussia, along the Saar and Upper Rhine, the Volkssturm performed useful security occupations that freed reserves for use elsewhere. On the Oder and Upper Rhine, in Fortresses such as Breslau, and in Berlin, East Prussia, and other places, Volkssturm units demonstrated they could fight as regular infantry when given adequate preparation and support. The Volkssturm, like the Home Guard, also contributed by taking over rear-area duties, thus allowing the military to focus on other tasks. The Volkssturm does not prove that militias are useless but indicates that they can succeed only if they are built upon a carefully planned and constructed foundation and are not hastily improvised under emergency conditions.

Indeed, the Volkssturm probably would have been more effective had it been founded earlier, had more time to prepare for combat, and been more limited in size. It would have been better run by the army, with the NSDAP restricting its own involvement to propaganda, registration, and other auxiliary functions. Also, without the complex and burdensome Levy System, the Volkssturm could have concentrated exclusively on true local defense, avoided some of the divisiveness engendered by the classification process, and freed the military draft apparatus to work exclusively on locating additional recruits for the Wehrmacht.

Although such measures might have made the Volkssturm a more effective auxiliary from a purely military perspective, this was not what Hitler, Bormann, and other Nazis sought to create. The Nazi leadership wanted a fanatic people's militia because, as they saw it, Germany's only alternative to annihilation was to continue resisting longer than the Allies were willing to attack. This required an iron will both in the trenches and on the home front. For the Nazi leaders, morale was the key to mastering the situation in late 1944 and early 1945, and the Volkssturm was to be a vital means both to restore morale and to protract the struggle. Why did they think this? Simply put, their ideological preconceptions strongly colored their thinking. This exposes the final reason for Volkssturm failure: there was a yawning gulf between Nazi ideological notions and reality.

One of the Nazis' erroneous assumptions was the belief that Germans inherently possessed martial qualities superior to those of any other nationality. German men, like everyone else, needed adequate weapons, logistical support and supervision, and coordination in battle; they could not simply receive a few hours of instruction in basic weapon usage, hear some propaganda, and go out to stop mechanized armies. Proper armament and training required time and could not simply be improvised on the spur of the moment by competition among political zealots or by sheer force of will.

A second major flaw in the assumptions behind the Volkssturm concerned the Nazis' assessment of NSDAP abilities. They wrongly believed that only the Party could ascertain the best interests of the German Volk. They were further mistaken in assuming that the Party had the ability and respect needed to convince Germans to follow their lead with blind fanaticism. In reality, by 1945 few Germans respected their local Party boss as a dynamic leader, and for many of those in doubt, the Volkssturm exposed just how factious, petty, incompetent, and/or brutal many of these Nazis were. In fact, Party control of the Volkssturm was predominantly negative, particularly where local officials exhibited selfishness or cowardice or fell back on brute force when their simplistic motivational appeals failed. Those Volkssturm men who did fight, with the exception of a few fanatics, acted not for National Socialism's preservation but out of fear, desperation, and the belief that they were protecting their homes, families, and country. The Volkssturm and the strategy of which it was a part failed because the leaders of the NSDAP had lost touch with the German people. These self-proclaimed experts in motivational leadership proved incapable of convincing all Germans that the interests of National Socialism and the German Volk were one and the same.

Finally, and perhaps most important, the Nazis' assumptions about their enemies were wrong. Contrary to Nazi perceptions, the Slavs were not racially inferior, nor were the Western democracies weak-willed. They both proved themselves capable of waging modern warfare every bit as effectively as Germans. Most important, the Allied coalition was not destined to collapse because of its contradictory ideologies. The Nazi leadership never fully convinced the German public—particularly that portion living in the western half of the country—that the consequences of a defeat would be the ultimate annihilation of the German Volk. The Nazis' actions earlier in the war had, however, successfully convinced their opponents what a German triumph would mean. The Allies—particularly the Soviets, eastern Europeans, and Jews—had Auschwitz, Oradour, Lidice, Babi Yar, Warsaw, Malmedy, and thousands of similar places to remind them of the brutally destructive, genocidal consequences of German victory. Hitler, Bormann, Himmler, and other Nazis never realized that as long as National Socialism existed, the Allies had a powerful motive to overlook their own differences and work for the Third Reich's total defeat. No matter how hard the Volkssturm's ragged and reluctant warriors fought, they could not alter this hard reality, and thus could do little to prevent Allied victory. Ironically, the miserably failed militia called the German Volkssturm points out that National Socialist ideology profoundly affected the strategic planning of both sides during World War II. Moreover, it shows how Nazi ideology largely superseded reality as the basis for decision making in the Third Reich.

Statistical Appendix

Like all evidence on the Volkssturm, statistical data are often fragmentary, scattered, skewed, and/or incomplete. The most detailed, broad, and accessible information on Volkssturm members is the German Red Cross's *Vermißtenbildliste* *(Pictorial Lists of the Missing in Action)*. The Red Cross compiled these after the war from information provided by missing individuals' relatives, friends, and unit comrades as a means of helping locate MIAs.[1] Arranged roughly by Gau and Kreis or unit, the Red Cross lists provide the name, 1939 town of residence, job, rank, and place and date where last reported of just under 31,000 Volkssturm men who were formally listed as missing in action. Unfortunately, Levy assignments are not included, although it is safe to assume a preponderance of Levy I men, since these were the first units armed and mobilized.

A second problem is that the vast majority of MIAs were from eastern Gaue, which might tend to skew results toward rural occupations (e.g., agriculture and crafts), although the presence of significant numbers of men from cites such as Berlin, Breslau, Danzig, and Königsberg offsets this. While by no means perfect, the Red Cross *Vermißtenbildliste* comprise the best available source on the Volkssturm's age and occupational profile, especially when the lists are used in conjunction with the few extant complete unit rosters or Levy assignment lists for an Ortsgruppe or a factory. Furthermore, because MIAs were by definition men on active duty and therefore away from their regular occupations, the Red Cross *Vermißtenbildliste* enable us to view more accurately the human composition of Volkssturm mobilizations and thereby gauge their impact on Germany's faltering war economy. Therefore, the *Vermißtenbildliste* provided much of the statistical basis for chapter 5.

The following tables are not based on sophisticated or complex statistical procedures, but some explanations are in order. Owing to the number of MIAs from eastern Gaue (East Prussia, Wartheland, Danzig–West Prussia, Pomerania, Mecklenburg, Upper and Lower Silesia, Brandenburg, Berlin, Sudetenland, Saxony, and the Austrian Gaue—for which there was very little information, since this was a postwar West German project), I employed a 20 percent sample of these men by selecting every fifth man in the *Vermißtenbildliste* from these Gaue (a total of 5,838 men). For the other, or western, Gaue, all 1,600 MIAs appearing in the lists are included; and of these, 1,010 men were members of Volkssturm special purpose (zbV) Levy I units, which fought in the east. To reflect proper proportions whenever national totals were needed and to ensure accurate east-west comparisons, the totals of eastern Gaue MIAs were weighted (i.e., multiplied by five), thus producing the rather artificially round actual numbers in the MIA-based tables.

Locating an accurate and comprehensive economic benchmark against which to compare information on Volkssturm units or MIAs is also challenging. For this study I utilized the sweeping overview provided by the *Wehrmachtersatzplan* (WEP) for 1945—except where indicated otherwise—because of this document's wealth of statistical information regarding age profiles and draft deferrals for the general labor pool, the date of the information (September 30, 1944), and because the Volkssturm Levy System was designed to use the same mechanisms and priorities as the regular conscription process.[2] Unfortunately, the WEP also has drawbacks. It employs one system of economic categories to assess the overall labor pool and another slightly different set for draft deferrals. Nor does the WEP fully explain its economic categories, and it lacks sufficient detail in some areas (e.g., skill levels or blue-collar/white-collar breakdowns). Finally, the plan cannot be harmonized fully with MIA data in every way; for example, the WEP lists workers by economic sector, but many MIAs are described only by job type.[3] In spite of such imperfections, the statistical information provided here, tempered by evidence cited in the text, provides the most comprehensive view of Volkssturm membership and its economic implications that anyone has attempted.

Volkssturm leader data are no more comprehensive, but Gau Bayreuth's surviving files contain considerable information on the men nominated for unit commands there. Data are again quite incomplete and vary from Kreis to Kreis within the Gau, and certainly the profile of Volkssturm leaders in other areas may have differed. Nonetheless, the Bayreuth information is the most significant extant evidence on the Volkssturm leadership corps that I uncovered, and it is sufficient to allow some important general conclusions about this group. Furthermore, there are also a few complete (or nearly complete) leader profiles for units from other parts of the country against which to compare—and generally confirm—conclusions drawn from the Bayreuth information. Thus, in a general sense, Volkssturm statistical data closely resemble all evidence on this organization—scattered and fragmentary, but adequate to support historical assessments.

Table 1. Volkssturm MIAs by Economic Sector

	EAST		WEST		NATIONAL	
	No.	Percent	No.	Percent	Percent	Index[a]
Job Type						
Banking/insurance	375	1.28	20	1.25	1.28	1.97
Tourism	520	1.78	14	0.87	1.73	1.63
Agriculture	8,435	28.90	214	13.88	28.09	1.35
Trade/professions	1,775	6.08	113	7.06	6.13	1.21
Forestry	280	0.96	11	0.69	0.95	1.11
Construction	1,665	5.71	143	8.94	5.87	1.02
Manufacturing/crafts	8,900	30.49	613	38.31	30.90	0.97
Government	2,020	6.92	126	7.88	6.97	0.56
Transportation/ communication	1,515	5.19	76	4.75	5.17	0.52
Mining	375	1.28	51	3.19	1.38	0.13
Utilities[b]	0	0.00	0	0.00	—	—
Uncategorizable						
White-collar	1,755	6.01	126	7.87	6.11	NA
Students	265	0.91	19	1.19	0.92	NA
Retirees	55	0.19	—	0.00	0.18	NA
No answer	1,255	4.30	76	4.62	4.32	NA
Totals	29,190	100	1,600	100	100	

The trade/professional category is combined as in the WEP. The uncategorizable white-collar employees could skew the results, but it is impossible to ascertain in precisely what economic sector these men—many listed simply as *Angestellter*—may have worked.

a. Index is national percentage for that sector divided by the national percentage of German men employed in that sector as shown in Tables 2 and 3. Thus an index greater than 1.0 means that sector's manpower tended to be overrepresented in the Volkssturm.

b. Although utility workers were not identified among MIAs, some may well have been in this group, although they did have extensive deferrals; GenInsp. für Wasser und Energie, "Runderlaß 75/44 LWA," Nov. 24, 1944, StA Bückeburg, L102b Stadthagen, Nr. 1876.

Table 2. All German Civilian Men by Economic Sector

| | 5/31/1939 | | 9/30/1944 | | CHANGE | |
| | | | | | Actual Percent | Percent of Total |
	No.	Percent	No.	Percent	Percent	
Mining	1,974,600	8.1	1,399,100	10.3	−29.2	+2.2
Government	2,407,700	9.8	1,696,400	12.5	−29.5	+2.7
Transportation/ communication	1,964,500	8.0	1,351,900	10.0	−31.2	+2.0
Utilities	213,700	0.9	144,500	1.1	−32.9	+0.2
Agriculture	4,836,700	19.8	2,805,700	20.7	−42.0	+0.9
Forestry	217,800	0.9	115,100	0.9	−46.9	−0.03
Manufacturing	8,174,800	33.4	4,324,200	32.0	−47.1	−1.4
Tourism	349,000	1.4	143,600	1.1	−58.9	−0.3
Banking/insurance	244,700	1.0	87,300	0.6	−64.3	−0.4
Trade/ professionals	1,917,500	7.8	68,700	5.1	−64.3	−2.7
Construction	2,175,900	8.9	77,600	5.7	−64.4	−3.2
Totals	24,476,900	100	13,528,100	100	−44.8	

The lone modification made to WEP figures was to move artisans engaged in construction from manufacturing/crafts to construction. The percentage given for 1944 (9.67) was applied to the 1939 number.

Table 3. Military Draft Deferrals by Economic Sector

| | DEFERRED | | ALL GERMAN MEN | | |
	No.	Percent	No.	Percent	Index[a]
Tourism	19,000	13.23	143,600	1.06	0.26
Trade/professions	215,200	31.43	684,700	5.06	0.62
Agriculture	928,700	33.10	2,805,700	20.74	0.65
Banking/insurance	41,900	48.00	87,300	0.65	0.94
Manufacturing/ craftworkers[b]	2,507,100	57.98	4,324,200	31.97	1.14
Government	1,008,200	59.43	1,696,400	12.54	1.16
Mining	930,200	66.49	1,399,100	10.34	1.30
Forestry	77,500	67.33	115,100	0.85	1.32
Utilities	107,500	74.39	144,500	1.07	1.46
Transportation/ communication	1,069,700	79.13	1,351,900	9.99	1.55
Totals	6,905,000	51.04	13,528,100	100	1.00

a. Index is percentage of deferred men in each sector divided by percentage of all German men deferred (51.04). An index greater than 1.0 means that personnel in that sector enjoyed higher than average rates of draft deferrals.

b. Construction sector included with craftsmen in the WEP.

Table 4. MIAs by Economic Sector and Draft Age (percentages)

	MIAs Non-DA	MIAs DA	MIAs NA	Sector DA	Index[a]
Tourism	67.22	30.91	1.87	13.23	2.34
Agriculture	44.57	55.19	0.24	33.10	1.67
Trade/professions	55.82	44.13	0.05	31.43	1.40
Mining	24.41	74.18	1.41	66.49	1.12
Manufacturing/construction[b]	46.78	52.81	0.41	57.98	0.91
Forestry	41.93	58.07	0.00	67.33	0.86
Transportation/communication	47.51	52.49	0.00	79.13	0.66
Government	68.40	31.13	0.47	59.43	0.52
Banking/insurance	75.19	24.81	0.00	48.00	0.51
Construction	(51.06)	(49.07)	(0.28)	NA	NA
White-collar	58.10	41.58	0.32	NA	NA
Students	67.25	32.75	0.00	NA	NA
Retired	72.72	27.28	0.00	NA	NA
NA	45.03	54.32	0.38	NA	NA
Overall	47.29	50.17	0.34	51.04	0.98

All ages are calculated from January 1, 1945.

a. Index is percentage of draft-age men among Volkssturm MIAs from each sector divided by percentage of all draft-age German men in the sector. An index greater than 1.0 indicates that the sector's personnel were overrepresented among Volkssturm MIAs. DA = draft age (men born in classes 1897–1927 inclusive)

b. Construction sector included with craftsmen in the WEP and those MIAs engaged in construction are included in the manufacturing/construction category. Construction MIAs are listed separately for informational and comparative purposes.

Table 5. Age Distribution of German Civilian Men Liable for Volkssturm Service

Birth Year	NATIONAL		VsMIAs	Index	VszbV	Index[a]
	No.	Percent				
1884–1896	4,890,000	35.69	46.03	1.30	33.16	0.93
1897–1900	1,823,000	13.30	20.09	1.51	26.24	1.97
1901–1905	2,104,000	15.35	17.16	1.12	25.45	1.66
1906–1927	3,092,000	22.56	12.92	.57	14.65	0.65
1928–1930	1,796,000	13.10	2.20	.17	0.30	0.02
Total	13,705,000	100	98.4[b]		99.6[c]	

In order to adapt WEP figures (this table's national data source) to the draft-age categories used in other tables, it was necessary to split an aggregated 1894–1900 grouping. This was accomplished by using the 1939 census to figure that 37.81 percent of the men in this 1894–1900 category were born in 1894–1896 and 62.19 percent in 1897–1900. The WEP's figure of civilian German men (2,931,000) born between 1884 and 1900 was then multiplied by these percentages to arrive at a rounded figure of 1,108,000 men born in 1894–1896 and 1,823,000 in 1897–1900. For 1939 census figures, see Germany, Statistisches Reichsamt, *Statistisches Jahrbuch 1941/42*, vol. 59 (Berlin: Verlag für Sozialpolitik, Wirtschaft und Statistik, 1944), 24.

The need for the 1897–1900 and 1901–1905 border categories comes from the fact that although the Wehrmacht was then drafting men from the 1897–1927 classes (ages seventeen to forty-seven) WEP priorities called for drafting fewer deferred men *(kriegverwendungsfähig* and *bedingt kriegverwendungsfähig)* from the 1897–1900 classes: 36 percent compared with 50 percent for the 1900–1927 classes. Also the pre-1906 classes had considerably fewer men in active Wehrmacht service (27.9 percent compared with the 80.2 percent in the 1906–1926 group).

a. Index is Volkssturm (Vs) MIA or Volkssturm zbV percentage, respectively, divided by national percentage. An index greater than 1.0 means that men from the birth year cohort were overrepresented among Volkssturm men.

b. The remaining 1.6% included 1.26% born prior to 1884 and 0.34% with birth year unknown.

c. The remaining 0.4% consists of men born prior to 1884.

Table 6. Age Distribution for Volkssturm Units

Company	Levy	Pre-1897 over DA	1897–1900 Border	1901–1905 Border	1906–1927 DA	Total DA	Average Age
Rastatt VII/3	I	57.97	18.84	12.32	10.87	42.03	48.8
Brieske	I	52.04	14.63	27.64	5.69	47.96	47.8
Rastatt VII/1	I	51.33	18.59	16.81	13.27	48.67	47.3
Rötz	I	42.20	17.34	19.07	21.39	57.80	44.5
Schaumburg-Lippe[a]	I	10.35	24.14	38.79	25.00	87.93	41.5
RMfVuP IV	II	17.78	11.11	33.33	37.78	82.22	41.1
Ludwigsfelde[b]	II	27.14	9.43	22.00	40.29	71.72	45.4
Eger	II	29.55	20.45	22.73	27.27	70.45	42.6
München-Ost[c]	II	50.85	16.10	11.02	22.03	49.15	46.5

Over DA = men born before 1897.

Border = men born in 1897–1905 classes from which some men were scheduled for conscription under the WEP.

All units were companies except the factory-affiliated Eger platoon and were selected because apparently complete rosters survived that specified the unit's Levy. 4. Komp., VsBtn. 16/37 (Brieske). "Stärkenachweisung," undated. LHA Postdam, PrBrRep. 61, Mark Brandenburg, Nr. 5.3.1; 1. and 3. Komp., Baden VsBtn. VII (Rastatt), "Namensliste," Nov. 27 and 28, 1944, both in Stadtarchiv Rastatt, Bürgermeisteramt Rastatt, A/3923; Og. Werne Oberland, "Liste," undated, T-81/95/108876–78; 7. VsKomp. Rötz, various lists in StA Amberg, NSDAP Krltg. Oberviechtach, Nr. 5; Kr. Schaumburg-Lippe Feldkomp., "Liste," undated, StA Bückeburg, L102b Stadthagen, Nr. 1877; 2. Komp., VsBtn. 16/374 (Ludwigsfelde), "Mob-Liste," Mar. 11, 1945, LHA Potsdam, PrBrRep. 2A, Regierung Potsdam, I Polizei, Nr. 2321; 2. Komp., VsBtn. 19/XVI (München-Ost), "Liste," undated. T-81/153/156331–32, 156339–42, and 156348–52; IV. Zug/I. Komp., VsBtn. 32/27 (Eger), "Liste," undated, T-81/94/108491; IV. Komp., VsBtn. Propagandaministerium, "Liste," undated, T-580/667/502.

a. The Schaumburg unit was a "field company" with pretensions of being an elite unit; therefore, it contained the youngest personnel available and is thus an exception among Levy I units. It listed two members for whom birth year could not be determined.

b. The Ludwigsfelde unit contained two members from the 1928 class who account for the other 1.14%.

c. The München-Ost formation is an anomaly, probably due to population or occupational peculiarities in the area.

Table 7. Ortsgruppe Levy Assignments by Draft Age

	Levy	Pre-1897 over DA	1897–1900 Border	1901–1905 Border	1906–1927 DA	Total DA	Average Age
Bramsche	I	58.78	19.08	12.98	9.16	41.22	49.2
Bramsche	II	51.02	18.56	16.15	14.09	48.88	47.5
Lingolsheim[a]	I	33.56	19.18	22.60	18.49	60.27	45.0
Lingolsheim[a]	II	41.96	11.61	16.07	30.36	58.04	44.8
Meinau[a]	I	27.27	23.38	25.98	22.08	71.44	43.8
Meinau[a]	II	30.34	15.73	21.35	32.58	69.66	42.7
Mühlenbeck	I	65.62	10.94	12.50	10.94	34.38	49.2
Mühlenbeck	II	44.23	15.87	22.11	17.79	55.77	45.8
Oberesch	I	51.02	10.20	19.05	19.73	48.98	45.7
Oberesch	II	41.66	16.67	16.67	25.00	58.34	44.3
Pullach[b]	I	30.00	10.00	20.00	35.00	65.00	40.7
Pullach[b]	II	36.97	20.61	21.21	20.61	62.43	44.5
Rheine	I	33.33	10.00	36.67	20.00	66.67	44.6
Rheine	II	23.44	21.87	29.69	25.00	76.56	44.1
Werne	I	40.41	30.30	16.16	13.13	59.59	45.4
Werne	II	7.79	8.04	22.86	61.31	92.21	38.4

These Ortsgruppen were selected because of their extensive, possibly even complete, listings of Levy I and II men. Og. Bramsche, "Erfassung der männlichen Bevölkerung zum Volkssturm," undated, StA Osnabrück, Dep. 59b, Nr. 1870: Og. Lingolsheim and Meinau, "Erfassungsliste," undated, T-81/95/109207–80; Og. Mühlenbeck, "Liste," undated, LHA Potsdam, PrBrRep. 61, Brandenburg, Nr. 5. 18.1; Og. Oberesch, "Erfassungsliste," undated, LA Saarbrücken, NS Mischbestand, Nr. 22, 46–49; Og. Pullach, "Liste," undated, T-81/94/108193–98; Og. Rheine "Aufführung," undated, T-73/21/3145048–52; Og. Werne Oberland, "Liste," undated, T-81/ 94/108876–78.

a. Meinau and Lingolsheim percentages do not total 100 due to men for whom no birth year was listed.

b. Pullach percentages do not total 100 because of members born after 1927.

Table 8. Volkssturm MIAs by Job Skills

	EAST		WEST		National MIA by Percent
	No.	Percent	No.	Percent	
White-collar and supervisory	7,655	26.22	474	29.63	26.40
Skilled workers	6,965	23.86	501	31.30	24.25
Farmers	6,580	22.54	144	9.00	21.84
Semiskilled or unskilled workers	5,865	20.09	359	22.44	20.21
Master craftsmen	550	1.89	29	1.81	1.88
Students	265	0.91	19	1.19	0.92
Retired	55	0.19	0	0.00	0.18
No answer	1,255	4.30	74	4.63	4.32

Statistical information on the entire German male workforce broken down by job skill categories is lacking for late 1944.

Table 9. Eastern MIA Workers by Area and Skill

Job Type	SEMISKILLED AND UNSKILLED No.	Percent[a]	SKILLED No.	Percent[a]	MEISTER No.	Percent[a]	TOTAL No.	Percent[a]
Other factory	2,405	41.00	230	3.30	—		2,635	19.69
Metalworking	10	0.17	1,695	24.33	30	5.45	1,735	12.97
Agriculture	1,635	27.86	—		35	6.36	1,670	12.48
Construction	150	2.56	1,335	19.17	75	13.64	1,560	11.66
Crafts	—		975	14.00	140	25.45	1,115	8.33
Food processing	20	0.34	810	11.63	140	25.45	970	7.25
Transportation/ communication	775	13.20	140	2.01	20	3.64	935	6.99
Machinery	35	0.60	430	6.17	25	4.55	490	3.66
Wood products	—		440	6.32	15	2.73	455	3.40
Boat/wagon fabrication	5	0.10	300	4.31	10	1.82	315	2.35
Mining	215	3.67	85	1.22	15	2.73	315	2.35
Printing	—		290	4.16	5	0.91	295	2.20
Services	200	3.41	55	0.79	—		255	1.91
Textiles	15	.26	165	2.37	35	6.36	215	1.61
Maintenance	180	3.07	—		—		180	1.35
Forestry	140	2.39	—		—		140	1.05
Security	30	0.51	15	0.22	—		45	0.34
Warehousing	35	0.60	—		—		35	0.26
Government	15	0.26	—		5	0.91	20	0.15
Totals	5,865	100	6,965	100	550	100	13,380	100

a. Percentages are the percentage of men employed in the listed industry out of the total number of men in that skill category (e.g., the 230 skilled "other factory" workers constituted 3.30% of all skilled workers among Volkssturm MIAs).

Table 10. Western MIA Workers by Area and Skill

Job Type	SEMISKILLED AND UNSKILLED No.	Percent[a]	SKILLED No.	Percent[a]	MEISTER No.	Percent[a]	TOTAL No.	Percent[a]
Other factory	153	42.86	35	6.96	1	3.45	189	21.27
Construction	16	4.48	111	22.07	7	24.13	134	15.07
Metalworking	1	0.28	119	23.67	3	10.34	123	13.85
Crafts	—		88	17.50	6	20.69	94	10.57
Agriculture	59	16.53	—		6	20.69	65	7.31
Transportation/ communication	51	14.29	2	0.40	—		53	5.96
Mining	43	12.04	5	0.99	—		48	5.40
Wood products	—		40	7.95	2	6.90	42	4.72
Machinery	2	0.56	37	7.36	2	6.90	41	4.61
Food processing	—		28	5.57	2	6.90	30	3.37
Printing	—		16	3.18	—		16	1.80
Textiles	2	0.56	11	2.19	—		13	1.46
Services	9	2.52	2	0.40	—		11	1.24
Maintenance	10	2.80	—		—		10	1.12
Boat/wagon fabrication	—		9	1.79	—		9	1.01
Forestry	8	2.24	—		—		8	0.90
Security	2	0.56	—		—		2	0.22
Government	1	0.28	—		—		1	0.11
Totals	357	100	503	100	29	100	889	100

a. Percentages are the percentage of men employed in the listed industry out of the total number of men in that skill category (e.g., the 111 skilled construction workers constitute 22.07% of all skilled workers among Volkssturm MIAs).

Table 11. National MIA Workers by Area and Skill (percentages)[a]

Job Type	Semiskilled and Unskilled	Skilled	Meister	All MIA Workers	Total MIAs
Other factory	41.12	3.55	0.17	19.79	9.17
Metalworking	0.18	24.29	5.70	13.02	6.04
Agriculture	27.24	0.00	7.08	12.17	5.65
Construction	2.67	19.36	5.53	11.88	5.50
Crafts	0.00	14.23	25.22	8.47	3.93
Food processing	0.32	11.22	24.53	7.01	3.25
Transportation/ communication	13.28	1.90	3.45	6.92	3.21
Machinery	0.59	6.25	4.66	3.72	1.72
Wood products	0.00	6.43	2.94	3.48	1.61
Mining	4.15	1.21	2.59	2.54	1.18
Boat/wagon fabrication	0.08	4.14	1.73	2.27	1.05
Printing	0.00	4.10	0.86	2.18	1.01
Services	3.36	0.76	0.00	1.86	0.86
Textiles	0.27	2.36	0.00	1.60	0.74
Maintenance	3.05	0.00	0.00	1.33	0.62
Forestry	2.38	0.00	0.00	1.04	0.48
Security	0.51	0.20	0.00	0.33	0.15
Warehousing	0.56	0.00	0.00	0.25	0.11
Government	0.24	0.00	0.86	0.14	0.06
% of total	43.60	52.34	4.06	100.00	46.34

a. Percentages are the percentage of men employed in the listed industry out of the total number of men in that skill category (e.g., other factory workers constituted 41.12% of all semiskilled and unskilled workers among Volkssturm MIAs).

Table 12. Comparison of Blue-Collar MIAs to 1940 Figures on Workers

Category	No. (East/West)	Percent of MIA Workers	Percent of All MIAs	Index1[a]	Index2[b]
Maintenance	180/10	1.33	0.62	2.15	1.44
Food processing	970/30	7.01	3.25	2.03	1.35
Miscellaneous	140/17	1.10	0.51	1.96	1.31
Printing	210/13	1.56	0.72	1.49	0.99
Arbeiter	2,405/153	17.93	8.31	1.45	0.96
Textiles	950/70	7.15	3.31	1.43	0.95
Wood products	920/61	6.88	3.19	1.33	0.88
Agriculture	1,670/65	12.16	5.63	1.22	0.81
Construction	1,115/105	8.55	3.96	0.94	0.62
Services[c]	320/21	2.39	1.12	0.91	0.61
Metalworking	3,030/225	22.81	10.57	0.86	0.57
Forestry	140/8	1.04	0.48	0.66	0.44
Transportation	935/53	6.92	3.21	0.51	0.34
Stone/glass	165/16	1.27	0.59	0.49	0.33
Mining	195/41	1.65	0.77	0.34	0.28
Chemical/rubber	35/1	0.25	0.12	0.16	0.11
All workers	13,380/889		46.36		0.67

The 1940 numbers were employed due to a lack of complete figures for later years, and although percentages would have changed somewhat, WEP draft deferral information (see appendix Tables 2 and 3) suggests the relative proportions between categories remained similar, thus providing an acceptable—though not ideal—yardstick for measuring representation.

a. Index1 shows the representation of MIAs among all German male blue-collar workers from that economic sector (percentage of MIA blue-collar workers in that category from this table divided by percentage of all German male blue-collar workers in that category in the entire economy from Table 13). An index greater than 1.0 indicates blue-collar workers in that sector were overrepresented among blue-collar Volkssturm MIAs.

b. Index2 shows the representation of MIAs from each sector among all German males in that economic sector (percentage of all MIAs in that category from this table divided by percentage of all German males in that category in the entire economy from Table 13). An index greater than 1.0 indicates that blue-collar workers in that sector among Volkssturm MIAs were overrepresented among all German males employed in that sector.

c. Services includes domestics, barbers, waiters, laundrymen, and similar occupations.

Table 13. Breakdown of German Male Workers as of July 5, 1940

Category	No.	Percent of Workers	Percent of Male Workforce
Metalworking	3,150,000	26.54	18.50
Transportation	1,600,000	13.48	9.40
Arbeiter	1,467,000	12.36	8.62
Agriculture	1,179,000	9.93	6.92
Construction	1,085,000	9.14	6.37
Wood products	615,000	5.19	3.61
Textiles	593,000	5.00	3.48
Mining	577,000	4.86	3.39
Food processing	411,000	3.46	2.41
Stone/glass	306,000	2.58	1.80
Services	247,000	2.08	1.45
Chemical/rubber	188,000	1.58	1.10
Forestry	186,000	1.57	1.09
Printing	125,000	1.05	0.74
Maintenance	74,000	0.62	0.44
Miscellaneous	66,000	0.56	0.39
All workers	11,869,000	100	69.71

Statistisches Jahrbuch 1941/42, vol. 59, 413.

Table 14. Keller and Knappich Machine Factory Employees

Job Type	LEVY I		LEVY II		TOTAL		Levy I Index[a]
	No.	Percent	No.	Percent	No.	Percent	
Unskilled workers	40	34.2	37	6.9	77	11.8	2.90
White-collar and supervisory	39	32.5	161	30.1	200	30.5	1.07
Skilled workers	40	34.2	303	56.6	343	52.4	0.62
Security	1	0.8	34	6.4	35	5.3	0.02
Totals	120	100	535	100	655	100	

Maschinefabrik Keller und Knappich, "Verzeichnis," Dec. 8, 1944, T-073/83/3230984–1003; "Antrag auf Anerkennung als Schlüsselkraft"; "Antrag auf Anerkennung als Fachkraft"; and "Antrag auf Anerkennung als Schlüsselkräfte," all Oct. 30, 1944, T-73/78/3223750–81.

a. Index is Levy I percentage divided by total percentage for that job skill type. An index greater than 1.0 indicates that individuals in that job skill category were overrepresented in Levy I within this factory.

Table 15. Transportation/Communication Sector MIAs by Job Skill and Employer

	Semiskilled and Unskilled	Masters Skilled	White-Collar	MIA Total	National Total[a]	Index
Reichsbahn	19.13	62.34	41.96	32.18	57.45	0.56
Reichspost	14.16	3.09	43.45	24.14	18.10	1.33
Other	66.71	34.57	14.59	43.68	24.45	1.79

a. National total = percentage of total number of German males employed nationally in the transportation/communication sector. Index is MIA total percentage divided by national percentage of German male employees in transportation/communication sector. An index greater than 1.0 indicates overrepresentation of that subsector's employees among Volkssturm MIAs.

Table 16. Western Levy I MIAs by Economic Sector

Job Type	No.	Percent	Index[a]
Banking/insurance	15	1.49	2.29
Construction	100	9.90	1.73
Trade/professions	78	7.72	1.53
Manufacturing	385	38.12	1.21
Forestry	9	0.89	1.05
Agriculture	132	13.07	.63
Government	70	6.93	.55
Transportation/communication	52	5.15	.52
Mining	21	2.08	.20
Uncategorized white-collar	90	8.91	NA
Students	3	0.30	NA
No answer	46	4.55	NA
Totals	1,001	100	

a. Index is national percentage of zbV unit members employed in the listed sector divided by the national percentage of German men employed in that sector as per Table 3. An index greater than 1.0 indicates overrepresentation of that sector's employees among MIAs from Volkssturm Battalion zbV (Levy I).

Table 17. Western Levy I (zbV) MIAs by Job Skill Type

Job Type	No.	Percent
White-collar/professional	310	30.69
Semiskilled and unskilled workers	217	21.49
Other skilled workers	181	17.92
Skilled factory workers	147	14.55
Farmers	91	9.01
Master craftsmen	15	1.49
Students	3	0.30
No answer	46	4.55

Table 18. Rastatt, Werne, and Rötz Levy I Units by Job Skill Type

	NO.			PERCENT		
Job Skill	Rastatt	Werne	Rötz	Rastatt	Werne	Rötz
White-collar/professional	50	30	2	44.26	30.30	4.88
Skilled factory workers	25	7	0	22.12	7.07	0.00
Other skilled workers	11	12	3	9.73	12.12	7.32
Semiskilled workers	6	40	4	5.31	40.41	9.76
Unskilled workers	7	3	9	6.20	3.03	21.95
Master craftsmen	11	4	10	9.73	4.04	24.39
Farmers	3	2	12	2.65	2.02	29.27
Others	0	1	1	0.00	1.01	2.43
Total	113	99	41	100	100	100

The Rastatt and Werne units are companies, the Rötz unit a platoon. I. Komp., Baden Vs. Btn. VII (Rastatt), "Namensliste der einberufene Männer," Nov. 27, 1944, Stadtarchiv Rastatt, Bürgermeisteramt Rastatt, A/3923; Og. Werne Oberland, "Liste," undated, T-81/94/108876–78; 7. VsKomp, Rötz, various lists in StA Amberg, NSDAP Krltg. Oberviechtach, Nr. 5.

Table 19. White-Collar/Professional Volkssturm MIAs

	EAST		WEST			Percent of All
Job Type	No.	Percent	No.	Percent	National (%)	MIAs
Office workers	1,460	19.07	111	23.42	19.34	5.09
Civil servants	1,430	18.68	87	18.36	18.66	4.93
Professionals	1,150	15.02	78	16.47	15.11	3.99
Merchants	1,124	14.63	77	16.24	14.73	3.89
Financial	375	4.90	20	4.22	4.86	1.28
Foremen	270	3.53	18	3.80	3.54	0.94
Managers	270	3.53	15	3.16	3.51	0.93
Postal employees	265	3.46	12	2.53	3.41	0.90
Technicians	245	3.20	28	5.90	3.36	0.89
Reichsbahn employees	245	3.20	8	1.69	3.11	0.82
Entertainers	190	2.48	2	0.42	2.36	0.62
Hotel/restaurant	120	1.57	3	0.63	1.51	0.40
Farm administrators	140	1.83	0	—	1.72	0.45
Foresters	130	1.70	2	0.42	1.62	0.43
Publishing	85	1.11	7	1.48	1.13	0.30
Owners	60	0.78	4	0.84	0.79	0.21
Contractors	35	0.46	1	0.21	0.44	0.12
Ship captains	20	0.26	1	0.21	0.26	0.07
Decorators	15	0.20	0	—	0.18	0.05
Streetcar employees	10	0.13	0	—	0.12	0.03
Religious jobs	10	0.13	0	—	0.12	0.03
NSDAP officials	10	0.13	0	—	0.12	0.03
Total	7,655	100	474	100	1,956 (100)	26.40

Table 20. Breakdown of Government Sector MIAs

	East/West MIAs	Overall MIAs (%)	OVERALL NATIONAL No.	Percent	Index[a]
Civil	1,860/120	6.43	947,900	7.01	0.92
Police	140/6	0.47	323,300	2.39	0.20
Wehrmacht	20/0	0.07	425,200	3.14	0.02
Total	2,020/126	6.97	1,696,400	12.54	0.56

The category of civil government includes party officials/employees. There are no separate WEP figures for NSDAP employees and deferrals, nor is the omission explained in the plan.
a. Index is overall national percentage of MIAs divided by overall national percentage of German men in each governmental sector. The index represents comparable underrepresentation of various sectors of government employees among Volkssturm MIAs.

Table 21. Volkssturm MIAs by Birth Year

	MIA EAST No.	Percent	MIA WEST No.	Percent	MIA Total (%)
Before 1884	380	1.30	8	0.50	1.26
1884–1889	5,080	17.40	109	6.81	16.85
1890–1894	6,000	20.55	248	15.50	20.29
1895–1899	6,855	23.49	394	24.63	23.54
1900–1904	5,625	19.27	444	27.75	19.71
1905–1909	2,420	8.29	190	11.87	8.48
1910–1914	1,000	3.43	81	5.06	3.51
1915–1919	350	1.20	31	1.94	1.24
1920–1924	440	1.51	40	2.50	1.56
1925–1931	940	3.22	50	3.13	3.22
NA	100	0.34	5	0.31	0.34
Average age	47.3		44.5		47.0

Table 22. Volkssturm Unit Leaders by Birth Year

	MIA COS		BAYREUTH COMPANY COS		BAYREUTH BATTALION COS	
	No.	Percent	No.	Percent	No.	Percent
Pre-1884	—	—	3	3.23	23	8.43
1884–1889	9	12.7	17	18.28	69	25.27
1890–1894	23	32.4	27	29.03	91	33.33
1895–1899	25	35.3	30	32.26	66	24.18
1900–1904	4	5.6	9	9.68	6	2.20
1905–1909	5	7.0	2	2.15	7	2.56
1910–1914	3	4.2	4	4.30	6	2.20
1915–1919	1	1.4	1	1.07	3	1.10
1920–1924	1	1.4	—	—	2	0.73
Average age	48.6 years		50.1 years		52.4 years	

The Bayreuth categories include all Kofü and Btnfü. With birthdates or ages listed in BA-Ko, NS 12, Nr. 1147, and StA Bamberg, M30, Nr. 838. The MIA column includes the seventy-one men with clearly identifiable Volkssturm ranks; few of these were battalion leaders, one factor behind their younger average age.

Table 23. Bayreuth Battalion Leaders' NSDAP Information

	Btns[a]	Total Btnfü	NSDAP Total[b]	P&Me[c]	Pg[d]	SA	SS	NSDAP Office	NA[e]
Gau	—	416	173	116	118	53	12	26	233
Bamberg	16	17	10	—	10	—	—	—	7
Bayreuth	22	22	13	13	9	4	2	8	9
Cham	9	13	10	5	10	—	—	—	3
Coburg	13	17	7	6	—	4	2	1	10
Kelheim	8	9	7	7	3	5	—	1	2
Kulmbach	7	8	6	6	3	3	—	2	2
Lichtenfels-Staffelstein	12	13	12	12	12	2	2	4	1
Mainburg-Naila	8	5	4	2	4	—	—	3	1
Passau	8	8	7	6	6	1	2	—	1
Regensburg	16	28	17	16	—	14	2	1	11
Rottenburg-Mallersdorf	7	7	4	4	4	—	—	3	3
Schwandorf-Nabburg	13	11	11	5	11	—	—	—	—
Weiden	15	32	16	6	16	—	—	—	16
Wolfstein	5	5	5	5	5	—	—	—	—

The Kreise in tables 23–26 were selected because they provided the most extensive political and military background on their unit leaders.

a. Btns = Minimum number of battalions in Kreis as per Gaustabsführung Bayreuth, "Starkenmeldung des Kreises," undated, in BA-Ko, NS 12, Nr. 1147. There may well have been more battalions organized in some areas, and almost certainly some men were not given battalion command; therefore, the total number of nominees does not match the minimum number of battalions.

b. Some men are listed in more than one category. The NSDAP total is the total number of individuals with membership in some Party organization.

c. P&ME = Number of men with both Party and military experience identifiable.

d. Pg = Parteigenossen, or party members.

e. NA = no information available.

Table 24. Bayreuth Company Leaders' NSDAP Affiliation

	Total Kofü	NSDAP Total[a]	Pg	SA	SS	NSKK	NA
Gau	682	97	58	29	5	6	585
Cham	50	35	33	2	—	—	15
Regensburg	96	34	—	23	5	6	62
Schwandorf-Nabburg	16	13	13	—	—	—	3

a. Some men are listed in more than one category. The NSDAP total is the total number of individuals with membership in some Party organization.

Table 25. Bayreuth Battalion Leaders' Military Background

	Gau Total	A	B	C	F	Ke	Ku	L	Pa	Pr	R	S	V	Wa	Wo	Z
General	1	—	—	—	—	—	—	—	—	—	1	—	—	—	—	—
Colonel	5	—	—	—	1	—	1	—	—	—	—	—	—	—	—	—
Major	32	1	—	1	—	—	—	—	—	1	9	1	1	1	—	—
Captain	67	4	6	4	—	—	1	4	1	1	3	3	5	1	1	2
Lieutenant	70	3	8	5	3	3	3	6	3	2	9	—	4	1	4	1
Sergeant	30	—	6	3	5	5	1	1	1	1	3	3	—	—	—	—
Corporal	5	—	—	2	1	—	—	1	—	—	—	—	—	—	—	—
Private	—	—	—	—	—	—	—	—	—	—	—	—	—	—	—	—
Other	3	—	—	—	1	1	—	—	—	1	—	—	—	—	—	—
SS	12	—	—	—	—	—	—	1	2	—	1	1	1	—	—	—
Unknown	191	4	2	2	5	—	2	—	1	3	2	2	1	1	—	1
Total	416	12	22	17	16	9	8	13	8	9	28	9	12	4	5	4
Battalions[a]	353	15	22	13	12	8	7	12	8	9	16	15	8	?	5	?

Kreise listed: A = Amberg, B = Bayreuth, C = Coburg, F = Fränkische Schweiz, Ke = Kelheim, Ku = Kulmbach, L = Lichtenfels-Staffelstein, Pa = Passau, Pr = Prachatitz, R = Regensburg, S = Straubing, V = Vilshofen, Wa = Waldmünchen, Wo = Wolfstein, Z = Zwiesel.
    a. This is the minimum number of battalions in the Kreis, although there certainly may have been more organized.

Table 26. Bayreuth Company Leaders' Military Background

	Gau Total	Kreis Kronach	Kreis Kulmbach	Lichtenfels-Staffelstein	Kreis Regensburg
Major	4	—	—	1	—
Captain	16	—	1	—	13
Lieutenant	41	1	7	8	15
Sergeant	83	12	14	27	22
Corporal	13	1	4	2	2
Private	6	1	1	1	—
Other	8	1	1	4	1
SS	5	—	—	—	2
Unknown	506	14	2	3	41

Table 27.   Eastern Volkssturm MIAs by Gau

	#MIA	%EMIA	%MIA	%Epop	Ind1	%Npop	Ind2
East Prussia	8,780	29.97	28.41	7.65	3.92	3.71	7.65
Lower Silesia	5,111	17.44	16.54	7.53	2.32	3.65	4.53
Pomerania	2,984	10.18	9.66	5.49	1.86	2.66	3.63
Berlin	2,691	9.18	8.71	9.94	0.92	4.82	1.81
Wartheland	2,441	8.33	7.90	10.51	0.79	5.10	1.55
Mark Brandenburg	2,211	7.55	7.16	6.89	1.09	3.34	2.14
Upper Silesia	1,648	5.62	5.33	9.95	0.57	4.83	1.10
Danzig–West Prussia	1,439	4.91	4.66	5.25	0.94	2.54	1.83
Sudetenland	804	2.74	2.60	6.75	0.41	3.27	0.80
Saxony	311	1.06	1.01	11.99	0.09	5.82	0.17
Vienna	162	0.55	0.52	4.42	0.12	2.15	0.24
General Government	156	0.53	0.50	—	—	—	—
Steiermark	65	0.22	0.21	2.56	0.08	1.24	0.17
Mecklenburg	53	0.18	0.17	2.06	0.09	1.00	0.17
Upper Danube	50	0.17	0.16	2.37	0.07	1.15	0.14
Lower Danube	34	0.12	0.11	3.89	0.03	1.89	0.06
Carinthia	1	0.00	0.00	1.03	0.00	0.50	0.01
Tirol-Vorarlberg	1	0.00	0.00	1.11	0.00	0.54	0.01
Salzburg	0	0.00	0.00	0.59	0.00	0.29	0.00
Uncategorizable and miscellaneous	358	1.22	1.16	—	—	—	—

Key:
#MIA = Number of Volkssturm MIAs (actual total, not a 20% sample).
%EMIA = Percentage of eastern Volkssturm MIAs.
%MIA = Percentage of all Volkssturm MIAs.
%EPop = Percentage of 1939 eastern population in Gau.
Ind1 = Index of representation of MIAs in eastern Germany.
%NPop = Percentage of 1939 total German national population.
Ind2 = Index of representation among all MIAs.

Map Appendix

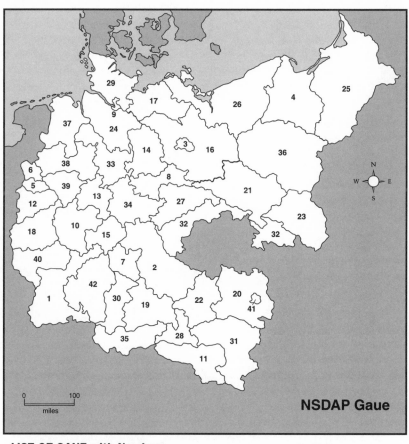

NSDAP Gaue

LIST OF GAUE with Numbers

1. Baden
2. Bayreuth
3. Berlin
4. Danzig-Westpreussen
5. Düsseldorf
6. Essen
7. Franken
8. Halle-Merseburg
9. Hamburg
10. Hessen-Nassau
11. Kärnten
12. Köln-Aachen
13. Kurhessen
14. Magdeburg-Anhalt
15. Mainfranken
16. Mark Brandenburg
17. Mecklenburg
18. Moselland
19. München-Oberbayern
20. Niederdonau
21. Niedersachsen
22. Oberdonau
23. Oberschlesien
24. Ost-Hannover
25. Ostpreussen
26. Pommern
27. Sachsen
28. Salzburg
29. Schleswig-Holstein
30. Schwaben
31. Steiermark
32. Sudetenland
33. Süd Hannover-Braunschweig
34. Thüringen
35. Tirol-Vorarlberg
36. Wartheland
37. Weser-Ems
38. Westfalen-Nord
39. Westfalen-Süd
40. Westmark
41. Wien
42. Württemberg-Hohenzollern

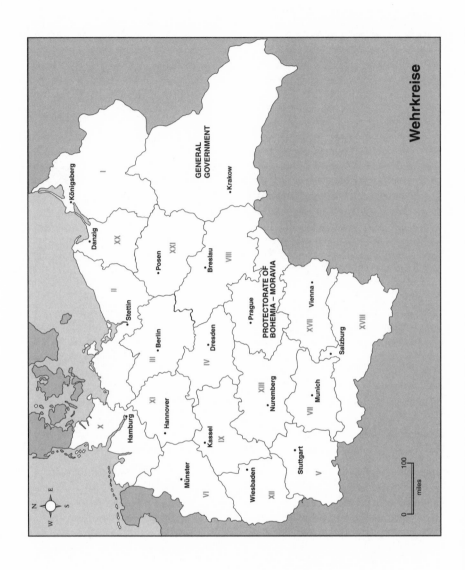

Wehrkreise

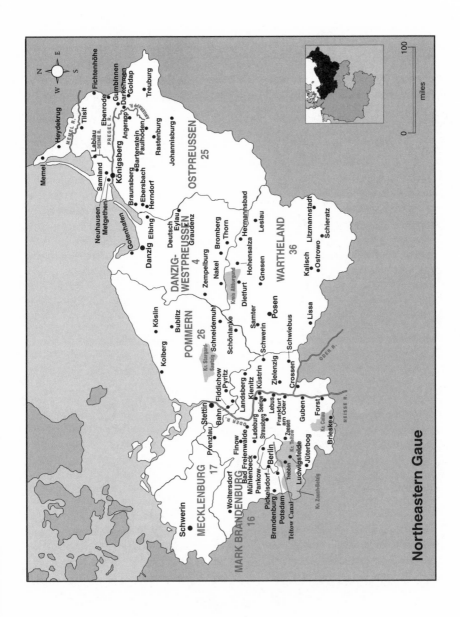

Northeastern Gaue

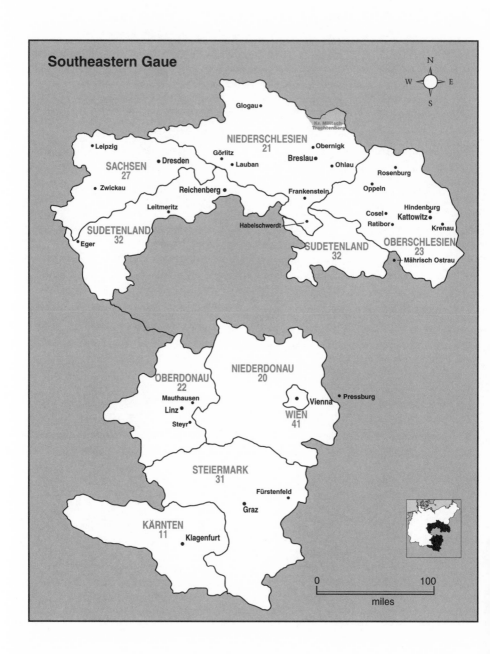

Southeastern Gaue

N
W — E
S

Glogau •

Kr. Militsch-
Trachtenberg

NIEDERSCHLESIEN
21

• Leipzig

Görlitz

• Dresden

• Obernigk

• Lauban

Breslau •

• Ohlau

SACHSEN
27

• Zwickau

Reichenberg •

Frankenstein •

Rosenburg •

Oppeln •

Leitmeritz •

Cosel •

Hindenburg •
Kattowitz •

• Eger

SUDETENLAND
32

Habelschwerdt

Ratibor •

Krenau •

SUDETENLAND
32

OBERSCHLESIEN
23

• Mährisch Ostrau

NIEDERDONAU
20

OBERDONAU
22

Mauthausen •

Linz •

Steyr •

Vienna •

• Pressburg

WIEN
41

STEIERMARK
31

Fürstenfeld •

Graz •

KÄRNTEN
11

• Klagenfurt

0   100

miles

Southwestern Gaue

N
W — E
S

MAINFRANKEN 15
• Steinwiesen
• Coburg
• Lohr am Main
Aschaffenburg
Obernberg
• Lichtenfels • Kulmbach
• Altenplos
• Bamberg • **Bayreuth**
Saarburg
• Serrig
• Hamm
Oberesch • Ensdorf
Neustadt
a.d.
Weinstrasse
Miltenberg • **Würzburg** • Heroldsbach • Waischenfeld
• Grafenwöhr
• Welden
WESTMARK 40
Neustadt
a.d. Aisch
Kr. Fränkische
Schweiz
• Pfreimd
Metz
Forbach
• Saarbrücken
Speyer
Germersheim
BADEN 1
• Heidelberg
Gerabronn
Crailsheim
Nuremberg •
Amberg•
Schwandorf
Nabburg
• Waldmünchen
• Rötz •
• Fürth im Wald
• Cham
LORRAINE 40
Karlsruhe
Ettlingen
Rastatt Pforzheim
NECKAR R.
Backnang
Ludwigsburg
Ansbach
FRANKEN 7
Regensburg
BAYREUTH 2
• Zwiesel •
• Prachatitz
Lichtenau Balz-
hofen
Strassburg
Bad Teinach
• **Stuttgart**
**WÜRTTEMBERG-
HOHENZOLLERN** 42
• Harburg
Bäumenheim
• Kelheim
• Mallersdorf
• Straubing
Wolfstein
Offenburg
Zell
Colmar
St. Georgen
Triberg
Baiersbronn
• Reutlingen
Denzingen
Ulm •
Welden
• Kicklingen
Mainburg
Dingolfing
• Passau
Vilshofen
ALSACE 1
RHINE R.
Freiburg
Villingen
Oberndorf
Augsburg •
SCHWABEN 30
Memmingen
Kaufbeuren
Fürstenfeldbruck
Anzing
• **Munich**
Bad Tölz •
**MÜNCHEN-
OBERBAYERN** 19
Lörrach
Konstanz
• Kempten
Anger •
Penzburg
• Salz-
burg
Lindau
Scheidegg
Nesselwang
Blaichach
• **Innsbruck**
SALZBURG 28
SÜD TIROL
TIROL VORARLBERG 35

JAGST R.

0   100

miles

189

Northwestern Gaue

Kiel
SCHLESWIG-HOLSTEIN
29

Aurich
Emden
Zeven
Hamburg
9

Oldenburg
Bremen-Walle
Bremen
OST-HANNOVER
24
Lüneburg
Soltau
WESER-EMS
37
Walsrode
Unterlüss
Celle
Bramsche
Schaumburg-Lippe
Gardelegen
Ibbenbüren
Stadthagen
Bückeburg
MAGDEBURG-ANHALT
14
Diesdorf
Rheine
Münster
Osnabrück
Kr.
Herford
Lippe
Wolfenbüttel
Hannover
SÜD
Salzgitter
Magdeburg
Anholt
Isselburg
Detmold
HANNOVER-
Dessau
Dorplck
Rees
Lüdinghausen
WESTFALEN-NORD
38
BRAUNSCHWEIG
33
Goslar
ESSEN
6
Essen
Werne
Recklinghausen
Kirchborchen
HALLE-MERSEBURG
8
Halle
Bochum
39
DÜSSELDORF
5
Ratingen
Ennepe-Ruhr
Kreis
WESTFALEN-SUD
Kassel
Merseburg
Nieder-krüchten
Gustorf
Düsseldorf
Bergheim
Rheinisch-Bergischer
Siegkreis
Sauerland
KURHESSEN
13
THURINGEN
34
Jena
Weimar
Aachen
Bonn
Cologne
Eisenach
KÖLN-AACHEN
12
Linz am Rhein
HESSEN-NASSAU
10
Zehla-Mellis
Suhl
Meiningen
Greiz
Remagen
Koblenz
Westerburg
Kr.
Oberlahn-Usingen
Kaisersesch
Rhens
Boppard
St. Goar
St. Goarshausen
Keppeshausen
Kaub
Frankfurt
Wittlich
Wiesbaden
Luxem-burg
MOSELLAND
18
St. Goarshausen
Trier
Saarburg

N
W E
S

0   100
miles

Notes

Introduction

1. HG Mitte Ia, "Tagesmeldung, 17.8.44, Nr. 14290/44 geh.," Aug. 18, 1944, National Archives Microfilm Series T-312, reel 248, frames 7803508–12 (hereafter, series no./reel no./frame no.).

2. The Volkssturm charge applied particularly to Martin Bormann; International Military Tribunal, *Trial of the Major War Criminals* (Nuremberg: IMT), vol. 1, 71; vol. 5, 310–11, 330.

3. For examples, see David M. Glantz and Jonathan M. House, *When Titans Clashed: How the Red Army Stopped Hitler* (Lawrence: University Press of Kansas, 1995), 292–300; or Norman Scarfe, *Assault Division: A History of the 3rd Division from the Invasion of Normandy to the Surrender of Germany* (London: Collins, 1947), 270.

4. Hans Kissel, *Der Deutsche Volkssturm 1944/45: Eine territoriale Miliz im Rahmen der Landesverteidigung* (Frankfurt am Main: E. S. Mittler und Sohn, 1962); Burton Wright III, "Army of Despair: The German Volkssturm 1944–1945" (Ph.D. diss., Florida State University, 1982). Both portray the Volkssturm as a traditional militia that failed as a result of Nazi incompetence. They devote most of their analysis to assessing the value of a civilian militia in modern war. Kissel wrote his book to prove the utility of militias in order to shape debate on the Bundeswehr. See Arbeitskreis Milizwesen, Arbeitskreis für Wehrforschung, "Aktennotiz über die erste Sitzung," Nov. 10, 1959, BA-MA, N426 (Nachlass Kissel), Nr. 56.

5. Franz Seidler, *"Deutscher Volkssturm": Das letzte Aufgebot 1944/45* (Munich: Herbig, 1989), is richly detailed, but its analysis differs little from earlier political assessments such as Dietrich Orlow, *The History of the Nazi Party 1919–1945*, vol. 2, *1933–1945* (Pittsburgh: University of Pittsburgh Press, 1973), 472–73. These political interpretations generally dismiss the role of ideology as just so much tired propaganda and portray the Volkssturm as a failed National Socialist people's army that owed its existence to the Nazi leaders' selfish or criminal desire to delay their inevitable defeat. It failed due to NSDAP ineptitude. Also see Alastair Noble, "The People's Levy: The Volkssturm and Popular Mobilisation in East-ern Germany, 1944–45," *Journal of Strategic Studies* 24, no. 1 (Mar. 2001): 165–87.

6. East Germans argued that the Volkssturm was intended to protect capitalists' skilled workers, evacuate their assets to the west, or prolong the war in hopes of convincing the Anglo-Americans to join the anti-Communist crusade. Klaus Mammach, *Der Volkssturm: Das letzte Aufgebot 1944/45* (Cologne: Pahl Rugenstein, 1981); Werner Grobosch, "Entstehung und Rolle des Deutschen Volkssturms" *Militärgeschichte* 6, no. 2 (1978): 180–92.

7. Gerhard L. Weinberg, *Germany, Hitler and World War II: Essays in Modern German and World History* (New York: Cambridge University Press, 1995), 274–86; Weinberg, *A World at Arms: A Global History of World War II* (New York: Cambridge University Press, 1994).

8. Perry Biddiscombe, *Werwolf! The History of the National Socialist Guerrilla Movement, 1944–1946* (Toronto: University of Toronto Press, 1998); Eleanor Hancock, *The National Socialist Leadership and Total War, 1941–45* (New York: St. Martin's, 1991).

9. See particularly Andreas Hillgruber, *Zweierlei Untergang: Die Zerschlagung des Deutschen Reiches und das Ende des europäischen Judentums* (Berlin: Siedler, 1986). For the basic positions in the ensuing controversy, see *Forever in the Shadow of Hitler? Original Documents of the Historikerstreit, the Controversy in Germany Concerning the Singularity of the National Socialist Annihilation of the Jews* (Atlantic Highlands, N.J.: Humanities Press, 1993).

10. On the impact of racial views, see Omer Bartov, *The Eastern Front, 1941–1945: German Troops and the Barbarisation of Warfare* (New York: St. Martin's, 1985); Bartov, *Hitler's Army: Soldiers, Nazis and War in the Third Reich* (New York: Oxford University Press, 1991). On the Volksgemeinschaft's role, see Jürgen Förster, "The Dynamics of Volksgemeinschaft: The Effectiveness of the German Military Establishment in the Second World War," in *Military Effectiveness*, vol. 3, *The Second World War*, ed. Alan R. Millett and Williamson Murray (Boston: Allen and Unwin, 1988), 180–220; Stephen Fritz, *Frontsoldaten: The German Soldier in World War Two* (Lexington: University Press of Kentucky, 1995); and Manfred Messerschmidt, "The Wehrmacht and the Volksgemeinschaft," *Journal of Contemporary History* 18, no. 4 (Oct. 1983): 719–44. Also see Volker Berghahn, "NSDAP und 'Geistige Führung' der Wehrmacht," *Vierteljahrshefte für Zeitgeschichte* 17 (1969): 17–71; Jürgen Förster, "The German Army and the Ideological War Against the Soviet Union," in *The Policies of Genocide: Jews and Soviet Prisoners of War in Nazi Germany*, ed. Gerhard Hirschfeld (London: Allen and Unwin, 1986), 15–29; Ian Kershaw, "How Effective Was Nazi Propaganda?" in *Nazi Propaganda: The Power and the Limitations*, ed. D. Welch (London: Croom Helm, 1983), 180–205; Theo Schulte, *The German Army and Nazi Policies in Occupied Russia* (Oxford: Berg, 1989); Christian Streit, *Keine Kameraden: Die Wehrmacht und die sowjetische Kriegsgefangenen* (Bonn: J.H.W. Dietz, 1991).

11. On the exhibit and the controversy, see Hamburg Institute for Social Research, *The German Army and Genocide: Crimes Against War Prisoners, Jews and Other Civilians, 1939–1944*, trans. Scott Abbott and Paula Bradish (New York: New Press, 1999).

12. Two solid examples include Lutz Klinkhammer, *Zwischen Bündnis und Besatzung: Das nationalsozialistische Deutschland und die Republik von Salò 1943–1945* (Tübingen: Max Niemeyer, 1993); and Walter Naasner, *Neue Machtzentren in der deutschen Kriegswirtschaft 1942–1945* (Boppard am Rhein: Harald Boldt, 1994). Also see Hancock.

13. See Keitel's claim that the Wehrmacht knew virtually nothing of the Volkssturm in International Military Tribunal, vol. 10, 597–98.

14. For example, Albert Kesselring, *Gedanken zum Zweiten Weltkrieg* (Bonn: Athenäum, 1955), 157.

1. Founding the Volkssturm

1. Quotation in OKH/GenStdH/Org. Abt. I, "Aufgaben und Richtlinien für die Kommandanten eines festen Platzes, GKdos. Nr. 2434/44," Mar. 8, 1944, T-77/ 782/5508841–43.

2. The Replacement Army (Ersatzheer) was the Wehrmacht entity that commanded all local garrisons, instructional schools, recruit depots, convalescents, prisoner-of-war camps, military police, construction units, and unattached regular formations within Germany proper. It was divided into nineteen regional commands *(Wehrkreise)*.

3. OKH/ChHRü and BdE/AHA Ia (IV), "GKdos. Nr. 2996/41," June 13, 1941, Records Microfilmed at Berlin Document Center, Box 873, bundle 799a, folder 1 (hereafter T-580/box no./bundle no./folder no.).

4. Himmler, "Schnellbrief, Okdo Io (4) Nr. 6/42," Jan. 17, 1942, T-175/1/ 2500049–54; "Schnellbrief, Okdo Io (3)1 Nr. 287/42," Nov. 9, 1942, LA Magdeburg, C 30 Ib XV: RVK, Nr. 4340.

5. It had lost eight killed and eighteen wounded in the course of its operations. Ordnungspolizei Kommandoamt, "Stärkemeldung," June 5, 1943; Ordnungspolizeichef Kurt Daluege, "FS Kdo. I, Org. (I) Nr. 7/44," Jan. 12, 1944, both in BA-Ko, R 19, Nr. 277.

6. SS Obergruppenführer Prützmann, "Schreiben, Tgb. Bd.S IV Nr. 501/44, geh.," Aug. 2, 1944, T-311/227/986; HSSuPF Rhein/Westmark, "Befehl, Tgb. Nr. 879/44, geh." Aug. 2, 1944, T-175/223/2761151–52; WK XIII Ia, "FS, Ia Nr. 20109/44, geh." Sept. 16, 1944, BA-MA, RH 53-13, Nr. 141.

7. Keitel, "Bestimmungen, WFSt/Qu./Org I Nr. 0013119/42 gKdos.," Sept. 2, 1942, T-175/242/2648248–50.

8. OKM/SKL, "KTB," Aug. 18, 1943, BA-MA, RM 7, Nr. 51, 325; Heinz Guderian, *Erinnerungen eines Soldaten* (Heidelberg: Kurt Vowinckel, 1951), 327.

9. WK XXI Kdr. Gen. Walter Petzel, "Militärische Vorbereitungen für die Verteidigung des Warthegaues," BA-Ko, Ost Dok 8/400; & "Volkssturm Wehrkreis XXI," BA-Ko, Ost Dok 8/402.

10. Gen. Georg von Hengl, "Report on the Alpine Fortress," MS B-461, 1–8; Franz Hofer, "The Alpine Fortification and Defense Line: A Report on German and U.S. Views of the 'Alpine Redoubt' in 1944," MS B-457, 9–10; Franz Hofer, "The National Redoubt," MS B-458, 6–8, all in *World War II Military Studies,* ed. Donald S. Detwiler, Charles B. Burdick, and Jürgen Rohwer, vol. 24, pt. X, "Special Topics," sec. D, "The National Redoubt and the Final Collapse" (New York: Garland, 1979).

11. OKH/GenStdH/Org. Abt. Nr.I, "FS Nr. 10560/44, geh.," Sept. 17, 1944, BA-MA, RH 2, Nr. 847b, 257; OB Südwest/ObKdo HG C Ia/Id, "GKdos. Nr. 2692/ 45," Mar. 8, 1945, T-311/8/7007369–79.

12. Rundstedt, "Entwurf, GKdos., OB West Ia Nr. 8787/44," Oct. 1, 1944. BA-MA, RH 19-IV, Nr. 77, 17–18; WK XVIII Ia/Ib, "GKdos., Nr. 1622/44," Nov. 16, 1944, T-79/292/459.

13. Hessen-Nassau Gaustabsamtleiter Linden, "FS," Dec. 8, 1941, T-580/873/799a/6.

14. Wahl to Bormann, "Abschrift von Schreiben," Sept. 30, 1943, BA-Ko, NS 19, Nr. 798; Bormann to Wahl, "Schreiben," Oct. 18, 1943, BA-Ko, NS 19, Nr. 798; Wahl to Himmler, "Schreiben," Dec. 22, 1943, BA-Ko, NS 19, Nr. 798.

15. Dietrich Orlow, *The History of the Nazi Party 1919–1945*, vol. 2, *1933–1945* (Pittsburgh: University of Pittsburgh Press, 1973), 437, 473.

16. PK Mobilization Abt. Chef Wilhelm Zander, "Aktenvermerk," Aug. 30, 1944, T-580/874/799b/6.

17. Max Domarus, ed., *Hitler: Reden und Proklamationen 1932–1945* (Wiesbaden: R. Lovit, 1973), 45, 269, 344, 424, 857, 2040; Adolf Hitler, *Mein Kampf*, ed. John Chamberlain et al. (New York: Reynal and Hitchcock, 1941), 792–95; Guderian, 326; Tim Mason, "The Legacy of 1918 for National Socialism," in *German Democracy and the Triumph of Hitler*, ed. Anthony Nicholls and Erich Matthias (New York: St. Martin's, 1971), 215–19.

18. The best works on the Eastern Front in summer 1944 are John Erickson, *The Road to Berlin: Continuing the History of Stalin's War with Germany* (Boulder, Colo.: Westview, 1983); Hermann Gackenholz, "The Collapse of Army Group Center in 1944," in *The Decisive Battles of World War Two: The German View*, ed. Hans-Adolf Jacobsen and Jürgen Rohwer, trans. Edward Fitzgerald (London: Andre Deutsch, 1965), 355–83; David M. Glantz and Jonathan M. House, *When Titans Clashed: How the Red Army Stopped Hitler* (Lawrence: University Press of Kansas, 1995), 195–233; Gerhard L. Weinberg, *A World at Arms: A Global History of World War II* (New York: Cambridge University Press, 1994), chaps. 12–13; Earl F. Ziemke, *Stalingrad to Berlin: The German Defeat in the East* (Washington, D.C.: Office of the Chief of Military History, 1968).

19. On the Western Front, see Martin Blumenson, *Breakout and Pursuit* (Washington, D.C.: Office of the Chief of Military History, 1961); Lionel F. Ellis and Alan E. Warhurst, *Victory in the West*, 2 vols. (London: HMSO, 1962–1968); Gordon A. Harrison, *Cross-Channel Attack* (Washington, D.C.: Office of the Chief of Military History, 1951); Charles B. MacDonald, *The Siegfried Line Campaign* (Washington, D.C.: Office of the Chief of Military History, 1963); Dieter Ose, *Entscheidung im Westen, 1944: Der Oberbefehlshaber West und die Abwehr der alliierten Invasion* (Stuttgart: Deutsche Verlags-Anstalt, 1982); Russell F. Weigley, *Eisenhower's Lieutenants: The Campaigns of France and Germany, 1944–1945* (Bloomington: Indiana University Press, 1980); and Weinberg, *World at Arms*, chaps. 12–13.

20. It should be noted that historians believe these figures are too low. OKH/GStdH/Org.Abt.Nr. I, "GKdos. Nr. 20737/44," Nov. 24, 1944; and "Notiz, Nr. 15412/44 geh.," Dec. 2, 1944, both T-78/411/6379655 and 6379655; OKH/HPA Amtsgruppe P1/1 (Zentral), Abt. IIc, "KTB Anlage: Vergleich des Verhältnissatzes der Fehlstelle," Dec. 11, 1944, BA-MA, RH 7, Nr. 638, 42.

21. See Alfred C. Mierzejewski, *The Collapse of the German War Economy, 1944–1945: Allied Air Power and the German National Railway* (Chapel Hill: University of North Carolina Press, 1988).

22. Note that the entire Replacement Army was smaller than the Wehrmacht's total 1944 casualties; Burckhardt Müller-Hillebrand, *Das Heer 1939–1945: Entwick-*

lung des organisatorischen Aufbaues, vol. 3 (Frankfurt am Main: E. S. Mittler und Sohn, 1969), 257.

23. United States War Department, *Handbook on German Military Forces: War Department Technical Manual TM-E30-454* (Washington, D.C.: U.S. Government Printing Office, 1945), sec. I, 46, 56.

24. OKH/GenStdH/Org. Abt. "Übersicht über die Entwicklung des Heeres," undated (probably Oct. 1944), T-78/423/6393229–352; Hans Kissel, *Der Deutsche Volkssturm 1944/45: Eine territoriale Miliz im Rahmen der Landesverteidigung* (Frankfurt am Main: E. S. Mittler und Sohn, 1962), 19–20.

25. Hermann Jung, *Die Ardennen Offensive 1944/45: Ein Beispiel für die Kriegführung Hitlers* (Göttingen: Musterschmidt, 1971), 101.

26. Guderian, "OKH/GenStdH/Org.Abt. A, FS Nrs. 623, 624, 625/44, geh.," Aug. 6, 1944, T-78/418/63577337–42; Guderian, 325–26.

27. Gen. Gunther Blumentritt, OB West Stabschef, "GKdos., Ia Nr. 7592/44," Sept. 2, 1944, BA-MA, RH 19 IV, Nr. 55, 38–42.

28. The U.S. First Army credited these fortress battalions with providing "much of the German tenacity in the West Wall." MacDonald, *Siegfried*, 16.

29. The name *Landsturm* came from the Prussian civilian militia units created in April 1813 for local use against Napoleon's troops in the War of Liberation. More recently it had been used as a designation for inactive reservists, but one can speculate that Guderian hoped to associate his proposed force with the older, somewhat romanticized image of German peasants rising to defend their homes against foreign domination.

30. Guderian, 326–27. Walter Warlimont, *Im Hauptquartier der deutschen Wehrmacht 1939–1945*, 3rd ed. (Munich: Bernhard und Graefe, 1978), 510–11, verifies Guderian's account.

31. Guderian, 326–27; Joseph Goebbels, *Die Tagebücher von Joseph Goebbels*, pt. 2, *Diktate, 1942–1945*, vol. 13, ed. Elke Fröhlich (Munich: K. G. Saur, 1995–1996), 438.

32. ObKdo HG Mitte, "FS," Sept. 11, 1944, T-312/251/7807769; Auswärtiges Amt, Abt. Inland II, "GRs. e.o. Inl. II 596," Oct. 5, 1944, T-120/1757/E0235343–44.

33. Koch to Bormann, "Abschrift von FS Nr. 80," Sept. 1944, T-581/6/151. Koch's claim that he created the Volkssturm idea is inaccurate, although some historians have accepted it. See Koch "Rede," Oct. 4, 1944, T-581/6/151; Michael H. Kater, *The Nazi Party: A Social Profile of Members and Leaders 1919–1945* (Cambridge, Mass.: Harvard University Press, 1983), 228.

34. Bormann, "Abschrift von FS," Sept. 14, 1944, BA-Ko, R 43 II, Nr. 692a, 3–6; Himmler, "Rede," Sept. 21, 1944, BA-MA, RH 14, Nr. 2; Bormann, "FS," Sept. 26, 1944, BA-Ko, NS 6, Nr. 763, 23; Hitler, "Führer Erlaß über die Bildung des Deutschen Volkssturms," Sept. 25, 1944, *Reichsgesetztblatt 1944*, pt.1, no. 52 (Oct. 20, 1944): 53.

35. See, e.g., Goebbels's August 3, 1944, speech in Helmut Heiber, ed., *Goebbels Reden*, vol. 2, *1939–1945* (Düsseldorf: Droste, 1972), 360–404.

36. Peter Hoffmann, *The History of the German Resistance 1933–1945*, trans. Richard Barry (Cambridge, Mass.: MIT Press, 1977), 337, 416–18.

37. Himmler apparently believed these positions would enable him to control the Volkssturm. Himmler, "Rede," Sept. 21, 1944, BA-MA, RH 14, Nr. 2.

38. Hitler, Bormann, and Lammers, "Erlaß des Führers über den totalen Kriegseinsatz," Jul. 25, 1944, T-84/175/1544827–28.

39. Bormann, "Ausführungsbestimmung zum Erlaß des Führers über die Ordnung und Lenkung des Ausserberuflichen Einsatzes," May 21, 1943, T-580/873/799a/6; Bormann, "RS 123/44, grs.," May 31, 1944, T-77/1432/360–66.

40. Quotation from Keitel, "OKW/WFSt/Qu.2/Verw.1 GKdos. Nr. 007715/44," Jul. 19, 1944, T-175/122/2648257–61. Also Hitler, Keitel, and Bormann, "Führer Erlaß über die Zusammenarbeit von Partei und Wehrmacht in einem Operationsgebiet innerhalb des Reiches von 13. Juli 1944," T-175/242/2648246–47.

41. Peter Longerich, "Jospeh Goebbels und der Totale Krieg: Eine unbekannte Denkschrift des Propagandaministers vom 18. Juli 1944," *Vierteljahrsheft für Zeitgeschichte* 35, no. 2 (1987): 307–8; also Eleanor Hancock, *The National Socialist Leadership and Total War, 1941–45* (New York: St. Martin's, 1991), 134.

42. Leiter Prop. i.V. Sondermann to Goebbels, "Berichte," Jul. 15, 1944, BA-Ko, R 55, Nr. 426, 28–31 and 34–35; Hitler, "Verfügung 12/44," Sept. 1, 1944, T-84/175/1544807; *Tagebücher von Goebbels*, pt. 2, vol. 13, 103.

43. SS Obergruppenführer and Gen. der Polizei Hofmann (Baden), "Aktenvermerk," Oct. 13, 1943, BA-Ko, NS 19, Nr. 798; SA Gruppe Kurpfalz, "Abschrift von Stärkenachweisung, FO 4 Br.B Nr. 303/44, geh.," Oct. 24, 1944, BA-Ko, NS 23, Nr. 235.

44. SA Gruppe Kurpfalz, "Abschrift von Auszüge aus dem Tagebücher der z.b.V. Stürme," various early October dates, BA-Ko, NS 23, Nr. 235; Niederdonau Gaustabsamtsleiter, "Schnellbrief," Oct. 16, 1944, T-581/33/folder 635; SA Gruppe Tannenberg, "Bericht," Oct. 24, 1944, BA-Ko, NS 23, Nr. 154; SA Gruppe Tannenberg, "Schreiben F-214/44," Nov. 1, 1944, T-580/874/799b/5; SA Gruppe Schlesien, "Bericht FO 1 Nr. 120/44, geh." Nov 24, 1944, T-580/849/108/151.

45. SA Gruppe Neckar, "Abschrift: Einsatz- und Tätigkeitsbericht," Sept. 19, 1944, BA-Ko, NS 23, Nr. 235; Hamburg Gltr. Karl Kaufmann, "FS," Oct. 6, 1944, T-580/872/799a/4; Chef der NSKK Führungsamt, "Abschrift von RS, Br.B Nr. 390/44, geh.," Oct. 12, 1944, T-581/20/folder 382; RPA Breslau, "Bericht: FS 14501," Oct. 20, 1944, BA-Ko, R55, Nr. 602, 111–12; Süd Westfalen Gltr. Albert Hoffmann, "FS 2573," Oct. 2, 1944, BA-Ko, NS 6, Nr. 313, 75; HJ Stabsführer Möckel, "FS," Aug. 2, 1944, BA-Ko NS 19, Nr. 219, 79–80; Gltg. Westmark, "RS," May 11, 1944, T-81/93/107778–84; Willy Timm, *Freikorps "Sauerland" 1944–45: Zur Geschichte des Zweiten Weltkriegs in Südwestfalen* (Hagen: Stadtarchiv Hagen, 1976).

46. Sondermann, "Bericht," Jul. 15, 1944, BA-Ko, R 55, Nr. 426, 28–31; Ostpreußen Gaustudentenführung, "Semesterbericht," Sept. 27, 1944, BA-Ko, NS 26, Nr. 151; Wehrwirtschaftsoffizier im WK I, "Tätigkeitsbericht, Nr. 206/44 geh.," Nov. 6, 1944, T-77/499/1665530.

47. Giesler, "Abschrift von FS," Sept. 29, 1944, T-580/872/799a/4; Peter Hüttenberger, *Die Gauleiter: Studie zum Wandel des Machtgefüges in der NSDAP* (Stuttgart: Deutsche Verlags-Anstalt, 1969), 190.

48. Note their emphasis was typically on the motivational and police—as opposed to military—aspects of a militia; Amtsrat Lemke to Sondermann, "Vorschlag," Jul. 13, 1944, BA-Ko, R 55, Nr. 616, 105; HJ Stabsführer Möckel, "FS," Aug. 2, 1944,

BA-Ko NS 19, Nr. 219, 79–80; *Tagebücher von Goebbels*, pt. 2, vol. 13, 438; James M. Diehl, "Victors or Victims? Disabled Veterans in the Third Reich," *Journal of Modern History* 59, no. 4 (Dec. 1987): 713.

49. Zander, "Vorlage" and "Aktenvermerk," Aug. 9 and 30, 1944, both T-580/874/799b/6.

50. Bormann, "RS 184/44, geh.," Aug. 16, 1944, T-580/17/179. For a discussion of this decree, see Thüringen Reichsverteidigungsausschuß, "Sitzungnotizen," Sept. 11, 1944, HStA Weimar, Reichsstattshalter, Nr. 477, 12–41.

51. Kaufmann remained liaison between the Gauleiters and Wehrkreis X, but this carried a good deal more responsibility than power. Hitler, "Befehl über Ausbau der deutschen Bucht, OKW/WFSt/Op. Nr. 773051/44 gK.Chefsache," Aug. 29, 1944; Jodl, "OKW/WFSt/Op. gK.Chefsache Nr. 773140," Aug. 31, 1944, in Walter Hubatsch, ed., *Hitlers Weisungen für die Kriegsführung 1939–1945: Dokumente des Oberkommandos der Wehrmacht*, 2nd ed. (Koblenz: Bernhard und Graefe, 1983), 276–79; Hitler, "Verfügung 12/44," Sept. 1, 1944, T-84/175/1544807; Hüttenberger, 190.

52. Bormann, "RS 229/44, geh." Sept. 10, 1944, T-580/17/180.

53. *Tagebücher von Goebbels*, pt. 2, vol. 13, 396; Guderian, 327; Albert Speer, *Inside the Third Reich*, trans. Richard Winston and Clara Winston (New York: Bonanza Books, 1982), 399; Jochen von Lang, *The Secretary, Martin Bormann: The Man Who Manipulated Hitler*, trans. Christa Armstrong and Peter White (New York: Random House, 1976), 270.

2. "Ein Volk steht auf": The Volkssturm in National Socialist Strategy, Ideology, and Propaganda

1. The works that most strongly influenced this chapter are Jay W. Baird, *The Mythical World of Nazi War Propaganda 1939–1945* (Minneapolis: University of Minnesota Press, 1974); Robert E. Herzstein, *The War That Hitler Won: The Most Infamous Propaganda Campaign in History* (New York: Putnam, 1978); Martin van Creveld, "War Lord Hitler: Some Points Reconsidered," *European Studies Review* 4, no. 1 (1974): 57–79; and the works of Bartov, Förster, Fritz, Hancock, Mason, Messerschmidt, Orlow, Schulte, Streit, and Weinberg that were previously cited. Also Joseph Goebbels, *Die Tagebücher von Joseph Goebbels*, pt. 2, *Diktate, 1942–1945*, vols. 13–15, ed. Elke Fröhlich (Munich: K. G. Saur, 1995–1996), proved valuable.

2. Hitler, "Führerbefehle," Nov. 25, 1944 and Mar. 19, 1945, in *1939–1945: Der Zweite Weltkrieg in Chronik und Dokumenten*, ed. Hans-Adolf Jacobsen (Darmstadt: Wehr und Wissen, 1959), 422–23.

3. Himmler, "Ansprache," July 29, 1944, BA-MA, RH 53-7, Nr. 878.

4. Hugh R. Trevor-Roper, ed., *The Bormann Letters: The Private Correspondence Between Martin Bormann and His Wife from January 1943 to April 1945*, trans. R. H. Stevens (London: Weidenfeld and Nicholson, 1954), 173.

5. Hitler, "Führer Erlaß über die Bildung des Deutschen Volkssturms von 25.9.44," in Hans Kissel, *Der Deutsche Volkssturm 1944/45: Eine territoriale Miliz im Rahmen der Landesverteidigung* (Frankfurt am Main: E. S. Mittler und Sohn, 1962), 97–98; Bormann, "Abschrift von FS," July 24, 1944, BA-Ko, NS 6, Nr. 1, 74–75;

Ian Kershaw, *Popular Opinion and Political Dissent in the Third Reich: Bavaria 1933–1945* (Oxford: Clarendon, 1983), 381–85.

6. Tim Mason, "The Legacy of 1918 for National Socialism," in *German Democracy and the Triumph of Hitler*, ed. Anthony Nicholls and Erich Matthias (New York: St. Martin's, 1971), 237–38.

7. Among the many examples, see Hitler, "Besprechung," Dec. 29, 1944, BA-MA, MSg 13, Nr. 32. Also Gerhard L. Weinberg, "Hitler's Image of the United States," *American Historical Review* 69, no. 4 (July 1969): 1006–21.

8. Hitler, "Verfügung 13/44," Sept. 12, 1944, BA-Ko, NS 6, Nr. 78, 47.

9. 3 PzAOK OB Gen. Raus, "Tagesbefehl," Oct. 21, 1944, T-313/324/8604839. Also Himmler, "Schreiben," July 21, 1944, in *"Reichsführer!...": Briefe an und von Himmler*, ed. Helmut Heiber (Stuttgart: Deutsche Verlags-Anstalt, 1968), 272–74.

10. Himmler, "Ansprache," July 29, 1944, BA-MA, RH 53-7, Nr. 878.

11. PzAOK 5, Ia "GKdos. 21660/44," Nov. 23, 1944, T-311/218/884–85.

12. Goebbels's July 26, 1944, and Feb. 28, 1945, radio addresses in *Goebbels Reden*, vol. 2, *1939–1945*, ed. Helmut Heiber (Düsseldorf: Droste, 1972) 356, 438–41. On the Ardennes Offensive, see Hermann Jung, *Die Ardennen Offensive 1944/45: Ein Beispiel für die Kriegführung Hitlers* (Göttingen: Musterschmidt, 1971); on the importance of the U-boat war, see Howard D. Grier, "Hitler's Baltic Strategy, 1944–45" (Ph.D. diss., University of North Carolina, 1991); and *Tagebücher von Goebbels*, pt. 2, vol. 13, 243, 248, 258–59, vol. 14, 269, vol. 15, 58; on the V-2, see Michael J. Neufeld, *The Rocket and the Reich: Peenemünde and the Coming of the Ballistic Missile Era* (New York: Free Press, 1995).

13. Sauckel, "Sitzungsprotokoll," Sept. 11, 1944, HStA Weimar, Reichsstatthalter, Nr. 477, 12–41; OBdM Adm. Karl Dönitz, "Abschrift von Kurzlagen, OBdM B Nr. 162/45 geh.," Mar. 4, 1945, BA-Ko, NS 6, Nr. 134, 3–6; *Tagebücher von Goebbels*, pt. 2, vol. 14, 230.

14. Richard Breitman and Shlomo Aronson, "The End of the 'Final Solution'? Nazi Plans to Ransom Jews in 1944," *Central European History* 25, no. 2 (undated): 177–203; Ingeborg Fleischauer, *Die Chance des Sonderfriedens: Deutsch-sowjetische Geheimgespräche 1941–1945* (Berlin: Siedler, 1986); Eleanor Hancock, *The National Socialist Leadership and Total War, 1941–45* (New York: St. Martin's, 1991), 36, 91–92, 111–12, 143–45, 186; Reimer Hansen, "Ribbentrops Friedensfühler im Frühjahr 1945," *Geschichte in Wissenschaft und Unterricht* 18 (1967): 716–30; Hansjakob Stehle, "Deutsche Friedensfühler bei den Westmächten im Februar/März 1945," *Vierteljahrshefte für Zeitgeschichte* 30 (1982): 538–55; and Gerhard L. Weinberg, *A World at Arms: A Global History of World War II* (New York: Cambridge University Press, 1994), 719–21, 780–84, 824.

15. Himmler, "Rede," Sept. 21, 1944, BA-MA, RH 14, Nr. 2, 8.

16. On Nazi views of Soviet strength, see Helmut Heiber, ed., *Hitlers Lagebesprechungen* (Stuttgart: Deutsche Verlags-Anstalt, 1962), 679; Gau Berlin Propagandaleiter, "Vertrauliches RS 9/45," Jan. 29, 1945, LHA Potsdam, PrBrRep. 61, Berlin, Nr. 14.4.5.

17. Hitler, "Besprechung," Dec. 29, 1944, BA-MA, MSg 13, Nr. 32; *Tagebücher von Goebbels*, pt. 2, vol. 14, 34–36; Weinberg, "Hitler's Image."

18. Hitler quoted in Weinberg, "Hitler's Image," 1018. Also see *Tagebücher von Goebbels,* pt. 2, vol. 13, 119.

19. Hitler, "Besprechung," Dec. 29, 1944, BA-MA, MSg 13, Nr. 32.

20. Goebbels, "RS," Feb. 5, 1945, T-81/23/220755–57.

21. RMfVuP, Chef des Propagandastabes, "Material für Propagandisten," BA-Ko, R 55, Nr. 793, 1–30, is a series listing propaganda guidelines and themes from late 1944 and 1945. Number 27 (Feb. 17, 1945) dealt extensively with the Nazis' views of their enemies.

22. RMfVuP, Chef des Propagandastabes, "Material für Propagandisten, #23–24," Jan. 12, 1945, BA-Ko, R 55, Nr. 793, 11; Gau Westfalen-Nord Propaganda-leitung, "Kennwortparolen," Dec. 21, 1944, StA Detmold, Bestand L 113, Nr. 523, 190–91; Gau Berlin Propagandaleiter, "Vertrauliches RS 9/45," Jan. 29, 1945, LHA Potsdam, PrBrRep. 61, Berlin, Nr. 14.4.5.

23. RMfVuP, Chef des Propagandastabes, "Material für Propagandisten, #27," Feb. 17, 1945, BA-Ko, R 55, Nr. 793, 1–3.

24. Gau Westfalen-Nord Propagandaleitung, "Bekanntmachung" undated (Oct. 1944); "Propagandahinweis Nr. 19," Nov. 3, 1944, both StA Detmold, Bestand L 113, Nr. 523, 170–80.

25. RMfVuP, Chef des Propagandastabes, "Material für Propagandisten," various dates, BA-Ko, R 55, Nr. 793, 1–30; Gau Berlin Propagandaleiter, "RS 75, 78, 79, 89/44 and 4, 5, 7/45," Sept. 27, Oct. 9, 11, Nov. 9, 1944, Jan. 17, 19, and 23, 1945, respectively, LHA Potsdam, PrBrRep. 61, Berlin, Nr. 14.4.5.

26. At least one set of propaganda guidelines stated this in so many words, Gau Westfalen-Nord Propagandaleitung, "Propagandahinweis Nr. 19," Nov. 3, 1944, StA Detmold, Bestand L113, Nr. 523, 176–80.

27. RMfVuP, Chef des Propagandastabes, "Material für Propagandisten," various dates, BA-Ko, R 55, Nr. 793, 1–30; Also see Bartov's work; Hancock, 49; Manfred Messerschmidt, "The Wehrmacht and the Volksgemeinschaft," *Journal of Contemporary History* 18, no. 4 (Oct. 1983): 735.

28. WK VII NSFO, "Abschrift: Führungsfernspruch Nr. 3," Feb. 10, 1945, T-84/160/1527026.

29. Gau Bayreuth Schulungsamt, "Vs. Schulungsunterlage 1," Jan. 1945, T-580/872/799a/1.

30. Hitler, "Abschrift von Führerbefehl, ObKdo HGr. B Ia GKdos. Nr. 7466/44," Sept. 16, 1944, T-311/3/7002349–50.

31. Hitler, "Führerbefehl," in "OKH/GenStdH/Org. Abt. I, "Aufgaben und Richtlinien für die Kommandanten eines festen Platzes, GKdos. Nr. 2434/44," Mar. 8, 1944, T-77/782/5508841–43; Hitler, "Führerbefehl," Nov. 25, 1944, in "OKW/WFSt/Qu. 2, FS Nr. 1409/44, geh.," Nov. 28, 1944, in *Hitlers Weisungen für die Kriegsführung 1939–1945: Dokumente des Oberkommandos der Wehrmacht,* ed. Walter Hubatsch, 2nd ed. (Koblenz: Bernhard und Graefe, 1983), 298–99.

32. Guderian, "OKH/GStdH/Ausb. Abt. (Ia) Nr. 3000/44, Merkblatt 18b/37: Alarmeinheiten," July 23, 1944, T-77/785/5513055–78; OKH, "Merkblatt: Verteidigung von Ortschaften," undated, BA-MA, RH 30, Nr. 4.

33. OKW/NSFO, "Die Möglichkeit der Stunde," *Die Politische Soldat,* Folge 3 (Feb. 1945), 4, BA-MA, RH 53-13, Nr. 154, 47–50.

34. Goebbels, "RS," Feb. 5, 1945, T-81/23/207555–57; author unknown (NSFO materials) "Persönliche Tapferkeit siegt über Masse und Material," Information für die weltanschauliche Führung, Folge 10 (Mar. 8, 1945), T-175/229/2767705–28.

35. WK VII NSFO, "Abschrift von Führerfernspruch Nr. 4," Feb. 13, 1945, T-84/160/1527024.

36. A rough prose translation reads: A wooden sword and bravery, protects goods and possessions, better than a cannon—without; *Oldenburgischen Staatszeitung,* cited in Herbert Schwarzwälder, *Bremen und Nordwestdeutschland am Kriegsende 1945,* vol. 2 (Bremen: Carl Schünemann, 1973), 55.

37. Herzstein's book provides a good, detailed explanation of Goebbels's view of the purpose of propaganda.

38. On the influence of the Party on military affairs, see Peter Hüttenberger, *Die Gauleiter: Studie zum Wandel des Machtgefüges in der NSDAP* (Stuttgart: Deutsche Verlags-Anstalt, 1969), 172–95; Manfred Messerschmidt, *Die Wehrmacht im NS Staat: Zeit der Indoktrination* (Hamburg: R. von Decker, 1969), chap. 5; Dietrich Orlow, *The History of the Nazi Party 1919–1945,* vol. 2, *1933–1945* (Pittsburgh: University of Pittsburgh Press, 1973).

39. On the NSFO, see Waldemar Besson, "Zur Geschichte der Nationalsozialistischen Führungsoffiziere," *Vierteljahrsheft für Zeitgeschichte* 9, no. 1 (Jan. 1961): 76–116; Messerschmidt, *Die Wehrmacht,* 441–80; and Gerhard L. Weinberg, "Adolf Hitler und der NS-Führungsoffizier," *Vierteljahrsheft für Zeitgeschichte* 12, no. 4 (Oct. 1964): 443–56.

40. WK VII NSFO, "National Sozialistische Führung," June 20, 1944, T-79/24/1163. On NSFO goals, see 708 VGDiv, Abt. NSFO, "Richtlinien für Weltanschauliche Erziehung," Sept. 30, 1944, BA-MA, RH 26-708, Nr. 33.

41. Himmler, "Ansprache," July 29, 1944, BA-MA, RH 53-7, Nr. 878.

42. On this, see Bartov's works and Mark Mazower, *Inside Hitler's Greece: The Experience of Occupation, 1941–1944* (New Haven, Conn.: Yale University Press, 1993), 208–10.

43. Gen. Ferdinand Schörner, OKW/NSFO Stabschef, quoted in Besson, 78.

44. Hitler, "Befehl von 13.3.45," in Bormann, "Anlage zu RS 148/45," Mar. 14, 1945, T-81/5/13030–33.

45. Bormann, "Anordnung 115/45," Mar. 6, 1945, BA-Ko, NS 6, Nr. 353, 134–35.

46. Bormann, "Anordnung 190/44," Aug. 23, 1944, T-580/17/179.

47. *Tagebücher von Goebbels,* pt. 2, vol. 13, 534–35, 573; Franken Gstbfü. Georg Dechant, "RS," Jan. 17, 1945, T-580/923/40.

48. Hitler, "Führer Erlaß über die Bildung des Deutschen Volkssturms von 25.9.44," in Kissel, 97–98.

49. Hessen-Nassau Gstbfü. Kurt Schädlich, "Ausbildungsbefehl 1/44," Nov. 10, 1944, HStA Wiesbaden, Abt. 483, Nr. 6462; Dechant, "RS," Jan. 17, 1945, T-580/923/40.

50. Note again the *Kampfzeit* and *Gleichschaltung* allusions, Kr. Hilpoltstein Schulungsleiter, "Bericht," Nov. 1, 1944, T-81/645/5448565.

51. Chef der Propagandastabes und Leiter Prop. i. V., Dr. Schäfer to Goebbels,

"Tätigkeitsberichte," Oct. 24, 1944, T-580/682/563, and Oct. 30, 1944, BA-Ko, R 55, Nr. 601, 193–202.

52. Quotation from GenKdo. VI Flakkorps (mot.) NSFO, "Befehl für die NS Führung," Mar. 1, 1945, T-84/159/1525947. The foundation for the local *Hoheitsträger*'s role is Bormann, "Einsatz der Partei im Invasionsfall, RS 123/44, grs." May 31, 1944, T-77/1432/360–66.

53. Koch to Bormann, "Abschrift von FS Nr. 80," Sept. 18, 1944, T-581/6/151; Hüttenberger, 212.

54. Bormann "Anordnung 98/45," Feb. 23, 1945, BA-Ko, NS 6, Nr. 353. 121–22.

55. For more on this, see chapter 6. PK Volkssturmstabschef Wilhelm Friedrichs to Bormann, "FS 933, Vorlage Bofinger," Oct. 11, 1944, BA-Ko, NS 6, Nr. 313, 143–46; PK Gruppe II F, "Entwurf von Arbeitstagung," Nov. 2, 1944, IfZG, Fa 91/1/11, 92–99.

56. PK Gruppe II F, "Entwurf von Arbeitstagung," Nov. 2, 1944, IfZG, Fa 91/1/11, 92–99.

57. Hauptschulungsamt der PK, *Der Dienstappell*, Folge 1 (Nov. 1944): back cover.

58. Quotation from WK XIII NSFO, "Gedänkenführung für das Monatsthema März," Mar. 10, 1945, BA-MA, RH 53-14, Nr. 154, 52–55; also see Messerschmidt, "Volksgemeinschaft"; and James M. Diehl, "Victors or Victims? Disabled Veterans in the Third Reich," *Journal of Modern History* 59, no. 4 (Dec. 1987): 705–36.

59. München-Ost Krstbfü., "Vsbefehl Nr. 2/45," Feb. 21, 1945, T-81/153/156215–18.

60. Bormann "RS 369/44," Nov. 1, 1944, T-580/53/285.

61. Friedrichs to Bormann, "FS 736," Sept. 22, 1944, BA-Ko, NS 6, Nr. 313, 160–73; Gerald Kirwin, "Allied Bombing and Nazi Domestic Propaganda," *European History Quarterly* 15, no. 3 (July 1985): 346–47.

62. Fritz M. Rebhann, *Finale in Wien: Eine Gaustadt im Aschenregen* (Vienna: Herold, 1969), 126.

63. *Gleichschaltung* refers to the effort by the NSDAP to harmonize German life in all its aspects with National Socialist ideas. It also refers to the attempt to bring all aspects of German life under the supervision of the Nazi Party.

64. Bormann "Anordnung 443/44," Dec. 12, 1944, T-81/95/109395–96.

65. Bormann, "RS 385/44," Nov. 7, 1944, T-81/1/11276–77.

66. PK Staff Befehlsleiter Dr. Klopfer to Bormann, "Vorlage, FS 15052," Nov. 30, 1944, T-580/872/799a/5; Bormann, "Anordnung 443/44," Dec. 9, 1944, T-81/95/1083395–96.

67. Bormann, "Anordnung 464/44 geh.," Dec. 22, 1944, BA-Ko, NS 6, Nr. 98, 105; PK's Dr. Römhold to Reichskanzleichef Dr. Hans Heinrich Lammers, "Vermerk zu Rk. 9743 E II," Dec. 12, 1944, BA-Ko, R 43 II, Nr. 692a.

68. On church services and chaplains, see Celle Krstbfü., "Vs. befehl Nr. 25/45," Feb. 9, 1945, T-81/95/109375–77, which invoked Bormann's instructions, although it did not further identify them. On clergy exemptions, see Bormann, "RS 362/44," Oct. 31, 1944, T-580/53/285; Bormann, "RS 374/44," Nov. 2, 1944, T-81/1/1273–74.

69. Ley, "Abschrift von Meldung 1381," Oct. 31, 1944, BA-Ko, NS 6, Nr. 168,

33–38; Bormann, "Aktenvermerk für II und III D," Nov. 1, 1944, BA-Ko, NS 6, Nr. 168, 33–38.

70. Bormann also scornfully added that churches could find female or older male substitutes, or "in individual cases church services could be conducted without organ music." Bormann "RS 13/45," Jan. 28, 1945, T-81/94/108085.

71. On Bormann's view of the churches, see Jochen von Lang, *The Secretary, Martin Bormann: The Man Who Manipulated Hitler*, trans. Christa Armstrong and Peter White (New York: Random House, 1976), 124–32.

72. Bormann, "RS 270/44," Sept. 26, 1944, T-580/53/285; Bormann to Zander, "FS," Oct. 15, 1944, T-580/872/799a/4.

73. Quotation from Bormann, "RS 353/44," Oct. 27, 1944, T-81/1/12755; Bormann "RS 350/44," Oct. 27, 1944, T-81/1/11249–50.

74. Bayreuth Gltr. Fritz Wächtler, "Durchsage," Jan. 26, 1945, BA-Ko, NS 12, Nr. 1147.

75. Reichpropagandaleitung der NSDAP, "Bildung eigener Volkssturm Einheiten durch bestimmte Personengruppen," *Rüstzeug für die Propaganda in der Ortsgruppe*, Folge 10 (Sondernummer Volkssturm, Nov. 10, 1944): 27.

76. Leiter der Staatlich Genehmigten Gesellschaft zur Verwertung musikalischer Urheberrechte to Goebbels, "Schreiben," Nov. 1, 1944, T-580/659/459.

77. Bormann to Zander, "FS," Oct. 15, 1944, T-580/872/799a/4.

78. Dechant, "RS BrB. Nr DVst 54/44," Nov. 23, 1944, StA Nuremberg, Bestand 593 Gltg, Nr. 139.

79. Quotation from Sauckel, "Befehl Nr. 2," undated, T-81/95/169723. Also Bormann, "Grundsätze der Mannschaftsführung, RS 349/44," Oct. 26, 1944, T-580/17/180.

80. Schuett to Bormann, "FS 845," Oct. 3, 1945, BA-Ko, NS 6, Nr. 763, 78; Reichpropagandaleitung der NSDAP, "Das beste Volkssturmlied," *Rüstzeug für die Propaganda in der Ortsgruppen*, Folge 10 (Sondernummer Volkssturm, Nov. 10, 1944): 28.

81. On Bartenstein's program, see Koch, "Abschrift von FS," Oct. 15, 1944, T-581/6/151; on Munich's, see Gau München-Oberbayern Propagandaleiter, "FS," Oct. 31, 1944, T-580/872/799a/4; on Berlin's, see Gstbfü. Günther Gräntz, "Vereidigungsprogramm," Nov. 8, 1944, T-580/667/502.

82. Herzstein called the Volkssturm oath ceremonies "the closest thing to the prewar Nürnberg Rallies that the Reich had seen in years," Herzstein, 250.

83. "Das ganze Volk tritt an," *Heidelberger Volksgemeinschaft*, Oct. 19, 1944, clipping in T-580/858/114/124.

84. Bormann, "FS," Oct. 15, 1944, T-580/872/799a/4; *Tagebücher von Goebbels*, pt. 2, vol. 14, 101.

85. Quotation from OB West, Abt. NS Führung, "Appell," Feb. 2, 1945, T-84/160/1527757–78. On the Party's perception of its role, see Orlow, vol. 2, 13–16.

86. Bormann "RS 369/44," Nov. 1, 1944, T-580/53/285. Also *Tagebücher von Goebbels*, pt. 2, vol. 14, 159.

87. Quotation from Friedrichs to Bormann, "FS 736, Aktenvermerk Zander," Sept. 22, 1944, T-580/872/799a/4; Koch to Bormann, "Abschrift von FS Nr. 80," Sept. 18, 1944, T-581/6/151.

88. Gau Köln-Aachen Hauptamtsleiter, "Nationalsozialistische Gaudienst, Folge 3034," Feb. 15, 1945, HStA Düsseldorf, RW 23, Nr. 104, 6–10; Diehl, 726–27.

89. Himmler's address badly overstated the *Landsturm*'s rather limited contribution to Napoleon's defeat; Himmler, "Rede" Oct. 18, 1944, BA-Ko, NS 19, Nr. 4016.

90. Gau Bayreuth Schulungsamt, "Vs. Schulungsunterlage Nr. 1," Jan. (no day), 1945, T-580/872/799a/1.

91. Friedrichs to Bormann, "FS 933," Oct. 11, 1944, BA-Ko, NS 6, Nr. 313, 143–46; Bormann, "RS 386/44, Kampfsätze," Nov. 8, 1944, T-81/1/11271.

92. Baden-Elsaß Gltr. Robert Wagner, "Abschrift von der Aufstellung des Volkssturms," Oct. 30, 1944, T-81/94/108261.

93. Bormann, "RS 386/44," Nov. 8, 1944, T-81/1/11271.

94. Bormann, "Abschrift von FS," Nov. 8, 1944, T-81/93/107678.

95. In fact, the propaganda machine simply could not get enough information on the East Prussian Volkssturm's exploits; Reichspressedienst Stabschef Helmut Sündermann to RPA Königsberg, "FS Pro. 299/7.11.44/28-4.7," Nov. 7, 1944, T-580/660/462.

96. Kriegsberichter Lt. Peter Kustermann, "Ostpreußischer Volkssturmmänner," Nov. 6, 1944, T-313/325/8605805–8, quoted here, is one of the many examples.

97. Chapter 6 examines Volkssturm unit leaders' actual qualifications. Bormann, "Anordnung 318/44," Oct. 12, 1944, in Kissel, 100–103; Bormann, "RS 28/45," Feb. 23, 1945, T-580/872/799a/3.

98. Hoffmann to Bormann, "FS 2573," Oct. 2, 1944, BA-Ko, NS 6, Nr. 313, 75; Koch, "Abschrift von BrB. 48/44 Kgeh.," Oct. 10, 1944, T-581/6/151.

99. "Das ganze Volk tritt an," *Heidelberger Volksgemeinschaft*, Oct. 19, 1944, clipping in T-580/858/114/124.

100. Bormann, "Grundsätze der Mannschaftsführung im Deutschen Volkssturm," Oct. 22, 1944, T-580/872/799a/4; Bormann, "RS 386/44," Nov. 8, 1944, T-81/1/11271.

101. On this, see Omer Bartov, *The Eastern Front, 1941–1945: German Troops and the Barbarisation of Warfare* (New York: St. Martin's, 1985), 38–69; Jürgen Förster, "The Dynamics of Volksgemeinschaft: The Effectiveness of the German Military Establishment in the Second World War," in *Military Effectiveness*, vol. 3, *The Second World War*, ed. Alan R. Millett and Williamson Murray (Boston: Allen and Unwin, 1988), 206–7.

102. Friedrichs to Bormann, "FS 937," Oct. 11, 1944, BA-Ko, NS 6, Nr. 313, 143–46.

103. Gau Berlin Propagandaleiter, "RS 10 & 11/45," Jan. 30 and Feb. 1, 1945, LHA Potsdam, PrBrRep. 61, Berlin, Nr. 14.4.5; Gau Bayreuth Schulungsleiter, "RS 9/45," Mar. 29, 1945, T-580/872/799a/1.

104. All company and battalion leaders received the NSFO weekly *Der politische Soldat* and a similar Volkssturm weekly called *Der Dienstappell* (samples are in BA-Ko, NS 6, Nr. 312, 56–79). On distribution of materials, see Moselland Gstbfü. Michael Broesl, "Anlage 7 zu RS, Abschrift von Bormann Anordnung 12/44," Nov. 23, 1944, T-81/94/108993.

105. Bormann, "Anordnung 1/45," Jan. 1, 1945, T-580/53/285.

106. Burton Wright III, "Army of Despair: The German Volkssturm 1944–1945" (Ph.D. diss., Florida State University, 1982), 101.

107. The differences, subtle and often more of degree than of kind, between a people's army and a traditional militia are as follows. Militias are more often the product of government decree and are structured to meet international legal requirements. They are more centrally controlled, standardized, and bureaucratized auxiliaries to regular military forces and administratively based on the government's territorial subunits. They tend to employ orthodox defensive tactics and activate only for short, fixed tours of duty. Their primary function is local defense. On the other hand, a people's army is motivated by the desire to implement or preserve a political agenda and relies on the devotion of its members to those goals for its cohesion and spirit. Often independent of professional military control, more loosely and locally organized and supervised, it tends to employ a wider range of improvised, irregular tactics in its struggle. Basically a people's army tends to reflect the ideology that created it, whereas a militia tends to reflect the government that decreed it. On this, see David K. Yelton, "The Last Reserves: Political-Military Aspects of the Structure, Function, and Composition of the German Volkssturm, 1944–1945" (Ph.D. diss., University of North Carolina, 1990), 12–16.

108. Jeremy Noakes and Geoffrey Pridham, eds., *Nazism 1919–1945: A History in Documents and Eyewitness Accounts*, vol. 1, *The Nazi Party, State and Society, 1919–1939* (New York: Schocken, 1983), 14–16.

109. OB West, Abt. NS Führung, "Appell," Feb. 2, 1945, T-84/160/1527757–78; Schörner, "OB der HGr Mitte, Ia/IIa, 840/45, geh.," Mar. 12, 1945, T-311/134/7179666–67.

110. Even in a National Socialist military reform proposal there was no call to supplant the professionals; no author, "Studie über eine nationalsozialistische Wehrreform," undated, but after Oct. 1944, T-78/382/6347343–59. Also Bormann, "RS 270/44," Sept. 26, 1944, T-580/874/799b/5.

111. Himmler, "Rede," Sept. 21, 1944, BA-MA, RH 14, Nr. 2, 18. Goebbels shared these sentiments, *Tagebücher von Goebbels*, pt. 2, vol. 13, 387, 393.

112. *Tagebücher von Goebbels*, pt. 2, vol. 14, 43–44, 55–56.

113. Herzstein, 199, 246–50.

3. National Administration

1. Hitler, "Führer Erlaß über die Bildung des Deutschen Volkssturms," Sept. 25, 1944, in Hans Kissel, *Der Deutsche Volkssturm 1944/45: Eine territoriale Miliz im Rahmen der Landesverteidigung* (Frankfurt am Main: E. S. Mittler und Sohn, 1962), 97–98.

2. Himmler, "Rede," Sept. 21, 1944, BA-MA, RH 14, Nr. 2, 5.

3. See points 6–8 in the "Führer Erlaß," Kissel, 97–98; Reichskanzlei to Bormann, "Entwurf von Verordnung über die Stellung der Angehörigen des Deutschen Volkssturms," undated, probably Nov. 1944, BA-Ko, R 43 II, Nr. 692, E424982–84.

4. Quotation from Bormann to Giesler, "FS," Oct. 31, 1944, T-580/872/799a/4; also Bormann to Friedrichs, "FS," Nov. 5, 1944, BA-Ko, NS 6, Nr. 764, 178–79.

5. Bormann, "FS," Oct. 29, 1944, BA-Ko, NS 6, Nr. 764, 123; Bormann to Giesler, "FS," Oct. 31, 1944, T-580/872/799a/4.

6. Bormann, "RS 278/44," Sept. 27, 1944, T-580/872/799a/5; and "RS 4/45," Jan. 6, 1945, BA-Ko, NS 6, Nr. 354, 22–23.

7. Bormann to Friedrichs, "FS," Sept. 26, 1944, T-580/872/799a/4; Bormann, "gRs.," Feb. 7, 1945, T-77/787/5515290–92; Bormann, "Anordnungen 11 & 34/45," Jan. 26, 1945, BA-Ko, NS 6, Nr. 99, 16, and Feb. 15, 1945, BA-Ko, NS 6, Nr. 353, 115–16.

8. Regensburg Regierungspräsident, "Schnellbrief Nr. 1234 h6," Dec. 4, 1944, StA Amberg, BzA Eschenbach, Nr. 4293.

9. For complete explanations of and citations for these events, see David K. Yelton, "The Last Reserves: Political-Military Aspects of the Structure, Function, and Composition of the German Volkssturm, 1944–1945" (Ph.D. diss., University of North Carolina, 1990), 128–33.

10. Himmler, "FS, Tgb. Nr. 4453/44," Oct. 1, 1944, T-580/872/799a/4.

11. The Volkssturm's Levy (Aufgebot) System is explored fully in chapter 5, but a general outline may help readers here. Levy I units could be mobilized for service anywhere within their home Gau and would thus be activated first. Levy II units—assignment to these units is the deferral mentioned in the text—could serve only in their home Kreis and would mobilize later. Assignment to Levies I and II was based on a man's occupation and the priority given it by those concerned with the war economy and conscription. Levy III units were for youths aged sixteen to nineteen, and Levy IV units were for men deemed physically fit only for guard duty.

12. Gerhard Rempel, "Gottlob Berger and Waffen SS Recruitment 1939–1945," *Militärgeschichtliche Mitteilungen*, no. 1 (1980): 116–17.

13. Bormann, "Anordnung 336/44," Oct. 19, 1944, T-580/872/799a/5; "RS 353," Oct. 27, 1944, T-81/1/11275.

14. Friedrichs to Bormann, "FS 736, Aktenvermerk Zander," Sept. 22, 1944, T-580/872/799a/4; Joseph Goebbels, *Die Tagebücher von Joseph Goebbels*, pt. 2, *Diktate, 1942–1945*, vol. 13, ed. Elke Fröhlich (Munich: K. G. Saur, 1995), 464–65.

15. Schepmann, "Tätigkeitsbericht," Dec. 1, 1944, BA-Ko, NS 23, Nr. 121. Also Schepmann, "RS," Aug. 23, 1944, T-81/90/103788–89; and "Rede," Aug. 23, 1944, T-81/90/103789–90.

16. Schepmann to Hitler, "Abschrift von Schreiben," Sept. 22, 1944, T-580/872/799a/4.

17. Bormann to Friedrichs, "FS," Sept. 26, 1944, BA-Ko, NS 6, Nr. 313, 174–77.

18. SA Oberste Führung Liaison Officer, Brigadeführer Wiczonke to Friedrichs, "Schreiben und Anlage," Oct. 3, 1944, T-580/874/799b/5; Wiczonke to Bofinger (PK Arbeitsstab V), "Entwurf von Einsatz der SA im Rahmen des Volkssturms," Oct. 19, 1944, T-580/874/799b/5; Bormann, "RS 357/44," Oct. 30, 1944, T-580/872/799a/5.

19. Friedrichs to Bormann, "FS 736, Aktenvermerk Zander," Sept. 22, 1944, T-580/872/799a/4; Obergruppenführer Kwalo (NSKK Berlin) to Kraus, "FS 250," Sept. 28, 1944, T-581/20/382; Berger, "RS, VsTgb. Nr. 517/44 geh., VoTgb. Nr. 41/44 geh.," Oct. 14, 1944, T-581/20/382.

20. Kwalo, "RS," Nov. 9, 1944, T-581/20/382; Friedrichs, "FS 1005," Oct. 20, 1944, T-580/872/799a/4.

21. Friedrichs to Bormann, "FS 1078," Oct. 28, 1944, T-580/872/799a/4.

22. He claimed such terminology could create the impression of a partisan force; Bormann to Friedrichs, "FS," Oct. 4, 1944, T-580/872/799a/4.

23. Bormann to Schepmann, "Schreiben," Sept. 26, 1944, BA-Ko NS 6, Nr. 763, 18. This grand title was practically meaningless; in fact, Bormann often railed about the need to curtail Volkssturm marksmanship training in favor of expanded antitank instruction.

24. Bormann to Friedrichs, "FS," Sept. 26, 1944, BA-Ko, NS 6, Nr. 313, 174–77; and Oct. 24, 1944, T-580/872/799a/4.

25. Oberste SA Führung, "Aktenvermerk," Nov. 13, 1944, T-580/874/799b/5; Schepmann, "Tagesbefehl Ch. Nr. 11. 100," Oct. 18, 1944, T-580/874/799b/5.

26. Friedrichs to Bormann, "FS Nr. 1078," Oct. 28, 1944, T-580/872/799a/4.

27. Berger, "1. Befehl für die Schießausbildung im Vs., VsTgb. Nr. 1372/44 gKdos., VoTgb. Nr. 65/44 gKdos.," Nov. 1, 1944, T175/122/2648014–16.

28. Schützenstandarte 3 (Berlin), "Standartenbefehl," Mar. 30, 1945, LHA Potsdam, PrBrRep. 61, SA, Nr. 18.310; Eigruber to Bormann, "FS," April 9, 1945, BA-Ko, NS 6, Nr. 277, 33–36.

29. Friedrichs, "FS Nr. 1005," Oct. 20, 1944, T-580/872/799a/4; Friedrichs to Bormann "FS Nr. 1013," Oct. 20, 1944, BA-Ko, NS 6, Nr. 763, 256–61.

30. RBDir. Regensburg, "Abschrift von RS," Oct. 20, 1944, BA-Ko, NS 12, Nr. 1147; Sudetenland Gltr. Konrad Henlein, "FS 1618," Oct. 25, 1944, T-580/872/799a/4; OKL/GenSt/Abt. GenQM, "GKdos. 13607/44," Oct. 23, 1944, T-580/872/799a/4.

31. Friedrichs to Berger, "Abschrift von FS," Oct. 20, 1944, BA-Ko, NS 6, Nr. 763, 262–64; Friedrichs to Bormann, "FS 1005," Oct. 20, 1944, T-580/872/799a/4.

32. A succinct list of Berger's offenses is in Friedrichs, "FS 1005," Oct. 20, 1944, T-580/872/799a/4. Also Bormann to Friedrichs, "FS," Oct. 22, 1944, T-580/872/799a/4; Bormann to Friedrichs, "FS," Oct. 25, 1944, BA-Ko, NS 6, Nr. 314, 50; Bormann, "RS 356/44," Oct. 26, 1944, T-580/17/180.

33. Friedrichs to Bormann, "FS 1062, Vorlage Friedrichs-Berger," Oct. 26, 1944, T-580/872/799a/4.

34. Sudetenland Stellvertretender Gltr. Neuburg to Friedrichs, "FS 1605," Oct. 25, 1944, T-580/872/799a/4; Berger, "Anweisung Nr. 2, VsTgb. Nr. 6670/44 geh., VoTgb. Nr. 144/44 geh.," Oct. 28, 1944, T-175/122/2618017–19; Bormann to Friedrichs, "FS," Oct. 29, 1944, T-580/872/799a/4; Bormann, "Anordnung 3/45," Jan. 26, 1945, T-81/94/108070–73.

35. Bormann to Friedrichs, "FS," Oct. 29, 1944, T-580/872/799a/4.

36. Bormann to Himmler, "FS, gRs.," Oct. 31, 1944, T-175/122/2648062–63.

37. In the largest single collection of documents (BA-Ko, NS 19, Nr. 3912)—a mere fifteen items—originating in Himmler's Volkssturm staff, Berger signed nine of them, Himmler only four.

38. Kissel, 21.

39. Friedrichs gleefully added that Berger reportedly dismissed Palm because he did "not possess enough force of argument against the Party Chancellery"; Friedrichs to Bormann, "FS 1213," Nov. 15, 1944, T-580/872/799a/5.

40. OKH/GenStdH/Ausb. Abt., "Skizze," Jan. 1, 1945, T-78/203/6148382.

41. Wilhelm von Grolmann (Leipzig police chief), "The Collapse of the German Reich as Seen from Leipzig (a Narrative)," MS B-478, in *World War II Military Studies,* ed. Donald S. Detwiler, Charles B. Burdick, and Jürgen Rohwer, vol. 24, pt. 10, "Special Topics" (New York: Garland, 1979).

42. Scholtz-Klink to Bormann, "FS 1065, geh.," Oct. 27, 1944, T-580/872/799a/4; Bormann, "Anordnung 422/44," Nov. 30, 1944, T-580/53/285.

43. Recall that Berger sought this same prize; Wilfred von Oven, *Finale Furioso: Mit Goebbels bis zum Ende* (Tübingen: Grabert, 1974), 395; Dietrich Orlow, *The History of the Nazi Party 1919–1945,* vol. 2, *1933–1945* (Pittsburgh: University of Pittsburgh Press, 1973), 468–70.

44. Friedrichs to Bormann, "FS 111," Oct. 19, 1944, T-580/872/799a/4; Friedrichs to Bormann, "FS 1052," Oct. 26, 1944, BA-Ko, NS 6, Nr. 314, 60–61; *Tagebücher von Goebbels,* pt. 2, vol. 14, 134.

45. RMfVuP Personnel Abt. Chef Stock to Goebbels, "Meldung," Dec. 13, 1944, BA-Ko, R 55, Nr. 914, 39; Stock, "Schreiben," Dec. 29, 1944, BA-Ko, R 55, Nr. 914, 29–30; Stock, "Meldung II 076," Jan. 2, 1945, BA-Ko, R 55, Nr. 914, 23; Reichsrundfunkgesellschaft to Stock, "Vermerk," Jan. 4, 1945, BA-Ko, R 55, Nr. 914, 28; Kofü., IV Komp. to Btnfü., Btn. Wilhelmplatz I, "Schreiben," Feb. 12, 1945, T-580/667/502; *Tagebücher von Goebbels,* pt. 2, vol. 14, 184.

46. On the Bormann-Speer feud, see Peter Hüttenberger, *Die Gauleiter: Studie zum Wandel des Machtgefüges in der NSDAP* (Stuttgart: Deutsche Verlags-Anstalt, 1969), 182–87; Alan S. Milward, *The German Economy at War* (London: Athlone, 1965), 115, 129; Orlow, vol. 2, 417–19, 434–36.

47. This included Speer's own headquarters' employees; RMfRuK Personalamt Bohr, "Vermerk," Oct. 21, 1944, BA-Ko, R 3, Nr. 1771, 15. Also Sonderbevollmächtige des Führers für die Donau, "RS 387/44," Oct. 25, 1944; RBDir. Regensburg, "Abschrift von RS," Oct. 20, 1944, both BA-Ko, NS 12, Nr. 1147; Müller (PK Arbeitsstab Vs.) to Klopfer, "FS," Oct. 22, 1944, BA-Ko, NS 6, Nr. 314, 185–86.

48. Friedrichs to Bormann, "FS 736, Aktenvermerk Zander," Sept. 22, 1944, T-580/872/799a/4; Ley to Bormann, "FS 2578," Oct. 24, 1944, T-580/872/799a/5; *Tagebücher von Goebbels,* pt. 2, vol. 13, 438, 464–65.

49. Bormann to Friedrichs, "FS," Oct. 24, 1944, BA-Ko, NS 6, Nr. 764, 43–44. Ley tried to salvage some role for the DAF by ordering that all factory units should be commanded by the local German Labor Front leader *(Werkscharführer).* If he was deemed unfit for this duty, he should resign and be replaced by the appointed Volkssturm commander; Ley, "Anordnung 25/44," Nov. 16, 1944, T-81/94/107876.

50. Bormann, "FS," Nov. 3, 1944, BA-Ko, NS 6, Nr. 764, 173; Speer to Bormann, "FS M 2893/44," Nov. 6, 1944, BA-Ko, Nr. 1573, 191; Bormann, "Anordnung 408/44," Nov. 20, 1944, in Kissel, 109–10.

51. On cooperation, see Bormann, "RS 460/44 geh.," Dec. 19, 1944, T-580/53/285; OKW/Chef Heeresstab, Org. Abt., "FS 308/45, geh.," Jan. 20, 1945, T-81/95/109868. On safeguarding personnel, see Speer, "Abschrift von RMfRuK RüA/Arb. VII RS," Nov. 20, 1944, StA Bückeburg, L102b Landratsamt Stadthagen, Nr. 1876.

52. Speer, "Auszüge aus Führerbesprechung, 28–29 Nov.," Nov. 29, 1944, BA-Ko, R 3, Nr. 1512, 64.

53. Bormann, "Anordnung 351/44," Oct. 27, 1944, T-580/872/799a/5; Artur Axmann, *"Das kann doch nicht das Ende sein"*: *Hitler's letzten Reichsjugendführer erinnert sich* (Koblenz: Bublies, 1995), 397.

54. Friedrichs to Bormann, "FS 833 & 897," Oct. 3 and 7, 1944, BA-Ko, NS 6, Nr. 763, 74–77 and 115–17; *Tagebücher von Goebbels*, pt. 2, vol. 15, 53–54.

55. See Gerhard Rempel, *Hitler's Children: The Hitler Youth and the SS* (Chapel Hill: University of North Carolina Press, 1989); and Richard E. Schroeder, "The Hitler Youth as a Paramilitary Organization (Ph.D. diss., University of Chicago, 1975).

56. Bormann, "Anordnung 351/44," Oct. 27, 1944, T-580/872/799a/5.

57. See Rempel, "Berger."

58. Quotation from Berger to Himmler, "GKdos. VsTgb. Nr. 196/45, Adj. Tgb. Nr. 50/45," Feb. 9, 1945, BA-Ko, NS 19, Nr. 3834. On SS influence in the WE-Lagers, see Rempel.

59. Quotation from Keitel, "GKdos., OKW/WFSt/Org. (III) Nr. 281/45," Jan. 28, 1945, T-77/783/5511454–55. Also Guderian, "OKH/GenStdH/Org. Abt. I Nr. 30518/44 geh.," Dec. 10, 1944, T-78/421/6390806.

60. On allocations, see Guderian, "GKdos., OKH/GenStdH/Org. I (P) Nr. 2138/45," Mar. 8, 1945, T-78/421/6390980. Friedrichs, "FS Nr. 570," Sept. 29, 1944, T-580/872/799a/4; Bormann, "Anordnung 101/45, gRs.," Feb. 21, 1945, BA-Ko, NS 6, Nr. 354, 141–42; OKW/QM Abt., "Vortragsnotiz, Staatssekretärbesprechung am 5.3.45, WFSt/Qu. Nr. 002263/45 gkdos.," Mar. 6, 1945, BA-MA, RW 4, Nr. 703.

61. The 1929 class began entering WE-Lagers in February, the 1930 class in April; Bormann, "Anordnung 29/45," Feb. 27, 1945, BA-Ko, NS 6, Nr. 99, 54; RVK Bayreuth, "Schnellbrief, 2564 b2 RVK," Apr. 4, 1945, StA Amberg, BzA Cham, Nr. 4434. On evacuating Levy III personnel, see Wendland, "OKH/GenStdH/OrgAbt I, Nr. 2/Nr. 1710/45 geh.," Apr. 11, 1945, BA-MA, RH 2, Nr. 849b, 192; Dr. jur. Hermann Schelling (former Levy III member), "Brief," Aug. 18, 1997, in the author's possession.

62. Bormann, "Anordnung 351/44," Oct. 27, 1944, T-580/872/799a/5; Hierl, "RS D3/Pers./RADwJ10163909/44," Oct. 28, 1944, T-81/110/129026–27; OKH/GenStdH/Org.Abt. I Chef Oberst Wendland, "GKdos. Nr. 624/45," Jan. 30, 1945, T-78/421/6390928–29.

63. Hierl to Bormann "Abschrift von FS," Sept. 28, 1944, T-580/872/799a/4. The RAD even cut back its economic duties because of its expanding role in military training; Gltg. Mark Brandenburg, "Schnellrundbrief 289/44," Oct. 5, 1944, LHA Potsdam, PrBrRep. 61, Mark Brandenburg, Nr. 1.2.

64. *Tagebücher von Goebbels*, pt. 2, vol. 13, 423, 589.

65. Keitel to Hitler, "GKdos., OKW/WFSt/Org (II), Nr. 3294/44," Oct. 29, 1944, T-78/421/6403396–97.

66. Also note that the ratio of army to Waffen SS recruits changed from 3.5:1 to 4.35:1. Oberst Fett, OKW/WFSt/Org (II) 2, Abt.Chef, "GKdos. Nr. 515/45," Feb. 19, 1945, BA-MA, RH 15, Nr. 126, 164; OKW QM Abt., "Vortragsnotiz, WFSt/Qu. Nr. 002263/45 gkdos.," Mar. 6, 1945, BA-MA, RW 4, Nr. 703.

67. February allocations called for the army to receive 75 percent of the total and the SS, 17.3 percent; OKW Wehrersatzamt, Abt. E (Id), "Abrechnung," Apr. (no day) 1945, BA-MA, RW 4, Nr. 26.

68. Jürgen Förster, "The Dynamics of Volksgemeinschaft: The Effectiveness of the German Military Establishment in the Second World War," in *Military Effectiveness*, vol. 3, *The Second World War*, ed. Alan R. Millett and Williamson Murray (Boston: Allen and Unwin, 1988), 189.

69. SS Führungsamt, Amt VI/Reit und Fahrwesen, "FS Az 34/11.44," Nov. 27, 1944, T-175/49/2562298.

70. Bormann, "FS," Sept. 27, 1944, T-580/872/799a/4.

71. Bormann, "RS 294/44," Oct. 1, 1944, T-580/872/799a/5; Keitel to Bormann, "OKW/WFSt/Qu. 3(Wi) FS Nr. 0824/45, geh.," Feb. 15, 1945, T-77/790/5518384–85; Keitel to Bormann, "OKW/WFSt/Qu. 2(I)/3(Wi) FS Nr. 01473/45, geh.," Mar. 2, 1945, T-77/790/5518376–77.

72. Dr. Anton (PK Arbeitsstab Vs) to Bormann, "FS 856," Oct. 4, 1944, BA-Ko, NS 6, Nr. 763, 82–83; Keitel to Bormann, "Abschrift von WFSt/Org III Nr. 4418/44 geh.," Oct. 25, 1944, T-77/783/5511550; OKW/Org. Abt. III Chef Oberst Fett, "Anordnung Nr. 6494/44 geh.," Nov. 11, 1944, T-77/783/5511521–24; Friedrichs to Bormann, "FS 1229," Nov. 19, 1944, T-580/872/799a/5.

73. Bormann, "RS 298/44" Oct. 2, 1944, T-580/17/180.

74. Unfortunately, there is no indication of Hitler's reaction to this proposal. AOK 19 Befehlshaber Gen. von Obstfelder, "Vortragsnotiz," Mar. 15–16, 1945, BA-MA, RH 20-19, Nr. 211, 15.

75. Guderian, "OKH/GenStdH/Org. Abt. A Nr. 1264/44 geh.," Oct. 8, 1944, T-78/418/6387582–84.

76. Percy Ernst Schramm, "The German Wehrmacht in the Last Days of the War (OKW Diary, 1 Jan. 1945–1 May 1945)," MS C-020, in Detwiler, vol. 11, 419; Gerhard Boldt, *Hitler: The Last Ten Days* (New York: Coward, McCann, and Geoghegan, 1973), 84–85.

77. Rundstedt, "GKdos. Nr. 9232/44," Oct. 15, BA-MA, RH 19 IV, Nr. 78, 130; WK XII Befehlshaber Danhauser, "Ia GKdos. Nrs. 2338/44," Oct. 17, 1944, BA-MA, RH 53-12, Nr. 27.

78. Hitler to Schörner, "FS," Feb. 27, 1945, T-78/350/6309386–87.

79. Volkssturm men could be conscripted only if their draft status (i.e., job) changed or their place of employment had fallen into enemy hands. OKW/WFSt/Org. (III), "Geheime FS Nr. 7659/44, geh.," Dec. 30, 1944, BA-MA, RW 4, Nr. 505, 50. Bormann, "RS 324/44," Oct. 14, 1944, T-580/872/799a/5.

80. See, e.g., OKH/GenStdH/Operations Abt., Abt. Landesbefestigung Chef von Bonin, "GKdos. Nr. 13079/44," Dec. 12, 1944, T-78/338/6294911.

81. OB West Chief of Staff, Siegfried Westphal, "Ia GKdos. Nr. 9299/44," Oct. 17, 1944, BA-MA, RH 19 IV, Nr. 78, 191; Ralph Bennett, *Ultra in the West: The Normandy Campaign 1944–1945* (London: Hutchinson, 1979), 173.

82. International Military Tribunal, *Trial of the Major War Criminals*, vol. 10 (Nuremberg: IMT), 597–98.

83. Friedrichs to Bormann, "FS 1052," Oct. 26, 1944, BA-Ko, NS 6, Nr. 314, 60–61.

84. The former quotation is from Bormann, "RS 324/44," Oct. 14, 1944, T-81/1/11229; the latter is from a letter of Sept. 27 to his wife; Hugh R. Trevor-Roper, ed., *The Bormann Letters: The Private Correspondence Between Martin Bormann and*

His Wife from January 1943 to April 1945, trans. R. H. Stevens (London: Weidenfeld and Nicholson, 1954), 124.

85. Bormann to Zander, "FS," Oct. 15, 1944, T-580/872/799a/4; Bormann to Friedrichs, "FS," Oct. 24, 1944, T-580/872/799a/4; Bormann, "Anordnung 358/44," Oct. 30, 1944, T-81/1/11260; Bormann, "Anordnungen 391 & 406/44," Nov. 7 and 18, 1944, BA-Ko, NS 6, Nr. 98, 61 and 64.

86. Bormann, "FS," Nov. 3, 1944, BA-Ko, NS 6, Nr. 764, 173; Speer to Bormann, "FS M 2893/44," Nov. 6, 1944, BA-Ko, Nr. 1573, 191.

87. Burgdorf to AOK 19 Befehlshaber Gen. Erich Brandenburger, "FS," Mar. 27, 1945, BA-MA, RH 20-19, Nr. 139, 90.

88. The Party Chancellery Volkssturm Staff contained representatives of the Wehrmacht, SA, SS, HJ, NSKK, Nationalsocialistische Volkswohlfahrt, and personal representatives of Goebbels, Ley, and Speer; Bormann to Friedrichs, "FS," Sept. 26 and 27, 1944, both T-580/872/799a/4.

4. Local Administration

1. Hitler, "Führer Erlaß über die Bildung des Deutschen Volkssturms," in Hans Kissel, *Der Deutsche Volkssturm 1944/45: Eine territoriale Miliz im Rahmen der Landesverteidigung* (Frankfurt am Main: E. S. Mittler und Sohn, 1962), 97–98.

2. On the Gauleiter, see Peter Hüttenberger, *Die Gauleiter: Studie zum Wandel des Machtgefüges in der NSDAP* (Stuttgart: Deutsche Verlags-Anstalt, 1969).

3. For a compilation of Volkssturm mobilization policy decrees, see OKH/GenStdH/Org. Abt. III, "FS Nr. 70675/45, geh.," Feb. 3, 1945, BA-MA, RH 2, Nr. 1114, 6.

4. Hüttenberger, 205; Dietrich Orlow, *The History of the Nazi Party 1919–1945*, vol. 2, *1933–1945* (Pittsburgh: University of Pittsburgh Press, 1973), 362, 436–38.

5. Bormann, "RS 324/44," Oct. 14, 1944, T-81/1/11229; Niederschlesien Gltr. Karl Hanke to Bormann, "FS 1388," Oct. 3, 1944, BA-Ko, NS 6, Nr. 763, 71.

6. Copies of each are in BA-Ko, NS 6, Nrs. 98 and 99.

7. Rostock OLGP, "Lagebericht 3130 Ea/56," Dec. 19, 1944, BA-Ko, R 22, Nr. 3385, 43–46; Speer, "Denkschrift," Mar. 18, 1945, T-73/180/3392523–26.

8. Mark Brandenburg Gltr. Emil Stürtz to Bormann, "FS 833," Oct. 21, 1944; Henlein to Bormann, "FS 1618," Oct. 25, 1944, both T-580/872/799a/4.

9. Hitler, "Verfügung 12/44," Sept. 1, 1944, T-84/175/1544807.

10. For example, he ordered Gauleitung Essen to cease using the names "Gausturm" and "Volkssturm Ruhr." Bormann to Friedrichs, "FS," Oct. 1, 1944, BA-Ko, NS 6, Nr. 313, 31; Bormann, "Anordnung 406/44," Nov. 18, 1944, BA-Ko, NS 6, Nr. 98, 64.

11. For example, see Gau Westmark Volkssturmstab, Abt. Ausrüstung und Bekleidung "RS," Oct. 26, 1944, LA Saarbrücken, NSDAP Mischbestand, Nr. 22, 31. On Bormann's resistance, see RMfRuK Planungsamt, "GRs. Nr. 1401/44, 48. Wochenbericht," Dec. 5, 1944, BA-Ko, R 3, Nr. 1957, 623–33.

12. Friedrichs, "FS 1005," Oct. 20, 1944, T-580/872/799a/4.

13. RMfRuK Stab Italien Dr. Walther Schieber, "Schreiben und Anlage,"

Nov. 28, 1944, T-77/790/5519097–100; Joseph Goebbels, *Die Tagebücher von Joseph Goebbels*, pt. 2, *Diktate, 1942–1945*, vol. 14, ed. Elke Fröhlich (Munich: K. G. Saur, 1995), 184; Otto Witek, "Meine Tätigkeit als Heeresgruppeintendant der Heeresgruppe G," MS# B-336, 58, 64, NA, RG 338, Box 19.

14. Speer to Kaufmann, "FS M2977/44g," Oct. 17, 1944, BA-Ko, R3, Nr. 1585, 96; Bayreuth Gstbfü. Josef Stigler, "RS 2/45," Jan. 2, 1945, T-580/872/799a/2; Hans Kissel, "Volkssturm," MS# B-627, 15–16, Duke, Location 58–G, Box 4.

15. OKH Heeresverwaltungsamtschef to Keitel, "OKH/HVA nr. 11/45 geh.," Feb. 28, 1945, T-77/790/5518378–79.

16. Berger, "Anweisung 1/45, Ia VoTgb. Nr 115/45," T-77/783/5511437; Keitel to Bormann, "WFSt/Qu. 3 (Wi.) Nr. 0824/45 geh.," Feb. 15, 1945, T-77/790/5518384; Berger, "Befehl, Ia VoTgb. Nr. 1988/45 geh.," Mar. 2, 1945, BA-Ko, NS 12, Nr. 1147.

17. Baden Gstbfü. Reinhard Burst, "Richtlinien," Nov. 10, 1944, T-81/220/474625–37; Gau Bayreuth Vs.Stab, "Stellenbesetzung," undated, BA-Ko, NS 12, Nr. 1147.

18. Friedrichs to Bormann, "FS Nr. 1052," Oct. 26, 1944, T-580/872/799a/4.

19. Bormann, "Anordnung 277/44," Sept. 27, 1944, in Kissel, 98–99.

20. Bormann, "Anordnung 290/44," Oct. 1, 1944, T-580/53/285.

21. Bormann to Friedrichs, "FS," Oct. 1, 1944, BA-Ko, NS 6, Nr. 313, 29; Friedrichs to Bormann, "FS 221 & 871," Oct. 2 and 6, 1944, BA-Ko, NS 6, Nr. 313; Friedrichs to Bormann, "FS," undated after Oct. 2, 1944, NS 6, Nr. 313, 3–9; Bormann to Wahl, "FS," Oct. 10, 1944, T-580/872/799a/4; Himmler to Berger, "Abschrift von FS," in Friedrichs to Bormann, "FS," Oct. 11, 1944, BA-Ko, NS 6, Nr. 313, 134; Bormann to Mainfranken Gltr. Otto Hellmuth, "FS," Oct. 22, 1944, BA-Ko, NS 6, Nr. 314, 150–51; Bormann to Wien Gltr. Baldur von Schirach, "FS," Oct. 31, 1944, T-580/872/799a/4.

22. Bormann to Köln-Aachen Gltr. Josef Grohé, "FS," Oct. 1, 1944, BA-Ko, NS 6, Nr. 313, 35; Scheel to Bormann, "FS 916," Oct. 1, 1944, BA-Ko, NS 6, Nr. 313, 42; Friedrichs to Bormann, "FS 221 & 871," Oct. 2 and 6, 1944, respectively, BA-Ko, NS 6, Nr. 313; Bormann to Danzig-Westpreußen Gltr. Albert Forster, "FS," Oct. 31, 1944, T-580/872/799a/4.

23. Bormann, "FS 112," Oct. 20, 1944, BA-Ko, NS 6, Nr. 314, 147; Bormann, "FS," Nov. 29, 1944, BA-Ko, NS 6, Nr. 764, 320.

24. Friedrichs to Bormann, "FS," undated, after Oct. 2, 1944, BA-Ko, NS 6, Nr. 313, 3–9.

25. Schwaben Gstbfü. Hans Geisser to Lindau Krltr., "Schreiben," Mar. 10, 1945, T-73/91/3242416.

26. Wahl to Bormann, "FS 533," Oct. 11, 1944, BA-Ko, NS 6, Nr. 313, 147–48.

27. Hellmuth to Bormann, "FS 603/44," Oct. 20, 1944, BA-Ko, NS 6, Nr. 314, 150–51; Jury to Bormann, "FS 1454," Sept. 30, 1944, BA-Ko, Nr. 313, 19.

28. This author uncovered information on forty-one of the forty-two men (all but Tirol-Vorarlberg's) who were *Gaustabsführer* in October 1944. The nominees of Wien, Schwaben, and Mainfranken are included, although Bormann expressly opposed their candidacy because there is no evidence as to who, if anyone, replaced them. A list is in PK, "Verzeichnis," undated (probably early Oct. 1944), T-580/53/Gruppe VIII/

285. Biographical information on the nominees comes from this folder and from BA-Ko, NS 6, Nrs. 313–14 and 763. Also useful in this regard was Great Britain, Ministry of Economic Warfare, *Who's Who in Germany and Austria* (London: Ministry of Economic Warfare, 1945); Gerhard von Seemen, *Die Ritterkreuzträger 1939–1945* (Friedberg: Podzun-Pallas, 1976); and Erich Stockhorst, *Fünftausend Köpfe: Wer war wer im Dritten Reich* (Velbert: Blick und Bild, 1967).

29. A seventh *Ritterkreuzträger*, Major Reinhard Burst, became Baden's Gstbfü. prior to mid-November 1944; Burst "Richtlinien," Nov. 10, 1944, T-81/220/4746225–37; Seemen, 101.

30. In fact, Bormann encouraged nominating men who had been released from the army due to wounds: Bormann, "RS 290 & 294/44," Oct. 1, 1944, T-580/53/285.

31. Omer Bartov's *Hitler's Army: Soldiers, Nazis and War in the Third Reich* (New York: Oxford University Press, 1991) and *The Eastern Front, 1941–1945: German Troops and the Barbarisation of Warfare* (New York: St. Martin's, 1985) provide the clearest examples of the National Socialist emphasis on the politicized junior officer's role in the war.

32. There were exceptions. Halle-Meerseburg's Schwub had recent staff experience as a Luftwaffe major general, and Bayreuth's Stigler had served as Gau liaison officer with WK XIII.

33. For example, Bormann's Ausführungsbestimmungen went no lower than the Kreis, where they were primarily implemented. Giesler, "RS," Jan. 10, 1945, StA Munich, Bestand NSDAP, Nr. 466c.

34. Bormann, "Anordnung 318/44," Oct. 12, 1944, in Kissel, 100–103.

35. Orlow, vol. 2, 362.

36. Karlsruhe Krstbfü., "Stabsbefehl Nr. 2/45," Mar. 1, 1945, T-81/95/108510. Also see the photos of the "Stoßtrupp Stadtverwaltung" in Josef Werner, *Karlsruhe 1945: Unter Hakenkreuz, Trikolore und Sternenbanner* (Karlsruhe: G. Braun, 1985), 96.

37. Dr. Paul Schröder, "Der Volkssturm," BA-Ko, Ost Dok 10/269.

38. For example, see "Volkssturm Erfassung weitgehend abgeschlossen," *Der Führer*, Nov. 20, 1944, clipping in Stadtarchiv Freiburg, Bestand C4 (Militärwesen), XI/27, Nr. 12.

39. Schönlanke Krstbfü. & Regierungsoberinsp. Gerhard Hohenhaus, "Die zivilen Verteidigungsmaßnahmen in Pommern im letzten Kriegsjahr," BA-Ko, Ost Dok 8/694.

40. Vilshofen Krltg., Dienststelle Vs., "RS," Oct. 16, 1944, BA-Ko, NS 12, Nr. 1147.

41. Schedlbauer to Stigler, "Meldung," Dec. 12, 1944, BA-Ko, NS 12, Nr. 1147.

42. Understandably, Schedlbauer's later reports reveal his growing frustration. Schedlbauer to Stigler, "Meldung," Jan. 9, 1945, BA-Ko, NS 12, Nr. 1147.

43. Westmark Gstbfü. Dr. Karl Caspary, "Abschrift von RS," Oct. 7, 1944, T-580/874/799b/5; Rheinisch-Bergischer Krltr., "Befehl Nr. 3," Oct. 23, 1944, T-81/94/108901–2.

44. For example, Kreisstab Bremen, "Kreisstabsführung Gliederung," undated, T-81/94/108367.

45. Bahninsp. Hans Quester, "Der Kampf um den Kreis Ohlau," BA-Ko, Ost Dok 10, Nr. 660.

46. Bormann, "RS 357/44," Oct. 30, 1944, T-81/1/11258.

47. Information on thirty of Gau Bayreuth's thirty-seven Kreisstabsführer is scattered throughout BA-Ko, NS 12, Nr. 1147, and StA Bamberg, M30 Gltg. Bayreuth, Nrs. 836–38. Data on Kr. Schwandorf-Nabburg's Kreisstabsführer are in a Nov. 23, 1944, letter in StA Amberg, Bestand NSDAP Krltg. Schwandorf, Nr. 6.

48. Bormann, "Anordnung 318/44," Oct. 12, 1944, T-580/872/799a/5.

49. Bormann, "Anordnung 318/44," Oct. 12, 1944, Kissel, 100–103; Zauch-Belzig Krltr., "Dienstanweisung Nr. 110," Oct. 20, 1944, LHA Potsdam, PrBrRep. 61, Mark Brandenburg, Nr. 5.17.1; Bremen Krltr., "RS 13/44," Oct. 26, 1944, T-81/94/108475.

50. Regierungspräsident Düsseldorf, "PI, Ia RS," Nov. 6, 1944, Stadtarchiv Ratingen, Nr. 2–726a; Bormann, "Anordnung 48/45," Mar. 27, 1945, T-580/53/285.

51. Koch to Bormann, "Abschrift von FS Nr. 80," Sept. 18, 1944, T-581/6/151.

52. Friedrichs to Bormann, "FS Nr. 898," Oct. 7, 1944, T-580/872/799a/4.

53. Zauch-Belzig Krltr., "Dienstanweisung Nr. 110," Oct. 20, 1944, LHA Potsdam, PrBrRep. 61, Mark Brandenburg, Nr. 5.17.1; Bayreuth Krltr., "40. Wochenbericht," Oct. 21, 1944, StA Bamberg, M33, Nr. 631.

54. Bremen Krltr., "RS 78/44," Oct. 17, 1944, T-81/94/108484; Zauch-Belzig Krltr., "Dienstanweisung Nr. 110," Oct. 20, 1944, & "RS H/G/g," Jan. 31, 1945, both in LHA Potsdam, PrBrRep. 61, Mark Brandenburg, Nr. 5.17.1 (there are numerous other examples in this file and Nr. 2.1.474); Lüdinghausen Krltr., "RS," undated (Feb. 1945?), T-81/94/108835–41.

55. HJ leaders, automatically in Levy III units, were exempt. Bormann, "Anordnung 427/44," Dec. 3, 1944, T-580/53/285.

56. Stigler, "RS 9/45," Jan. 4, 1945, T-580/872/799a/3; Stigler to Fränkische Schweiz Krstbfü., "Schreiben," Dec. 4, 1944; Wolfstein Krltr. to Stigler, "Schreiben," Jan. 3 and Jan. 8, 1945, both in BA-Ko, NS 12, Nr. 1147.

57. Niederdonau Gstbfü. Willi Fahrion, "Schnellbrief," Oct. 21, 1944, T-581/33/635; Gräntz, "RS F7-72/86/44," Dec. 12, 1944, T-580/667/502; Schädlich, "Abschrift von Befehl," Nov. 21, 1944, HStA Wiesbaden, Bestand 483, Nr. 6462.

58. 18. PzGrenDiv, "KTB," Nov. 6, 1944, BA-MA, RH 26-18, Nr. 125, 61.

59. Rheinisch-Bergischer Krltr., "RS 20/2/44." Oct. 24, 1944, T-81/94/108910.

60. SA Gruppe Weichsel, "Bericht, Br.B. Nr. 7407 Ch/Ma.," Nov. 24, 1944, T-580/867/128/411; membership lists of Gau Bayreuth's Kreis staffs in BA-Ko, NS 12, Nr. 1147.

61. Schepmann, "Verfügung, F Nr. 11090," Oct. 16, 1944, and "Verfügung, F Nr. 10050," Dec. 1, 1944, both BA-Ko, NS 23, Nr. 121; Berger, "1. Befehl für die Schießausbildung im Volkssturm, VsTgb. Nr. 1372/44 gKdos., VoTgb. Nr. 65/44 gKdos.," Nov. 1, 1944, T-175/122/2648014–16.

62. SA Gruppe Weichsel, "RS 6310/44," Oct. 17, 1944, T-580/874/799b/5; SA Gruppe Tannenberg, "Bericht F 214/44," Nov. 1, 1944, T580/874/799b/5; SA Gruppe Hansa, "Bericht F3," Nov. 4, 1944, BA-Ko, NS 23, Nr. 15; SA Gruppe Oberrhein, "Anruf," Nov. 14, 1944, BA-Ko, NS 23, Nr. 13, divider 314; Lüding-

hausen Krstbfü., "Befehl Nr. 1," Jan. 25, 1945, T-81/94/108824; various Bayreuth Krstbfü. reports in BA-Ko, NS 12, Nr. 1147.

63. SA Standarte 8 Berlin/Brandenburg, "RS," Oct. 24, 1944, LHA Potsdam, PrBrRep. 61, SA, Nr. 18.313.

64. Friedrichs, "Aktenvermerk," Nov. 13, 1944, T-580/874/799b/5.

65. Caspary, "Richtlinien," Nov. 3, 1944, LA Saarbrücken, Mischbestand Nr. 15, 11–19; SA Oberste Führung, "Entwurf," Nov. 1, 1944, T-580/874/799b/5.

66. Schädlich, "Abschrift: Eingliederung der SA zbV Einheiten," Nov. 21, 1944, HStA Wiesbaden, Bestand 483, Nr. 6462.

67. Sachsen Gltr. Martin Mutschmann, "RS G41/44," Oct. 10, 1944, T-580/874/799b/5.

68. Oberste SA Führung, "Vermerk, FO 2b Nr. 13704 Sch/tö," Nov. 1, 1944, BA-Ko, NS 23, Nr. 27; Schepmann, "Verfügung S 54200–07," Nov. 30, 1944, BA-Ko, NS 23, Nr. 121; Verwaltungschef der SA, "Verfügung," Dec. 5, 1944, BA-Ko, NS 23, Nr. 121; SA Gruppe Oberrhein, "Schießstände," Nov. 13 1944, BA-Ko, NS 23, Nr. 15.

69. Kwalo, "RS," Nov. 9, 1944, T-581/20/382; Kraus, "Richtlinien," Dec. 9, 1944, T-81/95/109664–77.

70. Gau Moselland Chef der motorisierten Volkssturmeinheiten, "Befehl, Br.B. Nr. 1/44 W/Sch, geh.," Nov. 21, 1944, T-81/94/108629; Motorstandarte 44 to Motorgruppe Thüringen, "Meldung Ia/45/Ma/We," Jan. 8, 1945, T-81/95/109644; Calau Krstbfü., "RS," Feb. 28, 1945, LHA Potsdam, PrBrRep. 61, Mark Brandenburg, Nr. 5.3.1; NSKK Motorsturmführer Eisenach, "Meldestaffellisten," Mar. 11, 1945, T-81/95/109586–92.

71. NSKK Motorgruppe Thüringen, "RS Ia/44/Ma/L2," Nov. 17, 1944, T-81/95/109627–32. Moselland Vs Gaustabschef der motorisierte Einheiten, "Befehl, Br.B. Nr. 2/44w/Sch geh.," Nov. 21, 1944, LA Rheinland-Pfalz, Bestand 662,5, Nr. 102; Stigler "RS 1/45," Jan. 4, 1945, T-580/872/799a/3.

72. Giesler, "RS," Feb. 14, 1945, StA Munich, Bestand NSDAP, Nr. 446c.

73. The unit was eventually disbanded and its planes scuttled to prevent their capture. Luftflotte 6, "Beitrag zum KTB," BA-MA, RL 7, Nr. 617, 175–78; Volker Reschke, "Eine fliegende Volkssturmeinheit," *Zeitschrift für Heereskunde* 198 (1965): 34–35.

74. Flugkäpitan Aschenbrunner to Himmler, "Schreiben," Oct. 27, 1944, T-175/122/3578014.

75. Kdr., SS Abschnitt IX/Würzburg to Stigler, "Schreiben," Nov. 20, 1944, BA-Ko, NS 12, Nr. 1147.

76. Insp. der Sicherheitspolizei und des SD, "gRs. 66/44 (3)," Oct. 30, 1944, T-175/404/2926406–7; Gestapoleitstelle Darmstadt, Abt. IV B b, "RS 28/44, Br.B. Nr. 8277/44 geh," Nov. 15, 1944, T-175/405/2928213–16.

77. Kdr., Ordnungspolizei Würzburg, "FS, Nr. 1150 Kdo(a)," Oct. 28, 1944, T-580/116/41; Regensburg Krstbsfü., "Verzeichnis," undated, StA Amberg, NSDAP Krltg. Regensburg, Nr. 72.

78. Bamberg Krltr. Strickler, "44. Wochenbericht," Nov. 25, 1944, StA Bamberg, Bestand M33, Nr. 631; Stigler to Friedrichs, "FS 93," Jan. 21, 1945, StA Bamberg, Bestand M30, Nr. 836.

79. RM des Innern, "Runderlaß, II RV 8118/45–500," *Ministerialblatt für die Innere Verwaltung*, Feb. 1, 1945, HStA Hannover, Hann 122a, Nr. 7054, 218–19.

80. Himmler, "Ausschnitte von Runderlass OW II f 1-3004/45, S III 143 Nr. 529/ 45," Jan. 23, 1945, HStA Munich, Bestand Reichstatthalter, Nr. 686.

81. Regierungspräsident Regensburg, "Abschrift von RS 1234 1 4," Nov. 13, 1944, StA Amberg, Bezirksamt Eschenbach, Nr. 4293.

82. DAF Gauverwaltung Essen, Hauptabt. Führung/Schulung, Werkscharen, "Aktenvermerk," Feb. 24, 1945, BA-Ko, NS 5, Nr. 214.

83. Düsseldorf DAF Gauobmann, "Abschrift von RS 87/44," Oct. 28, 1944, in Institut für Zeitgeschichte, *Akten der Partei Kanzlei der NSDAP: Rekonstruktion eines verlorengegangenen Bestandes* (Munich: Oldenbourg, 1983), nos. 117 08441, 117 08475–79.

84. Stigler, "RS Nr. 50/44," Dec. 11, 1944, IfZG, Db 202.02.

85. "Frauen schneiden für den Volkssturm," *Bayreuther Kurier*, Nov. 22, 1944, clipping in T-580/872/799a/2; Btnfü. Vs Btn. 19/XVI, "Befehl 7/45," Mar. 3, 1945, T-81/153/156250–54.

86. Btnfü., II Btn. Vs Kr. Oberlahn-Usingen, "1. Btnbefehl," Dec. 19, 1944, HStA Wiesbaden, Bestand 483, Nr. 6462.

87. On assistance, see Gltg. München-Oberbayern, "RS," Feb. 28, 1945, StA Munich, Bestand NSDAP, Nr. 466c; RAD Großinstandsetzungswerkstatt des Arbeitsgaues V Pommern West, "Bericht," Apr. 1, 1945, T-81/110/128793–98. On protecting personnel, see Dingolfing Krstbfü. to Stigler, "Schreiben," Nov. 15, 1944; Stigler to Dingolfing Krstbfü., "Schreiben," Dec. 13, 1944, both in BA-Ko, NS 12, Nr. 1147.

88. HJ Gebiet 22 (Bayreuth), "Schreiben," Oct. 18, 1944, BA-Ko, NS 12, Nr. 1147; Berger, "Abschrift von FS 423/00492 geh.," Oct. 19, 1944, BA-Ko, NS 12, Nr. 1147; Walkenhorst, PK VsStab to Bormann, "FS 14886," Oct. 25, 1944, T-580/ 872/799a/4.

89. Alfons Heck, *A Child of Hitler: Germany in the Days When God Wore a Swastika* (Frederick, Colo.: Renaissance House, 1985), 129, 140–43.

90. Between March 1942 and May 1944, the WE-Lagers had trained only 625,000 youths; Schroeder, 185. On HJ enrollment duties, see Dechant, "RS BrB. Nr. DVst 25/44," Nov. 10, 1944, StA Nuremberg, Bestand 503, Nr. 139.

91. Axmann, "Abschrift von Befehl," Oct. 3, 1944; Möckel, "Ausführungsbestimmungen," Oct. 3, 1944; Möckel, "Vermerk (with Berger and RAD representative)," Oct. 11, 1944, all in BA-Ko, NS 12, Nr. 1147; Gerhard Rempel, "The Misguided Generation: The Hitler Youth and the SS 1933–1945" (Ph.D. diss., University of Wisconsin, 1971), 575–78.

92. HJ Gebiet 22 (Bayreuth), "Schreiben," Oct. 30, 1944, BA-Ko, NS 12, Nr. 1147.

93. Berger to Axmann, "Abschrift von FS," Oct. 2, 1944, BA-Ko, NS 6, Nr. 763, 208–11.

94. HJ Gebiet Schwaben to OT Oberbauleitung Schwaben, "Schreiben," Nov. 11, 1944, T-76/1/663654; WE-Lager Harburg to WK VII, "Schreiben," Nov. 22, 1944, T-580/351/7.

95. WE-Lager Harburg II, "Personalaufstellungsliste," Nov. (no day) 1944,

T-580/351/7; Artur Axmann, *"Das kann doch nicht das Ende sein": Hitler's letzten Reichsjugendführer erinnert sich* (Koblenz: Bublies, 1995), 284–86; Schelling, "Brief," Aug. 18, 1997, in the author's possession; Ralf Roland Ringler, *Illusion einer Jugend: Lieder, Fahnen und das bittere Ende, Hitler Jugend in Österreich, Ein Erlebnisbericht* (St. Pölten: Niederösterreichisches Pressehaus, 1977), 125–26.

96. HJ Standort VIII/464 to Ortspolizei Niederkrüchten, "Schreiben," Dec. 29, 1944, HStA Düsseldorf, Dep. Niederkrüchten, Nr. 870; HJ Gefolgschaftsführer Stumpf to Memmingen HJ Bannführer, "Schreiben," Nov. 8, 1944, T-580/348/2, pt. 2.

97. Chapter 7 addresses both these issues in detail.

98. Himmler, "Abschrift von GKdos., BdE/AHA, Stab Ib, Bk/1 Nr. 9073/44," Nov. 11, 1944, T-81/95/109870–72; Keitel, "OKW/WFSt/Qu. 3 (Wi.) FS Nr. 824/45, geh.," Feb. 15, 1945, T-77/790/5518384–85. On Gauleiter complaints, see Pommern Gltr. Franz Schwede-Coburg, "FS 788/44," Dec. 18, 1944, BA-Ko, NS 6, Nr. 764, 324.

99. Himmler, "RS," Nov. 3, 1944, T-175/122/2648035.

100. WK XII Ia, Abt. Ausb., "Befehl, Nr. 1051/44, geh.," Oct. 18, 1944, BA-MA, RH 34, Nr. 146, 70; Geninsp. für den Führernachwuchs des Heeres, "FS Nr. 332/44 geh." Oct. 28, 1944, T-172/122/2648021–26.

101. Himmler, "Zusammenwirken von Wehrmacht und Deutschen Volkssturm, RFSS/BdE Ki/De VsTgb. Nr. 1359/44 gK, VoTgb. Nr. 103/44 gK," Nov. 23, 1944, in OKW/WEA/Abt. E (Ch a), "Anlage 7 zu gKdos. Nr. 975/44," Dec. 21, 1944, T-79/292/490.

102. For example, Wehrmachtstandortälteste Brandenburg, "Befehl Nr. 1 für die Verteidigung der Stadt Brandenburg," Tgb. Nr. 138/45 geh.," undated, 1945, T-84/242/6600911–14.

103. Gustorf Ortskommandantur files, Nov. 1944–Feb. 1945, T-312/521/8121567–709.

104. Friedrich Hossbach, *Schlacht um Ostpreußen: Aus den Kämpfen der deutschen 4. Armee um Ostpreußen in der Zeit vom* 19.7.1944–30.1.1945 (Überlingen am Bodensee: Otto Dikreiter, 1951), 50.

105. Genmaj. Kurt Anger, "WK XIII, Feb. 1–Mar. 1, 1945," MS B-226, 3, NA, RG 338, Box 14; Burgdorf to AOK 19 Befehlshaber Gen. Erich Brandenburger, "FS," Mar. 27, 1945, BA-MA, RH 20-19, Nr. 139, 90.

106. Hauptgemeinschaftsleiter Twittenhof (PK), "Bericht," undated (Apr. 1945), BA-Ko, NS 6, Nr. 169, 4–9; Oberbürgermeister der Stadt Leslau, "Bericht," Feb. (no day), 1945, BA-Ko, R 138 II, Nr. 7, 83–85. HG Weichsel Ia, "FS Nr. 5012/45, geh.," Apr. 2, 1945, T-311/69/7221416.

107. Caspary, "Bericht," Oct. 10, 1944, T-580/874/799b/5; RüKdo Augsburg Zentralgruppe UK Stellungen, "Aktenvermerk," Nov. 4, 1945, T-73/43/3176787–88.

108. WK VII (Munich) Ia, "Bestimmungen Nr. 19896/44, geh.," Dec. 19, 1944, T-79/22/694–97; WK XI, "Geschäftseinteilung," Feb. 1, 1945, BA-MA, RH 53-11, Nr. 21, 4; WK III (Berlin), "Erster Befehl für die Organisation der Abwehr im Wehrkreis III, Ia Nr. 85/45, geh.," undated (probably Feb. 1945), T-84/169/1537436.

109. Kdr., Schutzbereich München-West, "Anlage von Mob. Kalendar, Nr. 13/45, geh.," Mar. 20, 1945, T-84/239/6598074–75.

110. AOK 15/Korück, "Ausbau der Orte- und Panzersperren, Br. B. Nr. 298/45 geh.," Feb. 8, 1945, T-312/521/8121576–77.

111. Hossbach, "Erinnerungen von Gen. der Inf. Friedrich Hossbach," BA-MA, N24 (Nachlaß Hossbach), Nr. 39, Ch. IX, 36.

112. Ogltr. Bad Freienwalde/Oder, "Bericht," Feb. 4, 1945, LHA Potsdam, PrBrRep. 61, Mark Brandenburg, Nr. 2.1.475.

113. Michael H. Kater, *The Nazi Party: A Social Profile of Members and Leaders 1919–1945* (Cambridge, Mass.: Harvard University Press, 1983), 216–27.

114. Schedlbauer to Stigler, "Meldung," Dec. 20, 1944, BA-Ko, NS 12, Nr. 1147.

5. The Aufgebot System: Personnel Classification

1. Adult HJ WE-Lager personnel also served in Levy III; Bormann, "Anordnung 29/45," Feb. 27, 1945, T-580/53/285.

2. Quotation from Bormann, "Anordnung 318/44," Oct. 12, 1944, in Hans Kissel, *Der Deutsche Volkssturm 1944/45: Eine territoriale Miliz im Rahmen der Landesverteidigung* (Frankfurt am Main: E. S. Mittler und Sohn, 1962), 100–103. Also Bormann, "Anordnung 408/44," Nov. 20, 1944, in Kissel, 108–14; Himmler, "Befehl Nr. 1, VsTgb. Nr. 1360/44 gKdos., VoTgb.Nr. 104/44 gKdos," Nov. 24, 1944, T-79/292/491.

3. Bormann, "Anordnung 318/44," Oct. 12, 1944, in Kissel, 100–103.

4. Even Fritz Sauckel, Hitler's Plenipotentiary for Labor Allocations, had to beg Bormann to increase the deferral quota for his office's personnel; Sauckel to Bormann, "Abschrift von FS," Oct. 31, 1944, BA-Ko, NS 6, Nr. 168, 39–40.

5. Friedrichs to Bormann, "FS 822, Vorlage," Oct. 2, 1944, BA-Ko, NS 6, Nr. 763, 61–62.

6. Bormann, "Anordnung 407/44," Nov. 20, 1944, T-81/93/107752–53.

7. Bormann, "Anordnungen 379 & 408/44," Nov. 3 and 20, 1944, in Kissel, 104–5, 109–10.

8. Bormann, "RS 372/44," Nov. 3, 1944, T-580/17/180.

9. Economic officials freely admitted this; see Speer, RüAmt, Abt. Arb. E VII, "RS," Nov. 20, 1944, T-73/43/7176766–71; Gen. Insp. für Wasser und Engerie, "RS WI7RL 6627/44," Nov. 23, 1944, HStA Hannover, Hann. 122a, Nr. 7082, 12.

10. Bormann, "Anordnung 387/44," Nov. 8, 1944, T-81/93/107679–80.

11. Goebbels and Bormann, "Abschrift von Anordnung," Aug. 16, 1944, T-73/21/3145801–2; Klopfer to Bormann, "FS 883," Oct. 6, 1944, BA-Ko, NS 6, Nr. 763, 97–103; Bormann, "Anordnung 379/44," Nov. 3, 1944, in Kissel, 104–5; Speer, "RüAmt, Abt. Arb. E VII, RS," Nov. 20, 1944, T-73/43/7176766–71; Bormann, "Anordnung 50/45," Apr. 4, 1945, T-81/5/12976–79.

12. Gltg. München-Oberbayern, "RS," Jan. 10, 1945, StA Munich, Bestand NSDAP, Nr. 446c. Population figures are from Chef, OKW/Wehrmacht Ersatzamt, "GKdos.: Wehrmachtsersatzplan 1945," undated, late 1944, T-77/780/5506292–478.

13. Some Ortsgruppen placed such high priority on registration that they suspended all other work, including propaganda. Krltg. Wertheim, "Bericht, lfd. Beitrags Nr. 16/44, 2," Oct. 25, 1944, T-81/164/302152.

14. Caspary, "Abschrift von Bericht," Oct. 10, 1944, T-580/874/799b/5; Calau Krltr., "RS," Oct. 17, 1944, LHA Potsdam, PrBrRep. 61, Mark Brandenburg Nr.

5.3.1. Sample rosters can be found in Og. Lingolsheim & Og. Meinau (Kr. Strasburg), "Erfassungsliste," undated, T-81/95/109208–80.

15. Bormann, "Anordnung 443/44," Dec. 12, 1944, T-81/95/109395–96.

16. Bormann, "RS 385/44," Nov. 7, 1944, T-81/1/11276–77; Bormann to Friedrichs "FS," Oct. 22, 1944, T-580/872/799a/4.

17. München-Ost Krstbfü., "Merkblatt," Dec. 11, 1944, T-81/153/156382–83.

18. Company leaders had a voice in determining political unreliability, but the Gauleiter had to approve all exemptions; Bormann, "RS 362/44," Oct. 31, 1944, T-580/53/285; "Anordnung 443/44," Dec. 9, 1944, T-84/175/1544774–76; "Anordnung 464/44," Dec. 22, 1944, BA-Ko, NS 6, Nr. 98, 105.

19. Möckel, "Erlaß 2III.-39196," Nov. 1, 1944, StA Bückeburg, Bestand L4, Nr. 12512.

20. Caspary, "Abschrift von Bericht," Oct. 10, 1944, T-580/874/799b/5.

21. Friedrichs, "Bekanntgabe 33/45," Mar. 2, 1945, T-81/94/108156; Leitender Arzt im DtVs Gau Bayreuth, "RS 6/45," Mar. 1, 1945, T-580/872/799a/1.

22. Og. Brieske, "Erfassungsliste," undated, LHA Potsdam, PrBrRep. 61, Mark Brandenburg, Nr. 5.3.1.

23. Caspary, "Richtlinien," Nov. 3, 1944, LA Saarbrücken, NS Mischbestand, Nr. 15, 11–19.

24. Kr. Weiden Leitender Arzt, "Monatsbericht," Mar. 3, 1945; Kr. Vilshofen Leitender Arzt, "Monatsbericht, Feb. 1945," Mar. 16, 1945, both in BA-Ko, NS 12, Nr. 1147.

25. Dr. Carl Brenke, "Die Vorgänge in Königsberg seit Bedrohung der Stadt," BA-Ko, Ost Dok 8/518; Henry Bernhard, *Finis Germaniae: Aufzeichnungen und Betrachtungen* (Stuttgart: Kurt Haslsteiner, 1948), 244–45.

26. Kr. Wolfstein Leitender Arzt, "Monatsbericht, Feb. 1945," Mar. 3, 1945, BA-Ko, NS 12, Nr. 1147.

27. Some Gaue wisely forbade mixed Levy units; Caspary, "Richtlinien," Nov. 3, 1944, LA Saarbrücken, NS Mischbestand, Nr. 15, 11–19. At the opposite extreme, mixed Levy units initially constituted 286 of Gau Thüringen's 396 battalions; RVK Thüringen, "Liste," undated, HStA Weimar, Reichstatthalter, Nr. 478, 1–20.

28. One example is Möbelfabrik Konrad Wackerl & Co., "Schreiben," Dec. 4, 1944, T-73/76/3219929–30.

29. Stigler to Hof Krstbfü., "Schreiben," Mar. 3, 1945; Hof Krstbfü. to Stigler, "Bericht," Mar. (no day), 1945, both BA-Ko, NS 12, Nr. 1147.

30. Bormann, "Anordnung 379/44," Oct. 27, 1944, in Kissel, 104–5.

31. Süd Hannover-Braunschweig Gstbfü. Kaiser, "Anordnung Nr. 13," Dec. 12, 1944, StA Wolfenbüttel, 12 A Neu 13, Nr. 22264; Berlin Gaukommission, "Anweisung von Durchführung des Z-Karten System," Dec. 15, 1944, BA-Ko, R 55, Nr. 914, 37; RüKdo Recklinghausen, "RS 326, Az 67m(2), Nr. 14149/44," Dec. 14, 1944, BA-MA, RW 21–51, Nr. 18; RWM, "Abschrift von Runderlaß 339/44 LWa," Dec. 23, 1944, T-81/95/109846–49.

32. Berlin Gaukommission, "Anweisung von Durchführung des Z-Karten System," Dec. 15, 1944, BA-Ko, R 55, Nr. 914, 37; Reichsmin. des Innern, "Schnellbrief I 6538 II/44 [*sic*] 6000A," Jan. 5, 1945, LA Magdeburg, Rep C 20 Ib Oberpräsident, Nr. 3273.

33. Klopfer, "FS 883," Oct. 6, 1944, BA-Ko, NS 6, Nr. 763, 97–103; Stigler, "RS 50/44," Dec. 11, 1944, IfZG, Db 202.02.

34. Klopfer, "FS 883," Oct. 6, 1944, BA-Ko, NS 6, Nr. 763, 97–103; RüKdo Augsburg, Zentralgruppe to Firma Clemens Reifler (Nesselwang), "Schreiben," Feb. 22, 1945, T-73/84/3231591; and Krltg. Lippe's entire folder, StA Detmold, Bestand L113, Nr. 1024.

35. Klopfer, "FS 883," Oct. 6, 1944, BA-Ko, NS 6, Nr. 763, 97–103; RüKdo Recklinghausen, "RS 326, Az 67m(2), Nr. 14149/44," Dec. 14, 1944, BA-MA, RW 21–51, Nr. 18.

36. Ostpreußen Gstbfü. Knuth, "Abschrift vom Durchsage," Oct. 13, 1944, T-581/6/151; RüKdo Lüneburg, "RS, BrB. Nr. 211/45, geh., ZGrZ2," Jan. 26, 1945, T-73/22/3147511–15.

37. Schwaben DAF Gauobmann, "Schreiben," Feb. 9, 1945, T-73/81/3226657.

38. Bormann, "Anordnungen 19–21/45," Feb. 6 and 13, 1945, T-81/1/11138–45.

39. Dechant, "RS," Oct. 17, 1944, T-580/923/40.

40. Note the fifteen- to sixteen-year-olds among the missing from Levy I zbV units from Gaue Bayreuth, Hamburg, Mainfranken, and Kurhessen; Deutsche Rote Kreuz, Suchdienst, *Vermißtenbildliste*, vols. V[olkssturm] A, B, C, and Nachtrag (Munich: DRK, 1956–1966).

41. Evangelisch-Lutheran Landeskirchenamt, "Schreiben Nr. 6344," Oct. 31, 1944, StA Bamberg, M30, Nr. 837; Freiherr von Ketelhodt, "Bericht über den Einsatz des Vs Btns. Zempelburg in Bromberg vom 21.–26. Januar 1945," BA-Ko, Ost Dok 8/325.

42. Klaus Fuhrmann in *Geschäft ist Geschäft: Neun Deutsche unter Hitler*, ed. Louis Hagen (Hamburg: Merlin, 1969), 185–205.

43. Fahrion, "Gaubefehl 2/44," Nov. 13, 1944, T-581/33/635.

44. Among numerous examples is Og. Bischofsheim-West, "Ablieferungsnachweis," Nov. 21, 1944, T-81/95/109130.

45. In fact, it was a violation of policy for an Ortsgruppenleiter to make levy assignments; Pfulgriesheim Ogltr., "Erfassungsmeldung," Nov. 16, 1944, T-81/95/109141.

46. Reichsminister des Innern, "Schnellbrief II RV 10250/44–518," Dec. 9, 1944, LA Magdeburg, Rep. C 20 Ib Oberpräsident, Nr. 3273.

47. Gräntz, "Drahtrede," Feb. 26, 1945, BA-Ko, R55, Nr. 916, 112–14.

48. Fränkische Schweiz Krstbfü., "Bericht," Mar. 16, 1945, BA-Ko, NS 12, Nr. 1147; U.S. 1st Inf. Div., "G-2 Periodic Report Nr. 254," Mar. 2, 1945, G-2 Journal (1–3 Mar., 1945), NA, RG 407, Entry 427, Box 5741.

49. Krltr. Lüdinghausen, "RS," Jan. 25, 1944, T-81/94/1058834.

50. RüKdo Augsburg, file RMfRuK/705, T-73/44/3176793–939.

51. Bayreuth-Eschenbach Krstbfü., "Dienstanweisung Nr. 4," Dec. 22, 1944, StA Amberg, BzA Eschenbach, Nr. 4293; Btnfü., "Vs Btns 3/3 & 4, "Monatliche Stärkemeldungen," Feb., Mar., and Apr. 1, 1945, LHA Potsdam, PrBrRep. 61, Berlin, Nr. 11.10.

52. See, e.g., the Krltg. Lippe files in StA Detmold, Bestand L113, Nrs. 1023–25.

53. See, e.g., Kölnische Mode- und Textilgrossverhandlung to Kreiskommission Lippe, "Schreiben," Mar. 14, 1945; Lippe Krltr. to Kölnische Mode und Textilgross-

verhandlung, "Schreiben," Mar. 20, 1945, both in StA Detmold, Bestand L113, Nr. 968, 60–61.

54. Bormann, "Anlage zur Anordnung 55/45," Feb. 2, 1945, BA-Ko, NS 6, Nr. 353, 110–11; Bormann, "Anordnung 48/45," Mar. 27, 1945, T-81/5/12974–75.

55. See the numerous examples in Kr. Eberswald-Oberbarnim's file in LHA Potsdam, PrBrRep. 61, Mark Brandenburg 2.1.474.

56. RVK Magdeburg-Anhalt, "RS RVK 405/45," Feb. 19, 1945, LA Magdeburg, Rep C 20 Ib Oberpräsident, Nr. 3272.

57. Schulte, "Abschrift von Anordnung 1/45," Feb. 16, 1945, HStA Düsseldorf, RW 23, Nr. 273, 8.

58. SS-Postschutzbezirks Nürnberg, "Schreiben," Jan. 26, 1945, StA Bamberg, M30, Nr. 837; RB Dir. Nürnberg, "Schreiben Pr L48g/Rs/BmBerv(o)36Bbv," Feb. 5, 1945, StA Bamberg, M30, Nr. 837.

59. Freiburg im Breisgau Oberbürgermeister, "Besprechung," Feb. 9, 1945, Stadtarchiv Freiburg, Bestand C4 (Militärwesen), XI/27, Nr. 12; Vilshofen Krstbfü., "Meldung," Feb. 27, 1945, BA-Ko, NS 12, Nr. 1147.

60. Pfreimd Ogltr., "Schreiben," Feb. 2, 1945, StA Amberg, NS Krltg. Schwandorf, Nr. 6.

61. Krltr. Bayreuth, "Wochenbericht 3/45," Jan. 22, 1945, StA Bamberg, M30, Nr. 631.

62. Grafenwöhr Bürgermeister, "Abschrift von Schreiben," Dec. 6, 1944, StA Amberg, BzA Eschenbach, Nr. 4293; Fabrik Keufbeuren GmbH, "Schreiben, DrH/St. Nr. 709," Dec. 12, 1944, T-73/83/3230505; Detmold Landrat, "Schreiben," Feb. 3, 1945, StA Detmold, L113, Nr. 1023, 192–93.

63. Gen. Insp. für Wasser und Energie, "RS WI 7 RL 6627/44," Nov. 23, 1944, T-178/24/3679272–81; Collis Metalwerke, "Schreiben," Dec. 21, 1944, T-73/80/3227490; Dechentreiter Maschinenfabrik (Bäumenheim), "Schreiben," Feb. 14, 1945, T-73/80/3227918; Lage Levy I Btnfü. to Lippe Krltg., "Schreiben," Feb. 26, 1945, StA Detmold, Bestand L113, Nr. 1023, 10; Lippe Krltr. to Donop Ogltr., "Schreiben," Mar. 2, 1945, StA Detmold, L113, Nr. 773, 142; Stigler to RB Dir. Regensburg, "Schreiben," Mar. 27, 1945, StA Bamberg, M30, Nr. 836.

64. Bormann, "RS 30/45," Feb. 28, 1945, T-580/872/799a/1; Bamberg Krstbfü., "Schreiben," Feb. 16, 1945, BA-Ko, NS 12, Nr. 1147.

65. Speer, "Abschrift von FS Nr. 6949, geh.," Nov. 3, 1944, T-73/53/3189091.

66. The appearance that agriculture protected its German male workforce better than did manufacturing is due to agriculture's considerably lower proportion of draft-deferred men (see appendix Tables 3 and 4).

67. Mining is an exception, largely because it had an overwhelmingly draft-age population; any contribution it would make would come from this group. It also included some construction workers who were not particularly well shielded.

68. Berger, "Befehl, VsTgb. Nr. 488/45, VoTgb. Nr. 167/45, geh.," Jan. 17, 1945, T-580/872/799a/1.

69. Ortsgruppen Lingolsheim and Meinau, near Strassburg, drew up lists before proper guidelines existed; even so, their average ages fit the overall pattern. Pullach assignments are an anomaly, probably inaccurate because of the great imbalance in Levy sizes.

70. Full comparison is impossible without accurate 1944 data on job skills of civilian German men; however, figures on economic sectors strongly suggest these trends.

71. Maschinenfabrik Keller und Knappich, "Verzeichnis," Dec. 8, 1944, T-73/83/3230984–1003.

72. Bormann, "Anordnungen 432/44 & 2/45" Dec. 2, 1944, and Jan. 5, 1945, BA-Ko, NS 6, Nrs. 98, 90 and Nr. 99, 3, respectively.

73. Bayreuth Gauwirtschaftskammer, Handwerksabteilung, "Schreiben, Nr. 5280/Sch." Mar. 3, 1945, BA-Ko, NS 12, Nr. 1147.

74. On Dorpmüller, see Alfred C. Mierzejewski, *The Collapse of the German War Economy, 1944–1945: Allied Air Power and the German National Railway* (Chapel Hill: University of North Carolina Press, 1988), 156–57, 173–74.

75. Bormann, "Anordnungen 387, 407 & 408/44," Nov. 8 and 20, 1944, BA-Ko, NS 6, Nrs. 98, 52–59, 68–69, and Kissel, 108–14, respectively; "Anordnung," undated, T-178/24/3679234; "RS 51/45," Apr. 8, 1945, T-580/18/180.

76. See, e.g., J. N Eberle and Cie, "Schreiben," Feb. 15, 1945, T-73/43/3176451–52; RüKdo Oberrhein to Wagner, "Schreiben," Jan. 22, 1945, T-73/21/3145748.

77. There were eventually ten factory units in Kr. München-Ost; see Krstbfü., "Volkssturmbefehl 1/45," Feb. 9, 1945, T-81/153/156219–23. Also Bormann, "Anordnungen 387 & 408/44," Nov. 8 and 20, 1944, T-81/93/107679–80, and Kissel, 109–10, respectively; RMfRuK RüStab, Hauptwerksbeauftragter, "Bekanntmachung Nr. 3," Dec. 18, 1944, BA-Ko, NS 12, Nr. 1147.

78. Gesellschaft für Linnes Eismaschinen Höllriegelskreuth (Baiersbronn) file EAP 210–a/5, T-81/95/108065–191.

79. RMfRuK RüStab, Hauptwerksbeauftragter, "Bekanntmachung Nr. 3," Dec. 18, 1944, BA-Ko, NS 12, Nr. 1147.

80. Friedrichs, "RS 12/45," Jan. 26, 1945, T-81/94/108083–84; Giesler, "RS," Jan. 15, 1945, StA Munich, NSDAP, Nr. 466c.

81. See, e.g., Bezirksumschulungsausschuß Coburg, "Bericht," Feb. 2, 1945, BA-MA, RW 21–12, Nr. 12, 48.

82. Hitler, "Führer Erlaß," Jan. 31, 1945, T-73/180/3391953.

83. Speer, "RS, RMfRuK RüAmt, Arb. E VII-7579," Jan. 30, 1945, T-73/53/3188941; "FS, M 4402/45, geh.," Mar. 23, 1945, BA-Ko, R3, Nr. 122, 11.

84. RüKdo Augsburg files in T-73/43/3176391–502.

85. Allgäuer Schifabrik Hanser and Wilhelm (Scheidegg), "Schreiben," Feb. 15, 1945, T-73/81/3225531.

86. Baden's twenty-four active battalions contained 12,000 men by Feb. 1945. RüInsp Oberrhein, "Schreiben, Tgb. Nr. 983/45, geh.," Jan. 31, 1945, T-73/21/3145778. For Volkssturm mobilization impacts in East Prussia, see 4 AOK Wirtschaftsoffizier, "Aktenvermerk," Dec. 2 and 7, 1944, T-77/1113/130–33 and 135–37.

87. Krupp Nickelwerke Frankenstein, "Schreiben," Dec. 6, 1944, T-580/439/401/686; Allgäuer Baumwollspinnerei Blaichach, "Meldung," Dec. 8, 1944, T-73/74/3217482–83; RWK, "Zusammenfassung," undated (clearly 1945), BA-Ko, R11, Nr. 192, 70–71; Gau Baden Arbeitsamtpräsident, "Lage- und Tätigkeitsbericht," Jan. 31, 1945, T-81/646/5449650–55.

88. Bormann, "RS 437/44," Dec. 9, 1944, T-580/18/180; Dorpmüller, "Abschrift von FS K41–18610/44," Dec. 12, 1944, HStA Munich, Staatsministerium für Wirt-

schaft, Nr. 9390; Reichspostdirektion Nürnberg to Stigler, "Schreiben IIIE 8017–2," Feb. 5, 1945, StA Bamberg, M30, Nr. 837.

89. Armeewirtschaftsführer bei AOK 4, "Lagebericht, BrB. Nr. 466/44, geh.," Dec. 27, 1944, T-77/499/1666488–500.

90. Gau Schwaben RüKomm, "Niederschrift Nr. 9/45g.," Feb. 22, 1945, T-73/29/3157312–17.

91. Bormann, "Anordnungen 428–31/44,," all Dec. 2, 1944, "Anordnung 424/44," Dec. 4, 1944; "Anordnung 2/45," Jan. 5, 1945, all BA-Ko, NS 6, Nr. 98, 79–88; "Anordnung 21/45," Feb. 6, 1945, T-81/94/108126–27.

92. On the units, see, e.g., Rostock OLGP, "Lagebericht 3130 Ea/56," Dec. 19, 1944, BA-Ko, R22, Nr. 3385, 43–46. For Himmler's ban, see RM des Innerns, "Abt II RV Abschrift von RS, Nr. 9858/44-518," Nov. 14, 1944, Stadtarchiv Ratingen, 2, Nr. 807a.

93. Friedrichs to Bormann, "FS 1229," Nov. 19, 1944, T-580/872/799a/5; OKW/WFSt/Org. Abt. III, "FS Nr. 6494/44 geh.," Nov. 23, 1944, T-79/292/487–89; Bormann, "Anordnung 3/45," Jan. 26, 1945, BA-Ko, NS 6, Nr. 99, 5–6.

94. WK XIII (Nuremberg) Ia, "FS Nr. 20109/44, geh.," Nov. 22, 1944, BA-MA, RH 53-13, Nr. 141; Bamberg Krltr., "44. Wochenbericht," Nov. 25, 1944, StA Bamberg, Bestand M33, Nr. 631.

95. Og. Meinau and Og. Lingolsheim, "Volkssturm Erfassungsliste," undated, T-81/95/109208–80. Because the Red Cross compiled the MIA lists after the war, few NSDAP officials appear, since respondents would have been reluctant to admit that missing relatives or friends had been Party satraps.

96. AOK 4, OberQM, Abt. Qu. 1, "GKdos., Nr. 1089/44," Dec. 10, 1944, T-312/256/7813082–87.

97. According to the 1939 census, male and female employees in educational and religious occupations constituted only 1.78 percent of the workforce. Germany, Statistisches Reichsamt, *Statistisches Jahrbuch 1941/42*, vol. 59 (Berlin: Verlag für Sozialpolitik, Wirtschaft und Statistik, 1944), 186.

98. Reichsministerium für Wissenschaft, Erziehung und Volksausbildung, "Schnellbrief RV II 2/45," Feb. 27, 1944, BA-Ko, R21, Nr. 339.

99. Schulaufsichtsbezirk Goslar, "Verzeichnis," undated, StA Wolfenbüttel, Bestand 12 Neu 13, Nr. 22264; Kofü, Baden VsBtn. VII/1. Komp. (Rastatt), "Namensliste," Nov. 27, 1944, Stadtarchiv Rastatt, Bürgermeisteramt Rastatt, A/3923; Og. Werne, "Liste," undated, T-81/95/108876–78.

100. Schulrat Kr. Grafschaft Schaumburg, "Schreiben," Jan. 10, 1945, HStA Hannover, Hann 80 II E4, Nr. 188 I.

101. Bormann, "Anordnung 2/45," Jan. 5, 1945, BA-Ko, NS 6, Nr. 98, 3; RWM, Abt. II 3–A, "Abschrift von Runderlaß 339/44 LWa," Dec. 23, 1944, T-81/95/109846–49.

102. Bormann, "Anordnung 38/45," Mar. 9, 1945, T-580/53/285.

103. On civilian medical care during the war, see Michael H. Kater, *Doctors Under Hitler* (Chapel Hill: University of North Carolina Press, 1989). On Volkssturm medical arrangements, see Bormann, "Anordnung 393/44," Nov. 9, 1944, BA-Ko, NS 6, Nr. 98, 62.

104. Stigler to Ebermannstadt Krstbfü., "Schreiben," Feb. 6 and Mar. 12, 1945, both in BA-Ko, NS 12, Nr. 1147.

105. Bormann, "Anordnung 20/45," Feb. 6, 1945, BA-Ko, NS 6, Nr. 99, 44; Leiter des Planungsamts des Reichsforschungsrat, "RS Nr. 6," Feb. 12, 1945, T-175/273/2769805–9.

106. Interestingly, two of the fifteen deferred office workers were translators of Russian. Helmuth Sachse Luftfahrtgerätebau, Werk Kempten, "Antrag," Oct. 30, 1944, T-73/78/3223750–67 and 3223779–81; "Einschreiben," Dec. 7, 1944, T-73/78/3223688–89; Dec. 11, 1944, T-73/78/3223694–95; Dec. 13, 1944, T-73/78/3223696–99; and Jan. 11, 1945, T-73/78/3223685–87.

107. Maschinenfabrik Keller und Knappich, "Verzeichnis," Dec. 8, 1944, T-73/83/3230984–1003.

108. Wankel Versuchs Werkstätten, "Liste," undated, T-73/94/3246403.

109. Michel Werke, "Liste," undated, T-73/91/3242428–29; on Sachse, see note 106; on Keller and Knappich, see note 107.

110. Bormann, "Anordnung 424/44," Dec. 4, 1944, T-580/872/799a/5.

111. Wirtschaftsführer beim ObKdo der HG Mitte, "Lagebericht, BrB. Nr. 2520/45, geh.," Jan. 6, 1945, T-77/499/1666753–67; SD Leitabschnitt Königsberg, "Bericht, III D1-BrB. 2411/44, geh.," Dec. 7, 1944, T-175/274/2771765–70.

112. Westfalen Landesbauernfü., "Vierteljahresbericht," Jan. 5, 1945, BA-Ko, R 55, Nr. 602, 135–40; Bayreuth Landesbauernführer, "Schreiben, 2–326," Mar. 16, 1945, StA Bamberg, M30, Nr. 837.

113. Food processing totaled 3.25 percent of Volkssturm MIAs (appendix Tables 12 and 13). In July 1940, food processing accounted for only 2.91 percent of Germany's male civilian workforce, and one could expect the percentage to have been even lower by 1944; *Statistisches Jahrbuch 1941/42*, vol. 59, 417.

114. Freiburg Verwaltungsdir. to Krltr., "Schreiben," Dec. 2, 1944, Stadtarchiv Freiburg, C4 (Militärwesen), XI/27, Nr. 12.

115. Bormann, "Anordnung 33/45," Jan. 25, 1945, T-81/1/11136–37.

116. Bormann, "Anordnung 118/45," Mar. 6, 1945, NS 6, Nr. 353, 137; OKW/WFSt/QM Abt. Chef, "Auszug von Vortragsnotiz am 28.2.45, gKdos. Nr. 002045/45," Mar. 3, 1945, T-77/789/5517742–46.

117. RüKdo Recklinghausen, "RS Nr. 343, 67m (z), Nr. 14,420/45," Mar. 1, 1945, T-84/34/1310345–46.

118. Hohenhaus, BA-Ko, Ost Dok 8, Nr. 694.

119. Many also reasoned that farmers would fight harder to protect their land. Lüdinghausen Krltr., "RS," Jan. 25, 1944, T-81/94/108834.

120. Kissel, MS# B-627, Duke, Location 58-G, Box 4.

121. They received only a 30 percent deferral quota; Bormann, "Anordnung 424/44," Dec. 4, 1944, T-580/872/799a/5. Also Bayreuth Landesbauernfü., "Schreiben, 2–326," Mar. 16, 1945; Bayreuth Krltg., "Wochenbericht 6/45," Feb. 10, 1945, both StA Bamberg, M33, Nr. 631.

122. Stigler, "Schreiben," Feb. 7, 1945, StA Bamberg, M30, Nr. 837; Bayreuth Landesbauernschaft, Abt. IIIc, "Schreiben C 200W," Feb. 27, 1945, StA Bamberg, M30, Nr. 837; Bayreuth Landesbauernschaft, Abt. IIa, "Schreiben," Mar. 15, 1944, BA-Ko, NS 12, Nr. 1147.

123. Schulte, "Anordnung 1/45," Feb. 16, 1945, T-81/95/109907–13; Litzmannstadt Oberbürgermeister, "Bericht," Mar. 13, 1945, BA-Ko, R138 II, Nr. 7, 135–49.

124. Bormann, "RS 30/45," Mar. 1, 1945, T-580/18/181.
125. Firma Paraxol GmbH, Werk Welden, "Schreiben," Dec. 20, 1944, T-73/79/3224344.

6. Partisans or Combatants? The Volkssturm's Legal Identity

1. For the text of this speech, see Himmler, "Rede," Oct. 18, 1944, T-175/93/2614200–420.
2. A typical example is SD Leitabschnitt Stuttgart, "Stimmungsbericht," Nov. 8, 1944, T-81/95/109117–22.
3. Landrat Kr. Obernburg-Miltenburg, "Bericht," Oct. 27, 1944, T-175/227/2765882–91; Bamberg OLGP, "Bericht V 733–220 II," Dec. 1, 1944, BA-Ko, R 22, Nr. 3355, 100–105; Leitmeritz/Sudetenland OLGP, "Lagebericht 3130-12-168," Dec. 5, 1944, BA-Ko, R 22, Nr. 3376, 139–41.
4. Krltg. Freiburg im Breisgau, "Stimmungsbericht," Oct. 31, 1944; Krltg. Heidelberg, "Stimmungsbericht," Nov. 1, 1944, both BA-Ko, NS 6, Nr. 812.
5. Krltg. Pforzheim, "Bericht, lfd. Beitragsnr. 20," Oct. 20, 1944, T-81/164/302146–47; Jena OLGP, "Lagebericht 31320-2.12.44," Dec. 12, 1944, BA-Ko, R22, Nr. 3369, 123–24.
6. Schäffer, "Tätigkeitsberichte," Oct. 31 and Nov. 7, 1944, T-580/682/563; SD Leitabschnitt Stuttgart, "Stimmungsbericht," Nov. 8, 1944, T-81/95/109117–22.
7. Schäffer, "Tätigkeitsbericht," Nov. 7, 1944, T-580/682/563; SD Leitabschnitt Stuttgart, "Stimmungsbericht," Nov. 8, 1944, T-81/95/109117–22.
8. On German antipartisan policy, see Omer Bartov, *The Eastern Front, 1941–1945: German Troops and the Barbarisation of Warfare* (New York: St. Martin's, 1985); Bartov, *Hitler's Army: Soldiers, Nazis and War in the Third Reich* (New York: Oxford University Press, 1991); Mark Mazower, *Inside Hitler's Greece: The Experience of Occupation, 1941–1944* (New Haven, Conn.: Yale University Press, 1993); and Christian Streit, *Keine Kameraden: Die Wehrmacht und die sowjetische Kriegsgefangenen* (Bonn: J.H.W. Dietz, 1991).
9. First announced in Bormann, "Anordnung 277/44," Sept. 27, 1944, in Hans Kissel, *Der Deutsche Volkssturm 1944/45: Eine territoriale Miliz im Rahmen der Landesverteidigung* (Frankfurt am Main: E. S. Mittler und Sohn, 1962), 98–99.
10. Auswärtiges Amt Inland II Chef Rödiger, "Anlage 2 zu GRs. R222," Oct. 17, 1944, in Rödiger, "GRs Inl II 596," Nov. (no day), 1944, T-120/1757/E025351; Great Britain, Parliament, *Hansard's Parliamentary Debates (Commons)*, fifth series, vol. 361 (1940): 257–58, 268–70, 403–4, 1409.
11. Perry Biddiscombe, *Werwolf! The History of the National Socialist Guerrilla Movement, 1944–1946* (Toronto: University of Toronto Press, 1998), 119–21.
12. OKW, Allg. Abt. Kriegsgefangene, "2f24. 70 (Ia) FS Nr. 4733/44 geh.," Oct. 23, 1944, T-77/788/5516721–22.
13. Julius Stone, *Legal Controls of International Conflict: A Treatise on the Dynamics of Disputes and War-Law* (New York: Rinehart, 1959), 549–50.
14. Keitel, Bormann, and Himmler, "Verwendung des Deutschen Volkssturms, OKW/WFSt/Org.(III) Anordnung Nr. 1659/45 geh.," Mar. 28, 1945, T-77/783/5511402–6, summarizes Volkssturm duties.

15. XII SS AK, Abt. Ia, "Befehl, Ia Nr. 71/45, geh.," Jan. 9, 1945, T-354/120/3754322–26; Grohé, "Einsatzbefehl Nr. 1/45," Feb. 10, 1945, T-81/95/109916.

16. Compiled from No author, "Führerlagebesprechung," Jan. 27, 1945, BA-MA, RH 47, Nr. 65, Fragmente 24/25, 32–33; HSSuPF West, "Vortragsnotiz," Jan. 28, 1945, StA Bückeburg, L 102b Stadthagen, Nr. 1876; 180th Inf. Div. Ia, "Führungsanordnung Nr. 95, Nr. 413/45, geh.," Feb. 5, 1945, T-315/1539/53–54; Btnfü., VsBtn. 16/374, "Btnbefehl 6/45," Feb. 12, 1945, LHA Potsdam, PrBrRep. 2A, Regierung Potsdam, I Polizei, Nr. 2321; Berger, "Auszug von FS VsTgb. Nr. 475/45, geh.," Jan. 14, 1945 in OKW/WFSt/Org.(III), "FS Nr. 388/45," Feb. 12, 1945, T-77/783/5511438; Lippe Krltr., "RS 8/45," Feb. 21, 1945, StA Detmold, L113, Nr. 1023, 159; WK VII, "Ia GKdos. Nr. 1236/45," Feb. 24, 1945, T-84/240/6598515–19; RüKdo Augsburg, Zentralgruppe, "Aktenvermerk Nr. 735/45g," Mar. 13, 1945, T-73/58/3195770; SHAEF Psychological Warfare Div., Intelligence Sec., "Rept. 119983: The Volkssturm in Action," Mar. 15, 1945, NA, RG 226, Box 1334; Münster Krstbfü., "Befehl" Mar. 23, 1945, T-81/95/108286; OB West Kesselring, "GKdos. Nr. 4453/45," Apr. 27, 1945, T-321/19/4759895–96; Hans-Joachim Schmelzer, "Dokumentation zu den Geschehnissen vom Sommer 1944 bis zum 3.3.45 in und um Köslin zu Pommern," BA-Ko, Ost Dok 8/685; Petzel, Ost Dok 8/402; Ernst von Salomon, *Der Fragebogen* (Stuttgart: Europäisches Buchklub, 1951), 511; Rainer Fröbe et al., *Konzentrationslager in Hannover: KZ Arbeit und Rüstungsindustrie in der Spätphase des Zweiten Weltkrieges* (Hildesheim: August Lax, 1985), 396–97, 516, 539–44; Joachim Schultz-Naumann, *Mecklenburg 1945* (Munich: Universitas, 1990), 227; Herbert Schwarzwälder, *Bremen und Nordwestdeutschland am Kriegsende 1945*, vol. 1 (Bremen: Carl Schünemann, 1972), 64–65, 142.

17. "Protokoll von Landesgerichtsrat Dr. Julius Skalnik," in *Dokumentation zur Österreichischen Zeitgeschichte 1938–1945*, ed. Christine Klusacek, Herbert Steiner, and Kurt Stimmer (Vienna: Jugend und Volk, 1980), 545; Ernst Hornig, *Breslau 1945: Erlebnisse in der eingeschlossenen Stadt* (Würzburg: Bergstadtverlag Wilhelm Gottlieb Korn, 1986), 31–32.

18. Fröbe et al., *Konzentrationslager in Hannover*, 396–97, 516, 539–44; Gordon J. Horwitz, *In the Shadow of Death: Living Outside the Gates of Mauthausen* (New York: Free Press, 1990), 131–43, 154–55, 158–60; Streit, 294.

19. Speer, "Reisebericht, GenStdH/RMfRuK Nr. 8/45, gKdos.," Jan. 9, 1945, BA-Ko, R3, Nr. 1544, 81–84; Himmler, "FS," Jan. 28, 1945, T-311/167/7218660; OKH/FHO Chef Gehlen, "Vortragsnotiz," Jan. 31, 1945, T-78/304/6255670–71; Bonn Krstbfü., "Kreisstabsbefehl Nr. 8, Einsatzbefehl Nr. 2," Feb. 17, 1945, HStA Düsseldorf, RW 23, Nr. 273, 13; Burst, "Abschrift von RS," Feb. 27, 1945, BA-MA, RH 20-19, Nr. 4, 23; OB West, OberQM, "IVa-IIB1 Az gK 62 FS Nr. 1867/45, geh.," Mar. 1, 1945, BA-MA, RH 53-13, Nr. 148; Gltg. Schwaben, "Ernährungslage," Apr. 14, 1945, T-81/179/328886–87; Salomon, 511; Reinhold Maier, ed., *Ende und Wende: Das schwäbische Schicksal 1944–1946 in Briefe und Tagebuchaufzeichnungen* (Stuttgart: Rainer Wunderlich, 1948), 176.

20. Bormann, "RS 30/45," Mar. 1, 1945, T-81/94/108141–43.

21. Berger, "2. Ausbildungsbefehl, VsTgb. Nr 6674/44, geh., VoTgb. Nr. 172/44 geh.," Nov. 3, 1944, T-77/438/1302377; Himmler, "GKdos., VsTgb. Nr. 1359/44, VoTgb. Nr. 103/44," Nov. 23, 1944, T-175/122/2648011; Keitel, Bormann, and

Himmler, "Verwendung des Deutschen Volkssturms, OKW/WFSt/Org.(III) Anordnung Nr. 1659/45 geh.," Mar. 28, 1945, T-77/783/5511402–6.
22. Bormann, "Anordnung 318/44," Oct. 12, 1944, in Kissel, 100–103; Berger, "Abschrift von VsTgb. Nr. 6389/44, geh., VoTgb. Nr. 31/44, geh.," Oct. 14, 1944, T-580/874/799b/5; Auswärtiges Amt Inland II to Bormann, "Anlage 5 to gRs. R222," Oct. 17, 1944, T-120/1757/E025356–57; RFSS Vs. Staff, "FS 20563," Nov. 10, 1944, BA-Ko, NS 12, Nr. 1147.
23. RPA Lüneburg, "Ausschnitte von Stimmungsbericht," Jan. 15, 1945, T-580/656/449, teil 1.
24. Bormann, "FS," Sept. 26, 1944, T-580/872/799a/4; Bormann, "FS," Oct. 22, 1944, BA-Ko, NS 6, Nr. 764, 20.
25. OKW/WFSt/QM 2 (I), "FS Nr. 1318/45, geh." Feb. 23, 1945, BA-MA, RW 4, Nr. 709, Teil II, 186.
26. Bormann, "Anordnung 277/44," Sept. 27, 1944; "Anordnung 318/44," Oct. 12, 1944, in Kissel, 98–103; "Anordnung 406/44," Nov. 18, 1944, T-84/175/1544766–69.
27. Himmler, "GKdos., VsTgb. Nr. 1359/44, VoTgb. Nr. 103/44," Nov. 23, 1944, T-175/122/2648011.
28. Bormann, "FS," Oct. 4, 1944, T-580/872/799a/4. Each battalion's numerical designation consisted of the Gau number, a slash, and its own individual unit number assigned within the Gau; Bormann, "Anordnung 406/44," Nov. 18, 1944, T-84/175/1544766–69.
29. For Wehrmacht TO&Es, see U.S. Army Manual TM-E30-454, sec. 11, 35–41; and OKH/Org. Abt. Nr. I, "GKdos. Nr. 20100/44," Oct. 23, 1944, T-78/418/6387877–82. For Volkssturm formations, see Unknown, "Kriegsstärkenachweisungen," Nov. 20, 1944, T-81/95/109569–76.
30. Gau Bayreuth's battalions ranged from 425 to 1,455 men; most fell between 500 and 650; Stigler, "Starkenmeldungen," undated, BA-Ko, NS 12, Nr. 1147.
31. Bormann, "Anordnung 393/44," Nov. 9, 1944, T-580/872/799a/3.
32. Btnfü., VsBtn. Walsrode III, "Btn.befehl Nr. 9," Jan. 25, 1945, T-81/95/109807–8.
33. Westfalen-Süd Gstbfü. Setzer, "Kriegsstärkenachweisungen, Nov. 20, 1944," Jan. 10, 1945, T-81/94/107864–75; Unknown, "Kriegsstärkenachweisungen," Nov. 20, 1944, T-81/95/109569–76.
34. Bormann, "Anordnung 422/44," Nov. 30, 1944, BA-Ko, NS 6, Nr. 98, 78.
35. Setzer, "Kriegsstärkenachweisungen, Nov. 20, 1944," Jan. 10, 1945, T-81/94/107864–75.
36. Kraus, "RS," Oct. 14 and 27, 1944, T-580/872/799a/2; Gau Moselland, Chef der motorisierten Vs. Einheiten, "RS BrB. Nr. 2/44, Co/Sch, geh.," Nov. 21, 1944, T-81/94/108630–38; Kraus, "Richtlinien," Dec. 9, 1944, T-81/95/109664–77.
37. Magdeburg-Anhalt Gstbfü. Albert Heinz, "RS," Feb. 16, 1945, LA Magdeburg, Rep. C 20 Ib (XV: RVK), Nr. 3384; Schnellen VsBtn. Bonn, "Taktische Einstellung," undated, T-81/95/109893.
38. Caspary, "Richtlinien," Nov. 3, 1944, LA Saarbrücken, NSDAP Mischbestand, Nr. 15, 11–19; München-Ost Krstbfü., "Befehl," Mar. 16, 1945, T-81/153/156210.

39. Willy Timm, *Freikorps "Sauerland" 1944–45: Zur Geschichte des Zweiten Weltkriegs in Südwestfalen* (Hagen: Stadtarchiv Hagen, 1976).

40. Stigler, "RS 45/45," Feb. 27, 1945, BA-Ko, NS 12, Nr. 1147; HJ Ost-Hannover, "Anordnung 2300 Bl/Si, geh.," Mar. 23, 1945, T-81/102/119086–87. One Volkssturm unit conducted a successful raid on an American supply depot at Bad Teinach; Gltg. Württemberg-Hohenzollern, "Lagebericht," Apr. 18, 1945, T-580/43/Gruppe VIII/248.

41. On the Werewolf, see Biddiscombe.

42. Schörner, "FS Nr. 493/45 geh.," Jan. 23, 1945, T-311/167/7218542–43.

43. Wahl, "Rundspruch Nr. 11," Mar. 30, 1945, T-81/162/300554; OKW/WFSt/Op(H), "GKdos. Nr. 00344/45," Apr. 8, 1945, T-77/1423/937–38.

44. Friedrichs, "FS Nr. 869," Oct. 5, 1944, BA-Ko, NS 6, Nr. 763, 84–86; Bormann and Himmler, "Verordnung über eine Sondergerichtsbarkeit in Strafsachen für Angehorige des Deutschen Volkssturms," Feb. 24, 1945, *Reichsgesetzblatt*, 1945, pt. 1, no. 8; Bormann, "Abschrift von 1. Ausführungsbestimmung zur Verordnung über eine Sondergerichtsbarkeit in Strafsachen für Angehorige des Deutschen Volkssturms," Feb. 24, 1945, T-81/94/108151–53; Bormann and Himmler, "Anordnung 40/45," Mar. 16, 1945, T-81/94/108173–78.

45. Bormann and Himmler, "Verordnung über die Stellung der Angehörigen des Deutschen Volkssturms vom 1. Dez. 1944," Dec. 23, 1944, *Reichsgesetzblatt*, 1944, pt. 1, no. 65; Rudolf Absolon, *Wehrgesetz und Wehrdienst 1933–1945: Das Personalwesen in der Wehrmacht* (Boppard am Rhein: Harald Boldt, 1960), 9–11, 42.

46. Bormann and Himmler, "Verordnung über die Stellung der Angehörigen des Deutschen Volkssturms vom 1. Dez. 1944," Dec. 23, 1944, *Reichsgesetzblatt*, 1944 pt. 1, no. 65; Gestapo Regensburg, "RS 7702/44 IV 1b," Jan. 2, 1945, StA Amberg, BzA Neunberg, Nr. 2815; Friedrichs, "Bekanntgabe 16/45," Feb. 12, 1945, T-81/1/11146.

47. Btnfü., II Btn. Kr. Oberlahn-Usingen, "1. Btn. Befehl," Dec. 19, 1944, HStA Wiesbaden, Bestand 483, Nr. 6462; U.S. 70th Inf. Div., Task Force Herrin, "G-2 Periodic Rept. Nr. 31," Jan. 26–27, 1945, NA, RG 407, Entry 427, Box 11329; U.S. 9th Armored Div., "G-2 Periodic Rept. Nr. 11, Annex 2," Mar. 21, 1945, NA, RG 407, Entry 427, Box 15783.

48. Kdr., Ordnungspolizei Regensburg, "Abschrift von RFSS Befehl, Tgb. Nr. 49/45, KdO-Vs," Apr. 3, 1945, in Hans-Adolf Jacobsen, ed., *1939–1945: Der Zweite Weltkrieg in Chronik und Dokumenten* (Darmstadt: Wehr und Wissen, 1959), Nr. 162, 424–25.

49. One for squad leaders to four for battalion leaders; Bormann, "Anordnung 318/44," Oct. 12, 1944, in Kissel, 100–103; "Anordnung 391/44," Nov. 7, 1944, T-580/17/180. For similarities to army practices, see Bartov, *Barbarisation*, 38–39, 66–67; and Jürgen Förster, "The Dynamics of Volksgemeinschaft: The Effectiveness of the German Military Establishment in the Second World War," in *Military Effectiveness*, vol. 3, *The Second World War*, ed. Alan R. Millett & Williamson Murray (Boston: Allen and Unwin, 1988), 206–7.

50. Quotation from Bormann, "Anordnung 277/44," Sept. 27, 1944, Kissel, 98–99. Also see Bormann, "Anordnung 318/44," Oct. 12, 1944, Kissel, 100–103.

51. Quotation from Friedrichs to Bormann, "FS 933," Oct. 11, 1944, BA-Ko,

NS 6, Nr. 313, 143–46. Also see Bormann, "Anordnung 1/45," Jan. 5, 1945, T-580/ 53/285.
    52. OKH/HPA, "Tätigkeitsbericht," entry for Sept. 26, 1944, in T-78/39/1504; Bormann, "RS 294/44," Oct. 1, 1944, BA-Ko, NS 6, Nr. 98, 14.
    53. Bormann, "RS 350/44," Oct. 27, 1944, T-580/872/799a/4; Bormann "Anordnung 391/44," Nov. 7, 1944, T-580/17/180.
    54. Quotation from Dietrich Orlow, *The History of the Nazi Party 1919–1945*, vol. 2, *1933–1945* (Pittsburgh: University of Pittsburgh Press, 1973), 475. Similar sentiments are in Franz Seidler, *"Deutscher Volkssturm": Das letzte Aufgebot 1944/45* (Munich: Herbig, 1989), 169; and the memoirs of many Wehrmacht commanders, such as Kurt Dieckert and Horst Grossmann, *Der Kampf um Ostpreußen: Der umfassende Dokumentarbericht über das Kriegsgeschehen in Ostpreußen* (Stuttgart: Motorbuch, 1976), 64.
    55. Hoffmann, "FS 2573," Oct. 2, 1944, BA-Ko, NS 6, Nr. 313, 75; Koch, "Abschrift von Br. B. 48/44 Kgeh.," Oct. 10, 1944, T-581/6/151.
    56. Stigler's files are located in BA-Ko, NS 12, Nr. 1147; StA Bamberg, Bestand M30, Nr. 838, and StA Amberg's NSDAP Kreisleitung. records.
    57. OKH/HPA, 1 St. "Anlage zu GKdos. Nr. 3721/44," Nov. 12, 1944, BA-MA, RH 2, Nr. 3035, 26; Bartov, *Barbarisation*, 53.
    58. Confirming this age profile are Btnfü., Rastatt VsBtn. VII, "Liste," undated, Stadtarchiv Rastatt, Bürgermeisteramt Nr. A 1392; Oberesch Volkssturm, "Verzeichnis," undated, LA Saarbrücken, NSDAP Mischbestand, Nr. 22, 6; Kofu. 7. VsKomp. Rötz, "Liste," undated, StA Amberg, NS Krltg. Oberviechtach, Nr. 5; Bad Freienwalde, Ladeburg, Finow, Strausberg/West, and Strausberg Ogltr., "Meldungen," Oct. 6, 20, 21, 22, 23, 27, and Nov. 22, 1944, LHA Potsdam, PrBrRep. 61, Mark Brandenburg, Nr. 2. 1.474; Btnfü., VsBtn. 24/29, "Meldungen," various dates in EAP 210–c/2, T-81/95/109290–518; Krstbfü. Berlin-Pankow, "Liste," undated, LHA Potsdam, PrBrRep. 61, SA, Nr. 18.341.
    59. This trend is also noted among regular army field officers; see Bartov, *Barbarisation*, 49–52, 58–59.
    60. Btnfü., VsBtn. 24/29, "Meldungen," various dates in folder EAP 210-c/2, T-81/95/109290–518; Btnfü., Rastatt Btn. VII, "Liste," undated, Stadtarchiv Rastatt, Bürgermeisteramt Nr. A 1392.
    61. Hermann Riedel, *Villingen 1945: Bericht aus einer schweren Zeit* (Villingen/ Schwarzwald, Ring, 1968), 21–31; Riedel, *Ausweglos . . . ! Letzter Akt des Krieges im Schwarzwald, in der Ostbaar und an der oberen Donau, Ende April 1945* (Neckargemünd: Kurt Vowinckel, 1975), 145, 197.
    62. Gren. Btn. 77 "Westfalen," Abt. Ia "Meldung, Tgb. Nr. 81/45 geh.," Feb. 24, 1945, T-84/242/6600231–32; Bremen-Walle Ogltr., "Meldungen," Oct. 25 and Nov. 14, 1944, T-81/94/109479–81.
    63. Bad Freienwalde, Ladeburg, Strausberg, Strausberg/West, and Finow Ogltr., "Meldungen," Oct. 6, 20, 21, 22, 23, 27, and Nov. 22, 1944, LHA Potsdam, PrBrRep. 61, Mark Brandenburg, Nr. 2.1.474.
    64. Brieske Ogltr., "Bericht" Nov. 6, 1944, LHA Potsdam, PrBrRep. 61, Mark Brandenburg, Nr. 5.3.1; Btnfü., 1. VsBtn. Kr. Schaumburg-Lippe, "Schreiben," Nov. 10, 1944, StA Bückeburg, L 102b Stadthagen, Nr. 1877; Ltn. a.D. Hans Sturm

(Knight's Cross recipient and trainer at Grafenwöhr), "Letter," Feb. 22, 1993, in the author's possession.

65. SHAEF Psychological Warfare Div., Intelligence Section, "Interrogation of 13 Volkssturm Leaders," in OSS, "Report 119998," Mar. 14, 1945, NA, RG 226, Box 1334.

66. Btnfü., VsBtn. 24/29, "Meldungen," various dates in folder EAP 210–c/2, T-81/95/109290–518.

67. Schulrat, 5. Schulaufsichtsbezirk, "Verzeichnis," Feb. 13, 1945; Schulrat, Goslarer Schulsaufsichtsbezirk, "Verzeichnis," undated, both in StA Wolfenbüttel, Bestand 12 Neu 13, Nr. 22264.

68. Paul Flegel, "Bericht über die Volkssturmbataillone des Kreises Habelschwerdt," BA-Ko, Ost Dok 10/636.

69. Kr. Lippe, "Aufstellung des Bataillon und Kompanie Führer," undated, StA Detmold, L113, Nr. 1023, 84–86; Btnfü, Btn. 24/29, "Meldungen," various dates in folder EAP 210–c/2, T-81/95/109290–518; Oberesch Vs., "Verzeichnis," undated, LA Saarbrücken, NSDAP Mischbestand, Nr. 22, 6.

70. Bad Freienwalde, Ladeburg, Finow, Strausberg/West, and Strausberg Ogltr., "Meldungen," Oct. 6, 20, 21, 22, 23, 27, and Nov. 22, 1944, LHA Potsdam, PrBrRep. 61, Mark Brandenburg, Nr. 2.1. 474; Berlin-Pankow Krstbfü., "Liste," undated, LHA Potsdam, PrBrRep. 61, SA, Nr. 18.341.

71. As one Krltr. stated, commanders could have no military experience but should never be politically unqualified; Zauch-Belzig Krltr., "Dienstanweisung Nr. 110," Oct. 20, 1944, LHA Potsdam, PrBrRep. 61, Mark Brandenburg, Nr. 5.17.1.

72. Gstbfü. München-Oberbayern Heinz Hoffmann, "RS," Nov. 29, 1944, T-580/53/285.

73. Lüdinghausen Krltr., "RS," undated (probably Feb. 1945), T-81/94/108835–46. Also see Bremen-Walle Ogltr., "Meldung," Oct. 15, 1944, T-81/94/109481; Bad Freienwalde, Ladeburg, Finow, Strausberg/West, and Strausberg Ogltr., "Meldungen," Oct. 6, 20, 21, 22, 23, 27, and Nov. 22, 1944, LHA Potsdam, PrBrRep. 61, Mark Brandenburg, Nr. 2.1.474.

74. Including the dozen SS members who may well have been in the Waffen SS (only one was plainly identified as such) raises the percentage of battalion leaders with military backgrounds to 54.1 percent.

75. Sturm, "Letters," Feb. 22 and June 17, 1993, both in the author's possession.

76. Calau Krstbfü., "Anordnung 17," Jan. 11, 1945, LHA Potsdam, PrBrRep. 61, Mark Brandenburg, Nr. 5.3.1; Gerhard Hohenhaus, "Die zivilen Verteidigungsmassnahmen in Pommern im letzten Kriegsjahr," BA-Ko, Ost Dok 8/694; Siegfried Schug, "Bericht über die Kriese Stargard-Saatzig und Pyritz," BA-Ko, Ost Dok 8/637; Dr. Hans-Friedrich von St. Paul, "Kreis Militsch-Trachtenberg," BA-Ko, Ost Dok 8/718.

77. Berlin-Pankow Krstbfü., "Liste," undated, LHA Potsdam, PrBrRep. 61, SA, Nr. 18.341; Brieske Ogltr., "Bericht," Nov. 6, 1944, LHA Potsdam, PrBrRep. 61, Mark Brandenburg, Nr. 5.3.1.

78. All but one of the men listing no experience came from Finow, whose records did not provide military service data; of the others, some had not risen above enlisted status. Bad Freienwalde, Ladeburg, Finow, Strausberg/West, and Strausberg Ogltr.,

"Meldungen," Oct. 6, 20, 21, 22, 23, 27, and Nov. 22, 1944, LHA Potsdam, PrBrRep. 61, Mark Brandenburg, Nr. 2.1. 474.

79. Btnfü., Btn. 24/29, "Meldungen," various dates in folder EAP 210–c/2, T-81/95/109290–518.

80. Oberesch Vs., "Verzeichnis," undated, LA Saarbrücken, NSDAP Mischbestand, Nr. 22, 6.

81. 2. Komp., VsBtn. 19/XVI (Kr. München-Ost), "Liste," undated, T-81/153/ 156331–332 and 156339.

82. RB Dir. Nürnberg, "Übersicht über die Gliederung der Betriebsgebunden Einheiten des Deutschen Volkssturms," undated, StA Bamberg, M30, Nr. 838.

83. Reportedly, the ads quickly netted over forty men; Dotzler (PK Staff), "Vermerk für Pg. Friedrichs," Mar. 8, 1945, BA-Ko, NS 6, Nr. 135, 59–60; Btnfü., VsBtn. 16/279 (Trebbin), "Btn.befehl 1/45," Jan. 8, 1945, LHA Potsdam, PrBrRep. 2A, Regierung Potsdam, I Polizei, Nr. 2321.

84. Also 1. and 2. Züge, Vs. Bückeburg, "Liste," undated, StA Bückeburg, L 102b Stadthagen, Nr. 1877, shows all its squad leaders, save one, with military experience as enlisted men.

85. Förster, "Dynamics," 207, states that 45 percent of officer candidates between 1939 and 1942 were Party members.

86. See Bartov's works, especially, *Barbarisation*, 38–67; Förster, "Dynamics," 206–7; Mazower, 155–218; and Theo Schulte, *The German Army and Nazi Policies in Occupied Russia* (Oxford: Berg, 1989).

87. PzGren Ers. und Ausb. Btn. 12, "Schreiben," Dec. 22, 1944, BA-Ko, NS 12, Nr. 1147.

88. There was little correlation between former rank and course performance: two lieutenants had the highest average scores, but two privates also scored highly, and two other lieutenants performed as poorly as anyone; PzGren Ers. und Ausb. Btn. 12, "Verzeichnis und Beurteilung," Feb. 22, 1945, BA-Ko, NS 12, Nr. 1147.

89. Bormann, "RS 28/45," Feb. 23, 1945, T-81/94/108137–38.

90. Dr. Gerd Wunder (Kanzlei Rosenberg), "Beobachtung über die Kampfkraft des Volkssturmes," undated (after Jan. 1945), T-454/1/529–38; Hoffmann, "FS 2573," Oct. 2, 1944, BA-Ko, NS 6, Nr. 313, 75.

91. OSS, "Rept. 114828, Volkssturm Mobilization in the Konstanz Area," Feb. 21, 1945, NA, RG 226, Box 1270; Btnfü. Fischer to Unterabschnitt 3, Verteidigungsbereich Berlin, "Schreiben," Mar. 12, 1945, T-79/5/347.

92. Gnesen Krltr., "Bericht," in BA-Ko, Ost Dok 8/402.

93. In September, the army averaged an incredibly high loss rate of 317.5 officers daily; OKH/HPA Chef, Gen. Schmundt, "Tätigkeitsbericht," Oct. 9, 1944, in Dermott Bradley and Richard Schulze-Kossens, eds., *Tätigkeitsbericht des Chefs des Heerespersonalamtes, General der Infanterie Rudolf Schmundt 1.10.1942–29.10.1944* (Osnabrück: Biblio, 1984), 280; Schmundt, "OKH/HPA/1 St. GKdos. Nr. 3721/ 44," Nov. 12, 1944, BA-MA, RH 2, Nr. 3035, 26.

94. Bofinger (PK Vs. Stab) to Bormann, "FS 1134," Nov. 3, 1944, BA-Ko, NS 6, Nr. 764, 171–72; Schmundt, "Tätigkeitsbericht," Sept. 30, 1944, 141, in BA-MA, RH 7, Nr. 565, 149.

95. NSDAP Reichsschatzmeister Schwarz, "Anordnungen 27–29 & 33/44," Oct. 31,

Nov. 1, and 13, Dec. 6, 1944, T-580/872/799a/5 and T-81/220/474650–51; Berger, "RS, VoTgb. Nr. 1435/44, Dec. 15, 1944, T-77/783/5511486–94; Herford Kriestabsamtsleiter, "RS," Feb. 19, 1945, StA Detmold, Sammelbestand M15, Nr. 1; München-Oberbayern Gauschatzmeister, "RS," Feb. 23, 1945, StA Munich, Bestand NSDAP, Nr. 466c; Bormann, "1. Durchführungsbestimmmung zur Verordnung über die Stellung der Angehörigen des Deutschen Volkssturms," Mar. 6, 1945, in *Runderlaße für den inneren Dienst der Reichsversorgungsverwaltung,* Blatt 9, Mar. 6, 1945, 69–72, T-81/152/155469–84; Feig, "Befehl Nr. IVa 70/ 3 Mü/ Ho," Mar. 23, 1945, HStA Weimar, Reichstatthalter, Nr. 479, 3–4; Wächtler, "Durchsage," Mar. 28, 1945, BA-Ko, NS 12, Nr. 1147; Berger, "Merkblatt," undated, BA-KO, NS 12, Nr. 1147.

96. Typical volunteers were women or Levy IV men; Zauch-Belzig Krltr., "RS, eilt!," Jan. 17, 1945, LHA Potsdam, PrBrRep. 61, Mark Brandenburg, Nr. 5.17.1; Kofü, 7. VsKomp. Rötz, "Liste," undated, StA Amberg, NSDAP Krltg. Oberviechtach, Nr. 5.

97. Friedrichs, "Bekanntgabe 18/45," Feb. 8, 1945, T-81/94/108098–102; GenQM bei WK VII, "Richtlinien, Tgb. Nr. 45/45 geh.," Feb. 9, 1945, BA-MA, RH 34, Nr. 287; Verteidigungsbereich Berlin, QMzbV, "Besondere Anordnung für die Versorgung Nr. 4," Mar. 2, 1945, T-79/5/312–15; OKW Allgemeine Wehrmachtamt, "WVW II W, FS Nr. 765/45," Mar. 5, 1945, BA-MA, RW 6, Nr. 519, 8; Btnfü., Feldbtn. 38/VI, "Btn. Befehl 22," Mar. 11, 1945, T-81/95/109956; Friedrichs, "RS 43/45," Apr. 6, 1945, BA-Ko, NS 6, Nr. 99, 88.

98. Btnfü., VsBtn. 19/XVI, "Btn. Befehl 2/44," Dec. 8, 1944, T-81/153/156271–72; Btnfü., VsBtn. 4 (Heroldsbach), "Schreiben," Dec. 7, 1944, BA-Ko, NS 12, Nr. 1147; RPA Dessau, "Stimmungsbericht," Dec. 18, 1944, T-580/656/448; Btnfü.'s files, VsBtn. 16/374, LHA Potsdam, PrBrRep. 2A, Regierung Potsdam, I Polizei, Nr. 2321; Kofü. Paul Koallick, "Die letzten Erlebnisse in und um Pillau," manuscript in BA-MA, RH 24-25, Nr. 1(E), teil 2, 2.

7. Preparing for Battle

1. Berger, "Ausbildungsbefehl für den Deutschen Volkssturm, VsTgb. Nr. 6396/ 44 geh., VoTgb. Nr. 25/44, geh.," Oct. 16, 1945, T-81/95/109519–22; Bormann, "FS," Oct. 29, 1944, T-580/872/799a/4.

2. Berger, "2. Ausbildungsbefehl, VsTgb. Nr. 6674/44, geh., VoTgb. Nr. 172/ 44 geh.," Nov. 3, 1944, T-77/438/1302377.

3. Bormann, "RS 372/44," Nov. 3, 1944, T-73/43/3176771–72; Himmler, "Bekanntgabe 446/44," Dec. 13, 1944, T-84/175/1544777–79.

4. SA Gruppe Tannenberg "Bericht F-214/44," Nov. 1, 1944, T-580/874/ 799b/5; SA Gruppe Bayernwald, "RS 3/45," Jan. 2, 1945, T-580/872/799a/1.

5. Kraus, "RS und Anlagen," Oct. 14 and 27, 1944, T-580/872/ 799a/2; Kofü., Motor Komp. Forchheim, "Dienstplan für März," Feb. 1945, BA-Ko, NS 24, Nr. 29.

6. HSSuPF Main, SS Obergruppenführer Martin, "FS Nr. 1180," Nov. 30, 1944, BA-Ko, NS 12, Nr. 1147.

7. Himmler, "Befehl," Nov. 3, 1944, T-175/122/2648035. On the field army, see Befehlshaber AOK 4, Gen. Friedrich Hoßbach, "Ia FS Nr. 1922/44, geh.,"

Oct. 12, 1944, T-312/256/7813793. Even antiaircraft battery personnel were to join in; Flak Regt. 59(v) Ia, "GKdos. Nr. 59/45," Jan. 31, 1945, T-321/24/4767125.

8. SS Junkerschule Tölz, "Plan für die Ausbildung der Kofü," Oct. 22, 1944, T-580/874/799b/5; Gen. Insp. für den Führernachwuchs des Heeres, "FS Nr. 332/44," Oct. 28, 1944, T-175/122/2648024–26; Berger, "Führerausbildung in den Gauen, VsTgb. Nr. 6673/44, VoTgb. Nr. 171/44, geh.," Nov. 3, 1944, T-175/122/2648021–23; Stigler, "RS 49/45," Mar. 9, 1945, BA-Ko, NS 12, Nr. 1147.

9. WK XII, Ia, Abt. Ausbildung, "Befehl Az 34a 10 Nr. 1051, geh.," Oct. 18, 1944, BA-MA, RH 34, Nr. 146, 70; Zauch-Belzig Krltr., "Dienstanweisung 111," Nov. 1, 1944, LHA Potsdam, PrBrRep. 61, Mark Brandenburg, Nr. 5.17.1; Sturm, "Letter," Sept. 21, 1993, in the author's possession.

10. Fahrion, "Schnellbrief," Nov. 1, 1944, T-581/33/635; Kissel "Allgemeine Anordnung 2/45, VoTgb. Nr. 420/45," Jan. 15, 1945, T-580/53/285; Gltg. München-Oberbayern, "RS," Jan. 29, Mar. 3 and 7, 1945; Krltg. Fürstenfeldbruck, "Meldungen," Mar. 20 and 24, 1945, all in StA Munich, NSDAP, Nr. 466c; Stigler, "RS 49/45," Mar. 9, 1945, both in BA-Ko, NS 12, Nr. 1147; Btnfü., Btn. 19/XVI, "Btn. Befehl 9/45," Mar. 20, 1945, T-81/153/156242.

11. Berger, "Abschrift von FS," Feb. 6, 1945; Weiden Krstbfü., "Ausbildungs-plan," Mar. 19, 1945; Stigler, "Führer- und Unterführerlehrgänge," Apr. 7, 1945, all in BA-Ko, NS 12, Nr. 1147.

12. Berger, "Ausbildungsbefehl, VsTgb. Nr. 6673/44 geh.," Nov. 3, 1944, T-77/438/1302378; Berger, "Abschrift von RS," in Broesl, "Anlage 3 zur Anordnung 12/44," Nov. 23, 1944, T-94/81/108987; Kissel, MS# B-627, 17.

13. Gräntz, "Ausbildungsplan," Dec. 11, 1944, BA-Ko, R55, Nr. 1287, 47–48; Btnfü., Btn. I Ratibor, "Dienstplan, 22.11–22.12. 44," Nov. 23, 1944, BA-Ko, NS 30, Nr. 145.

14. Btnfü., Btn. 18/3 (Kaisersesch), "Erfahrungsbericht," Feb. 18, 1945, T-81/95/109890; Westfalen-Nord Gstbfü. Paul Faßbach, "Schreiben," undated (before Feb. 11, 1945), StA Detmold, L113, Nr. 1023, 62; Krltg. Vilshofen, "Auszug aus dem Wochenbericht," Mar. 17, 1945, BA-Ko, NS 12, Nr. 1147.

15. Schwede-Coburg, "FS 788/44," Dec. 18, 1944, BA-Ko, NS 6, Nr. 764, 324; RüKdo Recklinghausen, "RS 327," Dec. 21, 1944, T-84/34/1310371–72.

16. Berger's suggesting that Karl May novels might be useful lecture topics on how to fight "Indian style" was about as close to guerrilla warfare as Volkssturm training ever came. Berger, "RS, VsTgb. Nr. 6677/44, VoTgb. Nr. 235/44, geh.," Nov. 10, 1944, T-175/122/2648029–33.

17. Bock, "RS BrB. Nr. 585/45," Feb. 22, 1945, T-81/95/109283–90.

18. This was based on SA marksmanship training methods. See Berger, "1. Befehl für die Schießausbildung im Volkssturm, VsTgb. Nr. 1372, VoTgb. Nr. 65/44, gKdos," Nov. 1, 1944, T-175/122/2648014–16.

19. Koch, "Abschrift von GKdos., BrB. 48/44," Oct. 10, 1944, T-581/6/151.

20. SA Gruppe Bayernwald, "Richtlinien für die Ausbildung im Deutschen Volks-sturm, FO/B/OO," Feb. 9, 1945, BA-Ko, NS 12, Nr. 1147.

21. Berger, "FS, VsTgb. Nr. 8616/44, VoTgb. Nr. 577/44, geh.," Dec. 14, 1944, T-580/872/799a/5. An example of emphasis on parade ground drill is Btnfü.

Marquart (Zauch-Belzig), "Befehl," Nov. 22, 1944, LHA Potsdam, PrBrRep. 61, Mark Brandenburg, Nr. 5.17.1.

22. Himmler, "Bekanntgabe 446/44," Dec. 13, 1944, T-84/175/1544777–79; Friedrichs, "RS 4/45," Jan. 16, 1945, T-81/94/108074.

23. SA Gruppe Bayernwald, "Richtlinien," Feb. 9, 1945, BA-Ko, NS 12, Nr. 1147.

24. Kissel, "Befehl: Filme, VoTgb. Nr. 1113/44," Dec. 4, 1944, BA-Ko, NS 12, Nr. 1147.

25. Leiter RMfVuP Abt. Film/Reichsfilmintendant, "Schreiben," Dec. 20, 1944, BA-Ko, R55, Nr. 663, 25.

26. Krltg. Fürstenfeldbruck, "Ausbildungsplan," undated (probably Nov.–Dec. 1944), StA Munich, NSDAP, Nr. 466c.

27. Ebermannstadt Krstbfü., "Kreisstabsbefehl Nr. 2," Dec. 6, 1944, BA-Ko, NS 12, Nr. 1147, is but one example.

28. H. Kiessling & Co. (Denzingen), "Schreiben," Jan. 11, 1945, T-73/154/3321461; Landwirtschaftsrat Dr. Munde, "Organisation und Einsatz des Volkssturms in und um Landsberg am Warthe," BA-Ko, Ost Dok 8/704.

29. Stigler, "Führer & Unterführer Lehrgänge," Apr. 7, 1945, BA-Ko, NS 12, Nr. 1147; OKH/GenStdH/Org Abt., Nr. I, "FS Nr. 30838/44, geh.," undated (Dec. 25–31, 1944), T-78/421/6390885.

30. OKW/OberQM Staff, "FS 62v23 VsB (VIII 2)," Oct. 21, 1944, T-175/122/2648037; Kissel, "Aufstellung über Bedarf an Waffen," Nov. 30, 1944, T-81/94/108060–62.

31. OKH/GenStdH/GenQM, Abt. Qu. 3/z, "Berichte: Waffenbestand," Oct. 1, 1944, BA-MA, RH 3, Nr. 258, 33–38 and 72–76.

32. OKH/GenStdH/Org Abt. Nr. III, "Kriegsgliederungsskizzen," various from late 1944 to 1945, BA-MA, RH 2, Nrs. 1450–51.

33. The quotation is from Albert Speer, *Inside the Third Reich*, trans. Richard Winston and Clara Winston (New York: Bonanza, 1982), 450. Production figures for Sept. 1944 are in RMfRuK, "Statistische Schnellberichte, Feb. 1945," undated, T-73/182/3394389–403.

34. Stürtz, "Anordnung 9/44," Dec. 2, 1944, LHA Potsdam, PrBrRep. 61, Mark Brandenburg, Nr. 5.3.1.

35. Otto (Berger's Staff), "FS, Nr. 20563," Nov. 10, 1944, BA-Ko, NS 12, Nr. 1147; RFSS/BdE Beauftragter für Bewaffnung und Ausrüstung des Dt. Vs. SS, Standartenführer Purucker, "Besprechungsnotiz," Nov. 30, 1944, T-81/94/108063; Berger, "Anweisung 1/45," Jan. 5, 1945, in OKW/WFSt/Org. III, "FS Nr. 117/45," Feb. 12, 1945, T-77/783/5571437.

36. Keitel to Bormann, "WFSt/Qu. 3(Wi) Nr. 0824/45 geh.," Feb. 15, 1945, T-77/790/5518384; "WFSt/Qu. 2(I)/3(Wi) Nr. 1473/45 geh.," Mar. 2, 1945, T-77/790/5518376–77.

37. Hitler, "Abschrift von Führererlaß," Mar. 1, 1945," in Generalbevollmächtigter für die Reichsverwaltung, "RS II RV 8054/45g-518," Mar. 18, 1945, LA Magdeburg, Rep. C 20 Ib XV: RVK, Nr. 3384.

38. Speer, "FS M2977/44g," Oct. 17, 1944, BA-Ko, R 3, Nr. 1585, 96; Lippe Krltr., "Schreiben," Mar. 19, 1945, StA Detmold, L113, Nr. 1023, 42.

39. RMfRuK/RüStab Italien to Botschafter Dr. Rahn, "Schreiben & Anlage," Nov. 28, 1944, T-77/790/5519097–100; Berger to Karl Wolff, "Schreiben," Dec. 29, 1944, T-81/94/107962–63.

40. Generalbeauftragter RüStab Italien, "Kauf- und Finanzierungsprogram für Volkssturm Ostpreußen," Nov. 28, 1944, T-77/790/5519097–9100; OKW/WFSt/QM Abt. III(Wi), "Entwurf von FS Nr. 557/45, geh.," Jan. 25, 1945, T-77/790/5518396; Berger, Schieber (RMfRuK), Frank (OKH), Haylen (RWM), "Richtlinien für Volkssturm-Einkäufe," Feb. 2, 1945, T-77/790/5518391–93.

41. Schieber to Botschafter Rahn, "Schreiben," Nov. 30, 1944, T-77/790/5519090–94; OKW/WFSt/QM Abt. III(Wi), "Bericht," Jan. 6, 1945, T-77/790/5519046–48.

42. Speer, "FS 426," Jan. 20, 1945, T-81/95/109868.

43. Purucker, "Meldung," Feb. 10, 1945, T-81/94/107884–86.

44. Stigler, "Waffenmeldungen," Jan. 15 and Feb. 17, 1945, T-580/872/799a/1; OKH GenStdH/GenQM, Abt. Feldzeug In. Abt. 4 B/g(2), "FS, Az: 72a/n 60/83 Beute," Jan. 23, 1945, T-81/94/107906–7.

45. Koch, "Abschrift von RS BrB. Nr. 48/44, geh.," Oct. 10, 1944, T-581/6/151; IX AK Ia, "Meldung Nr. 4006/44, geh.," Nov. 11, 1944, T-313/326/8606409–10; Kissel, "Allgemeine Anordnung Nr. 2, VoTgb. Nr. 1312/44," Dec. 11, 1944, T-580/53/285; SHAEF G-2 Div., Combined Intelligence Objectives Subcommittee, Artillery and Weapons, "Report CIOS Target No. 2/637: Visit to Thuringia Small Arms Industry," Sept. 14, 1945, 3, copy in the author's possession via StA Meiningen, Außenstelle Suhl.

46. Reichsschatzmeister Franz X. Schwarz, "Vermerk," Oct. 4, 1944, T-580/815/243/88, teil 2; SA Sturmführer Cammin to Himmler, "Schreiben," Jan. 31, 1945, BA-Ko, NS 19, Nr. 668.

47. Berger, "FS, VsTgb. Nr. 6669/44, VoTgb. Nr. 133/44, geh.," Nov. 9, 1944, T-175/122/2648034.

48. Berger, "Anweisung Nr. 2," Oct. 28, 1944, T-175/122/2648017–19; Stigler, "FS Nr. 93," Jan. 21, 1945, StA Bamberg, M30, Nr. 836; Reichsschatzmeisterstab, "Vermerk von Telefongespräch," Jan. 26, 1945, T-580/830/252/221.

49. OKW/WFSt/QM 2 (I), "FS Nr. 1318/45, geh." Feb. 23, 1945, BA-MA, RW 4, Nr. 709, Teil II, 186.

50. OKH/GenStdH/GenQM Abt. I/A2, "FS Nr. I/3205/45, geh.," Jan. 24, 1945, T-77/790/5518405; Waldemar Magunia, "Der Volkssturm in Ostpreußen," BA-Ko, Ost Dok 8/592; Petzel, Ost Dok 8/402.

51. Zivilingenieur Franz Albrecht to Himmler, "Schreiben und Anlage," Nov. 10, 1944, BA-MA, RH 14, Nr. 3, 6–15.

52. Bock, "RS 585/45," Feb. 22, 1945, T-81/95/109288–90.

53. Speer, "Reisebericht," Nov. 1, 1944, BA-Ko, R 3, Nr. 1541, 4–25.

54. Explosives experimentation was also condemned as too dangerous. OKH RüStab Geräteaktion, "Schreiben BrB. Nr. 113/44, geh.," Dec. 20, 1944, T-81/94/108000–8001; Speer, "Abschrift von RS," undated, T-81/94/107974–75.

55. Sauckel to Bormann, "FS 1464," Oct. 23, 1944, T-580/872/799a/4.

56. Speer, "Besprechung beim Führer am 12 Okt. 1944," Oct. 13, 1944, T-77/10/721409–21; Speer, "RS TAE Nr. 9910614/44 & 9910682/44, geh.," Oct. 30 and 31,

1944, T-77/776/5502774–75 and 5502764–65; Speer, "Pünkte aus Führerbesprechung in den Zeit vom 1 bis 4 Nov. 44," Nov. 5, 1944, T-77/10/721394–408.

57. Speer, "Vermerk," Dec. 8, 1944, T-580/872/799a/1; "Niederschrift," Dec. 17, 1944, T-81/94/108005–7; Bormann, "RS 460/ 44, geh.," Dec. 19, 1944, T-580/53/285.

58. Purucker to Speer, "Besprechung über Volkssturmbewaffnung bei HDL Saur," Nov. 30, 1944, T-81/95/109869; Purucker, "SSD FS," Dec. 27, 1944, T-81/94/107976.

59. Terry Gander and Peter Chamberlain, *Weapons of the Third Reich* (Garden City, N.Y.: Doubleday, 1979), 15, 31, 36–37, 56, 65; Walter Harold Black Smith and James Smith, *The Book of Rifles* (Harrisburg, Pa.: Stackpole, 1963), 227.

60. RMfRuK Hauptausschuß Waffen/Zentrale Planungsstelle, "Mindesmonatsausstoß," Mar. 21, 1945, T-73/2/1047072; SHAEF G-2 Div., CIOS, "Thuringia Small Arms Industry," Sept. 14, 1945, 3, photocopy in author's possession via StA Meiningen, Außenstelle Suhl; RMfRuK Hauptausschuß Waffen/Zentrale Planungsstelle to Purucker, "Schreiben," Dec. 28, 1944, T-81/94/107970; RMfRuK RüAmt, Abt. Arbeitseinsatz Wirtschaft, "Schreiben," Jan. 25, 1945, BA-Ko, R 3, Nr. 1814, 46.

61. Beauftragte für das Munitionsprogramm, "FS B 257.1.45 Gr/B," Jan. 26, 1945, T-81/94/107909; Speer to Saur, "FS," Jan. 20, 1945, T-81/95/109868.

62. Bock, "RS 585/45," Feb. 22, 1945, T-81/95/109283–90.

63. Purucker, "Waffen und Munitionsmeldung," Feb. 10, 1945, T-81/94/107884–86; Speer, "Rede," Apr. 10, 1945, T-77/10/721851–66.

64. Krltg. Neustadt an der Aisch, "Meldung 11665/44–V/R," Dec. 12, 1944, T-580/933/799b/108; SHAEF Psychological Warfare Div., Intelligence Sec., "Rept. Nr. 120239, PW Interrogations in Brauweiler and Königsdorf [Königsau?]," Mar. 5, 1945, NA, RG 226, Box 1336.

65. Schwandorf Krstbfü., "RS 3/45," Jan. 22, 1945, StA Amberg, NSDAP Krltg. Schwandorf, Nr. 6; Calau Krstbfü., "Anordnung Nr. 18," date illegible, 1945, LHA Potsdam, PrBrRep. 61, Mark Brandenburg, Nr. 5.3.1.

66. Purucker, "Waffen und Munitionsmeldung," Feb. 10, 1945, T-81/94/107886.

67. E.g., Btnfü., 2. VsBtn. Rötz, "Btn. Befehl 4/44," Dec. 28, 1944, StA Amberg, NSDAP Krltg. Oberviechtach, Nr. 5.

68. Stigler, "Befehl," Nov. 9, 1944, and "RS 5/45," Jan. 2, 1945, both in BA-Ko, NS 12, Nr. 1147; Führer der Abt. Ausbildung bei Gstbfü. Hessen-Nassau, "Rahmenausbildung für Februar 1945," Jan. 13, 1945, HStA Wiesbaden, Abt. 483, Nr. 6462.

69. SA Gruppe Hansa, "Schreiben," Nov. 23, 1944, BA-Ko, NS 23, Nr. 21; Stigler, "RS 47/45," Dec. 11, 1944, T-580/872/799a/2; Kissel, "Allgemeine Anordnung Nr. 1/45, VoTgb. Nr. 181/45," Jan. 8, 1945, BA-Ko, NS 12, Nr. 1147.

70. Btnfü., 2. VsBtn. Rötz, "Btn. Befehl 4/44," Dec. 28, 1944, StA Amberg, NSDAP Krltg. Oberviechtach, Nr. 5; Calau Krstbfü., "RS," Jan. 24, 1945, LHA Potsdam, PrBrRep. 61, Mark Brandenburg, Nr. 5.3.1; Bonn Krstbfü., "Kreisstabsbefehl Nr. 11," Feb. 25, 1944, T-81/95/109904.

71. U.S. VII Corps, "G-2 Periodic Report #79," Mar. 20, 1945, in U.S. 1st Inf. Div. "G-2 Journal," NA, RG 407, Entry 427, Box 5746.

72. SHAEF Psychological Warfare Div., Intelligence Sec., "Rept. 119983: The Volkssturm in Action," Mar. 15, 1945, NA, RG 226, Box 1334; Kofü, 7. VsKomp.

Rötz, "Schießliste," Jan. 21, 1945, StA Amberg, NSDAP Krltg. Oberviechtach, Nr. 5.

73. Otto Albrecht, "Bericht," Mar. 15, 1945, BA-Ko, R 138 II, Nr. 7, 192–94.

74. Verwaltungschef der SA, "Verfügung," Dec. 5, 1944, BA-Ko, NS 23, Nr. 121; Keitel, "Entwurf von Schreiben," Jan. 26, 1945, T-77/789/5517839; United States War Department, *Handbook on German Military Forces: War Department Technical Manual TM-E30-454* (Washington, D.C.: U.S. Government Printing Office, 1945), sec. IX, 20.

75. U.S. 16th Inf. Regt., "S-2 Interrogation Rept.," Mar. 1, 1945, in U.S. 1st Inf. Div., "G-2 Journal, 1–3 Mar. 1945," NA, RG 407, Entry 427, Box 5741; Franz Seidler, *"Deutscher Volkssturm": Das letzte Aufgebot 1944/45* (Munich: Herbig, 1989), picture 79.

76. Magdeburg Landeswirtschaftsamt Oberpräsident, "Schnellbrief, LWA V/5-2859/44g-Kö," Oct. 28, 1944, LA Magdeburg, Rep. C 20 Ib XV: RVK, Nr. 3384; Oberste SA Führung, "Vermerk, FO 2b Nr. 13704 Sch Hö," Nov. 1, 1944, BA-Ko, NS 23, Nr. 26.

77. Magunia, Ost Dok 8/592; Hanns Baron Freytag von Loringhoven, *Das letzte Aufgebot des Teufels* (Nuremberg: self-published, 1965), 32.

78. Bormann, "Anordnung 11/45," Jan. 26, 1945, T-81/94/108081–82; Lippe Krltr., "Schreiben," Feb. 22, 1945, StA Detmold, L113, Nr. 954, 3.

79. Regierungspräsident, Landeswirtschaftsrat Fürth, "RS, 387/44," Oct. 27, 1944, BA-Ko, NS 12, Nr. 1147.

80. Bormann, "Anordnung 422/44," Nov. 30, 1944, T-580/53/285; Franken Gauschatzmeister, "RS" Feb. 20, 1945, StA Nuremberg, 503 Gltg., Nr. 139; Leiter des Arbeitsamts Memmingen, "Bericht," Apr. 3, 1945, T-73/110/3268741.

81. Btnfü., VsBtn. 34/19 to Feig, "Schreiben," Mar. 12, 1945; Feig to Btnfü., VsBtn. 34/19, "Schreiben IVa 75/1 Mü/Ho," Mar. 28, 1945, HStA Weimar, Reichstatthalter, Nr. 479, 1–2 and 6–7, respectively.

82. Bormann, "Anordnungen 462/44 & 463/44," Dec. 27–28, 1944, T-81/8/16196–97.

83. RMfVuP, Abt. Presse, "RS Nr. II/1/45," Jan. 6, 1945, T-84/167/1534745; Herford Kreisorganisationsamtsleiter, "RS," Jan. 10, 1945, StA Detmold, Sammelbestand M 15, Nr. 1; Hauptamt der Ordnungspolizei, "Anordnungen," 3. Jahrgang, Nr. 3, Jan. 11, 1945, BA-Ko, R 19, Nr. 3; SS Oberabschnitt West, "RS II Az 26g Me/Hü," Jan. 22, 1945, T-175/200/2741334.

84. RMfRuK Planungsamt/Arbeitsgebiet Bekleidung und Ausrüstung, "Wochenbericht für die Zeit vom 12.1. bis 18.1. 45, geh.," Jan. 19, 1945, BA-Ko, R 3, Nr. 1957, 745; RMfVuP Chef des Propagandastabs, "Tätigkeitsbericht," Feb. 21, 1945, T-580/682/563.

85. Gltg. Bayreuth, "Durchsage," Jan. 26, 1945, BA-Ko, NS 12, Nr. 1147; HSSuPF Verbindungsoffizier beim RVK Köln-Aachen, "Meldung," Feb. 5, 1945, T-175/224/1762603–8.

86. Herford Krltr., "RS," Jan. 27, 1945, StA Detmold, Sammelbestand M15, Nr. 1; Westfalen-Nord Gauschatzmeister, "RS 3/45," Feb. 5, 1945, StA Detmold, Sammelbestand M15, Nr. 306.

87. Kissel, "FS VsTgb. Nr. 8168/44, VoTgb. Nr. 465/44, geh.," Dec. 4, 1944, T-580/53/285; U.S. 3rd Armored Div., "G-2 Periodic Rept. #244," Feb. 27, 1945, NA, RG 407, Entry 427, Box 15063; U.S. 16th Inf. Regt., "S-2 Interrogation Rept.," Mar. 1, 1945, in U.S. 1st Inf. Div., "G-2 Journal, 1–3 Mar. 1945," NA, RG 407, Entry 427, Box 5741.

88. Kraus, "RS," Oct. 27, 1944, T-580/872/ 799a/2; RüInsp Oberrhein, "Schreiben," Jan. 13, 1945, BA-MA, RW 20–5, Nr. 56; Giesler, "RS," Feb. 7, 1945, StA Munich, NSDAP, Nr. 466c.

89. Teltow Krltr., "Vs. Befehl 15/45," Mar. 2, 1945, LHA Potsdam, PrBrRep. 2A, Regierung Potsdam I Polizei, Nr. 2321.

90. Schulte, "RS IVa/Sch/P/637/45," Feb. 2, 1945, T-81/95/109910; Bayreuth Gauschatzmeister, "RS 12/45," Feb. 19, 1945, T-580/872/799a/1; NSKK Motorsturm Eisenach, "Meldestaffellisten," Mar. 11, 1945, T-81/95/109586–92; Woltersdorf Bürgermeister, "Befehl," Apr. 19, 1945, LHA Potsdam, PrBrRep. 61, Mark Brandenburg, Nr. 5.25.27.

91. Rühle, "RS 13/45, geh.," Feb. 8, 1945, T-81/94/108237–38; Woltersdorf Bürgermeister, "Schreiben," Feb. 19, 1945, LHA Potsdam, PrBrRep. 61, Mark Brandenburg, Nr. 5.25.27.

92. Btnfu., Btn. zbV 2/4, "Bericht," Mar. 1, 1945, BA-Ko, NS 12, Nr. 1147; Lippe Krltr. to Kofü. Kellner, "Schreiben," Mar. 19, 1945, StA Detmold, L113, Nr. 1023, 42.

93. Burst, "Stabsbefehl Nr. 4, BrB. Nr. 135/44, geh.," Nov. 22, 1944, T-81/93/107794.

94. On propaganda shortages, see Dechant, "Schreiben," Feb. 12, 1945, T-580/923/40; on Party largesse, see Franken Gauschatzmeister, "RS," Nov. 2, 1944, and Jan. 24 and Feb. 20, 1945, both in StA Nuremberg, 503 Gltg., Nr. 139.

95. AOK 4, Ia, "Anlagen zum KTB: Einzelheiten zum Ia Tagesmeldung," Nov. 18, 1944, T-312/254/7811700–701.

96. British XXX Corps, "Intelligence Summary Nr. 625," Mar. 27, 1945, in U.S. 1st Inf. Div., "G-2 Journal, 28–31 Mar. 1945," NA, RG 407, Entry 427, Box 5747.

97. U.S. 3rd Armored Div., "G-2 Periodic Rept. Nr. 253," Mar. 8, 1945, NA, RG 407, Entry 427, Box 15063.

98. On morale, see USSBS, "The Effects of Strategic Bombing on Morale," in *The United States Strategic Bombing Survey*, vol. 1, ed. David MacIsaac (New York: Garland, 1976), 13–16, 50–52, 96–97; Ian Kershaw, *Popular Opinion and Political Dissent in the Third Reich: Bavaria 1933–1945* (Oxford: Clarendon, 1983), 382–85; Kershaw, *Der Hitler-Mythos: Volksmeinung und Propaganda im Dritten Reich* (Stuttgart: Deutsche Verlags-Anstalt, 1980), 90–91.

99. Clearly, many of these men would have been required to serve in the Volkssturm anyway; Ennepe-Ruhr Krstbfü., "Freiwilligenmeldung," Dec. 20, 1944, T-81/94/108565.

100. Krltg. Freiburg im Breisgau, "Stimmungsbericht," Oct. 31, 1944, BA-Ko, NS 6, Nr. 812; RPA Westfalen-Süd, "Tätigkeitsbericht," Nov. 14, 1944, T-580/683/563, pt. 2; OLGP Stettin, "Lagebericht 313 Ea-5–30g," Dec. 1, 1944, BA-Ko, R 22, Nr. 3386, 20–22; OLGP Leitmeritz/Sudetenland, "Lagebericht 3130-12-168," Dec. 5, 1944, BA-Ko, R 22, Nr. 3376, 139–41.

101. WK III, Abt. II/Wehrmachtpropaganda, "8. Bericht über den Sondereinsatz Berlin," Dec. 9, 1944, T-77/1037/6509530–34.

102. Kofü. Gerke, "Das Schicksal der Volkssturm Kompanie XXIII/482/4, Oppeln," in Pietsch, Ost Dok 10/812.

103. Schäffer, "Tätigkeitsbericht," Nov. 14, 1944, T-580/682/563; Krltg. Freiburg im Breisgau, "Bericht, lfd. Beitrags Nr. 1," Nov. 14, 1944, T-81/163/302155.

104. RPA Breslau, "FS Nr. 14501; Bericht," Oct. 20, 1944, T-580/657/449, pt. 2.

105. Karlsruhe Krstbfü, "Vereidigungsfeier," Feb. 11, 1945, GLA Karlsruhe, Best. 465d, Nr. 1362; Wehrmachtstandortältester Jüterbog, "Befehl," Mar. 10, 1945, BA-MA, RW 17, Nr. 28.

106. Dechant, "RS," Jan. 17, 1945, StA Nuremberg, 503 Gltg., Nr. 127.

107. Friedrichs to Bormann, "FS 933," Oct. 11, 1944, BA-Ko, NS 6, Nr. 313, 143–46; Bormann, "RS 383/44," Nov. 6, 1944, T-580/17/180; Bormann, "Anordnung 1/45," Jan. 5, 1945, T-580/53/285.

108. Bayreuth Gauschulungsleiter, "RS 1/45," Jan. 12, 1945, T-580/872/799/1; Dechant, "RS," Jan. 17, 1945, StA Nuremberg, 503 Gltg., Nr. 127; Zauch-Belzig Kreisschulungsleiter, "Schulungsanweisung DV Nr. 1," undated, LHA Potsdam, PrBrRep. 61, Mark Brandenburg, Nr. 5.17.1; Ernst von Salomon, *Der Fragebogen* (Stuttgart: Europäisches Buchklub, 1951), 508.

109. Bayreuth Gauschulungsleiter, "RS 1/45," Jan. 12, 1945, T-580/872/799/1.

110. RMfVuP "Deutsche Wochenschau" no. 738, Oct. 26; no. 740–41, Nov. 9–16, 1944; no. 748–55, Jan. 11–Mar. 23, 1945; originals in the Bundesarchiv-Filmabteilung.

111. Schäffer to Goebbels, "Schreiben," Oct. 16, 1944, BA-Ko, R55, Nr. 624; Bormann, "Anordnung 358/44," Oct. 30, 1944, T-81/1/11260; "RS 383/44," Nov. 6, 1944, T-580/17/180; SS Brigadeführer Bernt to Himmler, "Abschrift von Anregung," Nov. 16, 1944, BA-Ko, NS 19 neu, Nr. 839.

112. See chapter 2 for details.

113. Purported American atrocities were usually rapes, individual murders, and plundering, with black troops often portrayed as the culprits. Soviet atrocity reports often featured wholesale massacres of soldiers and civilians alike. RMfVuP, Chef des Propagandastabes, "Material für Propagandisten," various dates, BA-Ko, R 55, Nr. 793, 1–30; WK XIII NSFO, "Propagandahinweis," Nov. 11, 1944, BA-MA, RH 53-13, Nr. 154, 29.

114. At least six, and possibly seven, Volkssturm men won the Knight's Cross; Gerhard von Seemen, *Die Ritterkreuzträger 1939–1945* (Friedberg: Podzun-Pallas, 1976), 164, 170, 254, 259, 320, 339, 379. Also see Berlin Gaupropagandaleiter, "Vertrauliches RS 10/45," Jan. 30, 1945, LHA Potsdam, PrBrRep. 61, Berlin, Nr. 14.4.5; WK IX, NSFO, "Führungshinweis Nr. 6, Nr. 908/45," Feb. 20, 1945, T-84/161/1529297.

115. Genltn. Dittmar, "Abschrift von Rundfunkzvortrag," Oct. 24, 1944, in OKW/West/Amtsgruppe Wehrmachtpropaganda, "Schreiben," Nov. 9, 1944, T-84/160/1527248–31.

116. WK III, Abt. II/Wehrmachtpropaganda, "5. Bericht," Nov. 12, 1944, T-77/1037/6509518–20; RPA Lüneburg, "Bericht," Feb. 19, 1945, T-580/656/448.

117. SD Leitabschnitt Stuttgart, "Stimmungsbericht," Nov. 8, 1944, T-81/95/ 109117–22; RPA Lüneburg, "Stimmungsbericht," Jan. 29, 1945, BA-Ko, R55, Nr. 603, 104.

118. Tirol-Vorarlberg Gltr. Franz Hofer, "FS 98," Oct. 24, 1944, T-580/872/ 799a/4.

119. Swedish Military Attaché, "Bericht Nr. 745," Nov. 17, 1944, BA-Ko, R58, Nr. 107, 112–13.

120. NSFO Flakregt. 15 (mot.), "Abschrift von Führungshinweise," Nov. 24, 1944, T-84/160/15266898.

121. Schäffer to Goebbels, "Tätigkeitsbericht," Nov. 14, 1944, T-580/682/563; Coburg Krstbfü, "Bericht," Dec. 28, 1944, BA-Ko, NS 12, Nr. 1147; Fürstenfeldbruck Landwirtschaftsrat, "Bericht," Jan. 4, 1945, StA Munich, NSDAP, Nr. 466c.

122. Kofü., 3. Komp., VsBtn. Steinwiesen, "Bericht," Dec. 20, 1944, BA-Ko, NS 12, Nr. 1147.

123. WK III, Abt. II/Wehrmachtpropaganda "6. Bericht über den Sondereinsatz Berlin," Nov. 21, 1944, and Mar. 3, 1945, T-77/1037/6509521–24 and 6509411–27; RPA Innsbruck, "Bericht," Dec. 4, 1944, T-580/656/449, teil 1; Krltr. Bayreuth, "Wochenbericht 47," Dec. 16, 1944, StA Bamberg, M33, Nr. 631; Gendarmerie Posten Anger, "Monatsbericht für März," Mar. 19, 1945, StA Munich, LRA Berchtesgaden, Nr. 29656; Johannes Martini, "Das Volkssturmbattailon Cosel," BA-Ko, Ost Dok 10/790.

124. W. A. Francke to RMfVuP, "Schreiben," undated, T-580/655/441.

125. Willy Timm, *Freikorps "Sauerland" 1944–45: Zur Geschichte des Zweiten Weltkriegs in Südwestfalen* (Hagen: Stadtarchiv Hagen, 1976).

126. RPA Dessau, "Stimmungsbericht," Jan. 15, 1944, BA-Ko, R55, Nr. 603, 82.

127. Schäffer, "Tätigkeitsbericht," Nov. 14, 1944, T-580/682/563; Joseph Goebbels, *Die Tagebücher von Joseph Goebbels*, pt. 2, *Diktate, 1942–1945*, vol. 14, ed. Elke Fröhlich (Munich: K. G. Saur, 1995), 192.

128. The validity of this charge is difficult to assess, but the perception was widespread; see Friedrichs, "RS 12/45," Jan. 26, 1945, T-81/94/108083–84; Wolfstein Leitender Arzt, "Monatsbericht, Feb. 1945," Mar. 3, 1945, BA-Ko, NS 12, Nr. 1147.

129. RPA Niederdonau, "Ausschnitt vom Stimmungsbericht," Feb. 5, 1945, T-580/656/449, teil 1; Landratsamt Mährisch Schönberg, "Abschrift von Bericht," Feb. 17, 1945, BA-Ko, NS 6, Nr. 135.

130. WK III, Abt. II/Wehrmachtpropaganda, "16. Bericht über den Sondereinsatz Berlin," Feb. 1, 1945, T-77/1037/6509465–69; RPA Troppau, "Ausschnitt von Stimmungsbericht," Jan. 29, 1945, T-580/656/449, teil 1; SD Außenstelle Lörrach, "Stimmungs- und Meinungsbildung Bericht," Mar. 14, 1945, T-175/512/9378538–41.

131. RPA Nürnberg, "Stimmungsbericht," Jan. 23, 1945, BA-Ko, R55, Nr. 603, 99; RPA Dresden, "Stimmungsbericht," Feb. 5, 1945, T-580/656/449.

132. Schwede-Coburg to Bormann, "FS 594/44," Oct. 6, 1944, BA-Ko, NS 6, Nr. 313, 109; Emden Propagandaleiter to Goebbels, "Schreiben," Dec. 12, 1944, T-580/ 656/448.

133. WK III, Abt. II/Wehrmachtpropaganda, "19. Bericht über den Sondereinsatz Berlin," Feb. 23, 1945, T-77/1037/6509428–43.

134. SD Senica, "FS Nrs. 337 & 461: Tägliche Berichterstattungen," Feb. 19 and Mar. 5, 1945, both in T-175/553/9428992–95.

135. NSFO, WK VII, "Führerspruch Nr. 4," Feb. 13, 1945, T-84/160/1527024; RPA Bayreuth, "RS," Feb. 2, 1945, T-580/872/799a/1.

136. Kampfkommandant Ansbach, "Lagemeldung," Apr. 8, 1945, BA-MA, RH 30, Nr. 48; Salzburg Gltr. Gustav Adolph Scheel, "Lagebericht," Apr. 10, 1945, T-580/43/VIII/248.

137. Kofü., 2. Komp., VsBtn. 19/XVI, (München-Ost), "Meldungen" Dec. 17, 1944, Jan. 7 and 21, 1945, T-81/153/1056295, 1056315–16.

138. Luftwaffe Bekleidungsamt 1/71, "Schreiben," Jan. 12, 1945, StA Detmold, L113, Nr. 1023, 33; Stigler to Regensburg RB Präsident, "Schreiben," Mar. 27, 1945, StA Bamberg, M30, Nr. 836.

139. Kofü., 1. Komp., VsBtn. 40/12, "Meldung," Nov. 16, 1944, LA Saarbrücken, NSDAP Mischbestand, Nr. 22, 1; Kr. Wolfstein Leitender Arzt, "Monatsbericht, Feb. 1945," Mar. 3, 1945, BA-Ko, NS 12, Nr. 1147.

140. U.S. 89th Inf. Div., "G-2 Periodic Rept. #16," Mar. 20, 1945, NA, RG 407, Entry 427, Box 13224; U.S. 4th Armored Div., "G-2 Special Rept. #14," Oct. 26, 1944, NA, RG 407, Entry 427, Box 15184.

141. OSS, "Report 113180: Captured German Documents on Alsatian Volkssturm," NA, RG 226, Box 1248; *Tagebücher von Goebbels*, pt. 2, vol. 14, 233, 340–41.

142. Oberbefehlshaber der Marine, "Tagesniederschrift," May 3, 1945, BA-MA, RM 6, Nr. 375, 8; Radomir V. Luza, *The Resistance in Austria 1938–1945* (Minneapolis: University of Minnesota Press, 1984), 173, 224–25; Otto Molden, *Der Ruf des Gewissens: Der Österreichische Freiheitskampf 1938–1945* (Vienna: Herold, 1958), 245, 254.

143. Regierungspräsident Regensburg, "Monatsbericht Nr. VS 382g," Dec. 12, 1944, T-175/67/2582955–64; Generalstaatsanwalt Oldenburg, "Lagebericht, 3E 47/45 geh.," Feb. 5, 1945, BA-Ko, R 22, Nr. 3382, 54; Heike Bretschneider, *Der Widerstand gegen den Nationalsozialismus in München 1933 bis 1945* (Munich: Stadtarchiv München, 1968), 213; Martin Broszat, Elke Fröhlich, Anton Grossman, and Falk Wiesemann, *Bayern in der NS Zeit: Herrschaft und Gesellschaft im Konflikt,* vol. 1 (Munich: R. Oldenbourg, 1977), 679.

144. WK III, Abt. II/Wehrmachtpropaganda, "3. Bericht über den Sondereinsatz Berlin," Nov. 3, 1944, T-77/1037/6509512–14; Herbert Schwarzwälder, *Bremen und Nordwestdeutschland am Kriegsende 1945,* vol. 2 (Bremen: Carl Schünemann, 1973), 200.

145. On sabotage, see Helmut Bomm, "Die Backnanger Widerstand gegen die Nazis vor dem Einmarsch der Amerikaner am 20. April 1945," *Beiträge zur Geschichte der Stadt Backnang* 5 (1986): 154–68; on overall importance, see USSBS, European War Morale Div., "Rept. 64 b/t(8), Size and Composition of Anti-Nazi Opposition in Germany," NA, RG 243, Entry 6/7, Box 7.

146. Giesler, "Rundfunk Rede," Apr. 28, 1945, T-77/1051/6526518; Bretschneider, 225–39; Broszat et al., vol. 4, 374–80, 660–77.

8. Defending the Reich's Eastern Front

1. 3 PzAOK Stabschef Burckhardt Müller-Hillebrand, "Ia FS Nr. 10144/44, geh.," Oct. 18, 1944, T-313/324/8604684; Stürtz, "Rundspruch Nr. 110," Feb. 1, 1945, LHA Potsdam, PrBrRep. 61, Mark Brandenburg, Nr. 2.1.475.

2. Berger to Himmler, "GKdos. VsTgb. Nr. 196/45, VoTgb. 50/45," Feb. 9, 1945, NS 19, Nr. 3834.

3. Some have criticized the Volkssturm for increasing refugee hardships by leaving women, children, the elderly, and the infirm to flee alone; see Kurt Dieckert and Horst Grossmann, *Der Kampf um Ostpreußen: Der umfassende Dokumentarbericht über das Kriegsgeschehen in Ostpreußen* (Stuttgart: Motorbuch, 1976), 120. On the Volkssturm and evacuation, see Landrat des Kr. Samter, "Bericht," Feb. 23, 1945, BA-Ko, R 138 II, Nr. 7, 20–21; HG Mitte, OberQM Abt IVa/Qu. 2, "Befehl Nr. 16724/44, geh.," Nov. 16, 1944, T-311/229/1285–86.

4. WK I, "Ia FS Nrs. 3708, 3974, 3984, & 3995/44, geh.," Dec. 12 and 18 , 1944, T-311/218/3 and 12; Befehlshaber im Heeresgebiet GG, "Ia/Ic Tagesmeldung, Nr. 610/45, geh.," Jan. 11, 1945, T-501/218/1284; Oberltn. Gutjahr & Uffz. Burgel, "Berichte," Feb. 6 and 9, 1945, T-580/78/XIII/366; Btnfü., VsBtn. 16/374 (Ludwigsfelde), "Btn. Befehl 6/45," Feb. 12, 1945, LHA Potsdam, PrBrRep. 2A, Regierung Potsdam I Polizei, Nr. 2321; Fritz Brustat-Naval, *Unternehmung Rettung: Letztes Schiff nach Westen* (Herford: Kohler, 1970), 201.

5. 3 PzAOK OB, Gen. Erhard Raus, "Notizen zur Fahrt," Nov. 22, 1944, T-313/326/8606537; Kriminalpolizeistelle Magdeburg, "Anordnung," Mar. 16, 1945, LA Magdeburg, C30 Osterburg A, Nr. 1315; Kofü., 3. Komp., VsBtn. 16/122 (Kr. Eberswalde), "Komp. Befehl Nr. 24/45," Apr. 19, 1945, LHA Potsdam, PrBrRep. 61, Mark Brandenburg, Nr. 2.1.474.

6. Krltr. Wagner to PzAOK 3, OpAbt. (Ia), "Fernspruch," Oct. 7, 1944, T-313/323/8603552; HG Nord, Ia, "KTB entry," Oct. 10, 1944, BA-MA, RH 19 III, Nr. 330, 192; HG Mitte, "Ia Tagesmeldung für 22.10.44, Nr. 5433/44, geh.," Oct. 23, 1944, BA-MA, RH 20-9, Nr. 223; Dieckert and Grossmann, 48–50, 52, 55, 96.

7. Fallschirm Pzkorps Hermann Göring, Sturm Btn. "KTB Nr. 1," Oct. 22, 1944, entry, BA-MA, RL 32, Nr. 52, 34; Koch, "FS 225 & 229," Oct. 25–26, 1944, both in T-580/872/799a/4; AOK 4, Ia, "Lagekarten," Oct. 21–23 and 25, 1944, T-312/258/7816312–34; WK I, Wehrwirtschaftsoffizier, "Tätigkeitsbericht für die Zeit 1–31. Okt. 1944, Nr. 205/44, geh.," Nov. 6, 1944, T-77/499/1665530–44; Constanz von Jaraczewski, "Der Volkssturm des Kreises Angerapp (Darkehmen)," BA-Ko, Ost Dok 10/111.

8. AOK 4, Chief of Staff Dethleffsen, "Ia FS Nr. 2164/44, geh.," Oct. 31, 1944, T-312/256/7813351.

9. OKW, "Bericht," Oct. 26, 1944, T-312/254/7810689–91; Bruno Just, "KTB vom Volkssturm Einsatz Btn. Goldap 25/235," BA-Ko, Ost Dok 8/600; Dieckert and Grossmann, 57–71.

10. Koch, "Abschrift von Befehl Nr. 16, BrB. Nr. 108/44, Kgeh.," Oct. 29, 1944, T-581/151/16.

11. Gltg. Ostpreußen, "Abschrift von Meldekopf," Oct. 30, 1944, T-581/6/151; PzAOK 3, "Ia FS Nr. 11399/44, geh.," Nov. 19, 1944, T-313/326/8606407–8; HG Mitte Ia, "Ferngespräche," Dec. 22, 1944, T-312/258/7815847; AOK 4 OB Gen. Friedrich Hossbach, "Erinnerungen," BA-MA, Nachlaß Hoßbach N 24, Nr. 39, ch. ix, 36.

12. PzAOK 3, "Ia FS Nr. 11399/44, geh.," Nov. 19, 1944, T-313/326/8606407–8; Hossbach, "Ia FS Nrs. 2388 & 9717/44, geh.," Nov. 20 and 27, 1944, T-312/256/

7814143 and 7813784–85; Hossbach, "Ia Befehl Nr. 2422/44, geh.," Nov. 23, 1944, T-313/256/7814079.

13. XXXX PzKorps, "Ia FS Nr. 1991/44, geh.," Nov. 16, 1944, T-313/326/8606346; Raus, "Fahrtnotizen," Nov. 26, 1944, T-313/326/8606761–62; Dethleffsen, "Ia FS Nr. 24440/44, geh.," Nov. 24, 1944, T-312/256/7814042; IX AK, "Entwurf von Ia FS 3952/44, geh.," Nov. 7, 1944, T-314/436/1412.

14. Raus, "Notizen zur Fahrt," Nov. 1, 1944, T-313/325/8605500–582; Sicherheitspolizei/SD Sonderkommando 7b, "Meldung," Dec. 28, 1944, T-312/256/7813126–30.

15. Müller-Hillebrand, "FS," Dec. 20, 1944, T-313/327/8607719.

16. HöhArtKdo 313, "Ia FS Nr. 4261/44, geh.," Dec. 2, 1944, T-313/326/8607046. Also IX AK Ia, "Bericht Nr. 4430/44, geh.," Dec. 10, 1944, T-313/327/8607400–401.

17. These units were equipped with captured cannon. Guderian, "OKH/GenStdH/Org.Abt. Nr. I GKdos. Nr. 20377/44," Nov. 13, 1944, T-78/418/6387936–40; Guderian, "OKH/GenStdH/OpAbt/Abt. Landesbefestigung, GKdos. Nr. 13483/44," Dec. 25, 1944, T-78/338/6294818–19.

18. The mobilization included 90 East Prussian, 32 Wartheland, 24 Silesian, 20 General Government, and 10 Danzig–West Prussian Volkssturm battalions. OKH/GenStdH/Op/Abt. Landesbefestigung, "GKdos. Nr. 3021/45," Jan. 16, 1945, T-78/411/6379182–86; Befehlshaber im WK XXI, "Besetzung der B-1 Linie, Anlage 7 zum KTB," Jan. 19, 1945, BA-MA, RH 53-21, Nr. 15, 23–26.

19. Useful overviews include John Erickson, *Stalin's War with Germany*, 2 vols. (Boulder, Colo.: Westview, 1975–1983); David M. Glantz and Jonathan M. House, *When Titans Clashed: How the Red Army Stopped Hitler* (Lawrence: University Press of Kansas, 1995); Earl F. Ziemke, *Stalingrad to Berlin: The German Defeat in the East* (Washington, D.C.: Office of the Chief of Military History, 1968). More specific works are Dieckert and Grossmann; Heinz Magenheimer, *Abwehrschlacht an der Weichsel 1945: Vorbereitung, Ablauf, Erfahrungen* (Freiburg: Rombach, 1976); Hans von Ahlfen, *Der Kampf um Schlesien: Ein authentischer Dokumentarbericht* (Munich: Gräfe und Unser, 1961); and Erich Murawski, *Die Eroberung Pommerns durch die Rote Armee* (Boppard am Rhein: Harald Boldt, 1969).

20. WK XXI, "Feindlagekarte," Jan. 17–25, 1945, BA-MA, RH 53-21, Nr. 20K, Karte 10; HG A, "Morgenmeldungen," Jan. 22 and 24, 1945, BA-MA, RH 2, Nr. 321, 17–18, 92–97; Kr. Hohensalza Oberinsp., "Bericht," Mar. 21, 1945, BA-Ko, R 138 II, Nr. 7, 209–12; Kommandant, Festung Abschnitt 44 (B-1 Stellung), "Bericht," undated, BA-MA, RH 53-21, Nr. 18, 24–26; Wehrmeldeamt Ostrowo, "Bericht," undated, BA-MA, RH 53-21, Nr. 18, 22–23; Petzel, Ost Dok 8/402; Kissel, MS B-627, 19–20.

21. AOK 4, "Einzelheiten zur Ia Tagesmeldung vom 24.1.45," T-312/260/7818149; AOK 4, "Lagekarten," Jan. 27 and Feb. 3, 1945, T-312/260/781828994 and 262/7820713–16; Kurt Dieckert, "Einsatz von weiteren Einheiten des Heeres, der Waffen SS, Marine, und Luftwaffe," BA-Ko, Ost Dok 10/889.

22. HG Weichsel, "Ia, Lagekarten, GKdos. Nr. 375/44," Jan. 24–Feb. 21, 1945, T-311/171/7222784–958; Murawski, *Pommerns*.

23. HG Süd, "Ia KTB entries," Mar. 29 and 30, 1945," T-311/162/7214818–50.

24. AOK 4, "Einzelheiten zur Ia Tagesmeldung vom 25 & 26.1. 45," T-312/260/7818107–9 and 7818051–52; AOK 4, "Lagekarte," Jan. 27, 1945, T-312/260/7818289–94; Kr. Labiau Oberinsp. Eduard Knuth, "Mein Volkssturmeinsatz 1945," BA-Ko, Ost Dok 8/546; Magunia, Ost Dok 8/592; Kurt Dieckert, "Nachlaßmaterial über den Kampf um Ostpreußen," BA-Ko, Ost Dok 10/887; DRK Suchdienstdir. Max Heinrich, "Gutachten: Volkssturm Heydekrug," Apr. 9, 1972, both BA-MA, DRK Nr. 2; Otto Lasch, *So fiel Königsberg* (Stuttgart: Motorbuch, 1977), 42.

25. Hossbach, "Ia FS Nr. 839/45, geh.," Jan. 19, 1945, T-312/259/7817551.

26. AOK 4, "Ia Lagekarte, GKdos. 014/45," XXVI AK, "Ia Lagekarte, GKdos. 12/45," Jan. 25, 1945, T-312/262/7820686–88; Kurt Dieckert, "Die Einschließung und Belagerung von Königsberg," BA-Ko, Ost Dok 10/890, 86, 141.

27. OKW/WFSt/OrgAbt. (III), "FS Nr. 92/45, geh.," Jan. 8, 1945, T-77/783/5511478; Stürtz, "Rundruf 115," Feb. 2, 1945; Btnfü., VsBtns. 16/138 and 140 (both Finow), "Einsatzmeldungen," Feb. 6, 1945, all in LHA Potsdam, PrBrRep. 61, Mark Brandenburg, Nr. 2.1.475.

28. Teltow Krltr., "Vs. Kreisbefehl Nr. 3/45," Jan. 5, 1945, LHA Potsdam, PrBrRep. 2A I Polizei, Nr. 2321; Wehrmachtstandortälteste Brandenburg, "Befehl Nr. 1, BrB. Nr. 38/45," Feb. 4, 1945, T-84/242/6600911–14.

29. Calau Krltr., "RS 17/45," Feb. 9, 1945, LHA Potsdam, PrBrRep. 61, Mark Brandenburg, Nr. 5.3.1.

30. Landrat Paul Windels, "Militärische Vorbereitungen zum Schütze des Kreisgebietes und Räumung von Stadt und Land Stargard, 1944–45," BA-Ko, Ost Dok 8/674.

31. Wehrmeldeamt Schieratz, "Bericht," undated, BA-MA, RH 53-21, Nr. 18, 21–22.

32. Brandenburg Gausstabsführung, "RS VI Ge/Zü Folge 60/63/45," undated (1945), LHA Potsdam, PrBrRep. 61, Mark Brandenburg, Nr. 2.1.475; NSFO Sonderführer Lichtenberg, "Erfahrungsbericht," Mar. 22, 1945, T-580/78/XIII/366; Rudolf Pratsch, "Bericht über Volkssturm im Kr. Rosenberg, Oberschlesien," BA-Ko, Ost Dok 10/818; Heinrich, "Gutachten: Volkssturm Köslin (Pommern)," Feb. 7, 1972, BA-MA, DRK Nr. 2.

33. Land- und Forstwirt Hans-Jürgen von Wilckens, "Die Räumung und Besetzung der Kreises Zempelburg im Januar 1945," BA-Ko, Ost Dok 8/218.

34. Pratsch, Ost Dok 10/818.

35. Division Denecke, "KTB," reconstructed in 1955, BA-MA, RH 26-1010, Nr. 1; HG Weichsel, "Lagekarten," Jan. 24–Feb. 21, 1945, T-311/171/7222784–958; PzAOK 3, "Tagesmeldung," Feb. 26, 1945, T-311/168/7220167–69; OB AOK 2, "Ferngespräch mit Guderian," Feb. 28, 1945, T-311/168/7220292–93; Generalleutnant F. A. Schack, Kdt. XXXII AK, "Tagesbefehl," Apr. 7, 1945, BA-MA, RH 24-32, Nr. 1, 55; Steiermark Gltr. Sigfried Uiberreither, "Lagebericht," Apr. 16, 1945, T-580/43/VIII/248; Kissel, MS# B-627, 25.

36. HG Weichsel, "Lagekarten," Jan. 24–Feb. 21, 1945, T-311/171/7222784–958; RMfVuP Propagandastab, "Lage der Evakuierung," Feb. 8, 1945, BA-Ko, R 55, Nr. 616, 166–70; Genltn. F. A. Schack, Kdt. XXXII AK, "Tagesbefehl," Apr. 7, 1945, BA-MA, RH 24-32, Nr. 1, 55; XXXII AK, "Vorschlag," Apr. 22, 1945, BA-MA, RH 7, Nr. 310, 351–56; Div. Denecke, "KTB," reconstructed in 1955, BA-MA,

RH 26-1010, Nrs. 1 and 2; Stargard-Saatzig Krltr. Siegfried Schug, "Bericht über die Kreise Stargard-Saatzig und Pyritz," BA-Ko, Ost Dok 8/637.

37. Hitler, "Führerbefehl Nr. 11," Mar. 8, 1944, in *Hitlers Weisungen für die Kriegsführung 1939–1945: Dokumente des Oberkommando der Wehrmacht*, ed. Walter Hubatsch (Frankfurt: Bernhard und Graefe, 1962), 243–50.

38. OKH/GenStdH/AusbAbt. (II), "Entwurf von Nr. 50/45, geh.," Jan. 20, 1945, BA-MA, RH 11 III, Nr. 91, summarizes policies concerning Fortress defense.

39. OKH/GenStdH/Op. Abt./Landesbefestigung head Oberst Thilo, "Bericht," Apr. 6, 1945, BA-MA, RH 2, Nr. 335, 203–6.

40. Schörner, "Abschrift von FS," Feb. 9, 1945, T-78/304/6255683–85; Festungskommandant Gen. Hermann Niehoff, "Erfahrungsbericht, Nr. 1280/45, geh.," Mar. 18, 1945, T-311/9/7009293–303; Hans von Ahlfen and Hermann Niehoff, *So kämpfte Breslau: Verteidigung und Untergang von Schlesiens Hauptstadt* (Munich: Gräfe und Unser, 1961), 14, 25–28.

41. Niehoff, "Erfahrungsberichte, Nrs. 1214/45, geh. & 1280/45, geh.," Mar. 16 and 18, 1945, T-311/9/7009310 and 7009293–303; Niehoff, "GKdos. Nr. 4276/45," Apr. 6, 1945, T-78/305/6256897; OKH/GenStdH/OpAbt. III, "GKdos. Nrs. 4580 & 4702/45," Apr. 14 and 17, 1945, T-78/304/6254961–64 and 6255422–28; Ernst von Schaubert, "Der Volkssturm 68, Obernigk und Umgegend und meine Erlebnisse bei diesen," BA-Ko, Ost Dok Nr. 10/1394; Ahlfen and Niehoff, 25, 29–30, 37–39, 43, 48, 83, 125–27.

42. Bromberg Kreispropagandleiter, "Bericht," Jan. 26, 1945, T-580/670/509, teil 1; SD Abschnitt Lüneburg, "Bericht (on Posen)," Feb. 10, 1945, BA-Ko, R 58, Nr. 976, 105–7.

43. Adolf Klein, "Einsatz des Volkssturms in Königsberg 1945," BA-Ko, Ost Dok 8/598; Dieckert and Grossmann, 151–207; Lasch, *Königsberg*.

44. HG Weichsel, "Ia Tagesmeldung," Mar. 15, 1945, BA-MA, RH 19 XV, Nr. 8, 19; HG Weichsel, "Gefechtsbericht," Mar. 4–18, 1945, in HG KTB Anlagen, T-311/169/7221052–58.

45. Thilo, "Bericht," Apr. 6, 1945, BA-MA, RH 2, Nr. 335, 203–6; HG Weichsel, "Bericht: Durchbruch der 73. ID," undated, T-311/167/7218745–46; OKH/GenStdH/OpAbt. I/N, "Vortragsnotiz," Mar. 8, 1945, T-78/348/6306493; HG Weichsel, "Lagekarten," Jan. 24–Feb. 21, 1945, T-311/171/7222784–958; Volkssturm Btn. Deutsche Werke (Gothenhafen), "KTB," Feb.–Mar. 1945, BA-MA, RH 59, Nr. 3; Oberst Johann Albrecht von Bonin, "Die Festung Schneidemühl im zweiten Weltkrieg: Ausbau und Verteidigung 1944–45," BA-Ko, Ost Dok 8/700; Heinrich, "Gutachten: Volkssturm Danzig," Apr. 5, 1971, BA-MA, DRK Nr. 1; Tony Le Tissier, *Zhukov at the Oder: The Decisive Battle for Berlin* (Westport, Conn.: Praeger, 1996), 96–97.

46. Guderian, "OKH/GenStdH/Org. Abt. Nr. I GKdos. Nr. 20377/44," Nov. 13, 1944, T-78/418/6387936–40; Oberst Eberhard Schöpfer, "Der Kampf um Elbing," BA-Ko, Ost Dok 8/247.

47. Thilo, "Vortragsnotiz: Anruf der Stabschef WK XX," Jan. 27, 1945, BA-MA, RH 2, Nr. 331b, 47; Müller-Hillebrand, "Abschrift von PzAOK 3 Ia Nr. 1905/45, geh.," Mar. 16, 1945, BA-MA, RH 24-32, Nr. 1, 59–60.

48. These individuals retained Volkssturm membership, however. Hitler, "Befehl,"

Feb. (no day), 1945, T-311/171/7223248–49; Friedrichs, "Bekanntgabe 42/45," Mar. 29, 1945, T-81/179/328897–900.

49. Thilo, "Vortragsnotiz," Jan. 16, 1945, BA-MA, RH 2, Nr. 331b, 24.

50. Berger, "Befehl, VsTgb. Nr. 488/45, VoTgb. Nr. 167/45, geh.," Jan. 17, 1945, T-580/872/799a/1; Heinrich, "Gutachten: Volkssturm Frankfurt am Oder," Feb. 2, 1971; "Berlin," Feb. 8, Apr. 2 and 3, 1971; "Mark Brandenburg," Jan. 23, 1976, all BA-MA, DRK Nr. 1.

51. The Red Cross listed 712 MIAs from the Kurhessen, Bayreuth, and Hannover battalions that were destroyed here; *DRK Vermißtenbildliste*. On these units, see Heinrich, "Gutachten: Vs Btn. 13/17," May 19, 1971, BA-MA, DRK Nr. 1; "Gutachten: Volkssturm Hannover," Apr. 30, 1971, BA-MA, DRK Nr. 2; and Karl H. Mistele, "Zur Geschichte des Deutschen Volkssturms in Oberfranken," *Geschichte am Obermain* 12 (1979–1980): 110–23.

52. Theodor Busse, "Die letzte Schlacht der 9. Armee," *Wehrwissenschaftliche Rundschau* 5, no. 4 (Apr. 1956): 153.

53. AOK 9, "Gefechtsbericht," Feb. 7, 1945, T-312/350/7924434–35; HG Weichsel, "Gliederung: Unterstellten Einheiten," Feb. 10, 1945, T-311/167/7219192–94; General Rudolf Hofmann, "MS# P-114b, Pt. 9: Der Feldzug gegen die Sowjetunion im Mittelabschnitt der Ostfront 1941–45," NA, RG 338, Box 121.

54. There were also seven Volkssturm battalions in Fortress Frankfurt plus three other frontline units that may have been Volkssturm battalions but are not clearly identifiable as such. XL Panzer Korps, "Lagekarte," Feb. 7, 1945, T-311/171/7223414–21; Hofmann, MS# P-114b, Pt. 9, NA, RG 338, Box 121.

55. Four other frontline battalions were probably Volkssturm but are not positively identifiable as such; HG Weichsel, "Lagekarte, GKdos. Nr. 4044/45," Mar. 23, 1945, T-311/171/7223313–14 and 7223325–27; OKH/GenStdH/OpAbt., "GKdos. Nr. 4258/45," Apr. 5, 1945, T-78/305/6256916.

56. HG Weichsel, Ia, "Lagekarte, GKdos. Nr. 4044/45," Mar. 23, 1945, T-311/171/7223313–14; Gen. Hasso von Manteuffel, OB Pz AOK 3, "Hinweise für die Kampfführung, Ia Nr. 3389/45g," Mar. 26, 1945, BA-MA, RH 24-32, Nr. 1, 38–40; Hans-Joachim von Hopffgarten, "The Battle for the Lebus and Görlitz Bridgeheads on the Oder," *Military Review* 35, no. 12 (Mar. 1956): 99; Baron Hanns Baron Freytag von Loringhoven, *Das letzte Aufgebot des Teufels* (Nuremberg: self-published, 1965), 28–29, 51, 77–79.

57. Busse, "FS," Feb. 6, 1945, T-311/167/7219053; AOK 11, "Vermerk," Feb. 12, 1945, T-311/167/7219439.

58. Gen. Hellmuth Maeder, Führer Grenadier Div., "Bericht: Angriff im Raum Lauban," undated, BA-MA, RH 26-1012, Nr. 3; Le Tissier, *Zhukov*, 52.

59. Dr. Schäffer, RMfVuP, "Abschrift von Bericht des Ordonanzoffizier Thiess vom 1. Marschbataillon Hamburg," Feb. 9, 1945, T-580/659/459; HG Weichsel, "Ia Tagesmeldung, Nr. 4280/45, geh.," Mar. 20, 1945, T-311/169/7221102–4; Div. Denecke, "KTB" reconstructed in 1955, BA-MA, RH 26-1010, Nr. 1, 61, 69; Heinrich, "Gutachten: Btn. zbV Schleswig-Holstein," Feb. 15, 1971, BA-MA, DRK Nr. 1; "Gutachten: Btn. zbV Würzburg," July 31, 1972, BA-MA, DRK Nr. 2; Loringhoven; Le Tissier, *Zhukov*, 75.

60. Ltn. Kieslich, 1. Art. Komp., PzGren Ers. Bde. "Großdeutschland," "Der Kampf um Guben," undated (postwar manuscript), BA-MA, RH 54, Nr. 334; Max Florheim, "Der Einmarsch der Russen in mein Heimatgebiet Forst/Lausitz im Frühjahr 1945 und die dort durchgeführten Kämpfe 1945," BA-Ko, Ost Dok 8/711.

61. Sturm, "Letter," Sept. 21, 1993, in the author's possession.

62. On this campaign, see Le Tissier, *Zhukov.*

63. OKW/WFSt/QM, "GKdos. Nr. 2263/45," Mar. 6, 1945, BA-MA, RW 4, Nr. 703; Verteidigungsbereich Berlin, "Tagesmeldung," Apr. 21, 1945, T-311/170/7222127; Heinrich, "Gutachten: Volkssturm Berlin," Feb. 11, 1971, BA-MA, DRK Nr. 1.

64. Siegfried Knappe and Ted Brusaw, *Soldat: Reflections of a German Soldier, 1936–1949* (New York: Orion, 1992), 13–16.

65. Kr. Pankow-Weissensee had six armed battalions ready for action on February 12; two months later, only one remained, Pankow-Weissensee Krstbfü., "Berichte Nrs. 21 & 60/45," Feb. 12 and Apr. 12, 1945, T-79/5/233–36 and 163.

66. OKH/GenStdH, Adjutant des Chefs, "Notizen nach Führervortrag, Nr. 1456/45 gKdos.," Apr. 19, 1945, T-78/350/6308856.

67. OKH/GenStdH/OpAbt/Landesbefestigung, "Besatzung von Berlin," Apr. 19, 1945, T-78/305/6256495–96.

68. Oberst Hans Refior, "Der Endkampf um Berlin: Mein Berliner Tagebuch für die Zeit vom 18.3.–2.5.45," BA-MA, RH 53-3, Nr. 24, 4–10.

69. Gräntz, "Befehl für die Verteidigung der Reichshauptstadt," Jan. 31, 1945, T-79/5/73–74; WK III, "Befehl," Feb. 1, 1945, T-79/5/119–20.

70. Kdr., Unterabschnitt E, Innere Verteidigungszone von Berlin, "Bericht," Feb. 9 and 15, 1945, BA-MA, RH 53-3, Nr. 51, 3, 19; WK III, Ia, "Befehl Nr. 12/45," Feb. 15, 1945, T-79/5/231; Unterabschnitt E, Abt. IVa, "Bescheinigung," Feb. 15, 1945, BA-MA, RH 53-3, Nr. 51, 20; Kampfkommandant Schöneberg, "Ausbildungsbefehl," Feb. 20, 1945, BA-MA, RH 30, Nr. 2, 12; Kdr. Verteidigungsbereich Berlin, Genltn. Hellmuth Reymann, "Grundsätzlicher Befehl für die Vorbereitungen zur Verteidigung der Reichshauptstadt, Nr. 400/45, geh.," Mar. 9, 1945, BA-MA, RH 30, Nr. 3.

71. Pankow-Weissensee Krstbfü., "Berichte Nrs. 21, 24 & 42/45," Feb. 12, 17, and Mar. 10, 1945, T-79/5/233–36, 238–39, and 351–53.

72. Polizei Reviere 285, Untergruppe I, "Versorgungsanordnung I," Feb. 3, 1945, T-79/5/128.

73. WK III, "Befehl 9/45," Feb. 9, 1945, T-79/5/111; OKH/HPA, "Bericht," Mar. 6, 1945, T-78/40/6001842–43.

74. Although there were questions whether they would have fought British or American troops; Speer with Kommandanten der Festungsbereich Berlin, "Aktennotiz," Apr. 15, 1945, T-311/169/7221719.

75. Refior, "Endkampf," BA-MA, RH 53-3, Nr. 24, 11; Oberst Wilhelm Willemer, "MS# P-136: The German Defense of Berlin," Duke, Location 58-G, Box 14, 27, 29, 32, 40, 49; Heinrich, "Gutachten: Volkssturm Berlin," Jan. 29, 1971, BA-MA, DRK Nr. 1; Reinhard Lüdicke, "Straßenkämpfe im Südwesten Berlins 1945: Aufzeichnungen über seinen Volkssturmeinsatz vom 20. April bis 2. Mai, 1945," ed. Eckart Henning, *Der Bär von Berlin: Jahrbuch des Vereins für die Geschichte Berlins* (1977): 122; Ivan Konev, *Year of Victory* (Moscow: Progress, 1969), 177; Tony Le Tissier, *The Battle of Berlin 1945* (London: Jonathan Cape, 1988).

76. Lüdicke, 122–23; Willemer, 40.

77. Lüdicke, 124–26; Willemer, 27, 31; Gerhard Boldt, *Hitler: Die letzten zehn Tage* (Frankfurt am Main: Ullstein, 1973), 157.

78. OKW, "Berichte," Apr. 30 and May 4, 1945, T-77/775/5501725–29 and 5501736; Artur Axmann, *"Das kann doch nicht das Ende sein": Hitler's letzten Reichsjugendführer erinnert sich* (Koblenz: Bublies, 1995), 422–45; Nicolaus von Below, *Als Hitlers Adjutant 1937–45* (Mainz: Hase und Koehler, 1980), 419; Erich Kuby, ed., *Das Ende des Schreckens: Januar bis Mai 1945* (Hamburg: Ernst Kabel, 1984), 173, 189–90; Willemer, MS# P-136, 21; Knappe and Brusaw, 42, 50; Le Tissier, *Berlin*, 31, 136, 141, 145, 150, 170, 198.

79. Axmann, 407–16; Hans Kissel, *Der Deutsche Volkssturm 1944/45: Eine territoriale Miliz im Rahmen der Landesverteidigung* (Frankfurt am Main: E. S. Mittler und Sohn, 1962), 80–81; Niehoff and Ahlfen, 40, 82.

80. OKW, "Bericht aus dem Führerhauptquartier," Apr. 15, 1945, T-77/1431/157–63; Ralf Roland Ringler, *Illusion einer Jugend: Lieder, Fahnen und das bittere Ende, Hitler Jugend in Österreich, Ein Erlebnisbericht* (St. Pölten: Niederösterreichisches Pressehaus, 1977).

81. Joachim Schultz-Naumann, *Mecklenburg 1945* (Munich: Universitas, 1990), 92, 102; Knappe and Brusaw, 16.

82. Stürtz, "RS 72g/67/45," Feb. 21, 1945, LHA Potsdam, PrBrRep. 61, Mark Brandenburg, Nr. 2.1.474; Keitel, "Chef OKW/Id FS Nr. 22/45," Feb. 25, 1945, T-78/421/6390973–74; OKW/QM Abt., "Vortragsnotiz, WFSt/Qu. Nr. 002263/45 gKdos.," Mar. 6, 1945, BA-MA, RW 4, Nr. 703.

83. U.S. Seventh Army G-2, "Swiss Intelligence Report," Feb. 24, 1945, NA, RG 331, Box 107.

84. Küstrin-Königsberg Krltr., "Bericht," Apr. 5, 1945, T-580/78/XIII/366; Just, Ost Dok 8/600.

85. Ernst Hornig, *Breslau 1945: Erlebnisse in der eingeschlossenen Stadt* (Würzburg: Bergstadtverlag Wilhelm Gottlieb Korn, 1986), 105; Georges Starcky, *L'Alsacien: Le Drame des Malgré Nous* (Paris: Editions France-Empire, 1983), 220; Le Tissier, *Berlin*, 117, 153.

86. Willemer, MS #P-136, 20; HG Weichsel, "FS Nr. 5012/45, geh.," Apr. 2, 1945, T-311/169/7221416; Refior, "Endkampf," 11.

87. Dieckert, Ost Dok 10/887; Erich Dethleffsen, "Die Kämpfe der 4. Armee in Ostpreußen vom Mitte Januar 1945 bis zum Einstellen des Angriffs in Richtung auf die unteren Weichsel," BA-Ko, Ost Dok 8/529; Kurt Chill, "Koch 'ein wäckerer Kämpfer' und wie es wirklich war," BA-Ko, Ost Dok 8/523.

88. Gen. Insp. der Panzertruppen, "Bericht," Feb. 19, 1945, BA-MA, RH 10, Nr. 128, 60–64; Petzel, Ost Dok 8/400 and 402.

89. OKH/GenStdH/OpAbt/Abt. Landesbefestigung, "Besprechungsnotiz (with Berger), Nr. 249/45 geh.," Jan 5, 1945, T-78/339/6295334–35; HG A, "Ia FS Nr. 201/45, geh.," Jan. 12, 1945, T-501/218/1247; Befehlshaber im GG, QM, "Bericht," Jan. 17, 1945, BA-MA, RH 53-23, Nr. 47, 218.

90. Otto Albrecht, "Bericht," Mar. 15, 1945, BA-Ko, R138 II, Nr. 7, 192–94; Heinrich, "Gutachten: VsBtn. 13/17," May 19, 1971, BA-MA, DRK Nr. 1; Oberinsp. W. Heinisch, "Einsatz des Volkssturms in Polen 1945," BA-Ko, Ost Dok 8/749;

R. Podehl, "Erinnerungen an den Kampf um Labiau, Ende Januar 1945," BA-Ko, Ost Dok 10/177.

91. Himmler, "Befehl," Nov. 3, 1944, T-175/122/2648035.

92. WK XXI Befehlshaber, "Besetzung der B-1 Linie, Anlage 7 zum KTB," Jan. 19, 1945, BA-MA, RH 53-21, Nr. 15, 23–26; WK XXI, "KTB," Jan. 30, 1945," BA-MA, RH 53-21, Nr. 14, 67; Petzel, Ost Dok 8/402; Landrat Dr. Heinrich Groll, "Die Ereignisse im Kreise Krenau, Oberschlesien, während der russischen Offensive auf Oberschlesien im Januar 1945," BA-Ko, Ost Dok 8/768; Kissel, MS# B-627, 19–20; Klaus Schönherr, "Der deutsche Volkssturm im Reichsgau Wartheland 1944/45," *Militärgeschichtliches Beiheft zur Europäischen Wehrkunde* 2, no. 5 (Oct. 1987): 1–16; Karl Hielscher, "Das Kriegsende 1945 im Westteil des Warthelandes und im Osten der Neumark," *Zeitschrift für Ostforschung* 34, no. 2 (1985): 213–48.

93. AOK 4, "Lagekarte," Jan. 27, 1945, T-312/260/7818289–94.

94. Stellvertretender Landesplaner Posen, Dr. Kurt Eckert, "Bericht," Mar. 23, 1945, BA-Ko, R 138 II, Nr. 7, 205–7; Heinisch, Ost Dok 8/749; Podehl, Ost Dok 10/177.

95. PzAOK 3, "Ia FS Nr. 11399/44, geh.," Nov. 19, 1944, T-313/326/8606407–8.

96. Brandenburg Gaustabsführung, "RS VI Ge/Zü Folge 60/63/45," undated (1945), LHA Potsdam, PrBrRep. 61, Mark Brandenburg, Nr. 2.1.475; Konev, 177.

97. Krltg. Tilsit-Ragnit, "Stärkemeldungen," Nov. 10, 1944, T-314/436/431–32; XXXII AK, "Vortragsnotiz," Apr. 3, 1945, BA-MA, RH 24-32, Nr. 1, 45–50; Podehl, Ost Dok 10/177.

98. Otto Albrecht, "Bericht," Mar. 15, 1945, BA-Ko, R 138 II, Nr. 7, 192–94; Kr. Grätz Landrat, "Bericht," Apr. 5, 1945, BA-Ko, R138 II, Nr. 7, 223–26; Petzel, Ost Dok 8/402; Oberfinanzpräsident Erich Zerahn, "Erste Belagerung von Königsberg vom 30.1.–22.2.45," BA-Ko, Ost Dok 8/580.

99. Altburgund-Dietfurt Krltr., "Bericht," Mar. 5, 1945, BA-Ko, R 138 II, 77–78.

100. Kofü., Btn. 36/70 (Leslau), "Bericht," Feb. (no day), 1945, BA-Ko, R 138 II, Nr. 7, 103–5.

101. Raus, "Notizen über Fahrt," Nov. 20, 1944, T-313/326/8606453–55; XXXIX PzAK, "Ia FS Nr. 213/45, geh.," Jan. 18, 1945, T-312/262/7820221; Posen Stellvertretender Landesplaner, "Bericht," Mar. 23, 1945, BA-Ko, R 138 II, Nr. 7, 205–7; Friedrich von Helmigk-Pinnow, "Die Kämpfe in der Obrastellung zwischen Schwerin (Warthe) und Schwiebus," BA-Ko, Ost Dok 10/537.

102. Genltn. Brückner, OB, 6. VGDiv, "Die Division ab Juli 1944 bis Kriegsende," manuscript in BA-MA, RH 26-6, Nr. 112, 41; Pietsch, Ost Dok 10/812.

103. Heinrich, "Gutachten: Volkssturm Hermannsbad," Feb. 14, 1972, BA-MA, DRK Nr. 2.

104. See, e.g., SD Pressburg, "Stimmungsbericht," Mar. 25, 1945, T-175/549/9423856–68, on the use of Viennese Volkssturm battalions in Slovakian border areas. On rural Volkssturm units, see Petzel, Ost Dok 8/402.

105. Hitler, "OKW/WFSt/Op-Org GKdos. Nr. 00937/45," Jan. 28, 1945, in Hubatsch, *Weisungen*, 301.

106. At least 5,000 of these men were killed; Kissel, 88–89.

107. DRK, *Leitverzeichnis zur Vermißtenbildliste*, 228–80.

108. See appendix Table 19; Glantz and House, 367 n, 368–69 n; DRK *Vermißten-bildliste*, vol. VB and Nachtrag.

109. Schörner, "Meldung," Aug. 6, 1944, T-311/132/7177778; Joseph Goebbels, *Die Tagebücher von Joseph Goebbels*, pt. 2, *Diktate, 1942–1945*, vol. 13, ed. Elke Fröhlich (Munich: K. G. Saur, 1995), 580; Le Tissier, *Zhukov*, 146–48; Ziemke, 147.

110. Breslau's Hanke was a commonly cited example. See Berlin Gaupropaganda-leiter, "Vertrauliches RS 10/45," Jan. 30, 1945, LHA Potsdam, PrBrRep. 61, Berlin, Nr. 14.4.5.

111. Dokumentationsarchiv des österreichischen Widerstandes, *Widerstand und Verfolgung im Burgenland 1934–1945: Eine Dokumentation* (Vienna: Österreichischer Bundesverlag, 1979), 394; Maj. Seidel, WK XXI Auffangsstab, "Bericht," Jan. 22, 1945, BA-MA, RH 53-21, Nr. 18, 6; SD and Sipo bei AOK 2, "Meldung Nr. 112," Mar. 15, 1945, T-175/579/263–66; PK Volkssturm Stab to SS Richter beim RFSS, "Vermerk," Mar. 20, 1945, BA-Ko, NS 7, Nr. 126, 2.

112. Koch, "Abschrift von RS," Oct. 23, 1944, T-581/6/151; Kalisch Wehrersatzinsp. und Kampfkommandant, "Abschrift von Bericht," Feb. (no day), 1945, BA-Ko, R 138 II, Nr. 7, 128–34; Gen. Insp. der Panzertruppen, "Bericht," Feb. 19, 1945, BA-MA, RH 10, Nr. 128, 60–64.

113. SD Berlin, "FS #920," Feb. 1, 1945, T-175/06/9370800–801; Pztruppe Ers. & Ausb. Abt. F, "Bericht," Feb. 19, 1945, BA-MA, RH 54, Nr. 403; Knuth, Ost Dok 8/546; Magunia, Ost Dok 8/592; Dieckert, Ost Dok 10/890.

114. Lissa Stützpunkt Kommandant, "Bericht," undated, BA-MA, RH 53-21, 27; Gnesen Landrat Dr. Büttner, "Bericht," Feb. 28, 1945, BA-Ko, R 138 II, Nr. 7, 60–71; Kr. Hohensalza Oberinsp., "Bericht," Mar. 21, 1945, BA-Ko, R 138 II, Nr. 7, 209–12; Helmigk-Pinnow, Ost Dok 10/537.

115. SD Leitabschnitt Danzig, "Bericht," Dec. 26, 1944, BA-Ko, NS 19, Nr. 3828; OB KG Neumark, "Gefechtsbericht," Jan. 29, 1945, BA-MA, RH 30, Nr. 55; OKH/FHO Abt. III Propaganda, "Bericht," Feb. 9, 1945, T-78/571/378–85; Petzel, Ost Dok 8/400 and 402.

116. HG Weichsel, OberQM, "Notiz," Mar. 9, 1945, T-311/169/7220685; Gau Sachsen Schatzmeister, "Abschrift von Bericht," undated, T-580/78/XIII/366; Pietsch, Ost Dok 10/812; Loringhoven, 33, 35.

117. Lissa Stützpunktkommandant, "Abschrift von Bericht," Feb. (no day), 1945, BA-Ko, R 138 II, Nr. 7, 126; Petzel, Ost Dok 8/402.

118. Oberst Konrad Meyer, "Die Kämpfe 1945 im Kreis Cosel," BA-Ko, Ost Dok 10/790; Werner Haupt, *Berlin 1945: Hitlers letzte Schlacht* (Rastatt: Erich Pable, 1963), 45.

119. Feig to Weimar Wehrmachtkommandantur, "Schreiben IVa 75/3 Mü/Skon," Mar. 28, 1945, HStA Weimar, Reichsstatthalter, Nr. 479, 5.

120. Brandenburg Gltr. Stürtz found it necessary to order Volkssturm unit commanders not to surrender weapons to army units voluntarily or without orders; Stürtz, "RS 86g 170/45," Mar. 2, 1945, LHA Potsdam, PrBrRep. 61, Mark Brandenburg, Nr. 2.1.474.

121. Leitstelle Ost III für Frontaufklärung, "Festellung zur Feindlage, Nr. 2381/45, geh.," Feb. 16, 1945, T-78/571/326; Hornig, 60–61, 252, 259.

122. See, e.g., Frontaufklärungstrupp 325, "Bericht," Feb. 15, 1945, T-78/571/ 317; OKH/FHO Abt. IIb, "Anlagen zu FS Nr. 1813/45, geh.," undated, T-78/584/ 32–66.

123. Heinrich, "Gutachten: Volkssturm Oberschlesien," July 9, 1973, BA-MA, DRK Nr. 1, and "Volkssturm Köslin," Apr. 9, 1976, BA-MA, DRK Nr. 2.

124. Befehlshaber der SD und Sipo, "FS," Feb. 20, 1945, T-78/565/810–11; Kdr., Regt. Klotsche, "Letzte Feststellungen das Schicksal Hans Klotsche," Mar. 4, 1945, BA-MA, RH 26-1001, Nr. 3.

125. Dieckert, Ost Dok 10/890, 48.

126. Keitel, "FS Nr. 27/44," May 15, 1944, T-77/785/5513599–600; OKW/WFSt/ Org.Abt., "Vortragsnotiz Nr. 0791/45," Feb. 1, 1945, T-77/785/5513596–98.

127. Master craftsmen are included in these middle-class groups, as per Michael H. Kater, *The Nazi Party: A Social Profile of Members and Leaders 1919–1945* (Cambridge, Mass.: Harvard University Press, 1983); and David Schoenbaum, *Hitler's Social Revolution: Class and Status in Nazi Germany 1933–1939* (New York: Norton, 1980). On the NSDAP in the east, see Richard Bessel, *Political Violence and the Rise of Nazism: The Storm Troopers in Eastern Germany* (New Haven, Conn.: Yale University Press, 1984), 34.

128. Rita S. Botwinick, *Winzig, Germany, 1933–1946: The History of a Town Under the Third Reich* (Westport, Conn.: Praeger, 1992), esp. 12–14, 28; Knappe and Brusaw, 271.

129. Klein, Ost Dok 8/598; Helmigk-Pinnow, Ost Dok 10/537; Martini, Ost Dok 10/790; Stephen Fritz, "'We are trying . . . to change the face of the world'—Ideology and Motivation in the Wehrmacht on the Eastern Front: The View from Below," *Journal of Military History* 60, no. 4 (Oct. 1996): 697–99; Ian Kershaw, "How Effective Was Nazi Propaganda?," in *Nazi Propaganda: The Power and the Limitations*, ed. David Welch (London: Croom Helm, 1983), 180–205; Vejas Gabriel Liulevicius, *War Land on the Eastern Front: Culture, National Identity and German Occupation in World War I* (New York: Cambridge University Press, 2000).

130. This is similar to Schulte's explanation regarding the motivation of the average German soldier on the Eastern Front; Theo Schulte, *The German Army and Nazi Policies in Occupied Russia* (Oxford: Berg, 1989), 266–71. Also OLGP Breslau, "Lagebericht 3132 a-10-55," Dec. 3, 1944, BA-Ko, R22, Nr. 3358, 83–85.

9. Defending the Reich's Western Front

1. Rundstedt, "Ia GKdos. Nr. 9232/44," Oct. 15, 1944, BA-MA, RH 19-IV, Nr. 78, 130.

2. OB West Stabschef Gen. Siegfried Westphal, "Ia GKdos. Nrs. 9602 & 9678/ 44," Oct. 26 and 28, 1944, in BA-MA, RH 19 IV, Nr. 79.

3. 1. VsBtn. Metz, "Tätigkeitsbericht," Nov. 17, 1944, T-81/94/108310.

4. Zander to Bormann, "Vorlage," Nov. 11, 1944, BA-Ko, NS 6, Nr. 168, 2–4.

5. 1. VsBtn. Metz, "Tätigkeitsbericht," Nov. 17, 1944, T-81/94/108310; U.S. 5th Inf. Div., "G-2 Periodic Repts. 98–103," Nov. 17–22, 1944, NA, RG 407, Entry 427, Box 6754; Genltn. Hans Kittel, "Fragebogen Metz," MS B-079, NA, RG 338, Box 9.

6. Vs. Westmark/Sonderstab Lothringen, "Brief," Oct. 30, 1944, BA-Ko, NS 8, Nr. 172; OSS, "Rept. 113180: Captured German Documents from Alsace," undated, NA, RG 226, Box 1248; Eugène Riedweg, *Strasbourg: Ville occupé 1939–1945* (Steinbrunn-Le-Haut: Les Editions du Rhin, 1982), 138–40.

7. Mellenthin with Gltg. Baden-Elsaß, "Telefongespräch," Nov. 20, 1944, T-311/143/7189382–94; HG G, "Meldung," Nov. 22, 1944, T-311/30/7037818; Burst, "Stabsbefehl Nr. 4, BrB. Nr. 135/44, geh.," Nov. 22, 1944, T-81/93/107794.

8. Keitel, "Entwurf von OKW/WFSt/Op(Heer)/West GKdos. Nr. 14232/44," Dec. 2, 1944, T-77/782/5508809–11.

9. 180. Inf. Div., "Führungsanordnung Nr. 82," Jan. 25, 1945, T-315/1539/76–77; U.S. Army, Ninth Army, *Conquer: The Story of the Ninth Army 1944–45* (Washington, D.C.: Infantry Journal Press, 1947), 63.

10. OB West "Ia KTB Entry," Nov. 25, 1944," T-311/16/7017716–30; Gen. der Pioniere und Festungen, Abt. L Chef, "Niederschrift über die Besprechung beim Führer," Nov. 28, 1944, BA-MA, RH 11 III, Nr. 77, 122–26.

11. HG G Stabschef Städke with 559. VGD Ia, "Niederschrift von Telefongespräch," Dec. 5, 1944, T-311/144/7190024–25; U.S. 95th Inf. Div., "G-2 Periodic Rept. #48," Dec. 6, 1944, NA, RG 407, Entry 427, Box 13872; HG G OB, Gen. Hermann Balck, "Reisebemerkungen," Dec. 13, 1944, T-311/144/7190277.

12. 172. Reserve Div., "Tätigkeitsbericht," entries for Dec. 12 and 25, 1944, BA-MA, RH 26-172, Nr. 3, 26, 36; U.S. 95th Inf. Div., "G-2 Periodic Rept. Nr. 54," Dec. 12, 1945, NA, RG 407, Entry 427, Box 13873; Städke with HG G/QM Abt., "Niederschrift von Telefongespräch," Dec. 17, 1944, T-311/144/7190392; HG G, OB Gen. Johannes Blaskowitz, "Ia/F GKdos. Nr. 103/45," Jan. 25, 1945; T-311/145/7191582–84; Blaskowitz "Ia Befehl Nr. 293/45, geh.," Jan. 26, 1945, T-311/145/7191611.

13. HG G, "Ia KTB entry," Jan. 10, 1945, T-311/145/7190996; HG G, "Lagekarte AOK 1, GKdos. Nr. 629/45," Feb. 5, 1945, T-311/146/7192493–95; HG G OB, SS Obergruppenführer Paul Hausser, "Ia GKdos. Nr. 495/45," Feb. 1, 1945, T-311/145/7191739.

14. AOK 7, "Ia GKdos. Nr. 1405/45," Mar. 5, 1945, T-311/146/7192637–40; U.S. 45th Inf. Div., "G-2 Periodic Repts. #182–83," Mar. 21–22, 1945, NA, RG 407, Entry 427, Box 10897.

15. U.S. 95th Inf. Div., "G-2 Periodic Rept. #179," Dec. 14, 1944, NA, RG 407, Entry 427, Box 13872; U.S. 5th Inf. Div., "G-2 Periodic Rept. #126," Dec. 15, 1944, NA, RG 407, Entry 427, Box 6754; SHAEF, G-2, Counterintelligence Sub Div., Civil Security Section, "Weekly Intelligence Summary for Psychological Warfare #14," Dec. 30, 1944, NA, RG 331, Box 110; U.S. Mobile Field Interrogation Unit 2, "PW Intelligence Bulletin #2/48," Mar. 22, 1945, NA, RG 165, Box 717.

16. Städke with LXXXII AK Ia, "Niederschrift von Telefongespräch," Feb. 21 and 22, 1945, T-311/145/7192245–46 and 7192263; U.S. Seventh Army, "G-2 History: Chronology for Feb., 1945," NA, RG 407, Entry 427, Box 2584; Oberst Graf von Ingelheim, "Kampfhandlungen der LXXXII AK in der Zeit vom 2.12.44–27.3.45," MS B-066, NA, RG 338, Box 9, 26; United States, Seventh U.S. Army, *Report of Operations of the Seventh United States Army in France and Germany 1944–1945*, vol. 2 (Heidelberg: Aloys Gräf, 1946), 685.

17. U.S. 70th Inf. Div., "G-2 Journal, Entries 69, 74, & 75," Mar. 14, 19–20, 1945, NA, RG 407, Entry 427, Box 11329; U.S. 45th Inf. Div., "G-2 Periodic Rept. #181," Mar. 20, 1945, NA, RG 407, Entry 427, Box 10897.

18. Balck, "Reisebericht," Jan. 19, 1945, T-311/145/7191448–50; U.S. 45th Inf. Div., "G-2 Periodic Rept. #179," Mar. 18, 1945, NA, RG 407, Entry 427, Box 10897.

19. U.S. 42nd Inf. Div., "G-2 Periodic Rept. #30," Mar. 19, 1945, NA, RG 407, Entry 427, Box 10663.

20. Caspary, "Abschrift von Bericht," Oct. 10, 1944, T-580/874/799b/5.

21. Hans Kissel, *Der Deutsche Volkssturm 1944/45: Eine territoriale Miliz im Rahmen der Landesverteidigung* (Frankfurt am Main: E. S. Mittler und Sohn, 1962), 82.

22. OB West, "Tagesmeldung, Nr. 11038.44, gKdos.," Nov. 22, 1944, T-311/16/7017737–39; Burst, "Stabsbefehl Nr. 4, BrB. Nr. 135/44, geh.," Nov. 22, 1944, T-81/93/107794; OB West, "Lagekarte," Nov. 29, 1944, BA-MA, RH 19-IV, Nr. 96K, Karte 6; HG Oberrhein Ia, "Kriegsgliederung, Nr. 106/44 gKdos.," Dec. 7, 1944, T-78/411/6379207–8.

23. AOK 19 Id to HG Oberrhein Ia, "Notiz: Telefongespräch," Dec. 21, 1945, BA-MA, RH 20-19, Nr. 148, 107; HG Oberrhein OberQM, "Entwurf, FS Nr. 547," Dec. 28, 1944, T-311/172/7223716–17.

24. Brigade Baur Ia, "Kriegsgliederungsskizze, Nr. 32/45 gKdos.," Jan. 1, 1945, BA-MA, RH 2, Nr. 1453, 1; Brigade 1005, Kriegsgliederungsskizze, Nr. 9/45 geh.," Jan. 1, 1945, BA-MA, RH 2, Nr. 1453, 2.

25. Service was normally limited to six weeks, but it could be extended. Friedrichs, "Bekanntgabe 18/45," Feb. 8, 1945, T-580/872/799a/1.

26. HG Oberrhein, "Ia FS Nr. 559/45 geh.," Jan. 8, 1945, BA-MA, RH 20-19, Nr. 139, 7; AOK 19, "Ia FS Nr. 7105/45, geh.," Feb. 16, 1945, BA-MA, RH 20-19, Nr. 3, 37; Kissel, 82.

27. RüInsp Oberrhein, "Schreiben Tgb. Nrs. 927 & 983/45, geh.," Jan. 29 and 31, 1945, T-73/21/3145743–44 and 3145778.

28. HG G Ia, "KTB entry," Feb. 1, 1945," T-311/145/7191119; GenKdo. XVIII SS AK to Westphal, "Niederschrift von Telefongespräch," Feb. 2, 1945, T-311/145/7191791; Städke, "Ia FS Nr. 376/45, geh.," Feb. 28, 1945, BA-MA, RH 20-19, Nr. 198. 51; AOK 19 Ia, "KTB entry," Mar. 23, 1945," BA-MA, RH 20–19, Nr. 207, 68.

29. AOK 19 OB Rasp, "Ia GKdos. Nr. 931/45," Feb. 9, 1945, BA-MA, RH 20-19, Nr. 138, 16–20; Städke, "Ia/F Gkdos. 263/45," Feb. 24, 1945, T-311/145/7192338.

30. XVIII SS AK, "Ia Lagekarte," Feb. 1, 1945, T-311/172/7223765–68.

31. XVIII SS AK, "Lagekarte, Ia GKdos. Nr. 404/45," Apr. 4, 1945, LXIV AK, "Lagekarte, Ia GKdos. Nr. 582/45," Apr. 5, 1945, both BA-MA, RH 20-19, Nr. 230K.

32. See deployments in AOK 19 situation maps in BA-MA, RH 20-19, Kartenbände (identifiable by the "K" following their file number). On duties, see, e.g., LXIV AK, "Tagesmeldung," Feb. 20, 1945, BA-MA, RH 20-19, Nr. 193.

33. AOK 19 OB Gen. Erich Brandenberger, "Ia GKdos. Nr. 2681/45," Apr. 7, 1945, BA-MA, RH 20-19, Nr. 5, 22–23; HöhKdo Oberrhein, "Ausbau Befehle Nrs. 4 & 8, Ia Nrs. 379 & 400/45, gKdos.," Apr. 11 and 17, 1945, T-312/979/9171676–78 and 9171671.

34. AOK 19 Ia Brandstädter, "Entwurf von Ia FS Nr. 1170/45, geh." Feb. 19, 1945, BA-MA, RH 20-19, Nr. 139, 12.

35. AOK 1 OB Gen. Hermann Förtsch, "Befehl," Feb. 20, 1945, BA-MA, RH 20-19, Nr. 193.

36. Brandstädter, "Ia/Id GKdos. Nrs. 604 & 785/45," Feb. 24 and Mar. 5, 1945, BA-MA, RH 20-19, Nr. 139, 41–51.

37. Brandstädter, "Ia/Id GKdos. Nr. 604/45," Feb. 24, 1945, BA-MA, RH 20-19, Nr. 139, 41–49; Brandstädter to LXIV AK, "Notiz über Telefongespräch," Mar. 11, 1945, BA-MA, RH 20-19, Nr. 210, 47.

38. XVIII SS AK, "Ia FS Nr. 957/45, geh.," Mar. 16, 1945, BA-MA, RH 20-19, Nr. 139, 66.

39. LXIV AK Ic, "Bericht Nr. 970/45," Feb. 21, 1945, BA-MA, RH 20-19, Nr. 139, 30–31; Brandstädter, "Abschrift von Abschrift von Ia/Id GKdos. Nr. 604/45," Feb. 24, 1945, BA-MA, RH 20-19, Nr. 139, 41–49.

40. Hausser, "Ia/F GKdos. Nr. 212/45," Feb. 13, 1945, T-311/145/7192048.

41. Burst, "Befehl," Feb. 23, 1945, BA-MA, RH 20-19, Nr. 139, 36–40.

42. Brandstädter, "OberQM/Ia FS Nr. 2344/45, geh.," Mar. 26, 1945, BA-MA, RH 20-19, Nr. 4, 118.

43. Oberst Janke, Inf. Schule, "Erkundungsbericht über die Abwehrverhältnisse bei der 805. Inf. Div. (19. Armee)," Mar. 9, 1945, BA-MA, RH 20-19, Nr. 180, 45–49; AOK 19 OB, Gen. Hans von Obstfelder, "Ia GKdos. Nr. 2099/45," Mar. 20, 1945, BA-MA, RH 20-19, Nr. 4, 89; AOK 24 OB, Gen. Hans Schmidt, "GKdos. Nr. 559/45," Mar. 23, 1945, BA-MA, RH 20-19, Nr. 120.

44. Obstfelder, "Ia GKdos. Nr. 2099/45," Mar. 20, 1945, BA-MA, RH 20-19, Nr. 4, 89; Obstfelder, "GKdos. Nr. 2290/45," Mar. 25, 1945, BA-MA, RH 20-19, Nr. 4, 109; Chefadjutant des Führers Gen. Burgdorf, "FS," Mar. 27, 1945, BA-MA, RH 20-19, Nr. 139, 90.

45. Brandstädter with XVIII SS AK, "Notiz über Telefongespräch," Apr. 13, 1945, BA-MA, RH 20-19, Nr. 228, 117–18; AOK 19, "Ia KTB entry," Apr. 14, 1945, BA-MA, RH 20-19, Nr. 228, 165; AOK 19, "Tagesmeldung," Apr. 17, 1945, BA-MA, RH 20-19, Nr. 229, 81–84.

46. Brandstädter with LXXX AK Stabschef, "Notizen über Telefongespräch," Apr. 12, 1945, BA-MA, RH 20-19, Nr. 238, 3.

47. AOK 19, "Ia KTB entries," Apr. 5–7, 10–12, 15–16, 1945, BA-MA, RH 20-19, Nr. 225, 16, 21, 24, 26, 37, 42–43, 58, 64; AOK 19, "Ia Lagekarten: Nordfront," Apr. 7–10, 1945, BA-MA, RH 20-19, Nr. 231K; AOK 19, "Ia Tagesmeldung Nr. 2943/45, geh.," Apr. 12, 1945, BA-MA, RH 20-19, Nr. 228, 42–43; HöhArtKdo 321, "Ic Art. Tagesmeldung," Apr. 13, 1945, BA-MA, RH 20-19, Nr. 228, 157.

48. HöhArtKdo 321, "Ia FS Nr. 1080/45, geh.," Mar. 26, 1945, BA-MA, RH 20-19, Nr. 139, 83–84.

49. Sperrverband Hella to AOK 19, "Funkspruch Nr. 120," Apr. 7, 1945, BA-Ko, RH 20-19, Nr. 214, 11; or any AOK 19 "Ia Lagekarten" in KTB Anlagen in BA-MA, RH 20-19.

50. Kdr., Kampfbereich XII Nord, "Gliederungsskizze," Feb. 22, 1945, T-311/146/7192841.

51. 89. Inf. Div., "Kampfauftrage," Mar. 20, 1945, T-315/2040/472–74.

52. Gen. der Inf. Höhne, "Abwehrkämpfe des LXXXIX AK an der Rhein Front

vom 18.3. bis 28.3.45," MS# B-584, NA, RG 338, Box 29, 1, 4; Heinz Leiwig, *Finale 1945 Rhein-Main* (Düsseldorf: Droste, 1985), 44, 57.

53. U.S. 89th Inf. Div., "G-1 Periodic Rept. for 25–26 Mar.," in "G-2 Journal," Mar. 27, 1945; "G-2 Periodic Rept. Nrs. 16–17," Mar. 26–27, 1945, both in NA, RG 407, Entry 427, Box 13225; U.S. 89th Inf. Div., "G-2 After Action Rept. for 12–31 March 1945," Apr. 10, 1945, NA, RG 407, Entry 427, Box 13223; U.S. 87th Inf. Div., "Report," Mar. 25, 1945, in U.S. 89th Inf. Div., "G-2 Journal," Mar. 25, 1945, NA, RG 407, Entry 427, Box 13225.

54. Unit designation changed from Feldbtn. D to Feldbtn. VI to Btn. Thiet and finally to Btn. Rückriem. Feldbtn. D, "Meldung," Nov. 24, 1944, T-81/95/110048; Thiet, "Btn. Befehl Nrs. 1, 4–9, 11, 14," Nov. 28 and Dec. 27, 1944, Jan. 6, 14, 22, 26, 27, 29, and Feb. 9, 1945, T-81/95/110039–40, 109990, 109997–110021.

55. Korpstabsarzt, II Fallschirmjäger Korps, "KTB entries," Mar. 2 and 4, 1945, BA-MA, RL 33, Nr. 6, 130, 133; Rückriem, "Btn. Befehl Nr. 24," Mar. 17, 1945, T-81/95/109951–53; 2nd Canadian Corps, "Interrogation of PW Report," Mar. 31, 1945, Directorate of History, Canadian National Defence HQ, File 144.111009 (D9).

56. Rückriem, "Btn. Befehl Nrs. 17, 23–26," Feb. 18, Mar. 12, 17, 22, and 25, 1945, T-81/95/109942–55.

57. Genmaj. Rudolf Langhäuser, "The Fourth Commitment of the 6. Fallschirmjäger Division," MS# B-452, Duke, Location 58-G Box 4. Also Kofü, 1. Komp., Vs. Feldbtn. 38/7, "Bericht," Mar. 15, 1945, StA Detmold, L113, Nr. 1069, 5.

58. This was one reason why this unit left the most complete existing records of any active Volkssturm formation. Rückriem, "Btn. Befehl Nrs. 22, 24–25," Mar. 11, 17, and 22, 1945; "Bewaffnung des Bataillons" Mar. 14, 1945, all in T-81/95/109946–56.

59. Lionel F. Ellis and Alan E. Warhurst, *Victory in the West*, vol. 2 (London: HMSO, 1962–1968), 288–94; Rainer Pape, ed. *"bis 5 nach 12": Herforder Kriegstagebuch 1944/45* (Herford: Bussesche Verlagshandlung, 1984), 183–84; Charles P. Stacey, *The Victory Campaign: The Operations in Northwest Europe, 1944–1945* (Ottawa: The Queen's Printer and Controller of Stationery, 1960), 537–39.

60. Rückriem, "Btn. Befehl Nr. 26," Mar. 25, 1945, T-81/95/109942; Stacey, 538. Btn. 38/20 may have survived as 6. Parachute Div. continued to report two attached Volkssturm battalions on April 7. OKH/GenStdH/Org. Abt. IZ, "GKdos. Nr. 31672/45," Apr. 7, 1945, T-78/413/6381222–25.

61. Westphal, "OKW/OQu. GKdos. Nr. 115/44," Nov. 22, 1944, T-77/1427/123–31; Caspary, "Richtlinien," Nov. 3, 1944, LA Saarbrücken, NSDAP Mischbestand, Nr. 15, 11–19; Speer, "Reisebericht," Jan. 9, 1945, BA-Ko, R 3, Nr. 1544, 81–84; Burst, "Abschrift von RS," Feb. 27, 1945, BA-MA, RH 20-19, Nr. 4, 23; OB West, OberQM, "Abt. IVa-IIB, FS Nr. 1867/45, geh.," Mar. 18, 1945, BA-MA, RH 53-13, Nr. 148.

62. XII SS AK, Korück, "Befehl Nr. 1/45, geh.," Jan. 5, 1945, T-354/120/3754306–8; Btnfü., Btn. Walsrode 3, "Befehl," Jan. 18, 1945, T-81/95/109796; Vilshofen Krstbfü., "Meldung," Feb. 23, 1945, BA-Ko, NS 12, Nr. 1147; Franken Stellvertretender Gltr. Karl Holz, "RS," Mar. 8, 1945, T-1021/10/825.

63. Karlsruhe Krstbfü., "Befehl," Feb. 3, 1945, T-81/94/108525; 180. Inf. Div. Ia, "Führungsanordnung Nr. 95," Feb. 5, 1945, T-315/1539/53–54.

64. Gustorf Ortskommandant, "Kommandanturbefehl Nr. 1," Jan. 11, 1945, T-312/521/8121627.

65. Berger, "Anordnung 1912/1953/45," Jan. 25, 1945, in Rühle, "RS 10/45," Feb. 2, 1945, T-81/94/108239; no author, "Lagebesprechung mit dem Führer," Jan. 27, 1945, BA-MA, RH 47, Nr. 65, Fragmente 24/25, 32–33; Fröbe, 396–97, 539–44.

66. Münster Gestapostelle, Abt. IV c, "RS Nr. 3006/44," Jan. 17, 1945, T-175/468/2988423–27.

67. Balck, "Dienstanweisung, Ia/F Nr. 225/44 gKdos.," Dec. 16, 1944, T-311/144/7190343–49; WK VII, "Ia GKdos. Nr. 1236/45, & Anlagen" Feb. 24, 1945, T-79/76/386–401; Selb Ortskampfführer, "Ortsverteidigungsbefehl," Apr. 11, 1945, StA Bamberg, M30, Nr. 836; VsBtn. 19/91, "Btn. Befehl Nr. 6," Apr. 17, 1945, T-81/94/108215–17.

68. Heinz, "RS," Feb. 16, 1945, LA Magdeburg, Rep C 20 Ib XV: RVK, Nr. 3384; Stigler, "RS 45/45," Feb. 27, 1945, BA-Ko, NS 12, Nr. 1147.

69. Festungs Pionier Kdr. IV, "GKdos. Nr. 776/44," Dec. 13, 1944, BA-MA, RH 11 III, Nr. 205, 131.

70. Herbert Schwarzwälder, *Bremen und Nordwestdeutschland am Kreigsende 1945*, vol. 2 (Bremen: Carl Schünemann, 1973), 86.

71. GenKdo. XII SS AK, "Ia Befehl 71/45, geh.," Jan. 9, 1945, T-354/120/3754322–26; Hamburg Wehrmachtkommandantur, "Ib/Pz Befehl, Tgb. Nr. 1054/45 geh.," Mar. 22, 1945, T-81/94/108960; Ansbach Kampfkommandant, "Meldung," Apr. 8, 1945, T-84/241/6599834.

72. Gren. Btn. 77, "Tgb. Nr. 6/45, geh.," Jan. 28, 1945, T-84/242/6600364–65; "Ia Lagekarte, Nr. 14/45, geh.," Feb. 2, 1945, T-82/242/6600264; "Ia Meldung Nrs. 43 & 123/45, geh.," Feb. 9 and 19, 1945, T-84/242/6600294 and 6600246.

73. Gren. Btn. 77, "Ia Meldung Nrs. 8 & 16/45, geh.," Jan. 28 and Feb. 1, 1945, T-84/242/6600350 and 6600341; "Lagekarte," Feb. 2, 1945, T-84/242/6600264; Div. 466 Befehlshaber, "Divisions Tagesbefehl 3/45," Feb. 5, 1945, T-84/242/6600159–61.

74. Gustorf Ortskommandant, "Bericht," Nov. 11, 1944, T-312/521/8128697; "Meldungen," Nov. 16 and Dec. 22, 1944, T-312/521/8121692 and 8121649; "Stärkenachweisung," Dec. 15, 1944, T-312/521/8121655–56; Kofü., 1. Komp., VsBtn. 5/16, "Stärkemeldung," Jan. 19, 1945, T-312/521/8121616; AOK 15 Korück, "Ia GKdos. Nr. 51/45," Feb. 2, 1945, T-312/521/8121587; "Ia BrB. Nrs. 298 & 300/45, geh.," Feb. 8 and 9, 1945, T-312/521/8121576–77 and 8121583.

75. U.S. VII Corps, "G-2 Periodic Rept.," Mar. 1, 1945, in U.S. 1st Inf. Div., "G-2 Journal, 1–3 Mar. 1945," NA, RG 407, Entry 427, Box 5741.

76. 104th Inf. Div., "G-2 Journal, Entry 68," Mar. 1, 1945, NA, RG 407, Entry 427, Box 14637; U.S. Army, Third Armored Division, *Spearhead in the West 1944–45* (Frankfurt: Franz Joseph Heinrich, 1945), 165–68.

77. U.S. 3rd Armored Div., "G-2 Periodic Rept. #247," Mar. 2, 1945, NA, RG 407, Entry 427, Box 15063; 104th Inf. Div., "G-2 Journal, Entry 54," Mar. 3, 1945, NA, RG 407, Entry 427, Box 14637; U.S. 99th Inf. Div., "G-2 Periodic Rept. Nr. 114," Mar. 3, 1945, in U.S. 1st Inf. Div., "G-2 Journal, 4–6 Mar. 45," NA, RG 407, Entry 427, Box 5741.

78. George Blake, *Mountain and Flood: The History of the 52nd (Lowland) Division 1939–1946* (Glasgow: Jackson, Son and Co., 1950), 182–85; Ellis and Warhurst,

vol. 2, 305–6; Roger Evans, *The Story of the Fifth Royal Inniskilling Dragoon Guards* (Aldershot: Gale and Polden, 1951), 376–78; Günther Wegmann, *Das Kriegsende zwischen Ems und Weser 1945* (Osnabrück: N. Th. Wenner, 1983), 19–22, 34.

79. U.S. 10th Armored Div., "G-2 Periodic Repts. #85–86," Apr. 7–8, 1945, NA, RG 407, Entry 427, Box 15906; Meldeköpfe Feuchtwangen and Windsheim, "Lageberichte," Apr. 9 and 10, 1945, T-84/241/6599835–36; Friedrich Blumenstock, *Der Einmarsch der Amerikaner und Franzosen im nördlichen Württemberg in April 1945* (Stuttgart: Kohlhammer, 1957), 21–24, 188.

80. Joachim Brückner, *Kriegsende in Bayern 1945: Der Wehrkreis VII und die Kämpfe zwischen Donau und Alpen* (Freiburg im Breisgau: Rombach, 1987), 102, 169, 218–19; P. K. Kemp and John Graves, *The Red Dragon: The Story of the Royal Welsh Fusiliers 1919–1945* (Aldershot: Gale and Polden, 1960), 271–72; Norman Scarfe, *Assault Division: A History of the 3rd Division from the Invasion of Normandy to the Surrender of Germany* (London: Collins, 1947), 254; Schwarzwälder, vol. 2, 123, 152–54, 170–73.

81. U.S. 104th Inf. Div., "G-2 Periodic Rept. #157," Apr. 1, 1945, NA, RG 407, Entry 427, Box 14639; Charles B. MacDonald, *The United States Army in World War Two*, vol. 3, *The European Theater of War*, pt. 9, *The Last Offensive* (Washington, D.C.: Office of the Chief of Military History, 1973), 209, 214; Ken Hechler, *The Bridge at Remagen* (New York: Ballantine, 1957), 47, 85–88, 122–34.

82. Adelheid Bruder, ed., "Zu den letzten Kriegstagen 1945 in Backnang: Aufzeichnungen aus einem Tagebuch von Karl Bruder," *Beiträge zur Geschichte der Stadt Backnang* 6 (1987): 211; Edward N. Peterson, *The Many Faces of Defeat: The German People's Experience in 1945* (New York: Peter Lang, 1990), 40–47, 130–32; Walter Rinderle and Bernard Norling, *The Nazi Impact on a German Village* (Lexington: University Press of Kentucky, 1992), 177–89; Josef Werner, *Karlsruhe 1945: Unter Hakenkreuz, Trikolore und Sternenbanner* (Karlsruhe: G. Braun, 1985), 98–99.

83. Französische Kommandant der Stadt Reutlingen, "Verordnung Nr. 2," Apr. 22, 1945, in Gerhard Junger, *Schicksale 1945: Das Ende des 2. Weltkrieges im Kreise Reutlingen* (Reutlingen: Oertel und Spörer, 1971), 219; Gen. de Hesdin (CO 4th Morrocan Div.), "E-M 2 et 3me Bureau 1834/25," Apr. 24, 1945, in Hermann Riedel, *Villingen 1945: Bericht aus einer schweren Zeit* (Villingen/Schwarzwald: Ring, 1968), 68–69. Also see Junger, 104, 195–196; Riedel, *Villingen*, 5, 71.

84. U.S. 14th Armored Div. Combat Command B, "G-2 Journal, entry 36," Apr. 3, 1945, NA, RG 407, Entry 427, Box 16294; Seventh Army, *Report of Operations*, 3:778.

85. U.S. 95th Inf. Div., "G-2 Periodic Rept. #194," Feb. 16, 1945, NA, RG 407, Entry 427, Box 13879; Bürgermeisteramt Stadt Gerabronn, "Verlauf der Kriegsereignisse," Apr. 1, 1948, HStA Stuttgart, J170, Nr. 4/Crailsheim.

86. John Russell, *No Triumphant Procession: The Forgotten Battles of April 1945* (London: Arms and Armour, 1994), 230; Ulrich Saft, *Krieg in der Heimat: Das bittere Ende zwischen Weser und Elbe* (Langenhagen: Saft, 1992), 328–39; Schwarzwälder, vol. 2, 153, 168.

87. U.S. 100th Inf. Div., "G-2 Periodic Rept. #135," Apr. 7, 1945, NA, RG 407, Entry 427, Box 14219; MacDonald, *Last Offensive*, 415–18; Blumenstock, 23, 127, 169–70, 214–15.

88. Holz, "Lagebericht," Apr. 17, 1945, T-580/43/VIII/248; U.S. 3rd Inf. Div., "G-2 Periodic Repts. 219–22," Apr. 18–22, 1945, NA, RG 407, Entry 427, Box 6148; U.S. 45th Inf. Div., "G-2 Periodic Repts. 210–12," Apr. 17–19, 1945, NA, RG 407, Entry 427, Box 10897; Karl Kunze, *Kriegsende in Franken und der Kampf um Nürnberg im April 1945* (Nuremberg: Selbstverlag des Verein für Geschichte der Stadt Nürnberg, 1995), 117–24, 180, 203, 208, 211–13, 216, 219, 236–40, 266.

89. See Manfred Messerschmidt, "German Military Law in the Second World War," in *The German Military in the Age of Total War*, ed. Wilhelm Deist (Dover, N.H.: Berg, 1985), 323–35.

90. Brandstädter, "Ia FS Nr. 2960/45, geh.," Apr. 12, 1945, BA-MA, RH 20-19, Nr. 5, 53; Brandstädter with Korück 536, "Notiz über Telefongespräch," Apr. 12, 1945, BA-MA, RH 20-19, Nr. 238, 3; Brandenberger, "Ia GKdos Nrs. 2989 & 2990/45," Apr. 13, 1945, BA-MA, RH 20-19, Nr. 5, 69–71.

91. U.S. 45th Inf. Div., "G-2 Periodic Repts. #190–196," Mar. 29–Apr. 4, 1945, NA, RG 407, Entry 427, Box 10897; Oberst Graf von Ingelheim, "Kampfhandlungen des LXXXII AK in der Zeit vom 27.3–6.5.45," MS B-183, NA, RG 338, Box 13; Alois Stadtmüller, *Aschaffenburg im Zweiten Weltkrieg* (Aschaffenburg: Geschichts- und Kunstvereins Aschaffenburg, 1971), 153, 203, 243–310.

92. Befehlshaber der Auffangslinie IV, "Dienstanweisung," Apr. 25, 1945, T-175/223/2761165–67; Tuttlingen Krltr., "Schreiben," Apr. 17, 1945, T-81/178/327294.

93. Stigler, "RS 42/45," Feb. 23, 1945, BA-Ko, NS 12, Nr. 1147; Dechant, "Befehl," Mar. 22, 1945, BA-Ko, Sammlung Schuhmacher, Nr. 285; WK VII, "Korpsbefehl Nr. 3, Ia Nr. 6546/45 geh.," Apr. 18, 1945, T-79/17/110–13.

94. U.S. 83rd Inf. Div., "G-2 Journal, Entries 32–34, 40," Apr. 2, 1945, NA, RG 407, Entry 427, Box 12502; Heinz Meyer, *Damals: Der Zweite Weltkrieg zwischen Teutoberger Wald, Weser und Leine* (Preußisch Oldendorf: K. W. Schultz, 1980), 279.

95. Württemberg-Hohenzollern Gltg., "Lagebericht," Apr. 18, 1945, T-580/43/VIII/248.

96. Roscoe C. Blunt Jr., *Inside the Battle of the Bulge: A Private Comes of Age* (Westport, Conn.: Praeger, 1994), 126, 158, 167.

97. Quotation from U.S. 4th Armored Div., "G-2 Periodic Rept. (Special) #87," Apr. 27, 1945, NA, RG 407, Entry 427, Box 15183. On HJ resistance see U.S. V Corps, "G-2 Periodic Rept. #316," Apr. 20, 1945, in U.S. 1st Inf. Div., "G-2 Journal 19–24 Apr., 1945," NA, RG 407, Entry 427, Box 5752; U.S. 3rd Armored Div., Spearhead, 143; John Colby, *War from the Ground Up: The 90th Division in World War II* (Austin, Tex.: Nortex, 1991), 447; Alfons Heck, *A Child of Hitler: Germany in the Days When God Wore a Swastika* (Frederick, Colo.: Renaissance House, 1985), 165–68, and chaps. 10–11; Saft, 101, 430; Richard E. Schroeder, "The Hitler Youth as a Paramilitary Organization" (Ph.D. diss., University of Chicago, 1975), 278–79; Schwarzwälder, vol. 2, 51–52, and vol. 3, 161–62.

98. Hauptgemeinschaftleiter Twittenhof, "Bericht," undated (late Mar. 1945), BA-Ko, NS 6, Nr. 169, 4–9; Kr. Cham Gendarmerie, "Meldung Nr. 622," Apr. 5, 1945, StA Amberg, BzA Cham, Nr. 4431; Schelling, "Letter" Aug. 18, 1997, in author's possession.

99. E.g., the Volkssturm men buried in Koblenz's Main Cemetery averaged 49.6 years of age, with half (twenty of forty-one) over draft age and none younger than 24.

100. On Cologne, see U.S. 3rd Armored Div., "S-2 Periodic Rept. #184," Mar. 6, 1945, NA, RG 407, Entry 427, Box 15063; VII Corps, "G-2 Weekly Intelligence Review #10," Mar. 13, 1945, in U.S. 30th Inf. Div., "G-2 Journal," NA, RG 407, Entry 427, Box 9777. On Bonn, see U.S. 1st Inf. Div., "G-2 Periodic Repts. #260–61," Mar. 8–9, 1945, NA, RG 407, Entry 427, Box 5743. On Würzburg, see Max Domarus, *Der Untergang des alten Würzburgs im Luftkrieg gegen die deutschen Großstädte* (Gerolzhofen: Teutsch, 1969), 140–51, 181. On Aschaffenburg, see note 91; for Nuremberg, see note 88.

101. USSBS concluded that bombing did not usually stiffen resistance appreciably, but Nazi fanatics who had experienced heavy bombing had the highest morale of all Germans, and immediately after bombing raids, anti-Allied anger did increase. All this was perhaps a factor at Würzburg. USSBS, "The Effects of Strategic Bombing on Morale," in *The United States Strategic Bombing Survey,* ed. David MacIsaac (New York: Garland, 1976), vol. 1, 1–2, 12, 37, and vol. 2, 37. On Ulm, see Brückner, 123; on Wittlich, see Heck, *Child,* 161–64.

102. U.S. V Corps, "G-2 Periodic Rept. #311, 317," Apr. 14 and 21, 1945; U.S. 2nd Inf. Div., "G-2 Periodic Rept. #297," Apr. 18, 1945, both in U.S. 1st Inf. Div., "G-2 Journal, 15–24 Apr. 1945," NA, RG 407, Entry 427, Boxes 5751–52; U.S. 89th Inf. Div., "G-2 Periodic Repts. #38–39," Apr. 17–18, 1945, NA, RG 407, Entry 427, Box 13223; U.S. 104th Inf. Div. "G-2 Periodic Repts. #170–75," Apr. 14–19, 1945, and "G-2 Journal, entries 19, 36, 46," Apr. 22, 1945, NA, RG 407, Entry 427, Box 14639; U.S. 69th Inf. Div., "G-2 Periodic Repts. #65–66 & Journal," Apr. 18–21, 1945, NA, RG 407, Entry 427, Box 11307–8; U.S. 87th Inf. Div., "G-2 Periodic Repts. #118, 120," Apr. 19 and 21, 1945, NA, RG 407, Entry 427, Box 12886.

103. Grohlmann, in Donald S. Detwiler, Charles B. Burdick, and Jürgen Rohwer, eds., *World War II German Military Studies,* vol. 24, pt. X, sec. D, no. 6. (New York, 1979); Walter Görlitz, *Der Zweite Weltkrieg 1939–1945,* vol. 2 (Stuttgart: Steingruber, 1952), 551; MacDonald, *Last Offensive,* 394–95. On Holz, see Kunze, 215, 265–66.

104. U.S. 30th Inf. Div., "G-2 Intelligence Spot Rept.," Apr. 15, 1945, NA, RG 407, Entry 427, Box 8783.

105. AOK 1 Ia/Id, "GKdos. Nr. 982/45," Feb. 24, 1945, T-81/95/109548–49; WK XIII, "Ib Nr. 8270/45, geh.," Mar. 24, 1945, T-79/171/461–62; LXXX AK, "KTB entry," Mar. 28, 1945," BA-MA, RH 24-80, Nr. 70, 360.

106. NSFO Ruder, PK Abt. II F, "Bericht," Mar. 14, 1945, BA-Ko, NS 6, Nr. 169, 77–79; U.S. III Corps, "G-2 Periodic Rept. #103," Mar. 24, 1945, NA, RG 407, Entry 427, Box 3268; U.S. 6th Cav. Group, "S-2 Periodic Rept. #116," Mar. 26, 1945, in U.S. 89th Inf. Div. "G-2 Journal," Mar. 27, 1945, NA, RG 407, Entry 427, Box 13225; Hauptgemeinschaftsleiter Twittenhof, "Bericht," undated (late Mar. 1945), BA-Ko, NS 6, Nr. 169, 4–9.

107. Btnfü. Henkemeier to Lippe Krltr., "Schreiben," Mar. 18, 1945; Kofü. Kellner to Lippe Krltr., "Schreiben," Mar. 23, 1945, both in StA Detmold, L113, Nr. 1069, 203 and 173–74.

108. U.S. First Army, G-2, PW Combat Team Intelligence Section, "Weekly Intelligence Rept. #6," Mar. 5, 1945, in U.S. 104th Inf. Div., "G-2 Journal, 7–15 Mar. 1945," NA, RG 407, Entry 427, Box 14637.

109. OKH/GenStdH/OpAbt. III, "Tagesmeldung West vom 18.4.45," Apr. 19, 1945, T-78/339/6314512–16.

110. Some Volkssturm commanders were acutely aware of this; e.g., VsBtn. 19/91, "Btn. Befehl Nr. 6, Verteidigungsplan," Apr. 17, 1945, T-81/94/108215–17.

111. U.S. III Corps, "G-2 Periodic Rept. #83," Mar. 3, 1945, in U.S. 1st Inf. Div., "G-2 Journal, 14–16 Mar. 1945," NA, RG 407, Entry 427, Box 3268; Moselland NSFO Bereichsleiter Keitel, "FS Nr. 367," Mar. 19, 1945, T-580/79/369.

112. Schulte, "Einsatzbefehl 3/45," Feb. 11, 1945, T-81/95/109918; NSFO Ruder, "Bericht," Mar. 14, 1945, BA-Ko, NS 6, Nr. 169, 77–79; OKH/GenStdH/OpAbt. II, "GKdos. Nr. 4332/45," Apr. 8, 1945, T-78/354/6314595–602; Gen. Wolf Ewert, "Die Kämpfe der 338. Inf. Div. vom 1. Jan. bis 15. Apr. 1945," postwar manuscript, BA-MA, RH 26-338, 26.

113. U.S. 30th Inf. Div., G-2 "Periodic Rept. #271," Mar. 15, 1945, NA, RG 407, Entry 427, Box 8777; U.S. Seventh Army, *Report*, vol. 3, 829–30; Ernst von Salomon, *Der Fragebogen* (Stuttgart: Europäisches Buchklub, 1951), 530; HelmutBomm, "Die Backnanger Widerstand gegen die Nazis vor dem Einmarsch der Amerikaner am 20. April 1945," *Beiträge zur Geschichte der Stadt Backnang* 5 (1986): 154–68; Martin Broszat, Elke Fröhlich, Anton Grossman, and Falk Wiesemann, *Bayern in der NS Zeit: Herrschaft und Gesellschaft im Konflikt*, vol. 4 (Munich: R. Oldenbourg, 1981), 678; Junger, 159, 173, 181, 188, 197, 237, 248, 265–66; Werner Niehaus, *Endkampf zwischen Rhein und Weser: Nordwestdeutschland 1945* (Stuttgart: Motorbuch, 1983), 76, 183.

114. Civilians interrupting defense efforts were executed as saboteurs; HG B OB Model, Mar. 18, 1945, T-311/278/1097; GenKdo. XIII AK, "Ia Tagesmeldung," Apr. 12, 1945, T-354/120/3754360.

115. Btnfu., VsBtn. 18/3 (Kr. Cochem), "Erfahrungsbericht," Feb. 18, 1945, T-81/95/109890; Wehrmachtstreifengruppe zbV 10, "Bericht, BrB. Nr. 144, geh.," Mar. 7, 1945, T-311/146/7192892–94; NSFO Ruder, "Bericht," Mar. 14, 1945, BA-Ko, NS 6, Nr. 169, 77–79; SHAEF Psychological Warfare Div. Intelligence Section, "Rept. 119983: The Volkssturm in Action," Mar. 15, 1945, NA, RG 226, Box 1334; U.S. 6th Cavalry Group, "S-2 Periodic Rept. #116," Mar. 26, 1945, in U.S. 89th Inf. Div. "G-2 Journal," Mar. 27, 1945, NA, RG 407, Entry 427, Box 13225; Ansbach Kampfkommandant, "Lagebericht," Apr. 8, 1945, T-84/241/6599833; Hauptgemeinschaftsleiter Twittenhof, "Bericht," undated (late Mar. 1945), BA-Ko, NS 6, Nr. 169, 4–9.

116. Werner Meyer, *Götterdämmerung: April 1945 in Bayreuth* (Percha am Starnbergersee: Schutz, 1975), 115–16.

117. SHAEF, G-1, "Handling of Paramilitary Organizations (Treatment of Members of the Volkssturm)," NA, RG 331, Box 23; Eisenhower, "Teletype QX-31290, secret," Mar. 3, 1945, NA, RG 331, Box 114; U.S. Army Intelligence Center, *History of the Counterintelligence Corps*, vol. 19 (Baltimore: U.S. Army Intelligence Center, 1959), 79, app. 1–19, NA, RG 319.

118. Many Allied unit histories and memoirs mention this tactic, e.g., Blunt, 138–39; or Algernon T. M. Durand and R.H.W.S. Hastings, *The London Rifle Brigade 1919–1950* (Aldershot: Gale and Polden, 1952), 275–77.

119. A widely distributed Allied flysheet entitled "Es gibt nur eine Wahl" specifically warned of this; see Alois Stadtmüller, *Maingebiet und Spessart im Zweiten Weltkrieg: Überblick, Luftkrieg, Eroberung* (Aschaffenburg: Geschichts- und Kunstverein Aschaffenburg, 1983), Abbildung 70.

120. Military Intelligence Interrogation Team 421–G, "Interrogation of Civilians Rept. #48," Mar. 5, 1945, in U.S. 30th Inf. Div., "G-2 Journal," NA, RG 407, Entry 427, Box 8776.

121. Blunt, 138–39; Edgar Christoffel, *Der Endkampf zwischen Mosel, Saar und Ruwer 1944/45: Der Durchbruch der Amerikaner im südlichen Hunsrück zum Vormarsch nach Trier und zum Rhein* (Trier: Koch, 1985), 58.

122. SD Abschnitt Münster, "Stimmungs- und Meinungsbildung Bericht, Tgb. Nr. 1516 Th/Ht.," Mar. 20, 1945, T-175/272/2768917–21; SD Außenstelle Bad Canstatt, "Stimmungs- und Meinungsbildung Bericht," Mar. 27, 1945, T-175/272/2768876–80.

123. Hauptgemeinschaftsleiter Twittenhof, "Bericht," undated (late Mar. 1945), BA-Ko, NS 6, Nr. 169, 4–9; U.S. 12th Army Group, Publicity and Psychological Warfare Div., "Daily Summary of Intelligence," Mar. 11, 1945, in U.S. 1st Inf. Div., "G-2 Journal, 10–15 Mar. 1945," NA, RG 407, Entry 427, Box 5744.

124. SHAEF, Psychological Warfare Div., Intelligence Section, "Rept. 122220: Civilians Overflowing Front Line Towns," Feb. 28, 1945, NA, RG 226, Box 1363; U.S. 9th Armored Div., "G-2 Periodic Rept. #11," Mar. 21, 1945, NA, RG 407, Entry 427, Box 15782.

125. SHAEF, Psychological Warfare Div., Intelligence Section, "Rept. 122212: Two Reports on Erkelenz," and "Rept. 119988: Interrogation of Thirteen Volkssturm Leaders," Mar. 12 and 14, 1945, NA, RG 226, Boxes 1334 and 1363.

126. U.S. 84th Inf. Div., "G-2 Periodic Rept. Nr. 83," Feb. 8, 1945, NA, RG 407, Entry 427, Box 12646; U.S. Ninth Army, "Weekly Intelligence Summary," Mar. 22, 1945, in U.S. 30th Inf. Div., "G-2 Journal," NA, RG 407, Entry 427, Box 8778.

127. See Günther Bischof and Stephen E. Ambrose, eds., *Eisenhower and the German POWs: Facts Against Falsehood* (Baton Rouge: Louisiana State University Press, 1992). Page 24 reproduces an August 1945 report showing that 663,576 men, mainly Volkssturm members, had already been released from POW camps.

128. DRK, *Vermißtenbildliste* and *Leitverzeichnis nach Einheiten*, 226–280. The figure is arrived at assuming each of the 246 communities, mainly Kreise, mobilized a 500-man battalion and estimating the thirty-four battalions mentioned at 500 men each.

129. These sometimes-ridiculed obstacles played a "meaningful role" if properly placed and defended; OKH/GenStdH/Ausb. Abt. II, "Erfahrungsbericht Abwehr, Nr. 500/45, geh.," Feb. 1, 1945, BA-MA, RH 11 I, Nr. 25. For Allied views, see Donald A. Edwards, *A Private's Diary* (Detroit: self-published, 1994), 425; Hubert Essame, *The 43rd Wessex Division at War 1944–1945* (London: William Clowes and Sons, 1952), 248.

130. SHAEF, G-2, Psychological Warfare Div., Intelligence Section, "Rept. 119983: The Volkssturm in Action," Mar. 15, 1945, NA, RG 226, Box 1334.

131. E.g., transportation problems delayed Army Group G's order from the Oberndorf (Württemberg) Mauser factory of 5,000 carbines for Levy II units in the Black

Forest Border Position. OKH, with more political clout and available trucks and gasoline, ultimately won permission to move them across Germany to Neisse River Volkssturm units, although Oberndorf was only about fifty kilometers from AOK 19! Städke, "Niederschrift von Telefongespräch," Feb. 25 and 26, 1945, T-311/145/7192349 and 7192370–71.

Conclusion

1. See, e.g., Klaus Mammach, *Der Volkssturm: Das letzte Aufgebot 1944/45* (Cologne: Pahl Rugenstein, 1981), 148.

2. S. P. MacKenzie, *The Home Guard: A Political and Military History* (New York: Oxford University Press, 1995); David K. Yelton, "British Public Opinion, the Home Guard and the Defense of Great Britain, 1940–1944," *Journal of Military History* 58, no. 3 (July 1994): 461–80; A. D. Kolesnik, *Narodnoe opolchenie gorodov-geroev [People's Militia of the Hero-cities]* (Moscow: Nauka, 1974).

Statistical Appendix

1. DRK, *Vermißtenbildliste;* copies used belonged to the DRK Landesverband Rheinland-Pfalz in Mainz, though they are available at the BA-MA and the DRK Suchdienst in Munich.

2. Chef, OKW Wehrmacht Ersatzamt, "Wehrmachtersatzplan (WEP) 1945," undated, late 1944, T-77/780/5506292–478.

3. For example, assigning *Arbeiter* (literally, worker) to manufacturing is safe enough, but there is no way to identify exactly where the WEP categorized white-collar *Angestellter* (literally, staff or employee). In untangling the vagaries of German job skill categories, Detlev Mühlberger, *Hitler's Followers: Studies in the Sociology of the Nazi Movement* (London: Routledge, 1991), 11–25, proved invaluable.

Bibliography

Unpublished Primary Sources

ARCHIVAL SOURCES: GERMANY

Bundesarchiv Koblenz (BA-Ko)

NS 1	Gauschatzmeister der NSDAP
NS 5	Deutsche Arbeits Front (DAF)
NS 6	Parteikanzlei
NS 7	SS und Polizeigerichtsbarkeit
NS 8	Kanzlei Rosenberg
NS 12	Nationalsozialistische Lehrerbund
NS 19	Reichsführer SS, Persönlicher Stab
NS 20	NSDAP Kleine Erwerbungen
NS 22	Reichsorganisationsleiter
NS 23	SA
NS 24	NSKK
NS 26	NSDAP Hauptarchiv
NS 30	Einsatzstab Rosenberg
Ost Dok 8	Berichte in öffentlichen Leben tätig gewesener Personen aus den Gebieten östlich von Oder und Neiße zum Zeitgeschehen 1939–1945
Ost Dok 10	Berichte über Verwaltung und Wirtschaft in den reichsdeutschen Gebieten östlich von Oder und Neiße
R 3	Reichsministerium für Rüstung und Kriegsproduktion
R 7	Reichswirtschaftsministerium
R 11	Reichwirtschaftskammer
R 19	Chef der Ordnungspolizei
R 21	Reichsministerium für Wissenschaft, Erziehung und Volksbildung
R 22	Reichsjustizministerium
R 43 II	Reichskanzlei
R 55	Reichsministerium für Volksaufklärung und Propaganda
R 58	Reichsicherheitshauptamt
R 70/Lothringen	Polizeidienststellen
R 70/Elsaß	Polizeidienststellen
R 138 II	Behörden der Allgemeinen inneren Verwaltung und kommunalen Selbstverwaltung im ehemaligen Reichsgau Wartheland
Sammlung Schuhmacher	

Militärarchiv Freiburg (BA-MA)

N 24	Nachlass Friedrich Hoßbach
N 426	Nachlass Hans Kissel
RH 2	Oberkommando des Heeres (OKH)/Generalstab des Heeres
RH 3	OKH/General Quartiermeister
RH 7	OKH/Heerespersonalamat
RH 10	General Inspekteur der Panzertruppen
RH 11 I	General der Infanterie bei OKH/GenStdH
RH 11 III	General der Pioniere und Festungen in OKH
RH 14	Chef Heeres Rüstung und Befehlshaber des Ersatzheeres
RH 15	OKH/Allgeime Heeresamt
RH 19 II	Heeresgruppe (HG) Mitte
RH 19 III	HG Nord/Kurland
RH 19 IV	OB West
RH 19 VI	HG A/Mitte
RH 19 XII	HG G
RH 19 XV	HG Weichsel
RH 20-4	Armee Oberkommando (AOK) 4
RH 20-7	AOK 7
RH 20-9	AOK 9
RH 20-19	AOK 19
RH 21-3	PzAOK 3
RH 22	Befehlshaber rückwärtige Heeresgebiete
RH 23	Korück
RH 24-28	XXVIII Armeekorps (AK)
RH 24-32	XXXII AK
RH 24-48	XLVIII PzK
RH 24-55	XLV AK
RH 24-80	LXXX AK
RH 24-89	LXXXIX AK
RH 24-207	Höheres Kommando Oberrhein
RH 26-1	1. Infanterie Division
RH 26-6	6. Volksgrenadier Division
RH 26-18	18. Infanterie Division
RH 26-172	172. Reserve Division
RH 26-180	180. Infanterie Division
RH 26-338	338. Infanterie Division
RH 26-349	349. Infanterie Division
RH 26-551	551. Volksgrenadier Division
RH 26-708	708. Infanterie Division
RH 26-905	Division Nr. 905
RH 26-1001	Infanterie Division Bärwalde/Pommern
RH 26-1010	Division Dennecke
RH 26-1012	Führer Grenadier Division

RH 27-4	4. Panzer Division
RH 30	Taktische Befehlshaber, Feste Plätze, und Sonstige Stäbe, Verbände und Einheiten
RH 34	Truppenkommandanten
RH 53-3	Wehrkreis III
RH 53-4	Wehrkreis IV
RH 53-7	Wehrkreis VII
RH 53-11	Wehrkreis XI
RH 53-12	Wehrkreis XII
RH 53-13	Wehrkreis XIII
RH 53-21	Wehrkreis XXI
RH 53-23	Befehlshaber im Heeresgebiet GG
RH 54	Truppenteile des Ersatzheeres
RH 59	Deutscher Volkssturm
RHD 62	Miscellaneous Publications
RL 2 I	Oberkommando der Luftwaffe (OKL)/Generalstab der Luftwaffe, Chef
RL 2 II	OKL/Generalstab der Luftwaffe, Abt. I
RL 7	Luftflotten Kommandos
RL 33	Fallschirmtruppe
RM 6	Admiral beim Oberkommando der Marine (OKM)
RM 7	OKM, Seekriegsleitung
RS 2-12	XII SS AK
RS 2-18	XVIII SS AK
RW 4	Oberkommando der Wehrmacht (OKW)/Wehrmacht-führungsstab
RW 6	OKW/Allgeime Wehrmachtamt
RW 17	Wehrmachtkommandanturen
RW 20-5	Rüstungsinspektion Oberrhein
RW 21-21	Rüstungskommando Coburg
RW 21-51	Rüstungskommando Recklinghausen

Badisches Generallandesarchiv Karlsruhe (GLA Karlsruhe)
GLA 465

Bayerisches Hauptstaatsarchiv München (HStA München)
Reichstatthalter
Staatsministerium für Wirtschaft

Brandenburgisches Landeshauptarchiv Potsdam (LHA Potsdam)

PrBrRep. 2A	Regierung Potsdam I Polizei
PrBrRep. 61	NSDAP Teilbestand Gau Berlin
PrBrRep. 61	NSDAP Teilbestand Gau Mark Brandenburg
PrBrRep. 61	NSDAP Teilbestand SA der NSDAP

Deutsches Rotes Kreuz—Landesverbandstelle Mainz
DRK *Vermißtenbildliste*, vols. VA, VB, VC, and Nachtrag

Hauptstaatsarchiv Thüringen, Weimar (HStA Weimar)
Reichstatthalter in Thüringen

Hessisches Hauptstaatsarchiv Wiesbaden (HStA Wiesbaden)
Abt. 407   Polizeipräsidiums Frankfurt am Main
Abt. 483   Gau Hessen-Nassau

Institut für Zeitgeschichte, Munich (IfZG)
Db 202.02   Gauleitung Bayreuth
Fa 91/1/11   NSDAP Partei Kanzlei
Fa 91/2   NSDAP Partei Kanzlei
Fa 88/Fasz 151   Gauarchiv Ostpreußen

Landesarchiv Berlin (LA Berlin)
Rep 244   NSDAP Dienststellen, Acc. 2050 SA

Landesarchiv Sachsen-Anhalt, Magdeburg (LA Magdeburg)
Rep C20 Ib   Oberpräsident, XV Reichsverteidigungskommissar
Rep C30 Ib   XV Reichsverteidigungskommissar
Rep C30   Landratsamt Osterburg A
Rep C30A   Landratsamt Haldersleben

Landeshauptarchiv Rheinland-Pfalz, Koblenz (LHA Rheinland-Pfalz)
Nr. 654/5   Der Deutsche Volkssturm
Nr. 662.5   NSDAP
Nr. 700.145   Sammlung Wolff

Landesarchiv Saarbrücken (LA Saarbrücken)
Depositum Landeskommission für saarländische Landesgeschichte
Mischbestand NSDAP Westmark

Niedersächsisches Hauptstaatsarchiv Hannover (HStA Hannover)
Hann 80   Lüneburg III
Hann 89 II e4   Regierungspräsident zu Hannover, Nr. 188 II
Hann 122a   Oberpräsidium der Provinz Hannover
Hann 310 I K   Gauleitung Osthannover
Zeitgeschichtliche
    Sammlung

Niedersächsisches Staatsarchiv Osnabrück (StA Osnabrück)
Dep. 59b   Stadtarchiv Bramsche

Niedersächsisches Staatsarchiv Wolfenbüttel (StA Wolfenbüttel)
12 A Neu 13   Braunschweigisches Staatsministerium

Nordrhein-Westfälisches Hauptstaatsarchiv (HStA Düsseldorf)
Dep. Niederkrüchten
RW 23   NSDAP
RW 37   Höheres SS und Polizeiführer West

Staatsarchiv Amberg (StA Amberg)
Bezirksämter Amberg, Cham, Eschenbach, Neunberg v.W.
NSDAP Kreisleitungen Oberviechtach, Regensburg, Schwandorf, Weiden

Staatsarchiv Bamberg (StA Bamberg)
M 30   Gauleitung Bayreuth
M 33   Kreisleitungen der NSDAP

Staatsarchiv Bückeburg (StA Bückeburg)
Dep 9D   Stadt Bückeburg, Acc. 39/89
Dep 29   Obernkirchen
L 4   Schaumburg-Lippische Landesregierung
L 102b   Landkreis Stadthagen

Staatsarchiv Detmold (StA Detmold)
L 80   Ie Landesregierung Lippe, Gruppe IX Lippsche Polizei,
                        Titel I, Nr. 12, Band III
L 113   NSDAP und NS Organisationen in Lippe
Sammelbestand M15

Staatsarchiv Ludwigsburg (StA Ludwigsburg)
PL 502   Kreisleitungen, Gau Württemberg-Hohenzollern
K 110 SD   Dienststellen in Württemberg

Staatsarchiv München (StA München)
Landratsämter LRA   Berchtesgaden
  29656
Landratsämter LRA   Wolfratshausen
  39376
NSDAP Nr. 466a   Kreisleitung Fürstenfeldbrück

Staatsarchiv Münster (StA Münster)
Bestand NSDAP   Kreis- und Ortsgruppenleitungen

Staatsarchiv Nürnberg (StA Nürnberg)
Rep. 503   NS Mischbestand: Gauleitung Franken

Stadtarchiv Freiburg
Stadtrat Nrs. C4/XI/27/11–12

Stadtarchiv Rastatt
Burgermeisteramt Abt. A

Stadtarchiv Ratingen
2-677   Liste der gefallenen des Krieges 1939/45
2-726a   Regierungspräsident, Volkssturmverpflichtet von TN,
                        Feuerwehr und Schutzpolizei
2-807a–b   UK Stellungen
Germes, Jakob   *Ratingen: Geschichte in Geschichten* (unpublished
                        manuscript)

Thüringisches Staatsarchiv Meiningen, Außenstelle Suhl
Copy of SHAEF G-2 Division, Combined Intelligence Objectives Sub-Committee, Artillery and Weapons Team, "Report CIOS Target No. 2/637: Visit to Thuringia Small Arms Industry," Sept. 14, 1945 (archival location not given, copy in author's possession)

Württembergisches Hauptstaatsarchiv Stuttgart (HStA Stuttgart)
E 151a   Württembergische Innenministerium
J 170   Bericht von Gemeinde über die Kriegsereignisse 1945

UNITED STATES

National Archives (NA)
RG 165   War Dept., Army Chief of Staff, G-2 Division, Cap-
                    tured Personnel and Materials Branch, Enemy Pris-
                    oner of War Intelligence File, Boxes 716–17, 749.
RG 226   OSS, File 3.11 Germany (Volkssturm).
RG 243   USSBS, Entry 6/7: European War Morale Division,
                    Boxes 71, 73, 77.
RG 319   U.S. Army. Army Intelligence Center, *History of the
                    Counter Intelligence Corps.*
RG 331   SHAEF, G-1 Division, Allied Operational and Occu-
                    pation Headquarters, Decimal File Nrs. 383.2–2,
                    383.6/3–6 (Handling of Volkssturm prisoners),
                    Boxes 23, 26.
RG 331   SHAEF, General Staff, G-2 Division, Counter-Intelli-
                    gence Sub-Division, Civil Security Section, Boxes
                    107, 110, 117.
RG 331   SHAEF, Office of the Chief of Staff, Secretary General
                    Staff, Project Decimal File, Box 114.
RG 338   German Military Studies MS# B-066, 079, 083, 104,
                    108–10, 115, 119, 147, 158, 160, 183, 186, 193, 196,
                    219, 225-26, 238, 314, 317, 408, 463, 551, 565, 576,
                    584, 714, 735–36, 745, 785, 794, 811, 817–18, 821,
                    850; MS# P-065a-b, 114b; MS# T-9, Chaps. 17–19.
RG 407   Entry 427, World War II Operations Reports, G-2
                    records from October 1944 to May 1945 for the fol-
                    lowing units: Third, Seventh, and Ninth Armies; III
                    and XVI Corps; 1st, 3rd, 5th, 30th, 42nd, 45th, 69th,
                    70th, 83rd, 84th, 86th, 87th, 89th, 95th, 99th, 100th,
                    102nd, and 104th Infantry Divisions; and 2nd, 3rd,
                    4th, 9th, 10th, and 14th Armored Divisions.

National Archives Microfilm
T-73   Reich Ministry for Armaments and War Production
T-76   Organization Todt
T-77   German Armed Forces High Command (OKW)

T-78	German Army High Command (OKH)
T-79	German Army Areas (Wehrkreise)
T-81	NSDAP
T-84	Miscellaneous German Records
T-175	Chief of German Police and Reichsführer SS
T-178	Fragmentary Record of Miscellaneous Reich Ministries and Offices
T-311	Records of German Field Commands (Army Groups)
T-312	German Army Field Commands (Armies)
T-313	German Army Field Commands (Panzer Armies)
T-314	German Army Field Commands (Corps)
T-315	German Army Field Commands (Divisions)
T-321	German Airforce High Command (OKL)
T-354	Waffen SS Units
T-405	German Airforce Area Commands (Luftgaukommandos)
T-454	Reichs Commissioner for the Baltic States
T-501	German Army Field Commands (Rear Areas, Occupied Territories, and Others)
T-580	Miscellaneous Non-Biographic Material
T-581	NSDAP Hauptarchiv
T-608	German Navy High Command (OKM)
T-1021	German Documents Among the War Crimes Records of the Judge Advocate Division, HQ, U.S. Army, Europe

Duke University Manuscripts Department
Location 58-G, U.S. Army German Military Studies, MS# A-925, 934, 964–65; MS# B-080, 098, 124, 147, 190, 195, 309, 453, 627, 849; MS# P-136

University of North Carolina Map Collection
United States. Office of Strategic Services. "Greater Germany: Administrative Divisions," July 1, 1944.

CANADA

Canadian National Defence Headquarters, Directorate of History
File Nr. 144.111009 (D9)

CORRESPONDENCE *(in the author's possession)*

Schelling, Dr. jur. Hermann (former Volkssturm Levy III member)
Sturm, Ltn. (a.D.) Hans (former member of Berger's Volkssturm Staff)

Published Primary Sources

Ahlfen, Hans von. "Der Kampf der Festung Breslau." *Wehrwissenschaftliche Rundschau* 6, no. 1 (Jan. 1956): 20–39.
———. *Der Kampf um Schlesien: Ein authentischer Dokumentarbericht.* Munich: Gräfe und Unser, 1961.

Ahlfen, Hans von, and Hermann Niehoff. *So kämpfte Breslau: Verteidigung und Unter-gang von Schlesiens Hauptstadt.* Munich: Gräfe und Unser, 1961.

Andreas-Friedrich, Ruth. *Der Schattenmann: Tagebuchaufzeichnungen 1938–1945.* Berlin: Suhrkamp, 1947.

Anonymous. *A Woman in Berlin.* Translated by James Stern. New York: Harcourt, Brace, 1954.

Axmann, Artur. *"Das kann doch nicht das Ende sein": Hitler's letzten Reichsjugendführer erinnert sich.* Koblenz: Bublies, 1995.

Balck, Hermann. *Ordnung im Chaos: Erinnerungen 1893–1948.* Osnabrück: Biblio, 1981.

Bauer, Kaplan Fritz. *Würzburg im Feuerofen: Tagebuchaufzeichnungen und Erinner-ungen an die Zerstörung Würzburgs.* Würzburg: Echter, 1985.

Below, Nicolaus von. *Als Hitlers Adjutant 1937–45.* Mainz: Hase und Koehler, 1980.

Bernhard, Henry. *Finis Germaniae: Aufzeichnungen und Betrachtungen.* Stuttgart: Kurt Haslsteiner, 1948.

Blunt, Roscoe C., Jr. *Inside the Battle of the Bulge: A Private Comes of Age.* Westport, Conn.: Praeger, 1994.

Boelcke, Willi A., ed. *Deutschlands Rüstung im Zweiten Weltkrieg: Hitlers Konferenzen mit Albert Speer 1942–1945.* Frankfurt: Akademische Verlagsgesellschaft Athnena-ion, 1969.

Borkowski, Dieter. *Wer weiss, ob wir uns wiedersehen: Erinnerungen an eine Berliner Jugend.* Frankfurt: Fischer, 1980.

Boveri, Margaret. *Tage des Überlebens: Berlin 1945.* Munich: R. Piper, 1968.

Bradley, Dermott, and Richard Schulze-Kossens, eds. *Tätigkeitsbericht des Chefs des Heerespersonalamtes, General der Infanterie Rudolf Schmundt 1.10.1942–29.10.1944.* Osnabrück: Biblio, 1984.

Bruder, Adelheid, ed. "Zu den letzten Kriegstagen 1945 in Backnang: Aufzeich-nungen aus einem Tagebuch von Karl Bruder." *Beiträge zur Geschichte der Stadt Backnang* 6 (1987): 203–17.

Busse, Theodor. "Die letzte Schlacht der 9. Armee." *Wehrwissenschaftliche Rundschau* 5, no. 4 (Apr. 1956): 145–68.

Butcher, Harry C. *My Three Years with Eisenhower.* New York: Simon and Schuster, 1946.

Chandler, Alfred, Stephen E. Ambrose, Joseph P. Hobbs, Edwin Alan Thompson, and Elizabeth F. Smith, eds. *The Papers of Dwight David Eisenhower: The War Years.* Vol. 4. Baltimore: Johns Hopkins University Press, 1970.

Chuikov, Vasili I. *The End of the Third Reich.* Translated by Ruth Kisch. London: Panther, 1969.

———. *The Fall of Berlin.* Translated by Ruth Kisch. New York: Holt, Rinehart and Winston, 1967.

Deichelmann, Hans. *Ich sah Königsberg sterben: Aus den Tagebücher eines Arztes.* Aachen: Aachener Nachrichten, 1948.

Detwiler, Donald S., Charles B. Burdick, and Jürgen Rohwer, eds. *World War II German Military Studies.* 24 vols. New York: Garland, 1979.

Deutsche Gasolin A.G. *Leuna Zapfstellen Atlas.* Berlin: DGAG, 1938.

Dokumentationsarchiv des Österreichischen Widerstandes. *Widerstand und Verfolgung im Burgenland 1934–1945: Eine Dokumentation.* Vienna: Österreichischer Bundesverlag, 1979.

———. *Widerstand und Verfolgung in Tirol 1934–45: Eine Dokumentation.* Vol. 2. Vienna: Österreichischer Bundesverlag, 1984.

———. *Widerstand und Verfolgung in Wien 1934–45: Eine Dokumentation.* Vol. 3. Vienna: Österreichischer Bundesverlag, 1975.

Domarus, Max, ed. *Hitler: Reden und Proklamationen 1932–1945.* 2 vols. Wiesbaden: R. Lovit, 1973.

Edwards, Donald A. *A Private's Diary.* Detroit: Self-published, 1994.

Ein Mitkämpfer. "Das Volkssturmbataillon 591." *Allgemeine Schweizerische Militärzeitschrift* 3 (1948): 231–34.

Eisenhower, Dwight D. *Eisenhower's Own Story of the War: The Complete Report by the Supreme Commander.* New York: Arco, 1946.

Freytag von Loringhoven, Hanns Baron. *Das letzte Aufgebot des Teufels.* Nuremberg: Self-published, 1965.

Germany. Statistisches Reichsamt. *Statistik des Deutschen Reichs.* Vol. 550, *Amtliches Gemeindeverzeichnis für das Grossdeutsche Reich auf Grund der Volkszählung 1939.* Berlin: Verlag für Sozialpolitik, Wirtschaft und Statistik, 1944.

———. *Statistisches Jahrbuch 1941/42.* Vol. 59. Berlin: Verlag für Sozialpolitik, Wirtschaft und Statistik, 1944.

Germany, Federal Republic of. Bundesarchiv Zentralnachweisstelle—Korneleimünster. "Der Deutsche Volkssturm: Idee, Bildung, Organisation und Einsatz: Die Rechtstellung der Angehörigen des Deutschen Volkssturms," 1957.

———. "Sammlung wehrrechtlichen Gutachten und Vorschriften." Heft 20/21, Nr. 61, 135, "Fraueneinsatz im Deutschen Volkssturm," undated.

Goebbels, Joseph. *Die Tagebücher von Joseph Goebbels,* pt. 2, *Diktate, 1942–1945.* Vols. 13–15, Juli 1944–April 1945. Edited by Elke Fröhlich. Munich: K. G. Saur, 1995–1996.

Granzow, Klaus, ed. *Letzte Tage in Pommern: Tagebücher, Erinnerungen und Dokumente der Vertreibung.* Munich: Albert Langen–Georg Müller, 1984.

———. *Tagebuch eines Hitlerjungen, 1943–1945.* Bremen: Carl Schünemann, 1965.

Great Britain. *Weekly Political Intelligence Summaries,* Vols. 10–11, *July 1944 to June 1945.* Nos. 248–99. Millwood, N.Y.: Kraus International, 1983.

Great Britain. Parliament. *Hansard's Parliamentary Debates: Commons.* Series 5, vol. 404. 24 Oct.–28 Nov. 1944. London: HMSO, 1944.

Guderian, Heinz. *Erinnerungen eines Soldaten.* Heidelberg: Kurt Vowinckel, 1951.

Hagen, Louis, ed. *Geschäft ist Geschäft: Neun Deutsche unter Hitler.* Hamburg: Merlin, 1969.

Hartung, Hugo. *Schlesien 1944/45: Aufzeichnungen und Tagebücher.* Munich: Deutschen Taschenbuch, 1976.

Heck, Alfons. *The Burden of Hitler's Legacy.* Frederick, Colo.: Renaissance House, 1988.

———. *A Child of Hitler: Germany in the Days When God Wore a Swastika.* Frederick, Colo.: Renaissance House, 1985.

Heiber, Helmut, ed. *Goebbels Reden.* Vol. 2, *1939–1945.* Düsseldorf: Droste, 1972.

———. *Hitlers Lagebesprechungen.* Stuttgart: Deutsche Verlags-Anstalt, 1962.

———. *"Reichsführer!..." : Briefe an und von Himmler.* Stuttgart: Deutsche Verlags-Anstalt, 1968.

Heusinger, Adolf. *Befehl im Widerstreit: Schicksalsstunden der deutschen Armee 1923–1945.* Tübingen: Rainer Wunderlich Verlag Hermann Leins, 1957.

Hierl, Konstantin. *Im Dienst für Deutschland 1918–1945.* Heidelberg: Kurt Vowinckel, 1954.

Hitler, Adolf. *Mein Kampf.* Edited by John Chamberlain et al. New York: Reynal and Hitchcock, 1941.

Homsten, Georg, ed. *Die Berlin-Chronik: Daten, Personen, Dokumente.* Düsseldorf: Droste, 1984.

Hornig, Ernst. *Breslau 1945: Erlebnisse in der eingeschlossenen Stadt.* Würzburg: Bergstadtverlag Wilhelm Gottlieb Korn, 1986.

Hossbach, Friedrich. *Schlacht um Ostpreußen: Aus den Kämpfen der deutschen 4. Armee um Ostpreußen in der Zeit vom 19.7.1944–30.1.1945.* Überlingen am Bodensee: Otto Dikreiter, 1951.

Hubatsch, Walter, ed. *Hitlers Weisungen für die Kriegsführung 1939–1945: Dokumente des Oberkommandos der Wehrmacht.* Frankfurt: Bernhard und Graefe, 1962.

———. *Hitlers Weisungen für die Kriegsführung 1939–1945: Dokumente des Oberkommandos der Wehrmacht.* 2nd ed. Koblenz: Bernhard und Graefe, 1983.

Huber, Heinz, and Artur Müller, eds. *Das Dritte Reich: Seine Geschichte in Texten, Bildern, und Dokumenten.* Vol. 2, *Der Zusammenbruch der Macht.* Munich: Kurt Desch, 1962.

Institut für Zeitgeschichte. *Akten der Partei Kanzlei der NSDAP: Rekonstruktion eines verlorengegangenen Bestandes.* Munich: R. Oldenbourg, 1983 (microfiche collection).

International Military Tribunal. *Trial of the Major War Criminals.* Vols. 1, 5, and 10. Nuremberg: International Military Tribunal, 1947.

Jacobsen, Hans-Adolf, ed. *1939–1945: Der Zweite Weltkrieg in Chronik und Dokumenten.* Darmstadt: Wehr und Wissen, 1959.

Jacobsen, Hans-Adolf, and Werner Jochmann, eds. *Ausgewählte Dokumente zur Geschichte des Nationalsozialismus 1933–1945.* Vol. 3. Bielefeld: Neue Gesellschaft, 1961.

Jonca, Karol, and Alfred Konieczny, eds. *Festung Breslau.* Warsaw: Wroclawski Towarzystovo Naukowe, 1962.

Jordan, Rudolf. *Erlebt und Erlitten: Weg eines Gauleiters vom München bis Moskau.* Leoni am Starnbergersee: Druffel, 1971.

Kardorff, Ursula von. *Berliner Aufzeichnungen aus den Jahren 1942 bis 1945.* Munich: Biedenstein, 1962.

Kästner, Erich. *Notabene '45: Ein Tagebuch.* Berlin: Cecilie Dresden, 1961.

Kehrl, Hans. *Krisenmanager im Dritten Reich: Sechs Jahre Frieden—Sechs Jahre Krieg, Erinnerungen.* Düsseldorf: Droste, 1973.

Keitel, Wilhelm. *The Memoirs of Field Marshal Keitel.* Edited by Walter Görlitz. Translated by David Irving. New York: Stein and Day, 1966.

Kesselring, Albert. *Gedanken zum Zweiten Weltkrieg.* Bonn: Athenäum, 1955.

———. *Soldat bis zum letzten Tag.* Bonn: Athenäum, 1953.

Klusacek, Christine, Herbert Steiner, and Kurt Stimmer, eds. *Dokumentation zur Österreichischen Zeitgeschichte 1938–1945.* Vienna: Jugend und Volk, 1980.

Knappe, Siegfried, and Ted Brusaw. *Soldat: Reflections of a German Soldier, 1936–1949.* New York: Orion, 1992.

Koller, Karl. *Der letzte Monat: Die Tagebuchaufzeichnungen des ehemaligen Chef des Generalstabes der deutschen Luftwaffe vom 14. April bis 27. Mai 1945.* Mannheim: N. Wohlgemuth, 1949.

Konev, Ivan. *Year of Victory.* Moscow: Progress, 1969.

Kuby, Erich, ed. *Das Ende des Schreckens: Januar bis Mai 1945.* Hamburg: Ernst Kabel, 1984.

Lasch, Otto. *So fiel Königsberg.* Stuttgart: Motorbuch, 1977.

Lattre de Tasigny, Jean de. *The History of the French First Army.* Translated by Malcolm Barnes. London: Allen and Unwin, 1952.

Leeb, Emil. *Aus der Rüstung des Dritten Reichs (Das Heereswaffenamt 1938–1945): Ein authentischer Bericht des letzten Chef des Heereswaffenamt.* Frankfurt: E. S. Mittler und Sohn, 1963.

Lehmann, Fritz. *1939–1945: Beobachtungen und Bekenntnisse.* Hamburg: Hofmann und Campe, 1946.

Lehndorff, Hans Graf von. *Ostpreußische Tagebuch: Aufzeichnungen eines Artzes aus den Jahren 1945–1947.* Munich: Biederstein, 1961.

Lüdicke, Reinhard. "Straßenkämpfe im Südwesten Berlins 1945: Aufzeichnungen über seinen Volkssturmeinsatz vom 20. April bis 2. Mai, 1945." Eckart Henning, ed., *Der Bär von Berlin: Jahrbuch des Vereins für die Geschichte Berlins* (1977): 119–28.

MacIsaac, David, ed. *The United States Strategic Bombing Survey.* Vols. 1, 2, and 4. New York: Garland, 1976.

Maier, Reinhold, ed. *Ende und Wende: Das schwäbische Schicksal 1944–1946 in Briefe und Tagebuchaufzeichnungen.* Stuttgart: Rainer Wunderlich, 1948.

Montgomery, Jim. *B Company 776 Tank Destroyer Battalion in Combat.* Baltimore: Gateway, 1983.

Mühlen, Bengt von zur, ed. *Der Todeskampf der Reichshauptstadt.* Berlin: Chronos, 1994.

Nahm, Peter Paul. *Nach zwei Jahrzehnten: Erlebnisberichte über Flucht, Vertreibung und Eingliederung.* Wolfenbüttel: Grenzland Drückerei Rock, 1967.

Nationalsozialistischen Kraftfahr Korps (NSKK). *Strassen-Atlas von Deutschland.* Munich: Zentralverlag der NSDAP/Franz Eher Nachfolger, 1938.

Neumann, Peter. *The Black March: The Personal Study of an SS Man.* New York: William Sloane, 1959.

Noakes, Jeremy, and Geoffrey Pridham, eds. *Nazism 1919–1945: A History in Documents and Eyewitness Accounts.* 3 vols. New York: Schocken, 1983–1988.

Oven, Wilfred von. *Finale Furioso: Mit Goebbels bis zum Ende.* Tübingen: Grabert, 1974.

Pape, Rainer, ed. *"bis 5 nach 12": Herforder Kriegstagebuch 1944/45.* Herford: Bussesche Verlagshandlung, 1984.

Peikert, Paul. *"Festung Breslau" in den Berichten eines Pfarrers 22. Januar bis 6. Mai 1945.* Wroclaw: Ossolineum, 1968.

Petershagen, Rudolf. *Gewissen in Aufruhr.* Berlin: Verlag der Nation, 1958.

Pettenberg, Heinz. *Starke Verbände im Anflug auf Köln: Eine Kriegschronik in Tagebuchnotizen 1939–1945.* Cologne: J. P. Bachem, 1985.

Pöppel, Martin. *Heaven and Hell: The War Diary of a German Paratrooper.* Translated by Louise Willmot. New York: Hippocrene, 1988.

Präg, Werner, and Wolfgang Jacobmeyer, ed. *Das Diensttagebuch des deutschen Generalgouverneurs in Polen 1939–1945.* Stuttgart: Deutsche Verlags-Anstalt, 1975.

Rauschning, Hans, comp. *Das Jahr '45: Dichtung, Bericht, Protokoll deutscher Autoren.* Gütersloh: C. Bartelsmann, 1970.

Reschke, Volker. "Eine fliegende Volkssturmeinheit." *Zeitschrift für Heereskunde* 198 (1965): 34–35.

Ringler, Ralf Roland. *Illusion einer Jugend: Lieder, Fahnen und das bittere Ende, Hitler Jugend in Österreich, Ein Erlebnisbericht.* St. Pölten: Niederösterreichisches Pressehaus, 1977.

Sajer, Guy. *The Forgotten Soldier.* Translated by Lily Emmet. New York: Harper and Row, 1971.

Salomon, Ernst von. *Der Fragebogen.* Stuttgart: Europäisches Buchklub, 1951.

Schieder, Theodor. *Ein Bericht aus Ost- und Westpreußen 1945–47: Aufzeichnungen von Hans Graf von Lehndorff.* Bonn: Bundesministerium für Vertriebene, Flüchtlinge und Kriegsbeschädigte, 1960.

Schirach, Baldur von. *Ich glaubte an Hitler.* Hamburg: Mosaik, 1967.

Schmeling, Marianne. *Flee the Wolf: The Story of a Family's Miraculous Journey to Freedom.* Norfolk, Va.: Donning, 1978.

Schramm, Percy Ernst, ed. *Kriegstagebuch des Oberkommando der Wehrmacht.* Vol. 4. Frankfurt: Bernhard und Graefe, 1961.

Siemens-Schukertwerke. *Taschenatlas vom Deutschen Reich.* Gotha: Justus Perthes, 1927.

Smith, Walter Bedell. *Eisenhower's Six Great Decisions.* New York: Longmans, Green, 1956.

Speer, Albert. *Inside the Third Reich.* Translated by Richard Winston and Clara Winston. New York: Bonanza, 1982.

Springenschmid, Karl. *Die letzten Lützows: Wie 420 ostpreußische Hitlerjungen aus Kampf und Einsatz gerettet wurden.* Vaterstetten: Ardnt, 1977.

Stahlberg, Alexander. *Bounden Duty: The Memoirs of a German Officer 1932–1945.* Translated by Patricia Crampton. London: Brassey's, 1990.

Stannard, Richard M. *Infantry: An Oral History of a World War II American Infantry Battalion.* New York: Twayne, 1993.

Starcky, Georges. *L'Alsacien: Le Drame des Malgré Nous.* Paris: Editions France-Empire, 1983.

Steinhoff, Johannes. *The Last Chance: The Pilot's Plot Against Goering, 1944–1945.* Translated by J. A. Underwood. London: Hutchison, 1977.

Steinhoff, Johannes, Peter Pechel, and Dennis Showalter, eds. *Voices from the Third Reich: An Oral History.* Washington, D.C.: Regnery Gateway, 1989.

Stokes, Lawrence D., ed. *Kleinstadt und Nationalsozialismus: Ausgewählte Dokumente zur Geschichte von Eutin 1918–1945.* Neumünster: Karl Wachholz, 1984.

Studnitz, Hans-Georg von. *While Berlin Burns: The Diary of Hans-Georg von Studnitz 1943–45.* Englewood Cliffs, N.J.: Prentice-Hall, 1965.

Tams, Karl-Hermann. "Als Kompaniechef in Seelow im April 1945." *Militärgeschichte* 6 (1990): 565–75.

Trevor-Roper, Hugh R., ed. *The Bormann Letters: The Private Correspondence Between Martin Bormann and His Wife from January 1943 to April 1945*. Translated by R. H. Stevens. London: Weidenfeld and Nicholson, 1954.

————. *Final Entries 1945: The Diaries of Joseph Goebbels*. New York: Putnam, 1978.

Turnwald, Wilhelm. *Dokumente zur Austreibung der Sudetendeutschen*. Munich: Arbeitsgemeinschaft zur Wahrung Sudetendeutschen Interessen, 1952.

United States. Army. Office of the Chief Historian, European Command. *Disarmament and Disbandment of the German Armed Forces*. Frankfurt: Office of the Chief Historian, European Command, 1947.

United States. Army. Office of the Provost Marshal General, Prisoner of War Operations Division. *Historical Monograph*. Vol. 2. Washington, D.C.: Office of the Provost Marshal General, Prisoner of War Operations Division, 1945–1946.

United States. First U.S. Army. *Report of Operations 1 August 1944–22 February 1945*. 14 vols. Washington, D.C.: Department of the Army, 1946.

United States. Third U.S. Army. *After Action Report of the Third United States Army*. Wilmington, Del.: Scholarly Resources, 1983. Three reels of microfilm.

United States. Seventh U.S. Army. *Report of Operations of the Seventh United States Army in France and Germany 1944–1945*. Vols. 2 and 3. Heidelberg: Aloys Gräf, 1946.

United States Strategic Bombing Survey. Civilian Defense Division "Final Report (European Rept. #40)." In David MacIsaac, *The United States Strategic Bombing Survey*. Vol. 2. New York: Garland, 1976.

United States War Department. *Handbook on German Military Forces: War Department Technical Manual TM-E30-454*. Washington, D.C.: U.S. Government Printing Office, 1945.

Wahl, Karl. *". . . es ist das deutsche Herz": Erlebnisse und Erkenntnisse eines ehemaliges Gauleiters*. Augsburg: Selbstverlag Karl Wahl, 1954.

Warlimont, Walter. *Im Hauptquartier der deutschen Wehrmacht 1939–1945*. 3rd ed. Munich: Bernhard und Graefe, 1978.

Weidling, Helmut. "Endkampf um Berlin 1945." *Wehrwissenschaftliche Rundschau* 12, no. 1 (Jan. 1959): 40–52; 12, no. 2 (Feb. 1959): 111–18; 12, no. 3 (Mar. 1959): 169–74.

Wilckens, Hans Jürgen von, ed. *Die Große Not: Danzig-Westpreußen 1945*. Sarstedt/Hannover: Niederdeutscher Verlag Ulrich and Zeiss, 1957.

Wolff-Mönckeberg, Mathilde. *On the Other Side: To My Children from Germany 1940–1945*. Translated by Ruth Evans. London: Peter Owen, 1979.

Zhukov, Georgi. *Reminiscences and Reflections*. Vol. 2. Moscow: Progress, 1985.

Secondary Sources

Absolon, Rudolf. *Wehrgesetz und Wehrdienst 1935–1945: Das Personalwesen in der Wehrmacht*. Boppard am Rhein: Harald Boldt, 1960.

Ahlers, Conrad, et al. *Das Ende, das ein Anfang war*. Freiburg im Breisgau: Herder, 1981.

Allen, Peter. *One More River to Cross: The Rhine Crossings of 1945*. New York: Scribner, 1980.

Allen, William Sheridan. *The Nazi Seizure of Power: The Experience of a Single German Town 1922–1945.* Rev. ed. New York: Franklin Watts, 1984.

Ansbacher, Heinz. "Attitudes of German Prisoners of War: A Study of the Dynamics of National Socialistic Followership." *Psychological Monographs: General and Applied* 62, no. 1 (1948): entire issue.

Arndt, Werner. *Ostpreußen, Westpreußen, Pommern, Schlesien, Sudetenland 1944/45: Die Bild-Dokumentation der Flucht und Vertreibung aus deutschem Ostgebiet.* Friedburg: Podzun-Pallas, n.d.

Arntz, H. Dieter. *Kriegsende 1944/45: Zwischen Ardennen und Rhein.* Euskirchen: Kumpel, 1984.

Asprey, Robert. *War in the Shadows: The Guerrilla in History.* Garden City, N.Y.: Doubleday, 1975.

Bachor, Oskar-Wilhelm. *Der Kreis Gerdauen: Ein Ostpreußisches Heimatbuch.* Würzburg: Holzner, 1965.

Bacque, James. *Other Losses: An Investigation into the Mass Deaths of German Prisoners at the Hands of the French and Americans After World War II.* Toronto: Stoddard, 1989.

Baird, Jay W. *The Mythical World of Nazi War Propaganda 1939–1945.* Minneapolis: University of Minnesota Press, 1974.

Bartov, Omer. *The Eastern Front, 1941–1945: German Troops and the Barbarisation of Warfare.* New York: St. Martin's, 1985.

———. *Hitler's Army: Soldiers, Nazis and War in the Third Reich.* New York: Oxford University Press, 1991.

Bass, Michael. *The Story of the Century: The 100th Infantry Division.* New York: Century Association, 1946.

Battenberg, Friedrich, Jürgen Rainer Wolf, Eckhardt G. Wolf, and Fritz Deppert. *Darmstadts Geschichte: Fürstenresidenz und Bürgerstadt im Wandel der Jahrhundete.* Darmstadt: Eduard Rother, 1980.

Beck, Earl R. *Under the Bombs: The German Home Front 1942–1945.* Lexington: University Press of Kentucky, 1986.

Bennett, Ralph. *Ultra in the West: The Normandy Campaign 1944–1945.* London: Hutchinson, 1979.

Berghahn, Volker. "Meinungsforschung im 'Dritten Reich': Die Mundpropaganda-Aktionen der Wehrmacht im letzten Kriegshalbjahr." *Militärgeschichtliche Mitteilungen* 1 (1967): 83–119.

———. "NSDAP und 'Geistige Führung' der Wehrmacht." *Vierteljahrshefte für Zeitgeschichte* 17 (1969): 17–71.

Bergschicker, Heinz. *Deutsche Chronik 1933–1945: Alltag im Faschismus.* West Berlin: Elefanten, 1983.

Bessel, Richard. *Political Violence and the Rise of Nazism: The Storm Troopers in Eastern Germany.* New Haven, Conn.: Yale University Press, 1984.

Besson, Waldemar. "Zur Geschichte der nationalsozialistische Führungsoffiziere." *Vierteljahrsheft für Zeitgeschichte* 9, no. 1 (Jan. 1961): 76–116.

Besymenski, Lew. *Die letzten Notizen von Martin Bormann: Ein Dokument und sein Verfasser.* Translated by Reinhold Holler. Stuttgart: Deutsche Verlags Anstalt, 1974.

Biddiscombe, Perry. *Werwolf! The History of the National Socialist Guerrilla Movement, 1944–1946*. Toronto: University of Toronto Press, 1998.

Bischof, Günther, and Stephen E. Ambrose, eds. *Eisenhower and the German POWs: Facts Against Falsehood*. Baton Rouge: Louisiana State University Press, 1992.

Bishop, Leo, Frank J. Glasgow, and George A. Fisher. *The Fighting Forty-fifth: The Combat Report of an Infantry Division*. Nashville, Tenn.: Battery Press, 1978.

Blake, George, *Mountain and Flood: The History of the 52nd (Lowland) Division 1939–1946*. Glasgow: Jackson, Son and Company, 1950.

Blond, Georges. *The Death of Hitler's Germany*. Translated by Frances Frenaye. New York: Macmillan, 1954.

Blumenson, Martin. *The United States Army in World War Two*. Vol. 3, *The European Theater of War*. Pt. 5, *Breakout and Pursuit*. Washington, D.C.: Office of the Chief of Military History, 1961.

Blumenstock, Friedrich. *Der Einmarsch der Amerikaner und Franzosen im nördlichen Württemberg in April 1945*. Stuttgart: Kohlhammer, 1957.

Böddecker, Gunther. *Die Flüchtlinge: Die Vertreibung der Deutschen im Osten*. Munich: Herbig, 1980.

Boelcke, Willi A. *Die deutsche Wirtschaft 1930–1945: Interna des Reichswirtschaftsministerium*. Düsseldorf: Droste, 1983.

Boese, Karl. *Geschichte der Stadt Schneidemühl*. Würzburg: Holzner, 1960.

Boldt, Gerhard. *Hitler: Die letzten zehn Tage*. Frankfurt am Main: Ullstein, 1973.

———. *Hitler: The Last Ten Days*. New York: Coward, McCann, and Geoghegan, 1973.

Bomm, Helmut. "Die Backnanger Widerstand gegen die Nazis vor dem Einmarsch der Amerikaner am 20. April 1945." *Beiträge zur Geschichte der Stadt Backnang* 5 (1986): 154–68.

———. *Das Ende daß ein Anfang war: Der Zweite Weltkrieg und die letzten Kriegstage in Backnang und im Murrtal*. Backnang: Stadtarchiv und Stadtverwaltung Backnang, 1985.

Boon, J. T. *History of the South Wales Borderers and the Monmouthshire Regiment, 1937–1952*. Pt. 2, *The Second Battalion, The South Wales Borderers, D-Day 1944 to 1945*. Pontypool: Hughes and Sons, 1955.

Bosch, Heinz. *Der Zweite Weltkrieg zwischen Rhein und Maas: Eine Dokumentation der Kriegsereignisse im Kreise Geldern 1939–1945*. Geldern: Oberkreisdirektor des Kreises Geldern, 1970.

Boston, Bernard. *History of the 398th Infantry Regiment in World War II*. Washington, D.C.: Infantry Journal Press, 1947.

Botwinick, Rita S. *Winzig, Germany, 1933–1946: The History of a Town Under the Third Reich*. Westport, Conn.: Praeger, 1992.

Boyd, Carl. *Hitler's Japanese Confidant: General Oshima Hiroshi and MAGIC Intelligence 1941–1945*. Lawrence: University Press of Kansas, 1993.

Brandes, Detlef. *Die Tschechen unter Deutschen Protektorat*. 2 vols. Munich: R. Oldenburg, 1975.

Braunschweig, Günther, "Untergang in Königsberg." *Jahrbuch der Albertus Universität zu Königsberg/Preußen* 3 (1953): 182–231.

Bredenberg, Fritz. *Der Kreis Sensburg*. Würzburg: Holzner, 1960.

Breitman, Richard, and Shlomo Aronson, "The End of the 'Final Solution'? Nazi Plans to Ransom Jews in 1944." *Central European History* 25, no. 2 (undated): 177–203.

Bretschneider, Heike. *Der Widerstand gegen den Nationalsozialismus in München 1933 bis 1945*. Munich: Stadtarchiv München, 1968.

Briggs, Richard A. *Black Hawks over the Danube: The History of the 86th Infantry Division in World War II*. West Point, Ky.: Tioga, 1957.

Broszat, Martin, Elke Fröhlick, Anton Grossmann, and Falk Wiesemann. *Bayern in der NS Zeit: Herrschaft und Gesellschaft im Konflikt*. 4 vols. Munich: R. Oldenbourg, 1977–81.

Brückner, Joachim. *Kriegsende in Bayern 1945: Der Wehrkreis VII und die Kämpfe zwischen Donau und Alpen*. Freiburg im Breisgau: Rombach, 1987.

Brustat-Naval, Fritz. *Unternehmung Rettung: Letztes Schiff nach Westen*. Herford: Kohler, 1970.

Bukey, Evan B. *Hitler's Hometown: Linz, Austria 1908–1945*. Bloomington: Indiana University Press, 1986.

Burkert, Hans-Norbert, Klaus Matußek, and Doris Obschernitzki. *Zerstört, Besezt, Befreit: Der Kampf um Berlin bis zur Kapitulation 1945*. Berlin: Pädegogischen Zentrum, 1985.

Butterton, Meredith L. *Metric 16*. Durham, N.C.: Moore, 1972.

Byrnes, Lawrence G. *History of the 94th Infantry Division in World War II*. Washington, D.C.: Infantry Journal Press, 1948.

Carroll, Berenice. *Design for Total War: Arms and Economics in the Third Reich*. Paris: Mouton, 1968.

Cassidy, G. L. *Warpath: The Story of the Algonquin Regiment 1939–1945*. Toronto: Ryerson, 1948.

Christoffel, Edgar. *Der Endkampf zwischen Mosel, Saar und Ruwer 1944/45: Der Durchbruch der Amerikaner im südlichen Hunsrück zum Vormarsch nach Trier und zum Rhein*. Trier: Koch, 1985.

Clark, Alan. *Barbarossa: The Russian-German Conflict 1941–45*. New York: Morrow, 1965.

Clarke, Jeffery J., and Robert Ross Smith, *The United States Army in World War Two*. Vol. 3, *The European Theater of War*. Pt. 10, *Riviera to the Rhine*. Washington, D.C.: Center of Military History, 1993.

Colby, John. *War from the Ground Up: The 90th Division in World War II*. Austin, Tex.: Nortex, 1991.

Cole, Hugh M. *The United States Army in World War Two*. Vol. 3, *The European Theater of War*. Pt. 7, *The Ardennes: The Battle of the Bulge*. Washington, D.C.: Office of the Chief of Military History, 1965.

———. *The United States Army in World War Two*. Vol. 3, *The European Theater of War*. Pt. 1, *The Lorraine Campaign*. Washington, D.C.: Office of the Chief of Military History, 1950.

Cooper, John P., Jr. *The Story of the 110th Field Artillery*. Baltimore: War Records Division, Maryland Historical Society, 1953.

Cooper, Matthew. *The German Army 1939–1945*. New York: Stein and Day, 1978.

Cross, Robin. *Fallen Eagle: The Last Days of the Third Reich*. London: Michael O'Mara, 1995.

Dieckert, Kurt, and Horst Grossmann, *Der Kampf um Ostpreußen: Der umfassende Dokumentarbericht über das Kriegsgeschehen in Ostpreußen.* Stuttgart: Motorbuch, 1976.

Diehl, James M. "Victors or Victims? Disabled Veterans in the Third Reich." *Journal of Modern History* 59, no. 4 (Dec. 1987): 705–36.

Doerrbach, Hubert, and Herbert Meininger, *Stadtgeschichte und Bilddokumentation Karlsruhe.* Karlsruhe: Braun und Müller, 1984.

Dollinger, Hans. *The Decline and Fall of Nazi Germany and Imperial Japan.* Translated by Arnold Pomerans. New York: Bonanza, 1982.

Domarus, Max. *Der Untergang des alten Würzburgs im Luftkrieg gegen die deutschen Großstädte.* Gerolzhofen: Teutsch, 1969.

Domarus, Wolfgang. *Nationalsozialismus: Krieg und Bevölkerungsuntersuchungen zur Lage, Volksstimmung und Haltung in Augsburg während des Dritten Reiches.* Munich: R. Wölfe, 1977.

Draper, Theodore. *The 84th Infantry Division in the Battle of Germany.* New York: Viking, 1946.

Dunlop, J. K. "The Capitulation of Hamburg, 3 May, 1945." *Journal of the Royal United Service Institution* 94, no. 593 (Feb. 1954): 80–89.

Durand, Algernon T. M., and Maj. R.H.W.S. Hastings. *The London Rifle Brigade 1919–1950.* Aldershot: Gale and Polden, 1952.

Dyer, George. *XII Corps: Spearhead of Patton's Third Army.* N.p.: XII Corps Historical Association, 1947.

Eggert, Oskar. *Das Ende des Krieges und die Besatzungszeit in Stralsund und Umgebung 1945–1946.* Hamburg: Pommerschen Buchversand, 1967.

Ehrhardt, Traugott. *Die Geschichte der Festung Königsberg 1257–1945.* Würzburg: Holzner, 1960.

Ellis, Lionel F., and Alan E. Warhurst. *Victory in the West.* 2 vols. London: HMSO, 1962–1968.

Engelmann, Bernt. *In Hitler's Germany: Daily Life in the Third Reich.* Translated by Kristina Winston. New York: Pantheon, 1986.

Erickson, John. *Stalin's War with Germany.* 2 vols. Boulder, Colo.: Westview, 1975–1983.

Essame, Hubert. *The 43rd Wessex Division at War 1944–1945.* London: William Clowes and Sons, 1952.

Evans, Roger. *The Story of the Fifth Royal Inniskilling Dragoon Guards.* Aldershot: Gale and Polden, 1951.

Farquharson, J. E. *The Plough and the Swastika: The NSDAP and Agriculture in Germany 1928–45.* Beverly Hills, Calif.: Sage, 1976.

Flanner, Karl. *Widerstand im Gebiet von Wiener Neustadt 1938–1945.* Vienna: Europa, 1973.

Fleischauer, Ingeborg. *Die Chance des Sonderfriedens: Deutsch-sowjetische Geheimgespräche 1941–1945.* Berlin: Siedler, 1986.

Forever in the Shadow of Hitler? Original Documents of the Historikerstreit, the Controversy in Germany Concerning the Singularity of the National Socialist Annihilation of the Jews. Atlantic Highlands, N.J.: Humanities Press, 1993.

Förster, Jürgen. "The Dynamics of Volksgemeinschaft: The Effectiveness of the German Military Establishment in the Second World War." In *Military Effec-*

tiveness, Vol. 3, *The Second World War,* ed. Alan R. Millett and Williamson Murray, 180–220. Boston: Allen and Unwin, 1988.

———. "The German Army and the Ideological War against the Soviet Union." In *The Policies of Genocide: Jews and Soviet Prisoners of War in Nazi Germany,* Gerhard Hirschfeld, ed., 15–29. London: Allen and Unwin, 1986.

Fritz, Stephen. *Frontsoldaten: The German Soldier in World War Two.* Lexington: University Press of Kentucky, 1995.

———. "'We are trying . . . to change the face of the world'—Ideology and Motivation in the Wehrmacht on the Eastern Front: The View from Below." *Journal of Military History* 60, no. 4 (Oct. 1996): 683–710.

Fritzsche, Peter. "Machine Dreams: Airmindedness and the Reinvention of Germany." *American Historical Review* 98, no. 3 (June 1993): 685–709.

Fröbe, Rainer, et al. *Konzentrationslager in Hannover: KZ Arbeit und Rüstungsindustrie in der Spätphase des Zweiten Weltkrieges.* Hildesheim: August Lax, 1985.

Frohn, Robert. *Köln 1945–1981: Von Trümmerhaufen zur Millionenstadt.* Cologne: J. P. Bachene, 1982.

Gackenholz, Hermann. "The Collapse of Army Group Center in 1944." In *The Decisive Battles of World War Two: The German View,* ed. Hans-Adolf Jacobsen and Jürgen Rohwer, 355–83. Translated by Edward Fitzgerald. London: Andre Deutsch, 1965.

Gander, Terry, and Peter Chamberlain. *Weapons of the Third Reich.* Garden City, N.Y.: Doubleday, 1979.

Gause, Fritz. *Die Geschichte der Stadt Königsberg in Preußen.* Vol. 3, *Vom Ersten Weltkrieg bis zum Untergang Königsbergs.* Cologne: Böhlau, 1971.

Gellately, Robert. *The Gestapo and German Society: Enforcing Racial Policy 1933–1945.* Oxford: Clarendon, 1991.

Gellermann, Günther W. *Die Armee Wenck—Hitlers letze Hoffnung: Aufstellung, Einsatz und Ende der 12. deutschen Armee im Frühjahr 1945.* Koblenz: Bernard und Graefe, 1984.

Gersdorff, Ursula von. *Frauen im Kriegsdienst 1914–1945.* Stuttgart: Deutsche Verlags-Anstalt, 1969.

Glantz, David M., and Jonathan M. House, *When Titans Clashed: How the Red Army Stopped Hitler.* Lawrence: University Press of Kansas, 1995.

Görlitz, Walter. *Der Zweite Weltkrieg 1939–1945.* Vol. 2. Stuttgart: Steingruber, 1952.

Gosztony, Peter. *Endkampf an der Donau 1944/45.* Vienna: Fritz Molden, 1969.

Gottlieb, Günther, et al. *Geschichte der Stadt Augsburg: 2000 Jahre von der Römerzeit bis zur Gegenwart.* Stuttgart: Konrad Theiss, 1981.

Grant, D. W. *"Carry On": The History of the Toronto Scottish Regiment (M.G.) 1939–1945.* N.p, 1949.

Great Britain. Army. 23rd Hussar Regiment. *The Story of the Twenty-third Hussars 1940–1946.* Husum: 23rd Hussar Regiment, 1946.

Great Britain. Ministry of Economic Warfare. *Who's Who in Germany and Austria.* London: Ministry of Economic Warfare, 1945.

Grier, Howard D. "Hitler's Baltic Strategy, 1944–45." Ph.D. diss., University of North Carolina, 1991.

Grill, Johnpeter Horst. *The Nazi Movement in Baden 1920–1945*. Chapel Hill: University of North Carolina Press, 1983.

Grobosch, Werner. "Entstehung und Rolle des Deutschen Volkssturms." *Militärgeschichte* 6, no. 2 (1978): 180–92.

Groehler, Olaf, and Wolfgang Schumann. "Vom Krieg zum Nachkrieg: Probleme der Militärstrategie und Politik des faschistischen deutschen Imperialismus in der Endphase des Zweiten Weltkrieges." *Jahrbuch für Geschichte* 24 (1981): 275–97.

Grunberger, Richard. *The Twelve-Year Reich: A Social History of Nazi Germany 1933–1945*. New York: Holt, Rinehart and Winston, 1971.

Gurfein, M. I., and Morris Janowitz. "Trends in Wehrmacht Morale." *Public Opinion Quarterly* 10 (spring 1946): 78–84.

Gusovius, Paul. *Der Landkreis Samland*. Würzburg: Holzner, 1966.

Hamburg Institute for Social Research. *The German Army and Genocide: Crimes Against War Prisoners, Jews and Other Civilians, 1939–1944*. Translated by Scott Abbott and Paula Bradish. New York: New Press, 1999.

Hancock, Eleanor. *The National Socialist Leadership and Total War, 1941–45*. New York: St. Martin's, 1991.

Hansen, Reimer. "Ribbentrops Friedensfühler im Frühjahr 1945." *Geschichte in Wissenschaft und Unterricht* 18 (1967): 716–30.

Harrison, Gordon A. *The United States Army in World War Two*. Vol. 3, *The European Theater of War*. Pt. 2, *Cross-Channel Attack*. Washington, D.C.: Office of the Chief of Military History, 1951.

Hartmann, Erich. *Geschichte der Stadt Hohenstein in Ostpreußen*. Würzburg: Holzner, 1959.

Haupt, Werner. *Als die Rote Armee nach Deutschland kam: Der Untergang der Divisionen in Ostpreußen, Danzig, Westpreußen, Mecklenburg, Pommern, Schlesien, Sachsen, Berlin und Brandenburg*. Friedberg: Podzun-Pallas, 1981.

———. *Berlin 1945: Hitlers letzte Schlacht*. Rastatt: Erich Pable, 1963.

———. *Rückzug im Westen, 1944*. Stuttgart: Motorbuch, 1978.

Hechler, Ken. *The Bridge at Remagen*. New York: Ballantine, 1957.

Heiber, Helmut. *Goebbels*. Translated by John K. Dickinson. New York: Hawthorne, 1972.

Held, Walter. *Verbände und Truppen der deutschen Wehrmacht und Waffen SS im Zweiten Weltkrieg*. Osnabrück: Biblio, 1978.

Herzstein, Robert E. *The War That Hitler Won: The Most Infamous Propaganda Campaign in History*. New York: Putnam, 1978.

Hielscher, Karl. "Das Kriegsende 1945 im Westteil des Warthelands und im Osten der Neumark." *Zeitschrift für Ostforschung* 34, no. 2 (1985): 213–48.

Hillgruber, Andreas. *Zweierlei Untergang: Die Zerschlagung des Deutschen Reiches und das Ende der europäischen Judentums*. Berlin: Siedler, 1986.

Hirschfeld, Gerhard, ed. *The Policies of Genocide: Jews and Soviet Prisoners of War in Nazi Germany*. London: Allen and Unwin, 1986.

Hodemacher, Jürgen. *Salzgitter*. Düsseldorf: Droste, 1984.

Hoffmann, Peter. *The History of the German Resistance 1933–1945*. Translated by Richard Barry. Cambridge, Mass.: MIT Press, 1977.

Höhne, Heinz. *The Order of the Death's Head: The Story of Hitler's SS*. Translated by Richard Barry. New York: Ballantine, 1971.

Homze, Edward L. *Foreign Labor in Nazi Germany*. Princeton, N.J.: Princeton University Press, 1967.

Hopffgarten, Hans-Joachim von. "The Battle for the Lebus and Görlitz Bridgeheads on the Oder." *Military Review* 35, no. 12 (March, 1956): 98–107.

Horwitz, Gordon J. *In the Shadow of Death: Living Outside the Gates of Mauthausen*. New York: Free Press, 1990.

Hubatsch, Walter. *Die 61. Infanterie Division 1939 bis 1945: Ein Bericht in Wort und Bild*. Friedburg: Podzun-Pallas, 1983.

Hüttenberger, Peter. *Die Gauleiter: Studie zum Wandel des Machtgefüges in der NSDAP*. Stuttgart: Deutsche Verlags-Anstalt, 1969.

Institut für Marxismus-Leninismus. *Geschichte des Grossen Vaterländischen Krieges der Sowjetunion*. Vols. 4 and 5. Berlin: Deutsches Militärverlag, 1965–1967.

———. *Geschichte des Zweiten Weltkrieges 1939–1945*. 12 vols. East Berlin: Militärverlag der DDR, 1978–1985.

Jacobsen, Hans-Adolf, and Jürgen Rohwer, eds. *The Decisive Battles of World War Two: The German View*. Translated by Edward Fitzgerald. London: Andre Deutsch, 1965.

Jedlicka, Ludwig. "Das Milizwesen in Österreich." *Wehrwissenschaftliche Rundschau* 9, no. 7 (1959): 378–90.

Jung, Hermann. *Die Ardennen Offensive 1944/45: Ein Beispiel für die Kriegführung Hitlers*. Göttingen: Musterschmidt, 1971.

Junger, Gerhard. *Schicksale 1945: Das Ende des 2. Weltkrieges im Kreise Reutlingen*. Reutlingen: Oertel und Spörer, 1971.

Kaps, Johannes. *The Tragedy of Silesia 1945–1946: A Documentary Account with a Special Survey of the Archdiocese of Breslau*. Translated by Gladys H. Hartinger. Munich: Christ Unterwegs, 1952–1953.

Kardel, Hennecke. *Die Geschichte der 170. Infanterie Division 1939–1945*. Bad Nauheim: Hans-Henning Podzun, 1953.

Kater, Michael H. *Doctors Under Hitler*. Chapel Hill: University of North Carolina Press, 1989.

———. *The Nazi Party: A Social Profile of Members and Leaders 1919–1945*. Cambridge, Mass.: Harvard University Press, 1983.

Kemp, Anthony. *The Unknown Battle: Metz, 1944*. New York: Stein and Day, 1981.

Kemp, P. K. *The Middlesex Regiment (Duke of Cambridge's Own) 1919–1952*. Aldershot: Gale and Polden, 1956.

Kemp, P. K., and John Graves. *The Red Dragon: The Story of the Royal Welsh Fusiliers 1919–1945*. Aldershot: Gale and Polden, 1960.

Kershaw, Ian. *Der Hitler-Mythos: Volksmeinung und Propaganda im Dritten Reich*. Stuttgart: Deutsche Verlags-Anstalt, 1980.

———. "How Effective Was Nazi Propaganda?" In *Nazi Propaganda: The Power and the Limitations*, edited by David Welch, 180–205. London: Croom Helm, 1983.

———. *Popular Opinion and Political Dissent in the Third Reich: Bavaria 1933–1945*. Oxford: Clarendon, 1983.

Kieser, Egbert. *Danziger Bucht 1945: Dokumentation einer Katastrophe.* Esslingen am Neckar: Bechtle, 1978.

Kirwin, Gerald. "Allied Bombing and Nazi Domestic Propaganda." *European History Quarterly* 15, no. 3 (July 1985): 341–62.

Kissel, Hans. *Der Deutsche Volkssturm 1944/45: Eine territoriale Miliz im Rahmen der Landesverteidigung.* Frankfurt am Main: E. S. Mittler und Sohn, 1962.

Kitchen, Martin. *Nazi Germany at War.* New York: Longman, 1995.

Klabath, Rudolf. "Die Rolle der Seebrückenköpfe beim Kampf im Ostpreußen 1944–1945." In Militärgeschichtlichen Forschungsamt, *Abwehrkampf am Nordflügel der Ostfront 1944–1945.* Stuttgart: Deutsche Verlags-Anstalt, 1963, 271–451.

Klein, Burton. *Germany's Economic Preparation for War.* Cambridge, Mass.: Harvard University Press, 1959.

Klessmann, Eckart. *Geschichte der Stadt Hamburg.* Hamburg: Hoffmann und Campe, 1981.

Klietmann, K. G. "Der Deutsche Volkssturm im Tirol-Vorarlberg: Uniform und Abzeichen der Tiroler Standschützen 1944/1945." *Zeitschrift für Heereskunde* 47, no. 310 (1983): 157–58.

Klinkhammer, Lutz. *Zwischen Bündnis und Besatzung: Das nationalsozialistische Deutschland und die Republik von Salò 1943–1945.* Tübingen: Max Niemeyer, 1993.

Knickerbocker, Hubert R., et al. *Danger Forward: The Story of the First Division in World War II.* Washington, D.C.: Society of the First Division, 1947.

Koch, Johannes Hugo. *Heimatbuch Neustadt in Holstein.* Neustadt in Holstein: Selbstverlag, 1967.

Kolesnik, A. D. *Narodnoe opolchenie gorodov-geroev [People's Militia of the Hero-cities].* Moscow: Nauka, 1974.

Kösters, Hans G. *Essen Stunde Null: Die letzten Tage März–April 1945.* Düsseldorf: Droste, 1982.

Kraume, Hans-Georg. *Duisberg im Krieg, 1939–1945.* Düsseldorf: Droste, 1982.

Kropat, Wolf-Arno. *Hessen in der Stunde Null 1945/1947.* Wiesbaden: Selbstverlag der Historischen Kommission für Nassau, 1979.

Kuby, Erich, *The Russians and Berlin, 1945.* Translated by Arnold J. Pomerans. New York: Hill and Wang, 1968.

Kühling, Karl. *Osnabrück 1933–1945: Stadt im Dritten Reich.* Quakenbrück: Robert Kleinert, 1969.

Kunze, Karl. *Kriegsende in Franken und der Kampf um Nürnberg im April 1945.* Nuremberg: Selbstverlag des Vereins für Geschichte der Stadt Nürnberg, 1995.

Kurowski, Franz. *Armee Wenck.* Neckargemund: Kurt Vohwinckel, 1967.

Lachs, Johannes, and Friedrich Karl Reif. *Rostock.* Rostock: Hinstorff, 1968.

Lakowski, Richard. *Seelow 1945: Die Entscheidungsschlacht an der Oder.* Berlin: Brandenburgisches Verlagshaus, 1995.

Lang, Jochen von. *The Secretary, Martin Bormann: The Man Who Manipulated Hitler.* Translated by Christa Armstrong and Peter White. New York: Random House, 1976.

Laqueur, Walter. *Guerrilla: A Historical and Critical Study.* Boston: Little, Brown, 1976.

Lauen, Walter E. *Battle Babies: The Story of the 99th Infantry Division in World War II*. Baton Rouge: Military Press of Louisiana, 1951.

Leipner, Kurt. *Chronik der Stadt Stuttgart 1933–1945*. Stuttgart: Klett-Cotta, 1982.

Leiwig, Heinz. *Finale 1945 Rhein-Main*. Düsseldorf: Droste, 1985.

———. *Mainz 1933–1948: Von der Machtergreifung bis zur Wahrungsreform*. Mainz: Hermann Schmidt, 1987.

Lerner, Daniel. *Psychological Warfare Against Nazi Germany: The Sykewar Campaign, D-Day to VE Day*. Cambridge, Mass.: MIT Press, 1971.

Le Tissier, Tony. *The Battle of Berlin 1945*. London: Jonathan Cape, 1988.

———. *Zhukov at the Oder: The Decisive Battle for Berlin*. Westport, Conn.: Praeger, 1996.

Lindenblatt, Helmut. *Pommern 1945: Eines des letzten Kapitels in der Geschichte vom Untergang des Dritten Reiches*. Leer: Gerhard Rautenberg, 1984.

Liulevicius, Vejas Gabriel. *War Land on the Eastern Front: Culture, National Identity and German Occupation in World War I*. New York: Cambridge University Press, 2000.

Livet, Georges, et al. *Histoire de Colmar*. Toulouse: Editions Privat, 1983.

Longerich, Peter. "Joseph Goebbels und der Totale Krieg: Eine unbekannte Denkschrift des Propagandaministers vom 18. Juli 1944." *Vierteljahrsheft für Zeitgeschichte* 35, no. 2 (1987): 289–317.

Lorei, Madlen, and Richard Kirn. *Frankfurt und die drei Wilden Jahre: Ein Bericht*. Frankfurt: Frankfurter Bücher, 1963.

Lucas, James. *Germany's Elite Panzer Force: Großdeutschland*. London: MacDonald and Jane's, 1978.

Lüdde-Neurath, Walther. "Das Ende auf deutschem Boden." In *Bilanz des Zweiten Weltkrieges: Erkenntnisse und Verpflichtungen für die Zukunft*. Oldenburg: Gerhard Stalling, 1953.

Luza, Radomir V. *The Resistance in Austria 1938–1945*. Minneapolis: University of Minnesota Press, 1984.

MacDonald, Charles B. *The United States Army in World War Two*. Vol. 3, *The European Theater of War*. Pt. 6, *The Siegfried Line Campaign*. Washington, D.C.: Office of the Chief of Military History, 1963.

———. *The United States Army in World War Two*. Vol. 3, *The European Theater of War*. Pt. 9, *The Last Offensive*. Washington, D.C.: Office of the Chief of Military History, 1973.

MacKenzie, S. P. *The Home Guard: A Political and Military History*. New York: Oxford University Press, 1995.

Magenheimer, Heinz. *Abwehrschlacht an der Weichsel 1945: Vorbereitung, Ablauf, Erfahrungen*. Freiburg: Rombach, 1976.

Mammach, Klaus. *Der Volkssturm: Das letzte Aufgebot 1944/45*. Cologne: Pahl Rugenstein, 1981.

Manvell, Roger, and Heinrich Fraenkel. *Dr. Goebbels, His Life and Death*. New York: Simon and Schuster, 1960.

Mark, Wilhelm. "Miliz: Betrachtungen zu einer Geschichte des deutschen Volkssturms." *Allgemeine Schweizerische Militärzeitschrift* 128 (Dec. 1962): 693–97.

Mason, Tim. "The Legacy of 1918 for National Socialism." In *German Democracy and the Triumph of Hitler*, edited by Anthony Nicholls and Erich Matthias, 215–49. New York: St. Martin's, 1971.

Maurer, Helmut. *Konstanzer Stadtgeschichte im Überblick*. Sigmaringen: Jan Thorbecke, 1979.

Mazower, Mark. *Inside Hitler's Greece: The Experience of Occupation, 1941–1944*. New Haven, Conn.: Yale University Press, 1993.

McKee, Alexander. *The Race for the Rhine Bridges 1940, 1944, 1945*. New York: Stein and Day, 1971.

Messerschmidt, Manfred. "German Military Law in the Second World War." In *The German Military in the Age of Total War*, edited by Wilhelm Deist, 323–35. Dover, N.H.: Berg, 1985.

———. *Die Wehrmacht im NS Staat: Zeit der Indoktrination*. Hamburg: R. von Decker, 1969.

———. "The Wehrmacht and the Volksgemeinschaft." *Journal of Contemporary History* 18, no. 4 (Oct. 1983): 719–44.

Meyer, Heinz. *Damals: Der Zweite Weltkrieg zwischen Teutoberger Wald, Weser und Leine*. Preußische Oldendorf: K. W. Schultz, 1980.

Meyer, Werner. *Götterdämmerung: April 1945 in Bayreuth*. Percha am Starnbergersee: R. S. Schutz, 1975.

Meyerhoff, Hermann. *Herne 1933–1945: Die Zeit des Nationalsozialismus—Ein kommunalhistorischen Rückblick*. Herne: Stadt Herne, 1963.

Meyhöfer, Max. *Die Landgemeinden des Kreises Lötzen*. Würzburg: Holzner, 1966.

Mick, Allan H. *With the 102d Division Through Germany*. Washington, D.C.: Infantry Journal Press, 1947.

Mierzejewski, Alfred C. *The Collapse of the German War Economy, 1944–1945: Allied Air Power and the German National Railway*. Chapel Hill: University of North Carolina Press, 1988.

Mietzner, Franz. *Der Kreis Schloßberg: Ein ostpreußisches Heimatbuch*. Würzburg: Holzner, 1962.

Millett, Alan R., and Williamson Murray, eds. *Military Effectiveness*, Vol. 3, *The Second World War*. Boston: Allen and Unwin, 1988.

Milward, Alan S. *The German Economy at War*. London: Athlone, 1965.

Minott, Rodney G. *The Fortress That Never Was: The Myth of Hitler's Bavarian Stronghold*. New York: Holt, Rinehart and Winston, 1964.

Mistele, Karl H. "Zur Geschichte des Deutschen Volkssturms in Oberfranken." *Geschichte am Obermain* (1979/80): 110–23.

Molden, Otto. *Der Ruf des Gewissens: Der Österreichische Freiheitskampf 1938–1945*. Vienna: Herold, 1958.

Möller, Reiner. "Das Volkssturm im Kreis Steinberg." In *"Wir bauen das Reich": Aufstieg und erste Herrschaftsjahre des Nationalsozialismus in Schleswig-Holstein*, edited by Erich Hoffmann, and Peter Wulf. Neumünster: Wachholz, 1983.

Mühlberger, Detlev. *Hitler's Followers: Studies in the Sociology of the Nazi Movement*. London: Routledge, 1991.

Müller, Helmut. *Fünf vor Null: Die Besetzung des Münsterlandes 1945.* Münster: Aschendorff, 1983.

Müller, Rolf-Dieter, and Gerd R. Ueberschär. *Kriegsende 1945: Die Zerstörung des Deutschen Reiches.* Frankfurt: Fischer, 1994.

Müller, Rolf-Dieter, Gerd R. Ueberschär, and Wolfram Wette. *Wer zurückweicht wird erschossen! Kriegsalltag und Kriegsende in Südwestdeutschland 1944/45.* Freiburg im Breisgau: Dreisam, 1985.

Müller-Hillebrand, Burckhardt. *Das Heer 1933–1945: Entwicklung des organisatorischen Aufbaues.* Vol. 3. Frankfurt am Main: E. S. Mittler und Sohn, 1969.

Murawski, Erich. *Die Eroberung Pommerns durch die Rote Armee.* Boppard am Rhein: Harald Boldt, 1969.

Naasner, Walter. *Neue Machtzentren in der deutschen Kriegswirtschaft 1942–1945: Die Wirtschaftsorganisation der SS, das Amt des Generalbevollmächtigten für den Arbeitseinsatz und das Reichministerium für Bewaffnung und Munition/Reichsministerium für Rüstung und Kriegsproduktion im nationalsozialistischen Herrschaftssystem.* Boppard am Rhein: Harald Boldt, 1994.

Neillands, Robin. *The Conquest of the Reich: D-Day to VE-Day, A Soldier's History.* New York: New York University Press, 1995.

Neininger, Albert. *Rastatt als Residenz, Garnison, und Festung.* Rastatt: Selbstverlag, 1961.

Neufeld, Michael J. *The Rocket and the Reich: Peenemünde and the Coming of the Ballistic Missile Era.* New York: Free Press, 1995.

Nichols, Lester M. *Impact: The Battle Story of the 10th Armored Division.* New York: Bradbury, Sayles, O'Neill, 1954.

Nicolaisen, Hans-Dietrich. *Die Flakhelfer: Luftwaffenhelfer und Marinehelfer im Zweiten Weltkrieg.* Frankfurt: Ullstein, 1981.

Niehaus, Werner. *Endkampf zwischen Rhein und Weser: Nordwestdeutschland 1945.* Stuttgart: Motorbuch, 1983.

Noble, Alastair. "The People's Levy: The Volkssturm and Popular Mobilisation in Eastern Germany, 1944–45," *Journal of Strategic Studies* 24, no. 1 (Mar. 2001): 165–87.

North, John. *North-West Europe 1944–1945: The Achievement of 21st Army Group.* London: HMSO, 1953.

Orlow, Dietrich. *The History of the Nazi Party 1919–1945.* Vol. 2, *1933–1945.* Pittsburgh: University of Pittsburgh Press, 1973.

Ose, Dieter. *Entscheidung im Westen, 1944: Der Oberbefehlshaber West und die Abwehr der alliierten Invasion.* Stuttgart: Deutsche Verlags-Anstalt, 1982.

Overy, Richard. *War and Economy in the Third Reich.* New York: Oxford University Press, 1994.

Owings, Alison. *Frauen: German Women Recall the Third Reich.* New Brunswick, N.J.: Rutgers University Press, 1993.

Paul, Johann. *Vom Volksrat zum Volkssturm: Bergisch Gladbach und Bensburg 1918–1945.* Bergisch Gladbach: Heider, 1988.

Paul, Wolfgang. *Der Endkampf um Deutschland 1945.* Munich: Bechtle, 1976.

———. *Der Heimatkrieg 1939 bis 1945.* Esslingen am Neckar: Bechtle, 1980.

Persico, Joseph E. *Piercing the Reich: The Penetration of Nazi Germany by American Secret Agents During World War II.* New York: Viking, 1979.

Peterson, Edward N. *The Many Faces of Defeat: The German People's Experience in 1945.* New York: Peter Lang, 1990.

Podzun, Hans Henning. *Weg und Schicksal der 21. Infanterie Division.* Bad Nauheim: Hans Henning Podzun, 1951.

Preis, Kurt. *München unterm Hakenkreuz: Die Hauptstadt der Bewegung zwischen Pracht und Trümmern.* Munich: Ehrenwirth, 1980.

Prinz, Friedrich. *Trümmerzeit in München: Kultur und Gesellschaft einer deutschen Großstadt im Aufbruch 1945–1949.* Munich: C. H. Beck, 1984.

Prokofyev, N. "The Storm of Königsberg." *Soviet Military Review* 4 (Apr. 1969): 42–44.

Queen-Hughes, Robert W. *Whatever Men Dare: A History of the Queen's Own Cameron Highlanders of Canada 1935–1960.* Winnipeg: Bulman, 1960.

Rahier, Josef. *Jülich und das Jülicher Land in den Schicksaljahren 1944/45.* Jülich: Heimatverlag Josef Fischer, 1967.

Rauchensteiner, Manfred. *Krieg in Österreich 1945.* Vienna: Österreichischer Bundesverlag, 1970.

Rebentisch, Dieter. "Nationalsozialistische Revolution, Parteiherrschaft und totaler Krieg." In *Die Geschichte Hessens,* edited by Uwe Schultz, 232–48. Stuttgart: Konrad Theiss, 1983.

Rebhann, Fritz M. *Finale in Wien: Eine Gaustadt im Aschenregen.* Vienna: Herold, 1969.

Reitlinger, Gerald. *The SS, Alibi of a Nation 1922–1945.* New York: Viking, 1957.

Rempel, Gerhard. "Gottlob Berger and Waffen SS Recruitment 1939–1945." *Militärgeschichtliche Mitteilungen* no. 1 (1980): 107–22.

———. *Hitler's Children: The Hitler Youth and the SS.* Chapel Hill: University of North Carolina Press, 1989.

———. "The Misguided Generation: The Hitler Youth and the SS 1933–1945." Ph.D. diss., University of Wisconsin, 1971.

Reuth, Ralf Georg. *Goebbels.* Munich: Piper, 1990.

Richard, Felix. *Der Untergang der Stadt Wesel im Jahre 1945: Ein Gedenkbuch.* Düsseldorf: Rheinland, 1961.

Ricker, Leo Alexander. *Freiburg: Aus der Geschichte einer Stadt.* Karlsruhe: G. Braun, 1966.

Riedel, Hermann. *Ausweglos . . . ! Letzter Akt des Krieges im Schwarzwald, in der Ostbaar und an der oberen Donau, Ende April 1945.* Neckargemünd: Kurt Vowinckel, 1975.

———. *Marbach: Ein badisches Dorf bei Villingen im Schwarzwald und eine französische Kompanie im Wirbel des Kriegsende April 1945.* Marbach: Gemeinde Marbach, 1971.

———. *Villingen 1945: Bericht aus einer schweren Zeit.* Villingen/Schwarzwald: Ring, 1968.

Riedweg, Eugène. *Strasbourg: Ville occupé 1939–1945.* Steinbrunn-Le-Haut: Les Editions du Rhin, 1982.

Riess, Curt. *Joseph Goebbels.* Garden City, N.Y.: Doubleday, 1948.

Rinderle, Walter, and Bernard Norling. *The Nazi Impact on a German Village.* Lexington: University Press of Kentucky, 1992.

Rolf, David. *Prisoners of the Reich: Germany's Captives 1939–1945.* London: Leo Cooper, 1988.

Rose, Arno. *Werwolf 1944–45.* Stuttgart: Motorbuch, 1980.

Rossiwall, Theo. *Die letzten Tage: Die militärische Besetzung Österreichs 1945.* Vienna: Kremays und Scheriau, 1969.

Russell, John. *No Triumphant Procession: The Forgotten Battles of April 1945.* London: Arms and Armour, 1994.

Saft, Ulrich. *Krieg in der Heimat: Das bittere Ende zwischen Weser und Elbe.* Langenhagen: Saft, 1992.

Sauer, Paul. *Württemberg in der Zeit des Nationalsozialismus.* Ulm: Süddeutsche Verlagsgesellschaft, 1975.

Scarfe, Norman. *Assault Division: A History of the 3rd Division from the Invasion of Normandy to the Surrender of Germany.* London: Collins, 1947.

Schausberger, Norbert. *Rüstung in Österreich 1938–1945.* Vienna: Brüder Hollinek, 1970.

Schelling, Georg. *Festung Vorarlberg: Ein Bericht über das Kriegsgeschehen 1945 in unserem Land.* Bregenz: J. N. Teutsch, n.d.

Schmier, Louis Eugene. "Martin Bormann and the Nazi Party 1941–1945." Ph.D. diss., University of North Carolina, 1968.

Schnabel, Thomas, and Gerd Überschar. *Endlich Frieden! Das Kriegsende in Freiburg 1945.* Freiburg i.B.: Schillinger, 1985.

Schoenbaum, David. *Hitler's Social Revolution: Class and Status in Nazi Germany 1933–1939.* New York: Norton, 1980.

Schön, Heinz. *Die "Gustloff" Katastrophe.* Stuttgart: Motorbuch, 1984.

Schönherr, Klaus. "Der Deutsche Volkssturm im Reichsgau Wartheland 1944/45." *Militärgeschichtliches Beiheft zur Europäischen Wehrkunde* 2, no. 5 (Oct. 1987): 1–16.

Schott, Herbert. *Die Amerikaner als Besatzungsmacht in Würzburg 1945–1949.* Würzburg: Freunde Mainfränkischer Kunst und Geschichte, 1985.

Schroeder, Richard E. "The Hitler Youth as a Paramilitary Organization." Ph.D. diss., University of Chicago, 1975.

Schulte, Theo. *The German Army and Nazi Policies in Occupied Russia.* Oxford: Berg, 1989.

Schultz-Naumann, Joachim. *Mecklenburg 1945.* Munich: Universitas, 1990.

Schumann, Wolfgang, Olaf Groehler, et al. *Deutschland im Zweiten Weltkrieg.* Vol. 6, *Die Zerschlagung des Hitler Faschismus und die Befreiung des deutschen Volkes (Juni 1944 bis zum 8. Mai 1945.* Cologne: Pahl-Rugenstein, 1985.

Schwarz, Wolfgang. *Die Flucht und Vertreibung Oberschlesiens 1945–1946.* Bad Neuheim: Podzun, 1965.

Schwarze, Gisela. *Eine Region in demokratischen Aufbau: Der Regierungsbezirk Münster 1945/46.* Düsseldorf: Schwann, 1984.

Schwarzmaier, Hansmartin, et al. *Der deutsche Südwesten zur Stunde Null: Zusammenbruch und Neuanfang im Jahr 1945 in Dokumenten und Bildern.* Karlsruhe: Generallandesarchiv Karlsruhe, 1975.

Schwarzwälder, Herbert. *Bremen und Nordwestdeutschland am Kriegsende 1945.* 3 vols. Bremen: Carl Schünemann, 1972–1974.

———. *Das Ende an der Unterweser 1945: Bremerhaven (Wesermünde) und Umgebung am Kriegsende.* Bremerhaven: Nordwestdeutscher Verlag Ditzen, 1974.

Seaton, Albert. *The Fall of Fortress Europe 1943–1945.* London: B. T. Batsford, 1981.

Seemen, Gerhard von. *Die Ritterkreuzträger 1939–1945.* Friedberg: Podzun-Pallas, 1976.

Seidler, Franz. *"Deutscher Volkssturm": Das letzte Aufgebot 1944/45.* Munich: Herbig, 1989.

Selig, Wolfram, Ludwig Morenz, and Helmuth Stahleder. *Chronik der Stadt München.* Munich: Stadtarchiv München, 1980.

Siebel-Achenbach, Sebastian. *Lower Silesia from Nazi Germany to Communist Poland 1942–1949.* New York: St. Martin's, 1994.

Siebenborn, Kerstin. *Der Volkssturm in Süden Hamburgs 1944/45.* Hamburg: Verein für Hamburgische Geschichte, 1988.

Slapnicka, Harry. *Oberösterreich—als es "Oberdonau" heiß 1935–1945.* Linz: Oberösterreichischer Verlag, 1978.

Smelser, Ronald. *Robert Ley: Hitler's Labor Front Leader.* Oxford: Berg, 1988.

Smith, Walter Harold Black. *Basic Manual of Military Small Arms.* Harrisburg, Pa.: Military Service, 1945.

Smith, Walter Harold Black, and James Smith. *The Book of Rifles.* Harrisburg, Pa.: Stackpole, 1963.

Sorge, Martin K. *The Other Price of Hitler's War: German Military Losses Resulting from World War II.* Westport, Conn.: Greenwood, 1986.

Spiwoks, Erich, and Hans-Joachim Stöber. *Endkampf zwischen Mosel und Inn: XIII SS Armeekorps.* Osnabrück: Munin, 1976.

Sräga, Gudrun. "Singen 1945: Wiederbeginn des politischen Lebens unter französischer Besatzung." In *Siegründe: Beiträge zur Geschichte des Bodenseeraums,* edited by Dieter Schott and Werner Trapp. Weingarten: Drumlin, 1984.

Stacey, Charles P. *Official History of the Canadian Army in the Second World War.* Vol. 3, *The Victory Campaign: The Operations in Northwest Europe, 1944–1945.* Ottawa: The Queen's Printer and Controller of Stationery, 1960.

Stadtmüller, Alois. *Aschaffenburg im Zweiten Weltkrieg.* Aschaffenburg: Geschichts- und Kunstvereins Aschaffenburg, 1971.

———. *Maingebiet und Spessart im Zweiten Weltkrieg: Überblick, Luftkrieg, Eroberung.* Aschaffenburg: Geschichts- und Kunstverein Aschaffenburg, 1983.

Stehle, Hansjakob, "Deutsche Friedensfühler bei den Westmächten im Februar/März 1945." *Vierteljahrshefte für Zeitgeschichte* 30 (1982): 538–55.

Steiner, Herbert. *Gestorben für Österreich: Widerstand gegen Hitler.* Vienna: Europa, 1968.

Steinert, Marlis. *Capitulation 1945: The Story of the Dönitz Regime.* Translated by Richard Barry. London: Constable, 1969.

———. *Hitlers Krieg und die Deutschen: Stimmung und Haltung der deutschen Bevölkerung im Zweiten Weltkrieg.* Düsseldorf: Econ, 1970.

Stelzmann, Arnold. *Illustrierte Geschichte der Stadt Köln.* Cologne: J. P. Bachem, 1962.

Stockhorst, Erich. *Fünftausend Köpfe: Wer war wer im Dritten Reich.* Velbert: Blick und Bild, 1967.

Stone, Julius. *Legal Controls of International Conflict: A Treatise on the Dynamics of Disputes and War-Law.* New York: Rinehart, 1959.

Strangmeier, Heinrich, and Elizabeth Kraut. *Aus den letzten Kriegswochen 1945: Eine Dokumentation.* Hilden: Friedrich Peters, 1976.

Streit, Christian. *Keine Kameraden: Die Wehrmacht und die sowjetische Kriegsgefangenen.* Bonn: J.H.W. Dietz, 1991.

Strölin, Karl. *Stuttgart im Endstadium des Krieges.* Stuttgart: Friedrich, 1950.

Stuhlpfarrer, Karl. *Die Operationszonen "Alpenvorland" und "Adriatisches Küstenland" 1943–1945.* Vienna: Brüder Hollinek, 1969.

Taggart, Donald G. *History of the Third Infantry Division in World War II.* Washington, D.C.: Infantry Journal Press, 1947.

Taylor, Eric, and Willy Niessen. *Frontstadt Köln: Endkampf 1945 am Rhein und Ruhr.* Düsseldorf: Droste, 1980.

Tessin, Georg. *Verbände und Truppen der deutschen Wehrmacht und Waffen SS im Zweiten Weltkrieg 1939–1945.* 14 vols. Osnabrück: Biblio, 1973–1980.

Thorwald, Jürgen [Heinz Bongartz]. *Die Große Flucht.* Stuttgart: Steingruber, 1962.

Tieke, Wilhelm. *Das Ende zwischen Oder und Elbe—Der Kampf um Berlin 1945.* Stuttgart: Motorbuch, 1981.

Tiemann, Reinhard. *Geschichte der 83. Infanterie Division 1939–1945.* Bad Nauheim: Hans Henning Podzun, 1960.

Timm, Willy. *Freikorps "Sauerland" 1944–45: Zur Geschichte des Zweiten Weltkriegs in Südwestfalen.* Hagen: Stadtarchiv Hagen, 1976.

Tippelskirch, Kurt von. *Geschichte des Zweiten Weltkriegs.* Bonn: Athenäum, 1951.

Trevor-Roper, Hugh. *The Last Days of Hitler.* New York: Macmillan, 1947.

Tuider, Othmar. *Die Wehrkreise XVII and XVIII 1938–1945.* Vienna: Heeresgeschichtliches Museum, n.d.

U.S. Army. Second Infantry Division. *Combat History of the Second Infantry Division in World War II.* Nashville, Tenn.: Battery Press, 1979.

———. Third Armored Division. *Spearhead in the West 1944–45.* Frankfurt: Franz Joseph Heinrich, 1945.

———. Ninth Army. *Conquer: The Story of the Ninth Army 1944–45.* Washington, D.C.: Infantry Journal Press, 1947.

———. XVI Corps. *History of the XVI Corps: From Its Activation to the End of the War in Europe.* Washington, D.C.: Infantry Journal Press, 1947.

———. XX Corps. *The XX Corps: Its History and Service in World War II.* Halstead, Kans.: XX Corps, 1984.

———. 67th Armored Regiment. *History of the 67th Armored Regiment.* Brunswick, Germany: Georg Westermann, 1945.

———. 89th Infantry Division. *The 89th Infantry Division 1942–1945.* Washington, D.C.: Infantry Journal Press, 1947.

———. 106th Cavalry Group. *The 106th Cavalry Group in Europe 1944–1945.* Augsburg: J. P. Himmer, 1945.

———. 120th Infanty Regiment. *History of the 120th Infantry Regiment.* Washington, D.C.: Infantry Journal Press, 1947.

———. 376th Infantry Regiment. *History of the 376th Infantry Regiment Between the Years of 1921 and 1945.* Wupertal-Barmen: Carl Weddigen, 1945.

United States. Department of the Army. "Pamphlet #20-201: Military Improvisation During the Russian Campaign." Washington, D.C.: Office of the Chief of Military History, 1951.

van Creveld, Martin. "War Lord Hitler: Some Points Reconsidered." *European Studies Review* 4, no. 1 (Jan. 1974): 57–79.

Voelker, Johannes. *Die letzten Tage von Kolberg (4–18.3.45).* Würzburg: Holzner, 1959.

Vogl, Friedrich. *Widerstand im Waffenrock: Österreichische Freiheitskämpfer in der Deutschen Wehrmacht 1938–1945.* Vienna: Europa, 1977.

Wagener, Carl. "Kampf und Ende der Heeresgruppe B im Ruhrkessel, 22. März bis 17. April 1945." *Wehrwissenschaftliche Rundschau* 7, no. 10 (1957): 535–64.

Wagner, Dieter. *München '45 zwischen Ende und Anfang.* Munich: Süddeutscher Verlag, 1970.

Walter, Friedrich. *Schicksal einer deutschen Stadt: Geschichte Mannheims 1907–1945,* Vol. 2, *1925–1945.* Frankfurt: Knapp, 1950.

Wegmann, Günther. *Das Kriegsende zwischen Ems und Weser 1945.* Osnabrück: N. Th. Wenner, 1983.

Weigley, Russell F. *Eisenhower's Lieutenants: The Campaigns of France and Germany, 1944–1945.* Bloomington: Indiana University Press, 1980.

Weinberg, Gerhard L. "Adolf Hitler und der NS-Führungsoffizier." *Vierteljahreshefte für Zeitgeschichte* 12, no. 4 (Oct. 1964): 443–56.

———. *Germany, Hitler and World War II: Essays in Modern German and World History.* New York: Cambridge University Press, 1995.

———. "Hitler's Image of the United States." *American Historical Review* 69, no. 4 (July 1969): 1006–21.

———. *A World at Arms: A Global History of World War II.* New York: Cambridge University Press, 1994.

———. *World in the Balance: Behind the Scenes of World War II.* Hanover, N.H.: University Press of New England, 1981.

Werner, Josef. *Karlsruhe 1945: Unter Hakenkreuz, Trikolore und Sternenbanner.* Karlsruhe: G. Braun, 1985.

White, Wolfred K. "The Volkssturm: A Study of the German National Militia 1944–1945." M.A. thesis, Florida State University, 1963.

Whiting, Charles. *Bounce the Rhine.* New York: Stein and Day, 1986.

———. *Hitler's Werewolves: The Story of the Nazi Resistance Movement 1944–45.* New York: Stein and Day, 1972.

Wilke, Gerhard. "Village Life in Nazi Germany." In *Life in the Third Reich,* edited by Bessel Richard, 17–24. New York: Oxford University Press, 1987.

Williams, Jeffery. *The Long Left Flank: The Hard Fought Way to the Reich 1944–1945.* London: Leo Cooper, 1988.

Williamson, Gordon. *Infantry Aces of the Reich.* London: Arms and Armour, 1991.

Wissenschaftliche Kommission für deutsche Kriegsgefangenengeschichte. *Zur Geschichte der deutschen Kriegsgefangenen des Zweiten Weltkrieges.* Vol. 5, Kurt Bährens. *Deutsche in Straflagern und Gefängnissen der Sowjetunion.* Munich: Ernst und Werner Gieseking, 1965.

———. *Zur Geschichte der deutschen Kriegsgefangenen des Zweiten Weltkrieges.* Vol. X/2, Kurt Böhme. *Die deutsche Kriegsgefangenen in amerikanischer Hand— Europa.* Munich: Ernst und Werner Gieseking, 1965.

————. *Zur Geschichte der deutschen Kriegsgefangenen des Zweiten Weltkrieges.* Beiheft 1. Michael Rock. *Tagebuch aus sowjetischer Kriegsgefangenschaft 1945–49.* Munich: Ernst und Werner Gieseking, 1967.

Wright, Burton, III. "Army of Despair: The German Volkssturm 1944–1945." Ph.D. diss., Florida State University, 1982.

Wulf, Joseph. *Martin Bormann: Hitler's Schatten.* Gütersloh: Sigbert Mohn, 1962.

Yelton, David K. "British Public Opinion, the Home Guard and the Defense of Great Britain, 1940–1944," *Journal of Military History* 58, no. 3 (July 1994): 461–80.

————. "The Last Reserves: Political-Military Aspects of the Structure, Function, and Composition of the German Volkssturm, 1944–1945." Ph.D. diss., University of North Carolina, 1990.

Zeir, Hans Georg. *Geschichte der Stadt Pforzheim von dem Anfang bis 1945.* Stuttgart: Konrad Theiss, 1982.

Zelzer, Maria. *Stuttgart unterm Hakenkreuz: Chronik aus Stuttgart 1933–1945.* Stuttgart: Alektor, 1984.

Ziemke, Earl F. *Stalingrad to Berlin: The German Defeat in the East.* Washington, D.C.: Office of the Chief of Military History, 1968.

Zippel, Martin, "Untersuchungen zur Militärgeschichte der Reichshauptstadt Berlin von 1871 bis 1945." Inaugural diss., Westfälischen Wilhelms-Universität zu Münster, 1981.

Index